Aim for the Heart

Third Edition

This book is dedicated to Reverend Sidney Tompkins, my wife; and to Marion Tompkins, my mom, who proudly placed my books on her shelf even though she could not read them with her failing eyes. She drove me to my first radio job because I was too young to drive. Every time I moved in my career, she bought a taller TV antenna tower and turned it toward the city where I worked so she could watch me on TV. When I was a producer she didn't understand what I did at work so she told people I ran a TV station. When I reported stories each night, I tried to imagine I was talking just to her. Now that she is gone, I still talk to her, and I like to think she is still watching me.

Aim for the Heart

Write, Shoot, Report and Produce for TV and Multimedia

THIRD EDITION

Al Tompkins
The Poynter Institute

FOR INFORMATION:

CQ Press

An Imprint of SAGE Publications, Inc.

2455 Teller Road

Thousand Oaks, California 91320

E-mail: order@sagepub.com

SAGE Publications Ltd.

1 Oliver's Yard

55 City Road

London EC1Y 1SP

United Kingdom

SAGE Publications India Pvt. Ltd.

B 1/I 1 Mohan Cooperative Industrial Area

Mathura Road, New Delhi 110 044

India

SAGE Publications Asia-Pacific Pte. Ltd.

3 Church Street

#10-04 Samsung Hub

Singapore 049483

Printed in the United States of America

ISBN: 978-1-5063-1525-6

Acquisitions Editor: Terri Accomazzo

Editorial Assistant: Erik Helton

Production Editor: Bennie Clark Allen

Copy Editor: Robin Gold

Typesetter: C&M Digitals (P) Ltd.

Proofreader: Rae-Ann Goodwin

Indexer: Wendy Allex

Cover Designer: Candice Harman

Marketing Manager: Jillian Oelsen

Certified Chain of Custody
SUSTAINABLE   Promoting Sustainable Forestry
FORESTRY   www.sfiprogram.org
INITIATIVE   SFI-01268

SFI label applies to text stock

17 18 19 20 21 10 9 8 7 6 5 4 3 2 1

Brief Contents

Detailed Contents

Preface

Here we are with a third edition of *Aim for the Heart*. The changes in how we produce news and, more importantly, how people consume it require an update. This edition includes new chapters on reporting news for social media and online. I have added a new chapter on how to report stories that involve guns, and I have added a new focus on interviewing and critical-thinking skills.

We published the first edition of *Aim for the Heart* in 2002. The dust from the September 11 attacks had barely settled, and U.S. soldiers were shipping off to war. The United States still had not elected an African-American president, and New Orleans had no idea what chaos a hurricane named Katrina could cause. Internet journalism was just coming to bloom in 2001. There was no YouTube, Facebook or Twitter. Only the geekiest geeks sent instant messages. AOL chat rooms were the "social networks" of the time. The smartest phones delivered only e-mail and sports scores. BlackBerry was offering a revolutionary hand-held phone and mobile messaging device. Apple had just launched the iPod, and it did not play video.

As I teach in newsrooms across America and around the world, one thing I stress is that no matter what kind of screen your work shows up on, your most important job in journalism is to get the story right. The second job of the journalist is to be interesting, accurate and fair.

My experience has been that the majority of journalists who read my books are young, many are college students and some are new to the business. I hope my words will inspire you to enter this craft and encourage you to see it as an honorable and even vital part of a society. I am saddened by how many experienced journalists have left or been forced out of the profession. I worry about what the loss of their institutional knowledge will cost us when viewers need it most in times of uncertainty and chaos. To survive and thrive in journalism today you will have to be constant learners. Be honest, reliable and thick-skinned when others criticize you, and show compassion to the people you encounter. TV journalism is a glorious way to make a living. I would do it again without hesitation.

ACKNOWLEDGMENTS

Thanks to Vicki Krueger and Robin Gold, insightful editors who guided me through the birthing of this book.

About the Author

 **Al Tompkins** is the Senior Faculty for Broadcast and Online at The Poynter Institute in St. Petersburg, Florida.

Tompkins is a broadcast veteran who combines more than 25 years of newsroom experience plus nearly 20 years of teaching journalists around the globe. He has taught thousands of journalists in 49 states, Canada, Egypt, Denmark, Iceland, Cayman, South Africa and beyond. Tompkins has been awarded journalism's top prizes for his reporting, including the National Emmy, the Japan Prize, the Robert F. Kennedy Award, seven National Headliner Awards, three Gabriel Awards and the Governors Award from the National Academy of Television Arts & Sciences and being part of a team that won the Peabody Award. His work and teaching have been honored by the National Education Association, the American Bar Association, the National Press Photographers Association and the Radio Television Digital News Association, and he was inducted into the Kentucky Journalism Hall of Fame. He has helped to write national codes of ethics and coverage guidelines for the National Press Photographers Association and the Radio Television Digital News Association.

Tompkins has been interviewed and quoted by *CBS Evening News, NBC Nightly News, PBS NewsHour,* NPR's *Morning Edition* and *All Things Considered,* CNN, CBC's *The National,* South African Broadcasting Corporation Radio, *The Wall Street Journal, The Washington Post, The New York Times, The Dallas Morning News,* the *Los Angeles Times* and many others around the world.

Introduction

I often ask journalists that I teach, "What do you stand for as a journalist?"

I urge you to stop reading for a moment and consider that question.

Deep down in the quiet places of your heart, what do *you* stand for? Why do you want to be a journalist? What dreams do you have about righting wrongs, exposing corruption and giving voice to those who are voiceless?

After allowing my students to write, I ask them to share their thoughts with the entire group. The list they create generally includes these words:

WHAT WE STAND FOR AS JOURNALISTS

Tell the truth	Hold the powerful accountable
Illuminate	Give voice to the voiceless
Inform	Be relevant
Teach	Prompt viewer action/reaction
Inspire	Alert the viewer to danger
Effect change	Educate
Be clear	Be interesting
Be unbiased	Be sensitive
Be objective	Provide context
Be honest	Be balanced

It is quite a list.

Over the years, I have had the opportunity to ask dozens of focus groups of viewers what they think journalists *should* stand for. They generally create a list that looks like this:

WHAT WE WANT JOURNALISTS TO STAND FOR

(AND WHAT WE WANT JOURNALISTS TO DO)

Be truthful	Be tough
Be honest	Understand our community
Be fair	Be knowledgeable, be informed
Tell us the whole story	Follow up on stories
Tell us something we don't know	Find good news, not all bad
Don't exaggerate	Cover lots of topics
Don't brag	Be real and sincere
Respect privacy	Admit your mistakes

I am struck by the similarities of the lists.

So why is TV viewership declining? Why are so many journalists leaving the craft, no longer believing that their work matters?

The single most important reason, I think, is embedded in the next two lists that I often generate with my seminar participants.

When I ask journalists, "What are the most important issues facing our country and this community right now?" they say:

MOST IMPORTANT ISSUES FACING THE COUNTRY

The economy/jobs	Health care and insurance coverage
Terrorism	College costs
Immigration reform	Drug addiction
Housing costs	Gun crime
Traffic, transportation	Public education

Then I ask, "What stories have you given the most airtime to in the last 30 days?" The journalists make their list:

STORIES MOST OFTEN COVERED

Crime, usually drug related

Accidents and incidents, such as fires, floods, storms, traffic accidents

Planned community events and announcements

Political and governmental news conferences

Celebrity news and scandal

Health stories, health studies, "breakthroughs"

Government scandals

Consumer tips

Once in a while, a celebrity dies, a candidate says something provocative, racial tensions flair somewhere and the nation focuses on important conversations about meaty issues for a time. But the stories play out and newsrooms eventually settle into the same old coverage patterns.

Watch a local newscast, choose one in any time period in any city, and see how it stacks up with what you consider to be the most pressing issues in the community the station services. Last year my teaching took me to 65 cities, so I watched newscasts in every U.S. time zone in cities big and tiny. Most of what I watched seemed generic and optional. We can do better.

In 2016, the *Tampa Bay Times* newspaper (which is owned by The Poynter Institute) won a Pulitzer Prize for its coverage of the most underperforming public schools in the community. The paper dug deeply to discover the underlying reasons for the horrific performance of those schools and held the school board accountable for failing to act. Parents and community leaders demanded action, showed up for community meetings and the U.S. Secretary of Education flew in to demand the school board get its act together and fix the problems. I am grateful that the newspaper showed civic leadership and spent significant resources to dedicate two reporters, an editor, a photojournalist and a data expert to the project for most of a year. I was saddened that no local TV station had found a way to be so similarly bold. Somehow, television journalists have become convinced that the stories with gravity and complexity are "newspaper" stories and not good TV.

One of my favorite movies is *Citizen Kane*. In one scene Charles Foster Kane, a powerful and power-hungry newspaper publisher, stands in his office after putting out the first edition of his paper. He turns to his editors and says, "There is something I've got to get into this paper besides pictures and print. I've got to make the *New York Inquirer* as important to New York as the gas in that light."

Then, he writes out a Declaration of Principles to run on the newspaper's front page:

> I will provide the people of this city with a daily paper that will tell all the news honestly. They will get the truth in the *Inquirer*, quickly and simply and entertainingly and no special interests are going to be allowed to interfere with that truth. I will also provide them with a fighting and tireless champion of their rights as citizens and as human beings.

In the year I spent updating this book I have purchased a camera that records 360-degree video, I started learning how to fly a drone with an HD camera, and I finished a master's degree in digital design. My point is, to be a journalist you have to be a constant learner. You have to love learning new ways to reach viewers.

In this book, I hope to give broadcast journalists the tools they need to live out that same creed in a multimedia world that moves faster and touches more people than ever before. I can give you the skills to report stronger stories, but you have to find the courage and dedication within yourself to make it happen. Let's get started.

CHAPTER 1

Aim for the Heart

> *"I quite agree with you,"* said the Duchess, *"and the moral of that is—'Be what you would seem to be'—or if you'd like it put more simply—'Never imagine yourself not to be otherwise than what it might appear to others that what you were or might have been was not otherwise than what you had been would have appeared to them to be otherwise.'"*
>
> *"I think I should understand that better,"* Alice said very politely, *"if I had it written down: but I can't quite follow it as you say it."*
>
> *"That's nothing to what I could say if I chose,"* the Duchess replied, *in a pleased tone.*
>
> —Lewis Carroll,
> *Alice's Adventures in Wonderland*

Great stories hang in the viewer's ear and catch the viewer's eye. Great stories aim straight for the viewer's heart. The best news stories don't just inform: They teach, illuminate and inspire viewers.

As a reporter and later as a newscast producer, I feared that my viewers would be as confused and unable to decipher what I was saying as Alice is in the passage at the beginning of this chapter. At the end of a story, I wanted viewers to say, "Aha!" not "Huh?"

Before I write news stories, I glance at a simple little checklist I have kept for years. The list was written by former WSMV-TV news director and, later, general manager Mike Kettenring. After he left a long career in television, Kettenring became a Catholic priest, so it is no surprise that the checklist is built around the word "faith."

Fair

Accurate

Interesting

Thorough

Human

Have faith that the power of great storytelling will connect with the viewer's heart.

The checklist keeps stories from sounding like Sgt. Joe Friday on the TV show *Dragnet*. When Sergeant Friday was on the case, he would say, "Just the facts, ma'am."

News writing can be "just the facts." But the difference between *fact* telling and *story*telling is the difference between watching the stock ticker and hearing a story about an elderly woman who has lost every dime she needs for shelter and medicine because the market just tanked.

Storytelling has such power over us that it affects key regions of your brain. The words you read and hear even trigger responses in your brain if the writer uses metaphorical language—language that paints a picture, creates a link to something that is familiar to the audience. Emory University researchers reported in the research journal *Brain and Language* that when the writer uses such words as "She had a bubbly personality," the reader's sensory cortex, a part of the brain that senses touch, lights up. But bland descriptions such as "She had a lively personality" did not produce the same brain response.[1] Write the phrase "He fluffed his lines" and you are likely to get more brain response than "He forgot his lines." And "That man is oily" is more likely to produce greater sensory cortex response than "That man is untrustworthy."[2] Other researchers have found that the mere mention of the word "perfume" can light up the olfactory cortex, the part of the brain that senses smell.[3]

Researchers are also learning that storytelling seems to have the power to help humans become more understanding, more empathetic and more open to new ideas. One study said schoolchildren who had more stories read to them had a wider "theory of mind," which is the ability to understand other people's intentions. It turns out when you read to young children, you are not just expanding their vocabulary; you are teaching them to think. Stories connect deeply in our brains in ways raw facts cannot.

A British website, stayingaliveuk.com, helps clients "tell their stories" by turning facts into whiteboard animations. Part of the site's pitch includes this graphic describing how storytelling affects the human brain. The website tries to convince potential clients that the way to deeply connect with customers is to tell them a story. And it turns out that the advice is based on some pretty compelling science that has been building for decades.

The graphic shows four key activities that unfold when the listener/viewer/reader takes in a well-told story that connects intellectually and

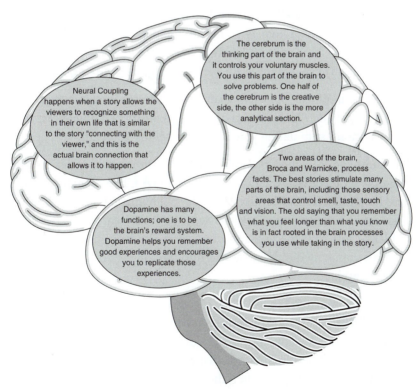

Source: By Hugh Guiney. https://commons.wikimedia.org/wiki/File:Human-brain.SVG; https://creativecommons.org/licenses/by-sa/3.0/deed.en. Text by Al Tompkins.

emotionally. The part of the brain known as Broca's area controls speech production. Wernicke's area handles how we understand the written and spoken word. (Both Pierre Paul Broca and Carl Wernicke were neuroscientists.) When you read a boring textbook (not this one) or watch a professor's bland PowerPoint lecture, you use these two areas of the cortex. But when the professor really fires up his or her creativity or when the writer uses descriptive language, other parts of your brain light up and you begin connecting with the information in surprisingly deep and memorable ways. Why? Because you are experiencing the story in ways that connect with your senses beyond your Broca's and Wernicke's areas. How cool is that?

Psychologists have a phrase for this connection: "narrative transport." The story transports the audience and connects consumers to their own experiences.

That brings us to the upper left portion of the graphic, which is another "wow." A Princeton research researcher named Uri Hasson discovered that when the storyteller powerfully connects with the listener, they actually "connect." There is something called neural coupling that shows up on an MRI scan of the brain. When the listener doesn't understand or doesn't care what the speaker is saying, the coupling vanishes.[4]

Let's apply all of this theory to a commercial to see how in just 30 seconds a brand such as Nike can aim for the heart by connecting with your emotions, stimulating your brain and selling you stuff.

The commercial features pro golfer Rory McIlroy, a golf sensation who at age 22 set records at the U.S. Open and PGA Championship. By the time he was 23, he had earned $10 million. He made it all look so easy. Nike could have shown this golfer wearing Nike gear and using Nike clubs and just told the viewer to buy stuff like Rory uses. That's not what the company did. Nike tapped into the mindset of an athlete or a wannabe athlete.

The gritty commercial shows Rory's alarm going off at 5:30 each morning. He lifts weighs, runs by himself down secluded rocky roads, stuffs vegetables into a blender and chokes down the green glob it produces each morning. Then he hits practice range golf balls into the dark of night, and he does it again when the alarm goes off at 5:30 the next day. Day after day, his story is about sweat and perseverance. The ad ends with him teeing off at a PGA tournament, the crowd roaring in awe, and the message appears: "Nike. Enjoy the Chase."

That's a story. That's the kind of story that Nike could expect would connect emotionally with anybody who has chased a dream and paid the cost. As Vanderbilt professor Jennifer Edson Escalas, who studies the psychology of advertising narratives, puts it:

> While some attention may occasionally be paid to features and benefits, the bigger picture in Nike ads revolves around a story of hard work, sweat, and perseverance; the result of the story is that Nike enables people to achieve their very best. Thus, Nike's story is about enabling consumers to achieve their personal quest for excellence. This story resonates with Nike's target consumers, who are athletic, fitness conscious individuals. Using Nike sports gear, the consumer can build his/her own personal story of accomplishment.[5]

Can Great Storytelling Make You Sexier?

And, get this: One study found that men's ability to tell stories "affects their attractiveness and perceived status."[6] If you learn to tell great stories, people may find you to be more attractive. One study found "individuals who can create compelling stories may be more persuasive and thus be able to influence others and gain social standing."[7]

And here's some good news for television and online video storytellers. The brain connections increase when the viewer can see the "meaningful" gestures that the storyteller makes telling the tale.[8]

At the risk of sounding like a late-night infomercial, I want to shout, "But wait, there's more." Storytelling is one of the qualities that separates us, so far as we know, from other species. Story narratives help us make sense of what is happening around us. They give our experiences order and perspective. When something newsworthy happens, we tend to want to know why, how, who it affected, and what came before and after. We want to know more than the factual "what happened" to get the "so what," which I would argue is the story beyond that facts.

This hunger for story has held true in every known culture from Sanskrit to Greek and Latin. The walls of Egyptian tombs and cave dwellings are covered with stories, not just facts. It's as though we are wired for stories. No child ever went to bed saying, "Daddy, read me some facts." It's as if we are prewired to want to hear stories. We want conflict and characters. We want context and resolution. Nobody told you the elements of a great story when you were a toddler, but you knew a great story when you heard one. In fact, if you were anything like my kids, you wanted to hear a great story over and over. The dopamine was flowing. Multiple cortexes fired up. Now we know why: We were making a neural coupling!

ALL THAT IS GREAT, BUT I'M ON A DEADLINE

I can almost hear TV reporters and producers protest, "Yea, Al, great. But we do TV. Our bosses want us to write short and tight. You can't be compelling and factual in a minute and 20 seconds."

It's not true. This whole book is about proving that.

Mark Twain, Dorothy Parker, F. Scott Fitzgerald, Edgar Allan Poe, Ernest Hemingway and John Steinbeck learned their craft by writing short stories. They all learned what broadcast journalists know: It is more difficult to write an interesting and contextually complete short story than it is to write a longer version of the story.[9]

French mathematician, physicist and philosopher Blaise Pascal wrote in a letter to a friend in 1657, "I have made this letter longer, because I have not had the time to make it shorter."[10]

With only a few words, the writer creates a hook and a complication, provides surprises, information and character development. On television, that hook (a) captures viewers' attention, (b) brings them up to speed and (c) leads them toward what is new in the story. Even in a 20-second story there should be at least one main character, tension and resolution.

Television stories and newscasts should tell tales, spin yarns, provide people with information they need to understand the world and teach viewers something they didn't know to keep them coming back.

This chapter will help you tackle those complex stories and tell them in a way that goes straight to the viewer's heart. In this chapter we will cover the following:

- How to find a tight story focus that connects to the viewer's heart
- How to use sound bites to reach the viewer's heart

FINDING FOCUS: AIM FOR THE HEART OF THE STORY

Anyone who has ever written a news story, a college term paper or even a second-grade class assignment knows how hard it is to find a tight focus for the story. Aiming for the heart of the story is essential to good storytelling.

My daughter MeiLin is a journalist. I should have known she would become a writer. When she was in second grade, she wrote a story for a class assignment called "My Luckiest Day." This 99-word tale is a clear example of what writers go through when they struggle to find a tight focus for a story. Watch what this young writer does right in the middle of the story to correct the course of a straying narrative. (I will include the spelling and punctuation she used for added flavor.)

"My Luckiest Day Ever"

MeiLin Tompkins, Second Grade

Lakeview Elementary School

My luckies day ever is today because my friend Kenna is coming to my house! Kenna lives in Tennese and I think it is my luckies day ever because she is my best friend and she likes it when I'm funny and so do I!

And I think I might want glasses not really but never mind about that because I'm spost to be talking about my friend Kenna will I can't wait tell she comes to my house to play fun games and watch TV and have some pop corn. I can't wait tell she comes!

My life as a journalist would have been so much easier if at age eight I could have learned what my daughter learned: Great writing is a process of selecting, not compressing, what goes into our stories.

As a reporter, I have found myself in the middle of a convoluted story, writing a sentence that sounded exactly like my daughter when she wrote, "Never mind about that—because I'm spost to be talking about . . ." Journalism is an endless process of editing out information and details.

The single most important question a writer can ask before he or she begins to type is, "What is this story about?" This book, for example, could have been about writing, but that would have been a broad book about all kinds of storytelling, from folktales to fairy tales to news writing. A book about writing might have covered how to write instructional manuals, technical documents and scientific journals.

This book could have been about broadcast writing, but that book might have covered everything from writing for sitcoms to documentaries. Instead, I chose to talk directly to people who write news stories. I have narrowed the focus. It is the first step in writing more powerful stories. Here is how my decision-making might look:

I sometimes think of stories as shapes. Think for a minute about your story as being a 1-minute 30-second box. Your box could look like this:

1:30

Or it could look like this:

1:30

The first box is the shape of a headline newscast. It would give you a lot of facts and details but would not drill down on any of them. It contains a little bit of information about a wide range of things. But the second box is narrow and deep. It focuses on a narrow subject.

News stories work best when they are narrow and deep, not wide and thin. Don't try to cram every detail you know into your story. Select, don't compress. Focus and get narrow. It usually means you will need fewer characters in your stories, but viewers will get to know the characters you include.

Teachers often tell students to get to the who, what, when, where, why and how of the story. How do you know if you have done that?

- The "who" is/are your main character(s).
- The "what" is the main action that affected the character(s).
- The "when" and "where" tell viewers about the setting, both in time and place.
- "Why" and the "how" set the story's context. This usually is the most newsworthy part of the story. Anybody can tell me what happened, but it takes a journalist to tell me how and why it happened.

THE FOCUS STATEMENT: THREE WORDS

By telling narrower but deeper stories, writers help viewers understand information more clearly. This process of finding focus is really about simplifying the story. To focus a story, the writer must fully understand it.

Here is a checklist that will help you start finding focus:

- What is the most interesting part about this story? (This is the main thrust of the story.)
- What surprised me? (This may be the lead.)
- What did I learn that I didn't know before? (This is a main surprise, which we usually put early in the story.)
- What will viewers want to know? In what order will they ask those questions? (This will determine the story frame.)
- What do I want viewers to remember and feel at the end of this story? (This is the most memorable sound bite.)
- What comes next? (This will lead you toward the end of the story.)
- Those details will help you answer the key question that will focus your story: "What is this story about?"

The answer should not be a long-winded account of all you know. Try to answer the question in one sentence.

Jon Franklin, a two-time Pulitzer Prize–winning writer, says writers should craft a focus statement about their story. The "focus statement," Franklin says, "should be three words in length." (You can get away with a free "an," "and" or "the.") Think of it as "who did what?"

Let's try out this idea.

Few stories have more complexities hidden in them than stories about war. The list of the possible stories we could do includes these:

- The generals
- The soldiers
- The civilians left at home
- The conflict involved
- The weapons
- The president in wartime
- The foreign policies that led to the fighting
- The history of the nations involved

- The strategy
- The diplomacy to end the fighting

It is tempting to believe that the most compelling war stories involve lots of shooting and bombing. People who have never been in a war may not understand what soldiers do. War is mostly not about shooting and bombing. It is about mind-numbing boredom and routine intermingled with moments of terror and adrenaline, followed by more tedious grunt work and sleep deprivation. To get to the real story of war, you have to get down to the level of the soldier. Everything the presidents, the diplomats and the generals do affects soldiers on the front line. War stories also involve war victims—the refugees who abandon their homes, huddle in camps and pray for peace.

> **POYNTER NEWSU E-LEARNING COURSE**
>
> Learn more about finding focus in *Aim for the Heart* at www.newsu.org/heart.

A college professor of mine loved to show us old black-and-white war documentaries. I figured they would be boring and slow. I settled in to endure one of the films and learned the principle that changed how I thought of "story focus" forever. It was an old Edward R. Murrow documentary from CBS News about the Korean War. CBS' *See It Now* program moved 15 reporters and cameramen to Korea for one week to attempt to capture the face of war. Here is how the program opened:

"Christmas in Korea"[11]

Edward R. Murrow (sound of a shovel digging into frozen earth in the background): This is Korea, where a war is going on. That's a Marine, digging a hole in the ground. They dig an awful lot of holes in the ground in Korea. This is the front. Just there, no-man's-land begins and, on the ridges over there, the enemy positions can be clearly seen. In the course of the next hour we shall try to show you around Korea a bit."

It was a stunning moment for me as a young television journalist.

Murrow's cameraman steadily photographed one Marine, chunking his shovel again and again against a frozen ground.

The documentary didn't include one general, not one government official. It told the complex story of the war by putting a face on the story. Murrow and producer Fred Friendly focused the story to the little person closest to it. They would repeat this technique over and over on *See It Now*. Almost 70 years later, it remains the central style of the most popular news magazine programs such as CBS' *60 Minutes*, ABC's *20/20* and *Nightline*, NBC's *Dateline* and NPR's *All Things Considered*.

Murrow and Friendly focused on the ordinary act of shoveling and the ordinary emotion of loneliness, which viewers at home understood.

My three-word summary of "Christmas in Korea" is "Soldiers endure war." The story was not about communism, it was not about foreign policy and it was not about the generals and politicians who got us into that war. Viewers learn a lot about the war's background, but "Christmas in Korea" had a laser-beam focus on the effect the war had on the soldiers and nurses who were closest to the pain, death and loneliness.

> **Murrow Interviews Airman Moriarty: I'm Airman Third Class Brendon M. Moriarty. I was born and raised in County Kerry, Ireland. I been used to mountains all my life, but it's the mountains (of) Killarney, not the mountains of Korea. I want to wish you all a Merry Christmas. Nora, I will be home in two hundred and ninety-two days, then we will celebrate Christmas, New Year's and St. Patrick's Day—we'll celebrate everything together. Okay darling, good-bye.**

The last line chokes me up.

I remember that sound bite from Airman Moriarty 40 years after I first saw it while sitting in a darkened college classroom. The viewer realizes that Airman Moriarty knows, to the day, how long it will be until he is back in Nora's arms. By the time the program ends, viewers will not remember the number of days (292) he has until he goes home. But they will always remember that he knows exactly how long it will be.

It is not enough for viewers to get information about the war. That's *fact* telling, not *story*telling. To make the story memorable, viewers have to feel something. My wife, who is a psychotherapist, tells me that people always remember what they feel longer than what they know.

A CENTRAL THEME: VIEWERS
REMEMBER WHAT THEY FEEL

More than 15 years after I watched that Murrow documentary, I put the lessons I learned to use. Christmas Eve, 1993, I found myself covering a story about soldiers and war. I was assigned to cover the predawn return to Fort Campbell, Kentucky, of soldiers from the 101st Airborne Division who were back from their tour of duty as "peacekeepers" in Somalia. It had been a particularly difficult and deadly mission. Americans entered Somalia with the good intention of feeding starving people, but soldiers were drawn into gunfights with local warlords. Somalis dragged soldiers' bodies through the streets. You may remember that from the book and movie *Black Hawk Down*. Now, most of the 101st were coming home.

I knew that, in all likelihood, there would be 12 or more television cameras at the event. I guessed that most of us were walking into the story with the same focus: Soldiers come home.

How could we do something different, something more memorable?

Driving to that story at 4 a.m. on that cold Christmas Eve, photojournalist Randy Palmer and I made a quick list of what we thought we might photograph and include in this story.

The list included the following:

- Families waiting
- People giving soldiers gifts
- A military band
- Tears and people crying
- The airplane
- Soldiers getting off the plane
- Officials making speeches
- Flags
- File and other historic pictures from Somalia
- People cheering

We knew that every other crew covering the story had a similar checklist in mind. We asked ourselves if there were other possibilities.

We considered these:

- Someone who is coming home but has no one waiting for him or her
- Going beyond the typical picture of a soldier coming home to find the husband of a female soldier who has been waiting for her return
- Whether families of soldiers who died in Somalia would be there
- Whether families of the soldiers still in Somalia would be there

The Army gave us no access to the waiting families until moments before the plane landed. All of the TV crews scrambled to get shots of the taxiing charter transport plane. Palmer also shot wide shots of the crowded tarmac and panned the cheering assembled crowd. All the while, I was walking through the crowd, looking for an interesting character. We stuck by the side of a woman and her young son who were standing there shivering in the cold, holding flowers for their solider. I wrote:

"Soldier Comes Home"

Al Tompkins and Randy Palmer[12]

Tompkins: Marla Denson has been here before on the airport tarmac . . . waiting. To be an Army wife, you have to get good at waiting.

Marla: Come on, you ready to go see Daddy?

(Close-up of shivering son)

Tompkins: Her husband, Charles, left for Somalia in August. When he left, the Army's mission in August was to feed a million starving Africans. (file tape) But the mission changed into an ugly shooting war. Marla knows that other families have waited in her same spot. Their husbands will never come home.

Marla: It's their jobs, they have to do it, they have to do it.

Tompkins: How do you get good at waiting?

Marla: Prayer, God, family and friends; them's the four things. If you don't have them, you can't make it.

Tompkins: Judy Gross has gotten good at waiting. She has spent twenty years waiting for her husband, the colonel, to come home from this place or that. This is an unexpected blessing, because nobody knew they were coming home until two days ago. (nat sd [natural sound] of cheering—people coming off the plane)

Judy Gross: Christmas when he was in Saudi, we just kept him in our thoughts and our prayers and we drank a toast to him on Christmas Eve, and that is about all you can do. You just have to think positive thoughts when they are not around.

Tompkins To Marla: What did you say when you heard he was coming in?

Marla: I love you. (laughs) I have to love him. He did his job and now it is over.

Tompkins: One by one, the reunions happened around her. (pictures of a mother screaming, then hugging her daughter) Parents screamed at the sight of their children. Husbands held closely to their wives in uniform. (picture of hands) But she waited. (picture of Marla straining to see the plane) She began to think, maybe he wasn't on this plane. (pause) Maybe there was a problem.

Marla (still looking past the camera, squinting, watching the last few soldiers come down the stairs from the plane): You have to be the mother and the father while they are gone. You have to do everything together. (in the distance—a man shouts, Hey—Hey!)

Marla: That's you! That's you! I love you, Charles! I love you, I love you, I love you, I LOVE you, Charles, I love you, I love you, I love you.

(She kisses him repeatedly as Charles struggles to hold his hand out to his young shivering son who has waited silently.)

Charles (to his son as he picks him up): Hey—Hey man, come here!

Tompkins: Corporal Charles Denson was home, home to be with his wife and his son. She brought him a rose, because, she said, he was always bringing her roses. She worried her hair didn't look right; she asked him a thousand times if he was okay. One hundred and fifty other Fort Campbell soldiers are still in Somalia tonight. What they wouldn't give to be where he is. He is home for Christmas.

Al Tompkins, Channel 4 News, Fort Campbell, Kentucky.

Take just a few minutes before you read further to answer a question about the focus of the story you just read. In one sentence, how would you describe what this story is about? How would you describe it in three words: a noun, a verb and an object? In other words, who did what?

You might come up with one of these:

- Soldier comes home
- Home for Christmas
- 101st comes home
- Families get present
- 101st completes mission
- Fort celebrates return
- Soldiers rescue Somalia

All of these could be good stories. They are not the story we produced.

I think our story was about Marla.

I think the main action Marla took was waiting.

She was waiting for Charles.

So the focus of the story was "Marla awaits husband." Or "Family awaits daddy."

The verb here is key. Let's see how and why we wove the theme of waiting through this story.

The first sentence said, "Marla Denson has been here before on the airport tarmac . . . waiting. To be an Army wife, you have to get good at waiting."

The second section of copy included, "Marla knows that other families have waited in her same spot. Their husbands will never come home." Then I ask Marla the question, "How do you get good at waiting?"

The third section of copy said, "Judy Gross has gotten good at waiting. She has spent twenty years waiting for her husband, the colonel, to come home from this place or that."

All of that waiting builds tension, so when Charles finally does come home, the viewers get a memorable emotional release.

Why did we choose waiting as a central theme? Palmer and I were looking for the common experience the people standing on that tarmac had with our viewers. We know most viewers are not in the military, most are not Army spouses. But everyone has waited. And remember, this was Christmas Eve, a time of waiting.

Waiting became the one experience that everyone who saw that story and everyone we met at that airport shared.

Now I could have focused the story on the fact that soldiers who have been at war came home. I could have recounted how many days they were gone, how many were on the plane, how happy they seemed to be home and how many people showed up to greet them. I could have reported that an officer was there to welcome them back. Those would all have been facts. I call that the "what happened" of the story. And let's stipulate that it's important to say what happened. But that's not what anybody is going to remember in this story. The viewer will be far more interested in the "so what" of the story than the "what." So I will load up the anchor lead-in with "what happened" (soldiers from the 101st Airborne Division came home after a bloody tour in Somalia). Then I will guide viewers through the "so what" of the story, the story that you cannot readily see or understand without my help. I believe this concept is key to how we will make our TV reporting relevant in a world where the "what" of the story arrives on my mobile phone nonstop. By the time I experience a newscast, there is a fair chance I know "what" the news is. But I still need a journalist to explain what it all means, why it is important, why it happened and what will happen next.

Focus your story to one sentence or even three words. Ask yourself, "Who did what?" Answer that question with a noun, a verb and an object. A tight focus will connect with the viewer's head and heart, and viewers remember what they feel longer than what they know. In breaking news, "what happened" is the most important information. But once the story spreads and the public knows "what" happened, journalists have to focus their energy on the "so what" of the story along with the "what's next" and "why this happened."

USE SOUND BITES THAT CONNECT TO THE VIEWER'S HEART

Great stories turn on great sound bites. Let's use the "Soldier Comes Home" story to study what makes a sound bite work well.

Here are the sound bites we used:

> Marla: It's their jobs, they have to do it, they have to do it.

> Marla: Prayer, God, family and friends; them's the four things. If you don't have them, you can't make it.

> Judy Gross: Christmas when he was in Saudi, we just kept him in our thoughts and our prayers and we drank a toast to him on Christmas Eve, and that is about all you can do. You just have to think positive thoughts when they are not around.

> Tompkins to Marla: What did you say when you heard he was coming in?

> Marla: I love you. (laughs) I have to love him. He did his job and now it is over.

> Marla (still looking past the camera, squinting, watching the last few soldiers come down the stairs from the plane): You have to be the mother and the father while they are gone. You have to do everything together. (in the distance—a man shouts, Hey—Hey!)

> Marla: That's you! That's you! I love you, Charles! I love you, I love you, I love you, I LOVE you, Charles, I love you, I love you, I love you.

Look carefully at those sound bites. What do you notice? None of the bites contain facts. They are opinions, emotions and observations from the people who are closest to the story. Nobody else could have said what those people said with the same authenticity. Be careful, though: Don't fall in love with a sound bite. If it does not relate to the main meaning of the story, drop it. Focus matters more than a sound bite.

Now let's look at the copy—the words I spoke as the reporter.

> Tompkins: Marla Denson has been here before on the airport tarmac . . . waiting. To be an Army wife, you have to get good at waiting.
>
> Tompkins: Her husband, Charles, left for Somalia in August. When he left, the Army's mission in August was to feed a million starving Africans. (file tape) But the mission changed into an ugly shooting war. Marla knows that other families have waited in her same spot. Their husbands will never come home.
>
> Tompkins: Judy Gross has gotten good at waiting. She has spent twenty years waiting for her husband, the colonel, to come home from this place or that. This is an unexpected blessing, because nobody knew they were coming home until two days ago.
>
> Tompkins: One by one, the reunions happened around her. (pictures of a mother screaming, then hugging her daughter) Parents screamed at the sight of their children. Husbands held closely to their wives in uniform. (picture of hands) But she waited. (picture of Marla straining to see the plane) She began to think, maybe he wasn't on this plane. (pause) Maybe there was a problem.
>
> Tompkins: Corporal Charles Denson was home, home to be with his wife and his son. She brought him a rose, because, she said, he was always bringing her roses. She worried her hair didn't look right, she asked him a thousand times if he was okay. One hundred and fifty other Fort Campbell soldiers are still in Somalia tonight. What they wouldn't give to be where he is. He is home for Christmas.
>
> Al Tompkins, Channel 4 News, Fort Campbell, Kentucky.

What do you notice about the copy? In this story, the copy includes all the facts and details that explain what viewers are seeing on the screen but would not understand if I didn't explain it.

I didn't say in the copy, "She hugged and kissed him. She was so happy to see him." Viewers could see that. I wanted viewers to know what Marla said she worried about (her hair); I wanted them to know why she brought him a rose (because he was always bringing her roses).

Once you learn and teach others this guideline of subjective sound (opinions and emotions) and objective copy (the facts and details), you won't have to settle for those awful and predictable interviews that producers too often see from police or public information officers. Anyone who has conducted an interview with a stiff-talking police officer knows what the typical interview includes:

Reporter: What do we have here, Officer?

Officer: We have a white male, shot twice with a large caliber weapon. The deceased died on the scene. An investigation is under way.

The only story focus that would come out of that line of questioning would be: "Shooting kills man." It is not a new or even interesting story.

Every producer groans when he or she hears that interview. Some news directors, in an act of frustration, have even banned interviewing officials in an attempt to get rid of the objective sound bite.

Questions that include the word "what" usually produce responses that are factual. "What time is it?" "What happened here?" They are important questions, but the answers usually produce better copy than sound bites.

Producers and photojournalists must coach their reporter colleagues to ask subjective questions.

How about this:

Reporter: Officer Jones, you were the first person on the scene. What went through your mind when you saw this body in the middle of the street?

Officer Jones: I said to myself, not again. This is the third murder this month.

Reporter: You have been working this side of town a long time. How safe is our town?

Officer Jones: I think the city is safe, but this area right here, these ten city blocks are a real problem. We've got to get a handle on this. This is crazy.

This interview might give us the basis for a much more interesting focus: "Murder troubles officer."

The subjective sound bite guideline also makes it easier to pick bites from speeches and long ceremonies. Be alert for the opinion, feeling or emotion. That is the bite that creates the lump in the viewer's throat.

I sometimes ask participants in my seminars and workshops whether any of them struggled with math. Invariably, hands shoot up (an interesting common trait of journalists; many of us are bad at math). I ask the participants if they remember being asked, in the fourth grade, to go to the board and work out a math problem in front of the class. Of course they do. I ask why they remember that, and the answers are touching. High-powered professional journalists confess in front of a crowd that they were embarrassed by how they felt when they got the answer wrong in front of their class. But then I ask a key question: "What was that problem you were trying to work out?" Of course, nobody remembers. The illustration is complete; they remember what they feel far longer than what they know.

I believe this ability to teach through feelings is the key strength of video, especially television. Other media have other strengths. There is something about the tactile nature of newspapers or even smartphones that allows me to learn by cognitively interacting with the information. I can read it again and again to understand the story and information more deeply. The internet allows me to learn by interacting with information on the screen. Radio allows me to learn by imagining. But television is unique in its ability to teach through emotions and sensory experiences.

NOTES

1. Author's email exchange with researcher Krish Sathian, MD, PhD, FANA, Professor of Neurology, Rehabilitation Medicine and Psychology, Emory University May 2016.

2. Simon Lacey, Randall Stilla, and K. Sathian, "Metaphorically Feeling: Comprehending Textural Metaphors Activates Somatosensory Cortex," *Brain and Language* 120, no. 3 (2012): 416–421, http://www.sciencedirect.com/science/article/pii/S0093934X12000028.

3. Anne Murphy Paul, "Your Brain on Fiction," *The New York Times*, March 17, 2012.

4. Greg J. Stephens, Lauren J. Silbert, and Uri Hassan, "Speaker Listener Neural Coupling Underlies Successful Communication," *Proceedings of the National Academy of Sciences of the United States of America*, 107, no. 32 (2010): 14425–14430.

5. Jennifer Edson Escalas, "How Marketing Managers Can Leverage the Psychology of Narratives," in *Cracking the Code: Leveraging Consumer Psychology to Drive Profitability*, ed. Steven S. Posavac (New York: Taylor & Francis, 2015), 81–199.

6. John K. Donahue and Melanie C. Green, "A Good Story: Men's Storytelling Ability Affects Their Attractiveness and Perceived Status," *Personal Relationships* 23, no. 2 (March 9, 2016): 199–213.

7. Beverly Davenport Sypher and Theodore E. Zorn, "Communication-Related Abilities and Upward Mobility: A Longitudinal Investigation," *Human Communication Research* 12, no. 3 (Spring, 1986): 420–431, doi:10.1111/j.1468-2958.1986.tb00085.x

8. Jeremy I. Skipper, Susan Goldin-Meadow, Howard C. Nusbaum, and Steven L. Small, "Gestures Orchestrate Brain Language," *Current Biology* 19, no. 8 (Apr. 28, 2009): 661–667.

9. Idea adapted from Jon Franklin, *Writing for Story* (New York: Atheneum, 1986).

10. Blaise Pascal, "Lettres provinciales," letter 16, 1657, http:\\www.quotationspage.com/quote/26931.html.

11. Dec. 29, 1953.

12. Dec. 24, 1993.

CHAPTER 2

The Shape of the Story

The smarter the journalists are, the better off society is. The better the teacher, the better the student body.

—Warren Buffett,
Billionaire businessman

W hen a news director is looking over your résumé or interviewing you, he or she has four main questions rattling around about you:

- How do you look and sound on the air?
- Can you write, report and tell a story?
- Can I trust you?
- Do you have the capacity to grow into a great talent?

I can't give you better hair, and I will leave the makeup tips to others. I will offer some thoughts on ethics and personal behavior later in this book. But the most important thing I can teach anyone who wants to be a journalist is how to write clearer and stronger stories. It does not matter how great you look, how nice you are or how many great story ideas you generate if you cannot tell the story in a clear and engaging way. Great stories may be magical, but writing them isn't magic.

In this chapter we will cover the following:

- The power of surprises in storytelling
- When and why to use different story frames
- How to write a powerful and memorable close
- How to write a stronger sentence by putting the power at the end

STORIES NEED SURPRISES: GIVE VIEWERS GOLD COIN MOMENTS

You reach the viewer's heart by sneaking up on it. Great writers embrace the element of surprise. I learned this lesson one day when Irving Waugh walked into my newsroom. Mr. Waugh was, quite simply, one of the most important people in Nashville, Tennessee. He was the retired CEO of the Grand Ole Opry and Opryland. The Opry had long been associated with WSM radio and television. Mr. Waugh cast a long shadow.

He didn't know me, but, boy, did I know him. I had seen his silver hair, athletic frame and distinguished face in WSM-TV's archive photographs. I was the newly installed news director of that station (now WSMV) when Waugh strode into the newsroom unannounced that morning. He walked confidently and wore a finely tailored gray suit. He was a man who thought big thoughts. His diction was perfect. He had been a radio correspondent reporting from the Philippines during World War II, and his voice still had that mellow bass radio announcer tone.

My insecurities kicked in. Was this a friendly visit or an inspection? I was sorry I had chosen a soup-stained tie to wear that day.

I offered him my sweaty hand, which he firmly shook, and timidly introduced myself.

"Lad, what's on the program tonight?" his voice boomed. He wanted to know what was going to be on this evening's news.

"Well," I stammered, "Tonight, we have a nice piece about . . ." He cut me off.

"Surprise me, lad," he said. "I don't get surprised much by what I see anymore." I don't recall him saying anything else as he turned on his polished heel and left.

I was hellbent on not disappointing him, that night or ever. From that day forward, the phrase "Surprise me, lad" shaped the way I thought about my writing and my story selection. Stories need surprises. Newscasts need surprises. Mr. Waugh needed surprises.

Think about how you would tell the story to your friends or your family over dinner. You would not start with how the story turns out.

Boyd Huppert, an outstanding storyteller and reporter at KARE-TV Minneapolis, says, "The little surprises in stories are like little gold coins that you can give to your viewer as a reward for staying with the story. Every ten seconds or so, writers should stick in one of those gold coin moments. Just treat the story as if it were a forest trail, sprinkling the gold coins down the trail. Don't put all of the coins at the beginning of the trail; there will be no reason to keep walking. Don't make viewers walk all the way to the end of the trail; they might never get there."

The gold coin metaphor works for newscast producers to use as well. Don't stick all of the gold coins in the first block of the newscast. Sprinkle the memorable gold coin stories and surprises throughout the newscast. One reason so many viewers tune out of newscasts at the end of the first quarter-hour is because they have become accustomed to producers putting all of the news in the first 10 or 15 minutes of the newscast. Viewers get wise to the fact that night after night some producers build newscasts in which the important news is followed by the weather; then come the fluff news, celebrity updates and sports. Get some gold coin stories deeper in the newscast to reward viewers for sticking with you.

■ ■ ■ REMEMBER

Stories need surprises so viewers will feel something. And when viewers feel something, they'll remember the story. Surprises and emotion are the ways you reward viewers for giving you their attention.

STORY FRAMES: STRUCTURE AND RESTRUCTURE

As I watch TV news, I find that so many stories look the same. Time is an enemy. Reporters write packages (a complete story with a reporter's narration, sound bites and natural sound), re-cuts (a new version of the same story) and internet versions. Producers write teases and stories, and some even write promotional copy and online news. TV journalists write so much in such a hurry that they may find themselves writing from formulas they have developed. The formulas swallow gold coin moments and never give them back. Formulaic writing gives viewers the sense that they have heard the story before, even if the details are new. The story "sounds like" a story they have heard before.

Any producer could tell you the formulas they write in a crunch. How many times have I written the words:

"A funeral was held today for . . ."

"Police are investigating . . ."

"A local family is lucky to be alive."

These formulaic phrases have no meaning. They jump out of our computers because, in a crunch, writers type whatever pops into their heads. And once a phrase works, it will pop out again and again when the writer feels crunched for time.

Memorizing formulas does not make you a writer any more than memorizing $E = MC^2$ makes you a physicist. Still, there are some formulas or, as writers sometimes call them, story frames, that endure. When producers and reporters are working on deadlines, story frames can help them quickly write clear and easy-to-follow stories.

THE G–I / B–E GRID

Don't be afraid. The headline makes this sound lot more complex and theoretical than it really is. I first heard this theory in a lecture that author Kurt Vonnegut delivered about story shapes. It was ridiculously simple and brilliant, and he urged the audience to use it and share it. So I have and I will.

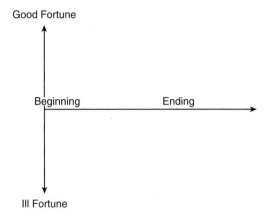

Imagine, Vonnegut said, that you have two axes on which to build your story. The vertical axis is the G–I axis. Good fortune sits at the top and ill fortune at the bottom.

The other axis on which we will map the story shape is the B–E axis, which represents the beginning and ending of the story.

The oldest stories ever told, the ones that audiences love more than any other, simply start with characters that people like, so they are slightly higher than the middle of the G/I axis. Then something awful happens to them. They sink to the bottom of the chart only to make a dramatic comeback just in time for the end of the story. Let's map *The Lion King* using Vonnegut's story axis.

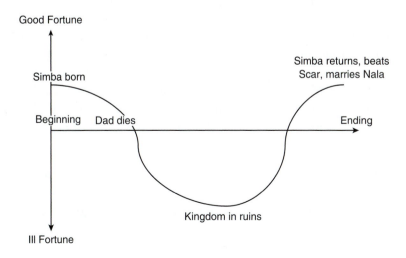

You can think of many examples of this shape, from *The Lion King* to *Frozen* and *The Wizard of Oz*, in which Dorothy actually goes up and down and up and down time and again.

You know this story shape well. Now let's try a variation on that shape, this time starting on the bottom end of the G–I axis. It is tough because most storytellers like to begin with an affable character that the audience does not have to warm up to.

We will use another story, Cinderella.

Now Cinderella has suffered lots of ill fortune. This story is so old that there are many adaptations over centuries. Somewhere around 7 B.C., a historian named Strabo wrote the story of "Rhodopis," sometimes called the "Egyptian Cinderella." Rhodopis was a young girl born in Greece, who had been kidnapped by pirates and sold into Egyptian slavery. She had beautiful blond hair, glowing green eyes and fair skin burned by the sun as she worked for an awful old man. Rhodopis' only friends were the animals who loved her. Sound familiar?

The Disney story stuck to the same story arc. Cinderella somehow ended up with a stepmother and some nasty-tempered stepsisters. We guess her mom died and her dad married this pig of a woman somehow, but the story does not get burdened with that. Suffice it to say Cinderella, who like Rhodopis is lovely, is about as far down the G-I line as you can go. And she stays there a while, until one day when she gets a visit from the fairy godmother. Things start looking up. Step by step, she gets some nice clothes including some fetching glass shoes (a foreshadowing if there ever was one), she gets transportation to and from a ball, she meets the prince and wows him. Then *bam*, it all falls apart fast. She loses track of time, rushes out the door and loses her shoe, and the prince never gets her name or mobile number. Cinderella sinks almost as low as she started on the G–I line, but she doesn't sink quite to the bottom because she still has the memories of her love for the prince.

Then the curve shoots to the top of the charts in a blissful ending that everyone sees coming but cannot resist. It is the same story as *The Little Mermaid* and a hundred other stories, but who's counting?

Let's chart the story of Cinderella:

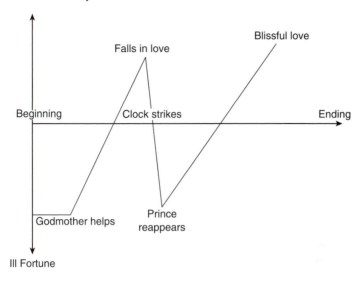

TRIED AND TRUE: SETTING, COMPLICATION, RESOLUTION, SUMMARY

As a reporter, when I was in a hurry and needed to write a story within minutes of an event, I relied on this storytelling structure. I realize now I was just using the old fairy tale structure.

Once upon a time . . . (the setting)

Suddenly . . . (the complication)

Fortunately . . . (the resolution)

As it turns out . . . (the closing/summary)

The story is easy on viewers' eyes and ears because the structure is so familiar. You heard it when you were a child in stories such as this one:

Once upon a time *there were three little pigs . . .*

Suddenly, *a big bad wolf appeared and planned to eat the pigs . . .*

Fortunately, *the third little pig made his house of bricks and the wolf could not blow it down . . .*

As it turns out, they were safe in the brick house. They sang "Who's Afraid of the Big Bad Wolf" and danced the night away.

Even old biblical tales follow this story frame. One of the oldest tales in the Bible, the story of Job, follows this frame exactly.

*There was once a rich and faithful man named Job. (**Once upon a time**)*

*Satan told God that if things turned badly for Job, then Job would turn on God. God said that was nonsense; Job would always remain faithful. The test began. (**Tension builds**)*

*Job lost his animals to raiders. A ball of fire fell from the sky and killed his servants. A big wind blew and killed all his children. (**Suddenly**)*

*Satan covers Job head to toe with boils. Job's friends try to convince Job that he must have done something wrong for all of this stuff to happen to him. Job struggles to figure out why his sweet life has turned so sour. He wants to die. He begs God for a just hearing. He can't understand why good things happen to bad people and bad things happen to good people like him. (**Complication**)*

*As it turns out, Job takes on God, face to face, demanding to know the meaning of all of this. God is not happy about it. God tells Job that as a man he can't understand why all of this bad stuff happens; it just does. Job learns that he doesn't know everything; he repents. (**Fortunately**)*

*In the end God gives Job a new family and fortune. Job lived another 140 years and saw four more generations before his death. (**As it turns out**)*

Now remember that is a story that is about 4,000 years old, and it follows the same frame as many of the things you write for the 6 o'clock news!

UPSIDE-DOWN: THE WHAT, BACKGROUND, MAIN ACTION, CONCLUSION

But sometimes, great stories can turn the old traditional story frames on their heads. They can look like this:

As it turns out . . . (what happened)

Once upon a time . . . (the background)

Suddenly . . . (the main action of the story)

Fortunately . . . (conclusion)

Here is a story that follows the upside-down story frame. KARE-TV's Boyd Huppert and photojournalist Gary Knox start this story in the present. They go back in time to give context and background; then the story returns to the present time.

This story started with a news release. Knox (who is a National Press Photographers Association Photographer of the Year) says one day he arrived early to work his 2 p.m. to 11 p.m. shift. As he skimmed through the story possibilities in the daily assignment desk folder, he saw a release that said:

To: All News Media

Re: Press conference

Where: 1030 Morgan Street

The City of Minneapolis will announce the demolition of a building that's been a problem in a Minneapolis neighborhood.

A Press Conference will be held at the site of the building at 3 p.m.

After the Press Conference, crews will begin to demolish 1030 Morgan.

The Mayor, the City Manager and the Police Chief will be on hand to answer media questions.

Knox and Huppert said they quickly asked to be sent out on the story. Knox said the assignment manager could not understand why one of America's best photojournalists and one of the country's most honored local reporters would ask to be assigned to cover a news conference. They clearly had a vision for the story that went far beyond a news conference.

This is the kind of story most photojournalists, reporters and producers hate because everyone already knows how the story will turn out. The city will destroy a building. Where is the suspense and storytelling opportunity in that?

Huppert and Knox knew the main story they wanted to tell was not centered on the news conference, the mayor, the city council or even the wrecking ball. They wanted to know why the city was making such a hoopla over the demolition of one old vacant building.

As you read this story, look for the story focus, the gold coins and the memorable moments. Look for the subjective sound and objective copy.

"1030 Morgan"

Gary Knox and Boyd Huppert

(Sound of a pile driver driving posts into the ground—pictures of a fence going up—pictures of broken windows in an old abandoned window)

Huppert: At 1030 Morgan, any sound but gunshots is good sound.

(More sound of pile driver—pictures of bullet holes in brick walls of the building)

Huppert: But these sounds qualify as music.

Neighbor: It is 1030 Morgan, the most notorious building in Minneapolis.

(Pictures of man putting up "Caution Do Not Enter" tape)

Huppert: An apartment house measured not just in units but in bodies. (File pictures of a shooting victim being carried out on a stretcher.)

Neighbor Number Two: People getting killed, violence and everything guns.

Huppert: In a six-month period last year, police answered 261 calls here.

Neighbor Number Three: It's just a bad building.

Men talking as bulldozer moves in.

Huppert: One of them, Denise Holland's.

Holland: One of them grabbed me, threw me down and said, "Give me your money." I told them I didn't have no money; the other one hit me. One stomped me and one cut me on my arm. (Picture of the scar on her arm)

Young Man: I seen this dude get his neck . . . (making a motion with his hand)

Neighbor Number Four: It's a demon; that is what I call it. That building ain't worth standing there.

(Sound and pictures of the bulldozer moving in)

Huppert: The demon at 1030 Morgan is about to be exorcised. (The arm of a front-end loader swipes across the front of the building, knocking a chunk out of the front wall; the crowd cheers)

Huppert: Neighbors fought for years to get to this day. (Woman uncorks a bottle of cheap champagne)

(Bystanders clink champagne glasses)

Bystanders: To 1030 Morgan—1030 Morgan.

Huppert: But it was the moment they savored.

Neighbor Number Four: I don't sit out here in no sun for nobody—I am going to sit and watch this building get tore down.

(The tractor's arm goes up for another swipe at the building—more bricks fall)

Huppert: Yet out of that sun came a symbol.

(The water from a firefighter's hose being used to settle dust helps to create a rainbow)

Neighbor Number Five: Do you see the rainbow? Yea.

Huppert: A sign of hope.

Denise: I think when that sucker comes down, people will start healing.

Huppert: Ten years of violence has ended (pictures of a black girl and a white boy standing side by side watching) with one last act of destruction.

(Man walking with a hunk of bricks he picked up)

Man With Bricks: This is for all the ones that passed away. I am going to take it home with me.

Huppert: The death of 1030 Morgan

A neighborhood woman talks to reporters.

Neighbor Number Two: Hallelujah.

Man With Bricks: For all the ones who ain't here. (He walks away with his arms full of bricks)

Boyd Huppert, KARE-11 News, Minneapolis.[1]

The typical frame for this story might have been this: City destroys building. But Knox and Huppert framed a more personal and intimate story. They framed the story about the demolition at 1030 Morgan as Neighbors celebrate demolition.

The story focuses *less on the building* at 1030 Morgan St. and *more on the people* who had been affected by the drug dealing and crime that had set up residence there. Because Knox and Huppert include the feelings and emotions of the people most closely affected by the demolition, the story becomes memorable and relevant, even to those of us who do not live near the neighborhood.

Their approach provides another important lesson. Journalists (and journalism students) should see every assignment as a story about people, not things. It does not matter if you are telling stories about students, athletes, politicians or crime bosses, your story will affect people's lives. Treat every story as Huppert and Knox did, with the sensitivity that you would hope for if the story were about you and your neighborhood. It is not just an assignment—it is a story.

DOTSON STORYTELLING: HEY, YOU, SEE, SO

Former NBC News/*Today* show correspondent Bob Dotson explained storytelling to me one day in the terms that he says a college professor taught him—advice that has helped shape one of the most known and honored storytellers in broadcasting. Dotson says every story should include these elements: "Hey," "You," "See," and "So."

- Every story begins with a "Hey," as in, "Hey, give me your attention."
- "You," the viewer should care about this story. We will make sure you see the relevance.
- "See" represents the two or three facts you have in your story that nobody else knows.
- "So" is why the viewer should care. In other words, "What does this story really mean?"

"When I write stories," Dotson says, "I always write the middle first. Then, if I have to cut the story for time, I cut a couple of the 'sees' and trim the 'so.'"

If he gets stuck for an opening line, Dotson says he often finds the second-best sound bite that he has but cannot use in the story because of time. Then he paraphrases it to make the lead sentence in the piece.

Dotson says his stories have four main parts:

- Scene setting
- Foreshadowing
- Conflict
- Resolution

Dotson says he is convinced that any story of any length can include these essential storytelling elements. "Even a 15-second commercial includes all four elements of scene: setting the scene, foreshadowing what is to come, establishing a conflict and resolving the conflict by selling you the product."

HOURGLASSES VERSUS PYRAMIDS: WHEN NARRATIVE RULES

We live in a time when viewers want to know the news quickly. Viewers have channel changer remotes at their fingertips, and they watch TV with mobile devices nearby too. So if you waste their time teasing a story they want to know about, they can find it online and ignore your story. That's why they rely on the inverted-pyramid style of "news first, details later." It's a reliable delivery system in breaking or spot-news reporting because getting the outcome of the story "up high" is vitally important to the viewer.

This time-honored news frame has been successfully used in stories for more than a century.

Former CNN assignment editor and now journalism professor and historian David T. Z. Mindich says that the inverted-pyramid style first may have been used in reporting of President Abraham Lincoln's death.[2]

There are many examples from that night. The Associated Press (AP) reported Friday April 14, 1865: "The President was shot in a theater to-night and perhaps mortally wounded."

AP writer Lawrence Gobright packed the most important news right in the opening sentence. Gobright filed a second dispatch that took readers on a chronology of the evening, but the opening sentence gave readers a reason to want to know why the reporter was writing about Lincoln's visit to Ford's Theatre.

The New York Herald and *The New York Times* reported the story the next morning. Both newspapers led their coverage not with stories written by reporters but with memos written by Secretary of War Edwin Stanton. Professor Mindich says Secretary Stanton's account of Lincoln's dying hours "may very well be one of the first inverted pyramids in history." The event in journalism history has its own irony because Stanton had a reputation for censoring the press during the Civil War.

On April 16, the *Herald* published Stanton's dispatch:

> This evening at about 9:30 p.m. at Ford's Theatre, the President, while sitting in his private box with Mrs. Lincoln, Mrs. Harris and Major Rathburn, was shot by an assassin, who suddenly entered the box and approached behind the President.
>
> The assassin then leaped upon the stage, brandishing a large dagger or knife and made his escape in the rear of the theatre.

The report was a little less direct than the stark AP version, but the main information still showed up in the first sentence.

The New York Times' lead story also was pyramid shaped but without the hard summary lead sentence and starts with an eyewitness account. The story that follows begins with the latest information. Even though it was reported more than 150 years ago, you can almost imagine Wolf Blitzer saying something like this at the top of his CNN show *The Situation Room* as urgent music plays under his words.

War Department, Washington

April 15—4:10 A.M.

To Major-Gen. Dix:

The President continues insensible and is sinking.

Secretary Seward remains without change.

Frederick Seward's skull is fractured in two places, besides a severe cut upon the head.

The attendant is still alive, but hopeless. Maj. Seward's wound is not dangerous.

It is now ascertained with reasonable certainty that two assassins were engaged in this horrible crime, Wilkes Booth being the one that shot the President, and the other companion of his whose name is not known, but whose description is so clear that he can hardly escape. It appears from a letter found in Booth's trunk that the murder was planned before the 4th of March, but fell through then because the accomplice backed out until "Richmond could be heard from." Booth and his accomplice were at the livery stable at six o'clock last evening, and there left with their horses about ten o'clock, or shortly before that hour.

It would seem that they had for several days been seeking their chance, but for some unknown reason it was not carried into effect until last night.

One of them has evidently made his way to Baltimore—the other has not yet been traced.

Edwin M. Stanton

Secretary of War

Some of the most remarkable breaking news reporting from that awful attack came from *The Star Extra*, which used the inverted-pyramid style along with some microscopic detail. *The Star Extra* reported,

> At 7:20 o'clock the President breathed his last, closing his eyes as if falling to sleep, and his countenance assuming an expression of perfect serenity. There were no indications of pain and it was not known that he was dead until the gradually decreasing respiration ceased altogether.
>
> Rev. Dr. Gurley, of the New-York Avenue Presbyterian Church, immediately on it being ascertained that life was extinct, knelt at the bedside and offered an impressive prayer, which was responded to by all present.
>
> Dr. Gurley then proceeded to the front parlor, where Mrs. Lincoln, Capt. Robert Lincoln, John Hay, the Private Secretary, and others, were waiting, where he again offered a prayer for the consolation of the family.
>
> The following minutes, taken by Dr. Abbott, show the condition of the late President throughout the night.
>
> 11:00 o'clock—Pulse 44.
>
> 11:05 o'clock—Pulse 45, and growing weaker.
>
> 11:10 o'clock—Pulse 45.
>
> 11:15 o'clock—Pulse 42.
>
> 11:20 o'clock—Pulse 45; respiration 27 to 29.
>
> 11:26 o'clock—Pulse 42.
>
> 11:32 o'clock—Pulse 48 and full.
>
> 11:40 o'clock—Pulse 45.
>
> 11:45 o'clock—Pulse 45; respiration 22.
>
> 12:00 o'clock—Pulse 48; respiration 22.

12:16 o'clock—Pulse 48; respiration 21; echmot. both eyes.

12:30 o'clock—Pulse 45.

12:32 o'clock—Pulse 60.

12:35 o'clock—Pulse 66.

12:40 o'clock—Pulse 69; right eye much swollen and echmoses.

12:45 o'clock—Pulse 70.

12:55 o'clock—Pulse 80; struggling motion of arms.

1:00 o'clock—Pulse 86; respiration 30.

1:30 o'clock—Pulse 95; appearing easier.

1:45 o'clock—Pulse 86; very quiet, respiration irregular. Mrs. Lincoln present.

2:10 o'clock—Mrs. Lincoln retired with Robert Lincoln to adjoining rooms.

2:30 o'clock—President very quiet; pulse 54; respiration 28.

2:52 o'clock—Pulse 48; respiration 30.

3:00 o'clock—Visited again by Mrs. Lincoln.

3:25 o'clock—Respiration 24 and regular.

3:35 o'clock—Prayer by Rev. Dr. Gurley.

4:00 o'clock—Respiration 26 and regular.

4:15 o'clock—Pulse 60; respiration 25.

5:50 o'clock—Respiration 28; regular; sleeping.

6:00 o'clock—Pulse failing; respiration 28.

6:30 o'clock—Still failing and labored breathing.

7:00 o'clock—Symptoms of immediate dissolution.

7:22 o'clock—Death.

The tiny details in the story, including the exact pulse rate, give readers vital information about how doctors hoped the president might pull through. At 5:50, there seemed to be a sign of hope. The president's breathing was regular and he was sleeping. Ten minutes later, hope began to fade with the note, "pulse failing"; we can see that in a period of minutes, Lincoln's condition grew more grave. Just after dawn, he died.

After the death of President Lincoln, Professor Mindich says, "The character of news writing changed." Newspaper reporters (and, later, TV and radio reporters) had discovered a formula for putting the most important news first. But the structure lacks the gold coins that pull readers and viewers through a story all the way to the end.

To build up to a pivotal moment in storytelling, writers have another shape at their fingertips: the hourglass. In the hourglass, the top of the story holds the important news but with a twist. It is followed by a transition to hold viewers' interest and supported by details of the event. The hourglass can hold the viewer's heart from top to bottom.

Let's look at a story by KARE-TV Minneapolis reporter Phil Johnston to see how these story frames play out in day-to-day reporting. Johnston and photojournalist Brett Akagi came across a car on fire. It was a fairly typical story except for one big detail—which they planted about a third of the way into the story.

This is a strong example of a daily news story that goes well beyond the inverted-pyramid style into an hourglass shape.

"What I've Got Is What I've Got"

Phil Johnston and Brett Akagi

(Sound of siren, pictures of flames, water spraying on the fire)

Paul Hawkins (Talking to firefighter): I pulled off the freeway and I saw smoke coming and I said, "Maybe just the pipe got hot."

Johnston: Almost as soon as Paul Hawkins' '89 Celebrity caught fire, on Hamlin Avenue near I-94, the St. Paul fire department had it out. But you would be amazed how quickly your world can change . . .

Hawkins: I stay in Minneapolis, but I live in my car.

Johnston: . . . when you are homeless.

Hawkins: Everything I own, my whole life, pictures of my mom, my family, my ID, everything I basically own.

Johnston: Since moving from Kentucky to Minnesota this winter, Paul Hawkins has made a home of his car while looking for work. For all practical purposes, for no apparent reason, his home was destroyed today.

Hawkins (With a disgusted look, he tosses burned belongings into the car): Well, what I got is what I got. I lost my gloves, my hats, every damn thing.

Johnston: And when you consider that Paul Hawkins' everything wasn't much to begin with . . .

Hawkins: My whole damn world.

Johnston: It kind of makes you wonder, why?

Hawkins (As he walks away from the burned-out shell of his car): You know, you take a forty-year-old male, ain't nobody gonna help me. I'm fixing to be on my own again.

Johnston: In St. Paul, Phil Johnston, KARE-11 News.

Johnston's story has an hourglass shape. It starts small, sets a conflict, then builds to a big surprise—the man lives in his car. The story gets small again, revealing all of the tiny details of what is in the car; then Hawkins begins to get emotional and frustrated. It is clear we are building to a dramatic finish. Paul Hawkins tosses a rag into the burned-out hull of the car and walks off in disgust, homeless and broke. Nobody is there to rescue him. The big surprise is that there is no hero to rush in and save him. It is just an afternoon of rotten luck.

Now, let's rewrite the story in a typical inverted-pyramid style. I suspect this is how most young journalists would tell the story. It would be all facts, following the who, what, when, where, why and how style, forgetting that stories require the storyteller to aim for the heart. Read this version:

Reporter: A car fire today destroyed everything that forty-year-old Paul Hawkins owned. Hawkins, who has been out of work, lived in his car. The 1989 Chevy Celebrity caught fire this morning while he was driving on Hamlin Avenue near I-94 in St. Paul. Nobody was hurt. But firefighters couldn't save Hawkins' belongings from the flames. He lost his hat, gloves, even pictures of his mother. Now he is left with nothing.

Paul Hawkins (With a disgusted look, he tosses burned belongings into the car): Well, what I got is what I got.

Reporter: Hawkins is not sure what he is going to do next. With no home and all of his belongings destroyed, he wondered how he can start over.

Hawkins: You know, you take a forty-year-old male, ain't nobody gonna help me. I'm fixing to be on my own again.

Reporter: Firefighters are not sure how the blaze started.

Hawkins (Talking to firefighter): I pulled off the freeway and I saw smoke coming and I said, "Maybe just the pipe got hot."

Reporter: In St. Paul, Joe Smith WXXX News.

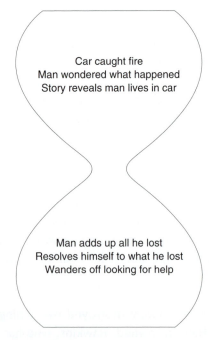

Car caught fire
Man wondered what happened
Story reveals man lives in car

Man adds up all he lost
Resolves himself to what he lost
Wanders off looking for help

Hourglass style. Starts small, sets a conflict and then builds to a big surprise.

This story shape looks like an inverted pyramid:

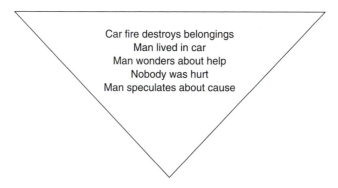

Car fire destroys belongings
Man lived in car
Man wonders about help
Nobody was hurt
Man speculates about cause

Inverted-pyramid style. Starts with all facts, followed by the who, what, when, where, why and how.

Which story do you think viewers will stick with and remember? What is the focus and three-word summary? How do sound bites help viewers feel, as well as hear, each story? When the writer makes a viewer feel the story, the writer has aimed for the viewer's heart.

If we had been telling the story of a horrible crash that killed a bunch of people, if we had been out there live telling the story of a wreck that tied up traffic for hours, then the inverted pyramid would have been exactly the right shape to use. It is a breaking-news shape. But most news stories are not breaking news. They are narrative stories and require the hourglass shape.

THE BIG CLOSE: RESOLVE THE STORY

Don't spend all of your energy on the first half of your story only to allow the piece to run out of gas. Save one last morsel for an "ear-catching close." It's the big finish. The close to the big sale. The grand finale of the fireworks display. What you show and say at the end of the story are often what lingers in the viewer's heart.

POYNTER NEWSU E-LEARNING COURSE

Learn more about story shapes in Aim for the Heart at www.newsu.org/heart.

As I think about what I will show, and the pictures that I will write to, I usually go for what a photojournalist friend, Don Cadorette, calls the "negative action shot."

At the end of the story Cadorette likes to have the subject walking away from the camera. If he used a zoom, he zoomed *out* at the close, not *in*. He wanted the viewer to physically detach from the story, as you would if you walked away at the end of a conversation. It is less jarring than a close-up or with someone walking toward you.

Be careful about what the viewer hears. When a story ends on a sound bite, be certain the sound bite does not tilt the story in some way that makes the story unfair. The last words in a story can color how the viewer thinks about the entire story.

Imagine a story about a college student suing a professor for giving her what the student says is an unfair grade. If you close your story with the tearful student saying, "I worked so hard on that project. It was so unfair. He just didn't like me," the story ends by giving the student the loudest voice. But if you close with the professor saying, "She has been a whiner since she arrived in my class. I made it clear what I expected, and she didn't do the work. It would be unfair to those who did the work well for me to be so charitable to her," then the professor gets the upper hand.

It is dangerous to close a story on a one-line outcue (the last line of the story) or a sound bite, because it can send an editorial tone that you didn't intend. It is usually better to end a story with narration. It may be a line that connects the bottom of the story with the top of the story.

When you are doing a live report, the best way to close a story is to "spin the story forward." Tell the viewer what is likely to happen next. If the city council just raised taxes, then the live stand-up story close might be when the tax increase takes effect, how to contact your council member, whether there is another vote or how to appeal your higher tax bill.

When Byron Pitts was assigned to produce the lead story for the *CBS Evening News* on the night of September 11, 2001, he said he knew it would be a historic assignment. He was worried not just about the content but the tone, especially on a night when the world was on the brink of war.

Pitts opened the story with a live stand-up saying:

"Without exaggeration, this part of Manhattan looks like a battlefield. We have seen blood, we have seen body parts, we have watched people die in front of our eyes. This was terrorism like we in America have never seen before."

At the end of the emotional and graphic story, Pitts came back on camera and spoke quietly.

"This morning when the first tower collapsed, I was standing about three blocks away with CBS news correspondent Mika Brzezinski. As the fireball rolled toward us, Mika grabbed her shoes, I grabbed her hand and we ran like hell. Thousands did. Except for a few sirens, I have never heard New York City this quiet. Graveyard quiet."

Pitts says, "I like a live close that moves the piece forward or paints the picture of that exact moment."[3]

Oddly, it was on September 11, 1998, when the tangled love story of a girl barely out of college nearly brought down the U.S. presidency. On that day the government issued the "Starr Report," which described the story of how President Bill Clinton kept up an illicit affair with a White House intern, Monica Lewinsky.

Although the country had heard of the affair and Lewinsky was one of the country's most recognized faces at the time, the story of who this young woman really was remained untold. CBS' Jerry Bowen started his story for the program *48 Hours* this way:

> **(Footage of Lewinsky walking through a group of reporters; Lewinsky entering a car)**
>
> **Bowen: Those who claim to know Monica Lewinsky say she always wanted to be the center of attention in the worst way.**
>
> **(Footage of Lewinsky walking through a group of reporters; Lewinsky at a dance)**
>
> **Bowen: And for the past eight months she has been. And those who claim to be her friends say it comes as no surprise.**[4]

Bowen told the story of Lewinsky's childhood, broken home, a five-year affair with "a drama instructor back at Beverly Hills High, a married man eight years her senior." The story built to this memorable closing line that ties the end of the story right back to the opening.

Bowen: And now the world knows about Monica Lewinsky, a child of affluence who grew up to be a woman at the center of a living nightmare; a young woman who behind the smile yearned to become somebody, and tonight, she has, in the worst way.

The worst endings are those that raise new questions and leave them to dangle. A close second is to end with a cliché such as "Time will tell" or "Nobody knows." It is as unsatisfying as a movie that ends with "It was all a dream." If you are struggling for an ending, go back in your story and see what questions you have not answered yet.

The closing works best if it connects with the opening in some way—closing the circle. The last sentence usually should be short and tight. It should contain only one main thought that summarizes the whole story. The last sentence should directly connect to the three-word focus statement you write for your story.

Good endings resolve the main theme of the story. The shorter the story, the stronger the surprise at the end should be. If you have a long story, viewers may resent you holding a big surprise until the end.

The best story close is like a good ending to a meaningful phone call. Don't repeat what you already said. Don't keep jabbering about nothing. Close it. But, like a good phone conversation, leave viewers with the knowledge and the feeling that you intended at the beginning.

"WELL, TIMMY": UNTIDY ENDINGS ARE OK

Former NBC News/*Today* show correspondent Bob Dotson says that most great stories have what he calls a "Well, Timmy" paragraph near the end.

"If you ever watch the old show *Lassie*," Dotson says, "then you will know what I am talking about. See, somewhere late in every episode, Dad sits down with little Timmy and sorts the story all out for him. 'Well, Timmy,' Dad might say, 'You see, the little birds have to learn to fly away from their mother, and even if we want to help them, they have to learn to be on their own, without our interference. Someday you will want to fly away from Mom and me, do you understand, son?'" Dad wisely resists the temptation to tidy up the fact that sometimes nature takes its painful course.

You see the same story frame on more recent shows such as *Game of Thrones, NCIS, Blue Bloods* and *Madam Secretary*. The shows build to a moment of understanding but end with a lingering tension.

Journalists also should resist the temptation to tidy up an untidy story. The good guy does not always win; sometimes stories do not resolve themselves. Sometimes bad guys get away with crimes, cops do bad things, nurses become addicted to drugs and soldiers are not brave. We must tell those stories or we risk being less than authentic.

We see a lot of "welcome home" stories when soldiers return from war, and it is good to celebrate such moments. But we also need to tell the stories about how difficult it is to adjust to civilian life after living in a war zone. War sometimes produces unexpected heroes, and we should find and tell those stories. We also owe it to the public to produce truthful storytelling about how hard it is to live without legs or with part of a brain missing because of a roadside bomb.

The "What I've Got Is What I've Got" story you read earlier in this chapter is an example of how journalists should resist tidying up an untidy story. Nobody rushes forward to rescue Paul Hawkins. At the end of the story, he has no shelter, no cell phone to call a friend to rescue him. The raw truthfulness adds power to the story because it is the way life is when the camera is not around.

I think Mr. Waugh would have liked that story.

■ ■ ■ REMEMBER

There are many kinds of story frames. The inverted pyramid is especially useful for covering breaking news that answers the question "What happened?" The hourglass frame is most useful when the story answers questions of context: "How often? Why? What else should I know?" Just before the story closes, summarize the main point in one sentence. Then, deliver the big close that comes back to the main conflict you established at the beginning of the story. But don't give in to pressure to make your ending something it isn't. Not all stories have happy endings. Some of them have ugly ones.

Sentences Have Shapes, Too: Power at the End

Just as stories have shapes, so do sentences. One way to write for the ear is to place the power of the sentence at the end.

My Poynter Institute colleague Roy Peter Clark was coaching a writer whose assignment was to tell the story of a memorial service for a whale shark named Ralph who died at an Atlanta aquarium. The reporter offered this sentence:

The crowd gathered and knelt around the 15-foot-long creature.

Clark said he could make the sentence stronger by not adding or subtracting a thing. He did that by asking the writer to place a number one next to the most important or surprising part of the sentence. The second most surprising element gets the number two, and the context, or "dull but important" part of the sentence, gets the number three. You try it.

The crowd gathered (___) and knelt (___) around the 15-foot-long-creature (___).

What surprises me most is that the crowd knelt around a dead whale shark. It shows reverence, respect and even sadness. So "knelt" gets the number one.

That there was a crowd at all is surprising and important to me. So that gets the number two. I already knew there was a dead whale shark involved in this story, so that gets the number three.

Clark teaches that the sentence should end with the number one, start with the number two and the context stays in the middle.

So, the new sentence is:

The crowd gathered (2) around the 15-foot-long creature (3) and knelt (1).

What an improvement!

Clark says there is nothing new about this technique, of course. As proof, he offers an example from Shakespeare's *Macbeth*. Which of these sentences do you think Shakespeare wrote for Macbeth's armor bearer, Seyton:

- "The Queen is dead, my lord."
- "The Queen, my lord, is dead."
- "My lord, the Queen is dead."

Shakespeare wrote the second sentence. Let's number his words by the power and importance of the information:

- "The Queen (2), my lord (3), is dead (1)."[5]

There is no question the death is the punch in the gut, so it goes at the end of the sentence (1). The word "Queen" catches your attention right off, so it belongs at the front (2). We know to whom Seyton is talking, so the courtesy title, my lord, is not nearly as important as what comes before or after it. That's why it gets ranked third and goes right in the middle of the sentence. (In fact, only a few lines before, Seyton calls Macbeth "my good lord," further diluting the importance of that reference later.)

Look at these other famous lines from the movies and see how the power goes at the end of the sentence. I numbered each sentence by each phrase's importance:

From *Gone With the Wind*

"Frankly (2), my dear (3), I don't give a damn (1)."

When Rhett Butler says, "Frankly," you know something big is going to come tumbling out of his mouth. "My dear" is condescending and sets up the powerful ending. I might argue that you could also write the sentence, "My dear (2), frankly (3), I don't give a damn (1)."

From *Forrest Gump*

"My mama always said (2), 'Life was like a box of chocolates (3); you never know what you're gonna get (1).'"

Mama was a key to his life, so what she said mattered. His life was a constant string of surprises, so "You never know what you're gonna get" belongs at the end. If he had said, "'Life is like a box of chocolates,' my mama always said. 'You never know what you are gonna get,'" then the fact that a grown man is still dependent on the wisdom of his mother gets lost. We have to know the source of the wisdom to understand the gravity in the punch line. The worst version would be "'Life is like a box of chocolates; you never know what you are gonna get,' my mama said." By the time you get to the end of the sentence, you have forgotten what mama said that was so wise.

From *Casablanca*

"Of all the gin joints (2) in all the towns in all the world (3), she walks into mine (1)."

Clearly the middle of the sentence, "in all the towns in all the world," is the most convoluted part of this thought. "Gin joints" is a great phrase, different from beer joints or whisky taverns. A gin joint is a smoky but sophisticated place with torch dancers, the kind of scene you would see in a Bogart movie. "Gin joints" sets up the sentence by setting a scene.

From *Silence of the Lambs*

"A census taker once tried to test me. I ate his liver (2) with some fava beans (3) and a nice Chianti (1)."

The crazy Dr. Hannibal Lecter is trying to make the point to Jodie Foster's character, FBI agent Clarice Starling, that cannibalism is no big thing to him. So Lecter put the "nice Chianti" at the end, as if his choice of wine were the big issue, not the fact that he ate another human.

The "fava beans" detail is so memorable because it is so shocking that a cannibalistic killer would think to prepare a side dish with his meal, as if to say, "Hmm, what would go well with a human body for dinner?" The writer also cleverly chose Dr. Lecter's name. "Hannibal" rhymes with "cannibal."

From *Mad Max*

"My name is Max (2). My world is fire (3). And blood (1)."

"Blood" is the power word. It is the human suffering. It comes last.

From *SpongeBob SquarePants*

"Squidward (2), I used your clarinet (3) to unclog my toilet (1)."

Comedy nearly always turns on the idea of power at the end of the sentence.

What if you are working with shorter sentences? Look at these:

From *Terminator 2*

"Hasta la vista (2), baby (1)."

No question about it. The sassy, in-your-face nature of the sentence is captured in the last word, "baby."

From *Captain America*

"You get hurt (2), hurt 'em back (1). You get killed (2), walk it off (1)."

The order of these two sentences is perfect. It is not "hurt them back if they hurt you." It is not "walk it off if they kill you." And the preposterous nature of the advice makes the passage jump. It is not out of the realm of possibility that somebody who was hurt could hurt somebody back but if you are dead, you won't be "walking it off." The passage implies that to be a superhero, you have to overcome anything, even death.

HOW TO SOUND LIKE MORGAN FREEMAN

Morgan Freeman is my favorite narrator. It is more than his smooth, deep voice. In movies and commercials, there is something about his style that breaks through the clutter. Let's figure out what it is.

First, let's look at a commercial he did for Visa. The commercial features Dan Jansen, a speed skater. Only seven hours before he was to race in the 1988 Olympics in Calgary, Jansen was on the phone with his sister who was taking her last breaths of life after a long bout with leukemia. Like Dan, Jane had been a speed skater. Dan had won a world championship race just before the Olympics. He was the hands-down favorite to win the gold medal in the 500-meter race. He wanted to win it for his sister. On the first turn, he crashed. Skidded across the ice. Sat crying with his head in his hands. The commercial showed all of that with this copy read by Morgan Freeman:

> Hours before his race in 88, Dan Jansen's sister Jane passed away.
>
> He'd promised her he'd win gold.
>
> He didn't.
>
> Until six years later.
>
> Then he skated a victory lap with his daughter Jane.

What do we notice about that passage?

For one thing, notice that the power words all come at the end of each sentence.

Passed away. Didn't. Jane.

Imagine if the copy had been written this way:

> Dan Jansen's sister Jane passed away hours before his race in 1988.
>
> He didn't win gold, even though he promised her he would.
>
> He skated a victory lap with his daughter Jane when he won six years later.

It sounds a lot like a news stories, doesn't it. And there is no heart in these sentences.

Let's try another Morgan Freeman commercial. This time Freeman is the voice of the commercial that Barack Obama ran during his re-election campaign. Obama was in big trouble at the time: the GOP was surging, the economy was sputtering, and although Osama bin Laden had been killed, the wars dragged on in Iraq and Afghanistan. Obama bailed out Wall Street and General Motors. Freeman needed to deliver a message to calm down the uncertainty.

> Every president inherits challenges. Few have faced so many.
>
> Four years later, our enemies have been brought to justice.
>
> Our heroes are coming home.

Assembly lines are humming again.

There are still challenges to meet, children to educate, a middle class to rebuild.

But the last thing we should do is turn back now.

The word order in these sentences is pure Morgan Freeman brilliance.

He delivers the memorable power words at the end of each sentence.

- "few have faced so many." The sentence acknowledges the job is tough no matter who serves. It does not say, "Barack Obama sure inherited a lot of problems."

- "brought to justice." That is a powerful phrase that avoids saying, "We killed him." Nobody opposes justice.

- "home." A more unifying word, not a phrase such as "We are pulling out of Iraq," which was controversial.

- "humming again." It does not mention the bailout, just the workers and work. Those are good things.

- "meet, educate, rebuild." These are all power words to punctuate phrases.

Let's look at some other examples of writing that put the power at the end of the sentence from the opening minutes of *March of the Penguins*. Sentence after sentence, the fluid and descriptive writing hangs in viewers' ears and creates vivid imagery. The words explain the video, rather than compete with it.

Here is how the film opens. Imagine Morgan Freeman's rich baritone voice reading these lines over scenes of Antarctic ice that towers like frozen cathedrals:

There are few places harder to get to in this world. But there aren't any where it is harder to live. The average temperature here at the bottom of the Earth is a balmy fifty-eight degrees below. That's when the sun is out.

It wasn't always like this; Antarctica used to be a tropical place, densely forested and teeming with life. But then the continent started to drift south, and by the time it was done drifting, the dense forests had all been replaced with a new ground cover—ice.

As for the former inhabitants, they'd all died or moved on long ago. Well, almost all of them.

Legend has it that one tribe stayed behind. Perhaps they thought the change in weather was only temporary, or maybe they were just stubborn. But whatever their reasons, these stalwart souls refused to leave. For millions of years they have made their home on the darkest, driest, windiest and coldest continent on Earth. And they have done so pretty much alone. So in some ways, this is a story of survival. A tale of life over death.

But it is more than that, really; this is a story about love.[6]

Let's look at those sentences.

There are few places harder to get to in this world. But there aren't any where it is harder to live.

The point of these sentences is that as difficult as it is to get to Antarctica, it is nearly impossible to live here—and, yet, the penguins do just that. The notion of living here is so unimaginable that it makes for a strong punch line revealed only after the writer points out how far away it is. How much weaker this would have been if the writer had said:

It is hard to get here and hard to live here. In fact, it is the hardest place in the world to live.

The movie said:

The average temperature here at the bottom of the Earth is a balmy fifty-eight degrees below. That's when the sun is out.

The second sentence is a surprise. It is a payoff. What if the writer had said:

Even when the sun is out, it is only fifty-eight degrees below zero.

It is factual but lacks the element of surprise. In truth, I doubt that viewers will ever remember the fact that it is 58 degrees below zero. They are seeing mountains of ice and just have to remember it is darn cold here. Since most of us have never experienced 58-degree-below weather, we cannot relate to conditions that cold. So the temperature is not the point of this passage; the fact that it is so cold and the sun is out is the point. You will remember what comes at the end of the sentence.

Let's look at one more sentence, and this time I will number it:

> **But then the continent started to drift south (2), and by the time it was done drifting (4), the dense forests had all been replaced with a new ground cover (3)—ice (1).**

It would be so much less effective to say:

> **Ice now covers what used to be dense forests. It all happened because the continent drifted so far south.**

The movie's narrative constantly explains what the viewer is seeing. You never hear Morgan Freeman say, "Look at all of this ice. There are mountains of it as far as you can see." Instead, he *explains* why there is so much ice. He never says, "Look, there are some penguins." Instead he explains how they got here and how they survive. The lessons are clear: Put the power at the end of the sentence and explain the video—don't just narrate it.

■ ■ ■ REMEMBER

Powerful stories have powerful sentences. Identify the most important or surprising part of every sentence and order the information accordingly.

NOTES

1. Photos © KARE-11. Used with permission.
2. David T. Z. Mindich, *Just the Facts: How "Objectivity" Came to Define American Journalism* (New York University Press, 1998), 65–67.
3. Interview with the author, Dec. 31, 2009.

4. CBS News, *48 Hours,* Sept. 11, 1998.
5. William Shakespeare, *Macbeth,* act 5, scene 5, line 19.
6. *March of the Penguins,* Warner Independent Pictures and National Geographic Films, Luc Jacquet, director; narration written by Jordan Roberts, 2005.

CHAPTER 3

Find Memorable Characters

> *What you're aiming at are people's ears rather than their eyes.*
>
> —Morley Safer,
> CBS *60 Minutes* correspondent

When a massive earthquake flattened Port-au-Prince, Haiti, in 2010, it is not an exaggeration to say that journalists had no words to adequately describe the damage, despair and death that surrounded them. Paul Hunter, of the Canadian Broadcasting Corporation (CBC), narrowed the focus of his stories. He told the story of one doctor who had worked day after endless day amputating quake victims' arms and legs. Hunter focused on a 9-year-old girl who had a badly broken left hand. A doctor pinned a tag on her dress. The message, written in English so the child could not know what she was in for, said, "Amputate hand." Hunter also showed a scene outside a clinic where a young woman was writhing in pain. Doctors had no painkillers to give to the woman as they set her broken arm. Rather than crying out in agony, she sang to God for saving her life. An attending medic sang along quietly.

Those arresting images of survival and exhaustion gave me the first real understanding I had about how awful the circumstances had become in that already struggling country.

Those small stories of compelling characters put a face on the story in a way no bureaucrat or elected official could. The characters made me "feel" the story, not just know about it.

Characters are usually people, but they can be objects, such as an old church, an overgrown cemetery or a pristine lake, or they can be animals, such as a dying swan. Each of these images evokes an emotion in the viewer. Characters are the mechanism we use to deliver information and tell the story. After all, people remember what they feel longer than what they know.

A story about the BP oil spill in the Gulf of Mexico is more memorable if you can tell me about a fisherman who can't feed his family because the fishing grounds are closed now, or if you tell me about an environmental worker who is dedicating her life to cleaning up the marshes.

Think of stories like ladders. The best stories move up and down the ladder.

At the top of the ladder is the wide story, the context. At the bottom is the specific, the character. You enter the story in the middle and it doesn't much matter where you go first, to the context or the character, just don't linger there.

In this chapter we will cover the following:

- How to use a memorable character to tell the story
- How to tell big stories through strong but small characters
- How to choose the number of characters you need to tell the story

PUT A FACE ON THE STORY: YOU REMEMBER WHAT YOU FEEL

From 1961 to 1998, ABC ran a program titled *Wide World of Sports*. Jim McKay voiced the opening over iconic images, including those of Muhammad Ali and a poor skier named Vinko Bogataj,[1] crashing down the slope. McKay's voiceover said, "Spanning the globe to bring you the constant variety of sports. The thrill of victory and the agony of defeat. The human drama of athletic competition. This is ABC's *Wide World of Sports*."

In that one show opening, ABC described what makes a story work. It didn't promise "scores and more." It promised human drama, thrills and agony. Characters become the delivery mechanism for information. I promise you that most viewers who are old enough to have watched that show have no idea who Vinko Bogataj is, but ask them about that *Wide World of Sports* show opening, and they will remember seeing him wipe out on that ski jump.

Make me feel the story and I will never forget it. Tell me a load of facts and they will be gone from my memory in seconds.

The best characters are "cool."

Colorful

Outgoing

Opinionated

Lively

And one more thing. The best characters give you access to the real person inside. They share their fears, hopes, disappointments and joys. You get to know what motivates and discourages them. Without this element, interviews feel superficial.

Winfield Dunn was a former Republican governor of Tennessee when he decided to run again for the office he once held. He was a delightful retired dentist who spoke in predictable sound bites. After covering him almost daily for months, I still didn't feel that I knew why he was running. He was a successful businessman, and his term as governor was generally considered to have been successful, especially for some areas of the state that Democrats had ignored for years. However, in this campaign he was running significantly behind in the polls. The crowds at his rallies were small, and campaign contributions were trickling in.

One day I asked Gov. Dunn why he was putting himself through a grueling campaign that, in all probability, he would not win. He said he was running because he "loved Tennessee."

I asked what I thought then was a dumb question: "How much do you love it?" He proceeded to tell me that when his first grandchild was born to his daughter, who was living in Oklahoma, he took a plastic bag of dirt with him to the meet the newborn. He says he emptied a bag of soil on a quilt that he had spread on the floor of his daughter's home. He then lifted the baby from her crib and dabbed her feet into the dirt. "I wanted her feet to touch Tennessee soil before they touched Oklahoman soil," the governor told me. There, finally, I had a window into the man. I couldn't help thinking that if he told that story in a campaign commercial, he could have been re-elected.

All of the campaign promises, all of the staged speeches, didn't tell me as much about the man as that one little story did. I barely remember what he promised in that campaign, although I must have heard those speeches a hundred or more times. I do remember how I feel about that one story concerning his granddaughter. It is so true: You remember what you feel longer than what you know.

Let's try this experiment. As best as you can, read this script without going backward to capture details. Just read the words as if you were reading them out loud. Then we will do some checking to see if my theory holds water.

"Lottery Jackpot Winners Speak"

CBS Evening News[2]

Bob Schieffer: Now the best story of the week. Eight Nebraska packinghouse workers won the biggest lottery jackpot in history. How did they react? Exactly as you would expect.

Eric Zornes: It was party time. (audience roars in laughter)

Schieffer: Eric Zornes is a maintenance mechanic at a Nebraska ham processing plant. Now he and seven co-workers are multi-millionaires.

Zornes: I have been retired for about four days now. (laughter)

Schieffer: Surprisingly, not everyone quit. Three of them, including David Gehle, worked as scheduled until 6:30 this morning.

Gehle: Well, they would have been short of help. (chuckling)

Schieffer: The winners are a cross-section of 21st century America. Three are refugees, two from Vietnam and one from Central Africa. They will divide the $365 million dollar jackpot

equally although after selecting a cash payout rather than an annuity, their individual winnings drop to about $22 million dollars, $15 and a half million after taxes. Naturalized American Quang Dao says he came here to be free. Now he is free and rich.

Dao: (heavy accent) This is a great country.

Schieffer: All of the winners seemed to react in their own special way.

(Chasity Rutjens standing at mic—question from audience) Are you married?

Rutjens: (shaking an oversized check in her hands) No, it's all mine.

Schieffer: Michael Terpstra took it all in stride.

Terpstra: I have been able to sleep; I just can't eat. (audience laughs)

Schieffer: Like a lot of people, he thought he would know what he would do if he ever won.

Terpstra: Oh, I am going to buy an island. I am going to buy an airplane. Reality, uh, gee, not a fan of flying, don't really like water. (laughter)

Schieffer: But it was Dung Tran, though he said the least, who spoke for all.

Tran: I happy![3]

Now remember, don't look back at the script you just read.

I have no doubt you remember nearly every sound bite word for word. They are so memorable: "It was party time," "Not a fan of flying, don't really like water," "No, it's all mine!" "They would have been short of help," "I can't eat," "I happy!" "This is a great country." You can name them all. Why? Because they are emotional. You will remember what you feel longer than what you know.

Let's try five questions about the facts of the story now.

- How many winners were there?
- What was the total jackpot?
- How many workers put in their normal shift despite winning?
- What was the total each person won before taxes?
- What was the total each person took home after taxes?

Why is this so difficult? Typically, when I show this story to a group of professional journalists or students, fewer than 5 percent can answer all of these questions correctly. I have had instances in which not one person could give me all five answers. But they can tell me every sound bite word for word.

You will remember what you *feel* longer than what you *know*. You will remember the characters in the story if you feel something for them.

(By the way, there were eight winners, the total jackpot was $365 million, three workers showed up for their regular shifts, individual winnings before taxes were $22 million, and the individual take after taxes was $15 and a half million.)

A great character is willing to tell you more than you can see. If you are standing outside a person's burned-out home, you don't need the person to tell you that the house is a total loss. A great character tells you what's in his or her heart, something like, "It's not the house that I will miss—it's the memories. I raised my family in that old house. Now they can't come home for Thanksgiving; it just won't feel like home without the house."

ONE EVENT, TWO STORIES: WIFE MOURNS LOSS

Kim Riemland, who worked as a masterful storyteller at KOMO-TV in Seattle, mined the richness of characters in her stories. One day, Riemland says, the station had asked her to "run by the courthouse and grab something" about a routine sentencing hearing in a murder case. The desk thought the story might be only 30 or 40 seconds on the newscast. Courthouse routines are usually dry and not worth much time on the air. When she got to the courthouse, however, she found a remarkable story. In fact, she plays off the "routineness" of this proceeding in her opening line. Then she puts a face on the routine hearing to make the story powerful and memorable.

"Sentencing Day"

Kim Riemland

KOMO-TV Seattle[4]

(Deputy leads handcuffed prisoner into courtroom)

Riemland: It is case number 96-dash-C-dash-07-dash-90-dash-9. That is how the courts see it. But to the woman in the second row, this is the day the man who killed her husband will be sentenced.

Alyce Loucks: David and I were partners in life. Not just another married couple (accused criminal hangs his head and leans on table in front of him while woman speaks), not just best friends, but inseparable souls, seeking our future together; our hearts were forever entwined.

Riemland: Alyce and David fell in love as kids, at Seattle University. As adults, they married. She was David's wife. Now, Alice Loucks tells the judge what it is like to be his widow.

Loucks: As surely as David suffered a torturous, cruel, physical death at the hands of Joseph Gardner and Shawn Swenson, so, too, have I suffered a torturous and cruel emotional death. The difference is David is now free from his pain, and I must live with mine every day for the rest of my life.

Riemland: David owned this North Seattle recording studio. It was here that he was living his dream. And it was here that he died. One night in March of 1995, two men tied David up, they beat him, strangled him, they put duct tape over his nose and mouth. They stole equipment from his studio, and they stole David from all the people in this courtroom. Alyce has thought about what David would say to the man who killed him.

Loucks: I wanted to make music, and live and love and laugh. And I would have helped you make music too, you fool. You didn't have to hurt me. Hell, I would have helped you carry those things out to your car, if you would have just let me keep my life.

Riemland: Those who loved David asked that Joseph Gardner get an exceptional sentence. But when he spoke to the judge, he did not ask for leniency.

Gardner: I did that and I never tried to sit there and fool myself or anybody else about it. I am willing to accept whatever the court is willing to give.

Riemland: The judge made her decision and, two and a half years after David's murder, case number 96-dash-C-dash-07-dash-90-dash-9 is over. Joseph Gardner will spend almost 30 years in prison. Alyce Loucks will spend the rest of her life without her husband.

At the King County courthouse, Kim Riemland, KOMO News 4.

Riemland chose the theme "Wife mourns loss." The story focuses almost exclusively on Alyce Loucks.

ONE EVENT, TWO STORIES: SENTENCING ENDS ORDEAL

The *Seattle Post-Intelligencer* covered the same hearing. Reporter Paul Shukovsky chose a different theme. He used minute details to paint the picture of the courtroom for the reader. For Shukovsky, the main character in the story was not one person but a collection of people who shared one emotion—sadness.

"Studio Owner's Killer Gets 29-year Sentence"

By Paul Shukovsky, Seattle Post-Intelligencer[5]

A 24-year-old man who pleaded guilty to the 1995 strangulation of a North Seattle recording studio owner was sentenced yesterday to almost 29 years in prison.

Joseph A. Gardner acknowledged that his role in the slaying of David G. Loucks, 34, was committed in the course of stealing his audio equipment.

Gardner's accomplice, Shawn Swenson, was found guilty of first-degree murder Tuesday.

On March 7, 1995, Swenson distracted Loucks by pretending to record a rap song at the studio, 4033 Aurora Ave. N. Meanwhile, Gardner slipped up behind Loucks and placed him in a chokehold, according to prosecutor Kerry Keefe.

Loucks was zapped by a stun gun, bound and gagged with duct tape and beaten while he was hogtied face down. Loucks' father, Allan Loucks, found his body the next day.

As family and friends sobbed softly, the elder Loucks yesterday told how discovering the body left an indelible mark of terror on him. And he beseeched King County Superior Court Judge Patricia Aitken to send Gardner to prison for life.

"I go to bed at night thinking of my poor son lying on the floor and being beaten by these animals."

The victim's wife, Alyce, told Aitken: "Two lives were lost that night. For just as he was tortured and murdered . . . so, too have I suffered a torturous and cruel emotional death. The difference is David is now free from his pain, and I must live with mine for the rest of my life."

Gardner, dressed in a red jail jumpsuit, stood before the bench with his head bowed, occasionally glancing toward Alyce Loucks.

Gardner reached for a tissue, wiped his nose, then told Aitken, "I did that. . . . I am willing to accept whatever the court is willing to give."

After Gardner's arrest, he cooperated fully with police and prosecutors and testified against Swenson during his trial.

Because of his cooperation, Keefe asked that Gardner be sentenced to 25 years.

But instead Aitken sentenced him to 347 months, saying that if not for his cooperation, she would have given him an even harsher sentence in excess of state sentencing guidelines.

Swenson will be sentenced Sept. 5.

The newspaper story focus might be summed up in three words as "Court sentences killer" or "Sentencing ends ordeal." Because the newspaper story was less focused on Alyce and focused more on the proceeding, Shukovsky included microscopic details about what went on in the courtroom.

"Gardner, dressed in a *red jail jumpsuit,* stood before the bench with *his head bowed . . .*"

And:

> "Gardner reached for a tissue, wiped his nose. . . ."

Even though the stories are very different in tone and focus, the reporters chose two of the same quotes/sound bites:

> "Two lives were lost that night. For just as he was tortured and murdered . . . so, too have I suffered a torturous and cruel emotional death. The difference is David is now free from his pain, and I must live with mine for the rest of my life."

And:

> "I did that. . . . I am willing to accept whatever the court is willing to give."

Both writers knew the power of a subjective sound bite. The quotes were thoughts, opinions, feelings and emotions that only could have come from the people closest to the story. Those sound bites allow the viewer to get into the skin of the characters, to share their pain, sense of loss, frustration and loneliness.

■ ■ ■ REMEMBER

The best characters are colorful, outgoing, opinionated and lively, and they give you access to their inner self, not just the public persona. Viewers will remember stories about these characters long after they forget the details of the event.

Little Pictures, Big Stories: Focus on People, Not Events

Edward R. Murrow's "Christmas in Korea" documentary for *See It Now* spends a half hour focusing on the names, faces, fears and hopes of soldiers stuck in the crossfire of war. The show ends with a platoon making plans to walk directly into harm's way. The ordinariness of the orders makes the plans seem all the more chilling.[6]

> Sergeant: I am gonna assign a recon patrol tonight, men, and these will be your jobs. Chambers, you will be number one scout. Ball will be number two, second man in the file. I'll be third scout. Wallace, you carry the AR, the basic load of ammunition. Archebeck, you follow Waley. Smith, you come after Archebeck, and Kim, follow Smith. Smothers behind Kim, and Lee carries the radio. Sisson, you pack the wire, and Sergeant Lammar, you are second in command. You will be in the rear. All right, let's move on.

One sound bite, a dozen young faces. Murrow's "put a face on it" style reminds viewers that *people*—not machines, not governments—fight wars. It is a war about people, ordinary people with names such as Waley, Smith and Chambers.

By putting a face on the story, you use the little picture to demonstrate the big picture. That skill is at the core of how Murrow took on Sen. Joseph McCarthy. Murrow's longtime producer, Fred Friendly, said, "We had always been under pressure to do something about McCarthyism, and he [Murrow] kept saying to people who came to see us about it, 'Look we're not preachers; we cover the news. When there is a good news story about McCarthy that will give us a little picture, we will do it. But we are not going to go make a speech about McCarthy.'"

That little picture came in the form of a newspaper clipping Murrow handed Friendly one day. "The story in the *Detroit Free Press* said, 'Radulovich fired,' and Ed said, 'This may be our McCarthy story.'"

The CBS *See It Now* team began looking into the case of Lt. Milo Radulovich, who had been tossed out of the U.S. Air Force Reserves in

1953 because his sister and father read a Serbian-language newspaper from time to time. Milo's father had immigrated to the United States 26 years earlier and liked the newspaper's Christmas calendars, Friendly said. The Air Force considered Radulovich a communist sympathizer because his sister and father read a newspaper that some considered "communist leaning." The program went right for the heart. It said, right up front, that nobody in the Air Force ever had a problem with Radulovich's loyalty or performance.

Here is the opening to the story that would signal the beginning of the end of Joseph McCarthy's rise to political power.

> **Murrow: This is the town of Dexter, Michigan, population, 1,500. This statue is at the head of Ann Arbor Street. "Erected by the citizens of Dexter to the heroes who fought and martyrs who died that the Republic might live." This is the story of Milo Radulovich—no special hero, no martyr. He came to Dexter one year ago, after ten years in the Air Force, won a general commendation for working on a secret weather station in Greenland. Now he is a senior at the University of Michigan eight miles away. His wife works nights at the telephone company. They live at 7867 Ann Arbor Street. This is Milo Radulovich.**

Murrow stripped the bark off the Air Force for the Radulovich case. He showed the government's case was built almost completely on unnamed sources whom Radulovich could not confront. Radulovich was not allowed to see the sealed documents the government said it had gathered that proved his guilt. *See It Now* interviewed townspeople, other so-called "little people," about what was happening to Radulovich. They interviewed John Palmer, the town's chief marshal, and Madeleine Lewis, who worked at the dry cleaning store down the street from where Radulovich lived. Murrow's team interviewed the town dentist and the gas station owner. To learn more about Radulovich's father, CBS interviewed the recording secretary for the United Auto Workers, of which Radulovich's father had been a member for two and a half decades.

The interviews were a masterful stroke. Each person interviewed had nothing to gain by sticking up for Radulovich, and they had so much to lose. They easily could have been branded as communist sympathizers for being critical of the government. But the theme of their comments cut to the heart of the story: "If this could happen to Lieutenant Milo Radulovich, it could happen to any American, and the people behind it should be stopped."

The program generated so much mail, so much heat, that five weeks after *See It Now* took on Radulovich's case, the secretary of the Air Force, Harold Talbott, reversed the government's decision with the simple statement, "He is not, in my opinion, a security risk." Radulovich had his life back.

"He [Murrow] believed this was a nation of little people, and he befriended them in real life and on television," Friendly said years later. "He loved little people who stood up against the crowd, and I think that is the essence of what Ed, who had a modest beginning and had to fight for a place in the sun, believed in."

This is a timeless technique. Jesus, in the New Testament, spoke in simple stories about everyday people. He told short stories, such as the one about the widow who gave all she had to the temple. He told the parable of a man and his prodigal son. He put a face on every lesson. He used simple examples to teach complex concepts.

The Chinese philosopher and teacher Confucius (whose real name was Kong Qiu) frequently taught his students in simple sentences, thoughts and stories. Often those stories were about the actions or obligations of one person, not all humanity. For example, "He who is not concerned about what is far off will soon find something worse nearby." And "To see what is right and not do it is cowardice."

Great storytelling clarifies complexity. When journalists cover the local planning and zoning meeting, they don't just tell viewers what the council decides; they explain how the decision will affect the community and who it will affect the most. Just as Murrow did, you should look for the little guy who is fighting city hall. Look for who will profit most and how they influenced the process.

When covering the tornado that rips through a county, focus less on the damaged barns and trees and more on the people who didn't have insurance and now have to find a way to rebuild. When you cover a flood, remember that high water is not interesting unless it affects someone. Who is fighting the rising water by building sandbag dikes? Who stayed up all night evacuating his home? The water is the *what* in the story, but the people are the *who*. Viewers will not remember how many feet the river rose; they will remember only that it rose enough to harm the elderly woman whose house got washed away.

How Many Characters Do You Need in a Story?

Choose the number of characters to include in your story based on the kind of story it is.

If you are trying to give a character great power and voice, then don't muck up the story with lots of other voices. A story about a rape victim, for example, might use only that victim. But if the story were about a person's false allegations about a man sitting in prison for a crime he did not commit, then two voices might be the right number. Two characters allow the viewer to see the contrast between characters, such as the challenger and the incumbent, the developer and the homeowner, the teacher and the student. If the goal of the story is to give viewers a sense of completeness, a larger experience or understanding of a complex issue or event, then use multiple characters to tell the story. A judge, for example, might say both the victim and the inmate are lying. Three or more voices give viewers a wider view, contrasting opinions, varying experiences. It is especially true when journalists cover protests or debates in which there are two artificial sides standing in front of them—those for and those against. To make sense of these two sides, viewers need to hear from other voices, too.

There is no one way to tell a story, whether it is a breaking news story or a feature. We often understand tragedy, heroism or joy through a single individual. At the same time, we sometimes need to see through many eyes, to understand the size of the situation.

Keep this in mind. If I watch your newscast, will I see, in each story, both the close-up and the wide shot? Will I understand the size of the situation and get close enough to someone to both know and feel the story? Great photojournalism includes a sequence of images: wide, medium, close-up and super-close-up shots (which we will explore in Chapter 9). Writing works the same way. The wide shot is the context, the big idea that this story represents. Close-ups are the characters who illustrate the situation or point of view. If the story is all wide shots, I don't feel anything. If it is all close-ups or characters, I miss the importance of the situation.

That 9-year-old girl in Haiti who was about to lose her hand made me care. Then the story told me how often that scene was repeated across the countryside. It gave me close-up and context.

Great writing helps viewers understand how nuclear power plants work (or fail), why countries fight, how viruses spread and why rivers flood. Edward R. Murrow said television journalism can "educate, illuminate and inspire." The surest way to reach that goal is to tell the big stories through small characters.

■ ■ ■ REMEMBER

Choose characters carefully. Don't clutter your story with too many characters, but use enough to give your story the close-up and the wide shot.

NOTES

1. "Chat Wrap: ABC's Terry Gannon": Interview on http://a.espncdn.com/abcsports/wwos/chatwrap/terrygannon.html.
2. *CBS Evening News,* Feb. 22, 2006.
3. Ibid.
4. Aug. 8, 1997.
5. Aug. 9, 1997.
6. *See it Now,* CBS News, Dec. 25, 1952.

CHAPTER 4

Write Inviting Leads

Do not put statements in the negative form.

And don't start sentences with a conjunction.

The passive voice should never be used.

Proofread carefully to see if you words out.

If you reread your work, you will find on rereading that a great deal of repetition can be avoided by rereading and editing.

Never use a long word when a diminutive one will do.

Unqualified superlatives are the worst of all.

If any word is improper at the end of a sentence, a linking verb is.

Avoid awkward or affected alliteration.

Last, but not least, avoid clichés like the plague.

—William Safire[1],
New York Times columnist

Former NBC News/*Today* show correspondent Bob Dotson tells this story:

Sometimes the opening line falls into my lap. A videographer I worked with once covered an all-night concert. I came to pick up his tape.

"Anything going on?" I asked.

"Not much," he answered. "Breakfast was either smoked or passed around in a bottle."

I grinned. "Bet you got pictures of that."

"Yep."

"Well," I chuckled. "Thanks for my opening line."

"Huh?"

"'Breakfast was either smoked or passed around in a bottle.' I think that kind of sums up this party, doesn't it?"

"Well . . ."

"Thanks," I said. "You're a helluva writer."

When we sang songs to our kids, I was always struck by how pointless the lead lines were. They sound like bad leads to news stories.

- "The wheels on the bus go round and round"
- "Old MacDonald had a farm"

To be a news story, the bus would have been recalled because the wheels were unsafe. If MacDonald's farm fell into foreclosure or he were arrested for growing marijuana, we might have an interesting story. News stories require a hook, a reason for the viewers to care. It is generally something unusual that happens or something usual that has an unusual twist or turn in it. Viewers are looking for a cue from you about whether they should stick around. The cue comes in the opening sentence.

Sweat the lead. The first sentence of your story sets the main conflict in motion. It reflects the focus. The lead deserves the energy you pour into it. The lead is a compass that points to the heart of the story.

Songwriters know that the lead is everything. In one of her biggest songs ever, Adele establishes tension right off the top:

Hello, it's me

I was wondering if after all these years you'd like to meet

To go over everything

They say that time's supposed to heal ya

But I ain't done much healing

How about Lady Gaga's "Bad Romance":

I want your ugly

I want your disease

I want your everything

As long as it's free

Read the first lines of these timeless songs. They all set tension right from the top, the way great stories do:

- "You never close your eyes anymore when I kiss your lips." (The Righteous Brothers)
- "She was just 17, and you know what I mean." (The Beatles)
- "I stay out too late, got nothing in my brain." (Taylor Swift)
- "I left my heart in San Francisco." (Tony Bennett)
- "I could have danced all night." (*My Fair Lady*)
- "Blame it all on my roots / I showed up in boots / And ruined your black tie affair." (Garth Brooks)
- "Shot through the heart, and you're to blame." (Bon Jovi)
- "We clawed, we chained, our hearts in vain, We jumped, never asking why." (Miley Cyrus)
- "You shake my nerves and you rattle my brain, too much love drives a man insane." (Jerry Lee Lewis)

Before you write, study your notes or the wire copy from which you are writing. Then, before your fingers hit the keyboard, put away your notes. The story you are about to write is in your head, not in your notebook. Check your notes for accuracy, but you will find that the details you have forgotten to include are probably best left out.

When our children were little, we used to watch *The Flintstones*. When Fred Flintstone tries to run, he jumps up in the air, his feet go round and round, underscored by the sound of a bongo drum. Then—zoom— he takes off like a shot.

Avoid writing what I call "Fred Flintstone leads." Don't allow your leads to run in place. Get right to the reason that viewers should spend some of their valuable time with you. You will immediately improve your live reporting.

In this chapter we will cover the following:

- Crafting leads that hook viewers
- Do's and don'ts for story leads
- Eliminating clichés in leads

FIRST IMPRESSIONS: GET THEM HOOKED

About every other month, my father drove my brothers and me "into town," where we would sit on the worn wooden benches of Charlie's Barbershop and wait our turn to get a buzz cut. There wasn't much happening outside the barbershop window in Fredonia, Kentucky, to distract a young boy from a long wait. The barbershop sat between Talley's Grocery and Cox's Feed Mill. For as long as I can remember, barber Charlie Phelps had a sign tacked to his wall. The sign featured a demure woman who wore pearls and a sensual black dress. She was looking over her shoulder as if she were leaving a cocktail party with somebody very lucky. Under her face, a caption read, "You never get a second chance to make a first impression. It pays to be well groomed."

All of those hours I spent fantasizing about that woman in the poster served me well when I became a journalist. Her lesson about good grooming applies to TV newswriting. The first sentence creates the viewer's first impression of the story. The lead should not overwhelm; it need not be the peak action of the story. But it should cast a wide net that captures as many viewers as possible.

Say you are doing a story about river pollution. You could open with cold statistics about how much toxic smoke belches each day from a nearby chemical plant. But consider starting with some copy about a bear who depends on this stream for its daily meals of salmon. I care about the bear. So I might stick around to hear how the factory's emissions hurt the bear or, worse, the people living nearby. I believe viewers see a story lead as the invitation to stay or the temptation to leave.

Veteran broadcast journalist Dow Smith says, "The most effective lead refers to some aspect of the story that is important or interesting to the audience—the hook."[2]

Smith says a lead about a tax increase, for example, should not start by saying, "The city council voted to raise property taxes by ten cents per one hundred dollars of assessed land value." The lead should tell viewers what the vote means: "The city council is raising your taxes $600." Smith says, "The best lead lines involve the audience by relating the news to them."

Great leads answer the viewer's questions: "So what? Why is this a story I should watch?"

The lead should not tell me how the story will turn out. The lead is not the story. The lead is the gateway to the story. It is the lure. It is your best pitch to get viewers to invest a little more time with you.

WHAT MOTIVATES VIEWERS: THE BASICS AND BEYOND

The lead has to speak to what motivates viewers to sit and watch.

For generations, marketers have tried to figure out what motivates people to act. Ministers, politicians, athletics coaches and military leaders all have to know what motivates the people they are trying to lead. This is a key question for journalists because we have to find ways to make dull or complicated stories interesting.

What motivates consumers to buy a box of cake mix rather than a prepared cake? Is it the cost of one versus the other? Are they motivated by wanting to bake the cake themselves as a sign of dedication and love? In the late 1950s, cake mix companies were mystified why women were not using cake mixes when the mixes were so much easier than baking from scratch. Marketing guru Ernest Dichter said women felt "self-indulgent" for using cake mixes and needed to feel as though they were really doing something for their families. Dichter said if women could add eggs to the mix, they would feel as if they were making a cake, rather than just pouring stuff from a box and adding water.[3]

Pillsbury tapped into that emotion with a commercial that included the line, "Nothin' says lovin' like something from the oven, and Pillsbury says it best." Pillsbury clearly understood the "family" motivation that sells cake mixes just as it sells news stories.

From Sigmund Freud to Steven Reiss to Abraham Maslow, there is no end to the number of big thinkers who have tried to figure out what motivates people. Freud came up with theories on sexual drive. Reiss produced a list of 16 drivers. Maslow said there were five main human motivations that can be explained in a pyramid:

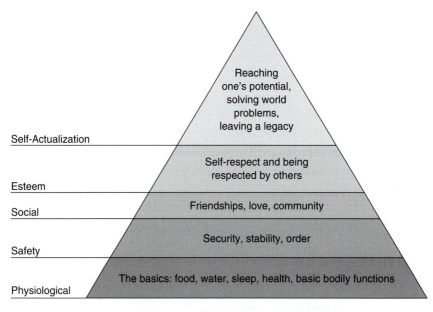

Source: Based on Abraham Maslow, "A Theory of Human Motivation," 1943.

From top to bottom, those needs are:

- Self-actualization—reaching one's potential, solving world problems, leaving a legacy
- Esteem—self-respect and being respected by others

- Social—friendships, love, community
- Safety—security, stability, order
- Physiological—the basics: food, water, sleep, health, basic bodily functions

Maslow believed that you move from the bottom of the pyramid to the top. If you can't meet basic needs, if you don't have enough to eat or if you don't have a safe place to sleep, you probably are not going to spend a lot of time thinking about the meaning of life.

When I see Maslow's list, I think about what kinds of stories would speak to each need. Clearly the lowest need, "physiological," is the kind we would cover in health stories. We cover stories about cancer, obesity, Alzheimer's, healthcare and heart disease. We cover stories about water and air quality. These all speak to this basic motivator.

We address the "safety" motivator in crime stories, in stories about unsafe cars and even in stories about texting or talking on the phone while driving.

The "social" motivator might be the stories we do about crumbling communities, the rise of social networks and the push for neighborhood schools.

The "esteem" motivator shows up in feature stories about the people around us who do remarkable things.

And once in a while, we find extraordinary stories about remarkable people who make a difference in this world. These people change us and challenge us to be more than we are. These are stories that speak to the "self-actualization" motive.

So, you see, this high-minded theory stuff shows up in our stories in important ways.

Just a little more theory, then I am going to boil this down to the "news" level.

In his book *First Things First,* Stephen Covey said we are all motivated by four main urges:

- To live
- To love
- To learn
- To leave a legacy

Like Maslow, Covey says the lowest motivator is simply to have the basics of life. But as those needs are met, we can move toward legacy building, leaving something behind when we are gone.

AL'S EIGHT MOTIVATORS

I have come to believe that there are five, and maybe as many as eight, main motivators for why somebody would watch a news story on TV or read it on the web.

In no particular order, they are as follows:

- Money
- Family
- Safety
- Health
- Community

Over the years I have identified three other motivators, but they are not nearly as strong as the first five:

- Moral Outrage/Unfairness
- Curiosity
- Trending and Topical

The "moral outrage" motivator is the story that any reasonable person would watch and be enraged. It is the thief who steals gifts from under somebody's Christmas tree; it is the lying politician or even the story of refugees trying to find a safer place to live and dying on the journey. Of course, outrage stories usually lean on one of the other motivators including money, family and safety. The tricky part of using the outrage motivator is that not everyone sees the same things as outrageous. One person may think it is outrageous that some want to allow guns on college campuses, another may see it is outrageous that we wouldn't allow teachers and students to defend themselves on campus. Issues of abortion, same-sex rights and immigration are examples of stories that sometimes turn on outrage but miss the mark with viewers because they don't see the story the same way you do. Moral outrage requires the journalist to lean toward editorializing. The journalist must decide what is right and what is wrong. It is treacherous ground.

Curiosity is what I think of as "the coolness motivator." Some stories have little real news value but they make me say "wow." I am thinking of a story my friend photojournalist Ali Ghanbari from WJW-TV in Cleveland produced about a teacher who had no arms. Ghanbari showed us how this high school math teacher wrote on a white board, managed pencils and drove her car using her feet. The story had no larger lessons except that this person who had a disability was an extraordinary teacher whom her students admired, not just because she had no arms, but because she was a caring teacher.

As you craft your lead, in fact as you craft the entire story, write to one (or, even better, more than one) of those motivators.

A city council meeting about a tax increase is clearly about *money*.

"You are about to pay $1,000 a year more in taxes."

But if the tax increase is going to pay for more police officers, it might be a story about *safety*.

"Police say, thanks to a tax hike that the City Council passed tonight, the police can finally hire more officers to patrol Nicetown schools." It also could ring the *community* bell.

CBS' *60 Minutes* may be the champion of hooking stories to motivators. Look at these snippets from one show's open. Let's identify the motivators for each one:

> **Ron Noble: Al-Qaida has said they want to kill four million of us.**
>
> **Steve Kroft: Ron Noble is the first American to ever run Interpol, and he allowed us a rare look into the inner workings of one of the oldest and most famous law enforcement agencies in the world. Its command center is the clearinghouse for international crime and maintains the world's largest database for known terrorists . . . 11,000 names. Noble doesn't believe that the international community is doing enough to prevent the next terrorist attack. And when we asked him about that, we were surprised that he broke down in tears.**

Wow!

The head of Interpol in tears? On national TV? What is the motivator? I would say it is *safety*. It might also be *family* if he knows something that will endanger my family or loved ones. If *60 Minutes* were just going after the much weaker *curiosity* motivator, the promotion might have said something like "Tonight, an exclusive inside look at Interpol, a secret police agency." But if you didn't care about Interpol, you would turn away and watch *The Simpsons*.

Here is another segment from that same *60 Minutes* show.

> **Morley Safer: It's the annual gathering of the National Inventors Hall of Fame, which honors America's visionary tinkerers: Patsy Sherman, who invented Scotchgard to protect the rug and the furniture; Dr. Harry Coover, who invented Super Glue to hold your stuff together; and Dr. Klaus Schmiegel, who invented Prozac to hold your head together. And standing tall among them, the subject of our story tonight: Forrest Byrd, a remarkable American original. Chances are, his invention has saved the life of someone you know.**

How is that for a tease that hooks you? A story about inventions may be a tough sell if the inventions didn't affect you in some way. But quickly we learn the faces and names of people who invented stuff we all use: Scotchgard and Super Glue. So Safer is using a "curiosity" motivator before he puts the tastiest bait in the water. He says this other inventor saved the life of somebody you know. That trades on health, safety and family (if you allow me to use family as a family of choice as well as a birth family).

Imagine how this would have been different if the lead had just said, "Tonight, meet the man who invented the respirator." Talk about a turnoff.

Safer was especially good at finding the part of the story that would resonate with the everyday viewer. He sparked a firefight with the high-brow art world when he did stories mocking the stratospheric prices some art lovers were paying for contemporary art, including "baby-blue bathroom fixtures" mounted in frames and hung in a pricy art fair display, and a VW van overflowing with ripe bananas. "It was one of the most controversial stories we have done in 44 years on the air," Safer said in 2012. The stories turned on an outrage motivator, but also tapped curiosity and money motivators.

A note of caution: When you write story leads, don't play games with the viewer. *Saturday Night Live* included a skit in which the TV anchor says, "The president is dead, but president of what? We'll have that story coming up."

Of course, that's just silly. Don't bury critically important information just to build suspense.

■ ■ ■ REMEMBER

Find the motivators—money, family, safety, health, community—that will hook viewers and get them to watch your story. Make sure your lead answers the question, "So what?"

Some Do's and Don'ts for Leads: Don't Stall; Get On With It

ATTRIBUTION BEFORE ACTION

First, tell viewers who is talking, so they will know whether they believe the source.

Not: "It was a case of arson, according to police."

Better: "Police say an arsonist set the fire."

NO MORE FRED FLINTSTONE LEADS

Not: "First up tonight," "Our lead story tonight," "Topping the news tonight," "The big story tonight," "In the news tonight," "As we have been telling you," "As we told you," "We start tonight with the latest on this still developing story."

Just get on with it. Author and writing teacher Merv Block asks, "Why do writers tell viewers they have been telling us a story for days? If the viewer does not know that, then telling us you told us does not help us."

THE LIVE SHOT LEAD

By the time viewers come to you live on the scene of a story, the anchor has already set the hook of the story and, most likely, has said where you are.

"Get some news in the first sentence," my former Poynter colleague and news director Jill Geisler told her reporters at WITI-TV in Milwaukee. "Don't stand in the convention hall and tell me you are live at the Joe Blow for governor's campaign headquarters. Tell me where he is, what he is doing, tell me what he will do next. Give me some news in the first sentence."

"HOME" IS WHERE THE VIEWER IS

Not: "Here at home," "Closer to home." Drop those "running in place" phrases. I once worked at a station that covered four states. "Here at home" to our anchors meant here in Paducah, Kentucky, where our studios were. But "here at home" could have meant here in Missouri, Illinois or Tennessee to our viewers who lived in those states.

DO NOT CONTINUE TO
USE THE WORD "CONTINUES"

Not: "The jury continues to deliberate tonight." News is what's new. If something continues, it is not new; it is just a continuation of what is old. Use the lead to tell viewers what is new. Think how you would tell me the "newest news" if you came home to dinner and tried to tell me what you did at work today. "The people standing outside the county courthouse are asking each other why the jury has been out so long." "The D.A. is wondering whether he should have taken this case to trial." Find something new and get it in the lead.

AVOID "IF YOU"

Not: "If you have children, watch this story." This means if I don't have children, I can turn away. "If you like Jell-O . . ." What if I hate Jell-O? Can I watch TV Land instead and not miss anything? Don't give viewers a chance to change the channel. They'll do it. The only "if you" lead I can think of that might hold viewers is, "If you have a pulse, you should watch this story." That would cover pretty much everyone we are trying to serve.

SELDOM START WITH A NUMBER, NAME OR PLACE

Let's start with ages.

Not: "49-year-old Joan Johnson is angry that the county wants to raise her taxes." You have given me a reason to care about her. Her age should not be in the story unless it matters to the story. If officials are raising her taxes *because* she is 49, then the age stays in the story, just not in the lead. Let's turn the sentence around. "The county wants to raise her taxes, and Joan Johnson is angry."

Think back to "Little Red Riding Hood." How old was Red Riding Hood? It doesn't matter. She was little. That's all I need to know.

Scott Libin, a grammar-loving news director and former colleague at The Poynter Institute, would ask reporters, "Would you say, 'I'm going over to see my grandmother tonight. The 78-year-old widow is not feeling well'"?

Libin says he is convinced reporters include ages and dates in their leads because it makes copy look more complete—and it makes reporters and producers think they are including important details in their stories. Libin says, "When age matters, use it."

"If a 10-year-old robs a bank, then the age belongs in the lead. If a 30-year-old robs a bank, the age is probably not newsworthy."

And then there's the problem with names.

Give information before identification. Not: "Reginald M. Demarcus is in jail tonight, charged with burglary." Viewers associate details about the person with the person's name, but they need the details first. Think how much easier it is to remember somebody's name at a cocktail party when she says, "Hi, I'm Joey's cousin, Sylvia," rather than, "I'm Sylvia, Joey's cousin." You can almost hear yourself saying, "Oh, Joey's cousin, now what's your name again?"

Not: "In Las Vegas, the rain is coming down." If I missed the city name, I missed the whole story. Maybe something like, "You don't expect floods in the desert, but Las Vegas flooded today."

KILL THE CLICHÉS: ESPECIALLY THE CLICHÉS OF THOUGHT

Not: "Candidates for governor *hit the campaign trail* today." It's not nice to hit.

Not: "It was *every mother's worst nightmare*." What exactly *is* a mother's worst nightmare?

Not: "*apprehended.*" Can we just say "arrested" or "caught"?

Not: "Investigators are *sifting through the rubble* tonight looking for clues." Really? My grandmother sifted flour. I have covered a lot of fires, but I have never seen firefighters sift rubble.

Not: "Eighteen people are *confirmed dead.*" If they are not confirmed, let's not call them dead.

Not: "Negotiators *held talks* today." Why not say they "met"?

When we report on car wrecks, why do writers feel a need to say somebody "*suffered contusions and abrasions*"? Could we just simplify it to "cuts, bumps and bruises"?

Not: "Negotiators sat down at the *bargaining table* today." The company and the union started negotiating; they talked or met. There is no special table around which negotiators meet called a "bargaining table."

Not: "Police are on high-alert tonight, this *in the wake of* . . ." Wake is for water and funerals: Just say "after."

Not: "Police suspect *foul play* in the death of a young girl." Murder is not play; it is serious. Police say somebody killed the young girl.

Not: "Police are looking for an *armed suspect* tonight." A suspect is a specific person police have in mind. If cops do not know for whom they are looking, then journalists should label the person by the criminal type, such as a robber, burglar or rapist.

Not: "*deceased.*" Let's be honest, the guy is "dead." Same for *slain* and *fatalities.* Somebody or something killed them.

Why say "*incarcerated*" when you could say "in jail"?

Why do writers call them "*hot water heaters*"? If the appliance in your garage heats water, shouldn't we call it a water heater?

Other phrases that could *suffer a tragic death:* "the right stuff," "out stumping," "ground zero," "a real horse race," "warts and all," "bandwagon," "bargaining chip," "pins and needles," "rank and file," "some say," "officials say," "reportedly," "tempers flared," "hot and heavy," "changes hands," "close call," "a new lease on life," "innocent bystander," "innocent victim," "firestorm," "lone gunman," "disturbing," "surprising," "shocking," "fantastic," "stunning," "denies allegations," "confirms allegations," "the Bible Belt," "Old Man Winter," "lucky to be alive," "amazing," "breathtaking," "sigh of relief," "it's a miracle," "major breakthrough," "medical miracle," "Iraqi [or insert other country] strongman," "time will tell," "too soon to tell," "last but not least" and, my least favorite of all, "totally destroyed."

Why do so many writers call Martin Luther King Jr. "the slain civil rights leader" on second reference? Why do we have to have cute names for weather events such as "the white stuff," "the wet stuff" and "thunder boomers?"

Perhaps even worse than using clichés in writing is when we use "clichés of thought" to frame our stories. You know these tired old crutches:

- All soldiers are brave.
- Farmers are hardworking.
- Booking-room sergeants are rude and condescending.
- Senior citizens are frail and fearful.
- Teenagers are self-absorbed.
- People of faith are self-righteous.
- Politicians are liars.

I feel like Cher in the movie *Moonstruck* when she smacked Nicolas Cage and yelled, "Snap out of it!" Stories that break these cliché frames are so much more memorable. Murrow showed us soldiers who probably were brave, but he focused on their tender, loving side. I crave stories about honest hard-working politicians who dedicate their lives to public service at great cost. There are such people. Remember that movie *Rudy* about a kid who struggled to get into Notre Dame and tried to walk on to the football team. Through his grit and determination he makes the practice team and wanted one thing, to just wear the uniform on game day, on the field. The story resonates with people partly because most of us are not football stars: We identify with the guys on the bench who just want a shot at life. I like stories about people of faith who have lots of questions and struggle with how to live their lives.

The story of the great boxer Muhammad Ali was more compelling because this world-class athlete, at the end of his life, was frail with Parkinson's disease. Despite his illness, he would show sparks of humor and charity. I noticed that when he died, news stories focused more on his struggles overcoming racism, his conversion to Islam, his arrest for refusing the military draft and his attempt to regain his title at an age far beyond the point at which most fighters retire. Here was a man who was world famous for bragging but in his senior years could not talk or walk without assistance. The fighting that made him a global icon caused his brain injury and eventually his death.

The struggles of life seldom have black-or-white answers. Stories that wade around in the gray of people's lives may be less tidy but nearly always are more interesting and authentic.

The craft of writing demands precision. Mark Twain said, "The difference between the almost right word and the right word is really a large matter. 'Tis the difference between the lightning bug and the lightning."

■ ■ ■ REMEMBER

Active leads, written with precise language, invite viewers to stay with you and watch the story. Go past the clichés to tell stories viewers will remember.

Notes

1. William Safire, "On Language," *The New York Times*, Nov. 4, 1979.
2. Dow C. Smith, *Power Producer* (Washington, DC: Radio-Television News Directors Association, 2000), 43.
3. "Something Eggstra," Snopes.com, http://www.snopes.com/business/genius/cake mix.asp.

CHAPTER 5

Verbs and Adjectives

I once used the word OBSOLETE in a headline, only to discover that 43 percent of housewives had no idea what it meant. In another headline, I used the word INEFFABLE, only to discover that I didn't know what it meant myself.

—David Ogilvy[1],
Advertising executive sometimes called
"The Father of Advertising"

One evening my wife and I watched an evening newscast in which the big story was a forest fire that had burned thousands of acres and seemed destined to grow larger. The story opened with dramatic pictures of the flames. Helicopters swooped as the correspondent said,

"Smoke rising, firefighters tiring, water running out."

I looked at my wife and said,

"Verbs missing, story unclear, set off."

Television journalists are disguising verbs as gerunds. You can spot the phony verbs because they usually have an "ing" behind them. It has become so common that I have called friends of mine at networks and asked whether they have been ordered not to use verbs. None admits to it.

Think about how silly you would sound if you came over to my house for dinner, walked through the front door, turned your nose to the air and pronounced, "Pot roast cooking, smelling good, hungering for dinner." How did all of this start? What happened to verbs? God knowing. In this chapter I will argue that journalists use too many adjectives and not enough active verbs. My concerns are about journalism more than style.

In this chapter we will cover the following:

- The difference between verbless style and active writing
- Ways to use "to be" verbs with precision
- The difference between subjective and objective adjectives, and why journalists should avoid subjective adjectives

THE THING ABOUT "ING": A PASSIVE, VERBLESS STYLE

Every few years, television reporters and producers adopt some new way of writing that they think "juices up" copy and makes it sound more urgent. Most often, trendy writing sacrifices active verbs for false present verbs.

They write,

> "President Obama, in Washington tonight, considering what to do about health care."

The past, the present and the future seem to meld together. If you watch the evening news, it might appear that all news is live; none of the information is past tense. However, almost all news, by definition, is past tense. The president might be considering what to do about Social Security right now, but he also might be taking a nap, eating dinner or taking a bath.

Here is a story I saw on the *NBC Nightly News*.[2] Notice how the journalist uses only seven complete sentences but all of the people she interviews speak in complete sentences. I put her complete sentences in *italics*.

Kelly O'Donnell: Today the farewell. *In West Palm Beach, Florida, those who loved Barry Grunow, those who learned from him in the classroom, come together to remember.*

Student: It was really sad; he was a great guy. I really miss him a lot.

O'Donnell: A teacher for nearly thirteen years, a husband to Pamela for nine, a father to 5-year-old Sam, 9-month-old daughter LeeAnn.

Friend: He has a huge heart and he loved to work with kids.

O'Donnell: At 35, Grunow killed by a bullet fired just minutes before the school year ended Friday. The accused shooter, 13-year-old Nathaniel Brazill, a boy in whom Mr. Grunow actually saw promise, just recently recommending Brazill be named a peer mediator next year, helping other students resolve conflicts.

But on Friday the honor student was sent home for horsing around with water balloons. Police say he returned with this 25-caliber handgun. Today, school officials mystified, the student showed no signs of trouble, no history of behavior problems.

Nat Harrington (West Palm Beach schools): We still don't have any of the answers that people will ultimately get to in terms of why.

O'Donnell (standup): One area under examination, the boy's home life, reports of domestic violence between his mother and her now ex-husband and later a boyfriend. *Police say officers were called to the home seventeen times in the last six years, but no one was ever arrested or charged.*

Tonight the school fence filled with tributes to Grunow, an English teacher who left an affluent suburban district five years ago to teach here in Lake Worth, a working-class neighborhood where friends say he felt he could do more good.

Parent, Richard Rathell: You know, he was a guy of integrity. He loved his family; he cared enough about his community to come back to his community to teach.

O'Donnell: *For his family, the loss renews old wounds. Grunow's dad died on this same day 18 years ago. Now his two children will know the same pain.*

Kelly O'Donnell, NBC News, Lake Worth, Florida

O'Donnell says she intentionally writes in the "verbless" style. "If a story is complicated, sometimes a writer has to use more words and a more traditional style. But other times I want to convey emotion and experience. I want to shift some attention from what I am saying. It is like poetry where words are collected together to create feelings and ideas. Those stories are different from how prose is written. I want viewers to hear things and fill in some of the gaps so long as it is clear and understandable," she says.[3]

But there is a danger in allowing viewers to fill in the gaps. Viewers get distracted. Viewers don't watch TV news the same way journalists watch TV news. At home, viewers might watch news while they prepare a meal. They might be only half-listening to the news with a screaming child in the background. Every morning I read the paper with the TV on in the background. I contend that the verbless style with gaps, as O'Donnell calls them, makes understanding more difficult.

She makes the case that the kind of "watching" TV that I do makes her style more useful, not less useful.

"People are bombarded by images," O'Donnell says. "When they are under time constraints, I say the fewer words the better, so long as it is understandable. This style gives people an opportunity, a way of giving equal weight to consider the script, the sound and the pictures."

But the passive and verbless style creates other problems. By not saying in the copy who sent the boy home, we do not know the possible motivation the boy had for shooting Mr. Grunow. The story says,

"But on Friday, the honor student *was sent* home for horsing around...."

The viewers ask, "*Who* sent him home?"

The passive verb phrase "was sent" prevents the sentence from supplying the vital information of who sent the boy home. It is an example of

AIM FOR THE HEART

how passive and verbless writing becomes not so much a *stylistic* issue. To me it is a *journalistic* issue.

"To Be" or Not "To Be": Verbs Drive Sentences

Whether journalists use verbs is not just an issue of style. Writing that does not include active verbs runs counter to everything journalists say they stand for.

Let's look at a passive sentence and an active one based on the same facts:

"We are afraid." Nobody would argue that the sentence is bad grammar. But it could be so much better.

"The storm scares us." This is an active sentence that tells me that you are afraid and now we know why. Great writing tells me who (or what) did what. So this chapter is not just about a matter of style but also about telling me who (or what) did whatever you are reporting.

All passive verbs are derived from the verb phrase "to be." My grammar teacher in high school called them "state of being" verbs. If something is in a "state of being," it means it is not taking action. State of being verbs include "am," "is," "are," "was," "were," "be," "being," "been."

But be careful: Not all "to be" verbs are passive. (Yes, you read that right. All passive verbs are "to be" verbs, but not all "to be" verbs are passive. It is similar to saying all birds have wings but not everything that has wings is a bird.)

Passive voice: The body was found on Oak Street.

Active voice: Jack found the body on Oak Street.

Passive voice: It is being called the most important bill that Congress will take up all year.

Active voice: President Trump calls it the most important bill that Congress will consider all year.

Passive voice: Mistakes were made.

Active voice: The Pentagon made mistakes.

Passive voice: I was lead to believe.

Active voice: Al led me to believe.

A word of caution: The words "is" and "are" speak in a present tense voice; the rest are past tense. So if we say, "The president tonight is considering . . ." then we must know for sure it is something he is doing right now. If we don't know whether he has stopped considering the issue—maybe he has made up his mind—then we cannot say he is still considering tonight. It implies the matter is still up for debate.

So, put yourself on a "to be" diet.

Notice that I didn't say to never use "to be" verbs, but ask yourself whether there is a more active way to write the sentence.

When I was teaching producers at a Michigan TV station, I saw some copy that a producer wrote for the evening news. The story read,

> "The suspicious device was found in a school bathroom."

> I asked the producer, "Who found the bomb?"

> "Oh," he said, "a third-grader did."

So the new sentence said,

> "A third-grader found the suspicious device in a school bathroom."

Active verbs tell the viewer "who did what." Verbs drive sentences. They infuse sentences with energy. Precision writers use active verbs. I find that when journalists use passive voice, they usually do so because they don't know "who did what."

Let's go back to Kim Riemland's "Sentencing Day" story in Chapter 3 to see how active verbs give power to stories. I italicized the active verbs.

> David *owned* this North Seattle recording studio. It was here that he was living his dream. And it was here that he *died*. One night in March of 1995, two men *tied* David up, they *beat* him, *strangled* him, they *put* duct tape over his nose and mouth. They *stole* equipment from his studio, and they *stole* David from all the people in this courtroom. Alyce has *thought* about what David would say to the man who killed him.

In that passage we can find nine active verbs in six sentences. The active verbs give life to an event that happened months earlier.

As a young writer I admired the work of CBS correspondent Charles Kuralt. He and photographer Izzie Bleckman traveled around in an RV and told stories about ordinary people who were remarkable, usually in some folksy way. When Kuralt was about to retire, he went back to his 12 favorite places in America to spend one full month in each place. He wrote about his farewell travels in his book *Charles Kuralt's America*.[4] For the month of February, he chose Key West, Florida. Read this opening passage and pay attention to the verbs, which I will highlight. How do the verbs add action, energy and precise information?

"February: Key West"

It is a speck of rock in a pastel sea.

Palms **whisper**, songbirds **sing**.

The place has never known a frost.

People **spend** their days at rest in wicker chairs on gingerbread verandas.

Flowers **bloom** all year and love is free. Without a hint of irony, everybody **calls** it "paradise."

Key West **seduced** me and **changed** me.

I **arrived** wearing a blue blazer, gray trousers and polished black shoes. The first day I **shed** the jacket. The second day I **changed** to canvas boat shoes. The third day, still feeling overdressed,

I **dug** around in my duffle bag. I **found** my shorts and a polo shirt. A day or two later, except for excursions into town, I **gave up** the shorts for a bathing suit and **took off** the shirt and the shoes and **stopped** shaving.

Imagine how easy it would be to weaken the passage with a few passive verbs. He could have written, "I was seduced and changed by Key West." Not horrible but not perfect. "Key West seduced me and changed me" paints a picture for me. And go back to Chapter 1 when we discovered that metaphoric writing, the kind of words that stir personal connections between the listener and the writer light up multiple parts of the brain. We go beyond understanding to "feeling." When you are too warm, you "shed" your clothes. When you have a duffle bag, you dig around in it to find stuff deeply buried. The most powerful of all of those verbs was "seduced." How much less brain activity we could expect if the writer had said, "Key West is really nice. I liked it a lot."

To write in this descriptive way, why say "sits" if you could say "slouches"?

Why say "put" if you could accurately say "tossed" or "slammed"?

Avoid complicated verbs like "acknowledged," when you could just say "said."

But be careful: The verb you choose must be true. Did the person really "slouch"? If you say a candidate "admitted" that he had traveled to Las Vegas, it implies that he revealed the information grudgingly.

The verb you choose also can reveal a bias. For example, see how the verbs in these sentences telegraph a bias:

"America rescued Iraq."

"America occupied Iraq."

"America invaded Iraq."

"America helped Iraq."

"America attacked Iraq."

Put your stories on a "to be" diet. Ask "Who did what?" to help yourself avoid passive verbs. The difference between active and passive verbs is the difference between "the gun was found" and "the boy found the gun."

WORDS MATTER: WHEN AN "ACCIDENT" IS A "CRASH"

Mark Rosekind was a man on a mission when he showed up to speak at the Harvard School of Public Health's driver safety conference in May 2016. His mission was to get us all to stop using the words traffic "accident" when we really should be saying "crash."

He told the crowd, "When you use the word 'accident,' it's like 'God made it happen.'" Rosekind is the head of the National Highway Traffic Safety Administration (NHTSA) and pointed out that nearly all crashes are not accidents. Most car crashes, he said, are caused by drinking, distracted driving and other neglect behind the wheel. Only six percent of crashes, he said, are caused by weather, vehicle malfunctions, a car hitting a deer in the road or other truly accidental causes. The words we use to describe car crashes matter, he says, because there is widespread apathy toward the issue while deadly crashes kill 38,000 people in the U.S. each year.[5]

Rosekind is only echoing what his agency has been saying since 1997 when NHTSA launched its first "crashes are not accidents" campaign. And still the language persists.

Rosekind is gaining some support for the cause, and Nevada and Massachusetts lawmakers removed the word "accident" from dozens of state statues to insert the word "crash." In 2013, New York City police adopted a policy to stop using the word "accident" to describe traffic collisions. A few months later, San Francisco city cops adopted similar guidelines.

The wording may sound like a minor difference, but it could make a big difference to juries and insurance companies examining claims if a police investigator said a collision was an avoidable crash, not merely an accident. "Accident" implies nobody is to blame. Stuff happens.

The movement to stop using the word "accident" as a catch-all for traffic collisions has roots in families who are most affected by the pain from highway crashes. The advocacy group Families for Safe Streets compared the use of the word "accident" in preventable crashes to how factory owners whitewashed preventable injuries that happened in unsafe workplaces and called them "accidents." The group even launched an online petition asking the public to promise to stop misusing the word. The Families for Safe Streets campaign is based on the simple premise that "language shapes policy."

Nineteen years after NHTSA launched its campaign to recognize the difference between traffic crashes and true accidents, The Associated Press, on April 2, 2016, tweeted a new advisory to journalists saying, "Avoid accident, which can be read by some as a term exonerating the person responsible."

Rosekind was right when he said in that Harvard speech, "In our society, language can be everything."

■ ■ ■ REMEMBER

Language matters. Be precise in your word choice to reflect the accuracy of the event.

Avoid "Fantastic, Unbelievable, Gut-Wrenching" Subjective Adjectives

Mark Twain offered some advice about using adjectives. "Substitute 'damn' every time you're inclined to write 'very'; your editor will delete it and the writing will be just as it should be."

We each see the world through our own lens. The lens is colored by many factors such as where we grew up; how much education we have; our race, gender, and ethnicity; and, for those of us with brothers and sisters, where we fall in our sibling order. We all have our own biases and experiences.

All of those points of view show themselves in our writing, especially when we use subjective adjectives. Go on a search-and-destroy mission to edit them out of your news copy.

I differentiate between "subjective" and "objective" adjectives because there is nothing wrong with using adjectives that are provably true and add valuable information.

An example of subjective adjectives might be this sentence:

> It was an *awful* scene. The *terrifying* woman slammed her husband with a *huge* frying pan.

It is the writer's opinion that the scene was "awful," that the woman was "terrifying" and that the pan was "huge."

If I used objective adjectives I might write:

> The *three elementary school–age* children watched as their mother whacked their *drunken* dad's head with a *seven-pound cast iron* frying pan.

The facts prove that the children were of elementary school age, that the man was drunk and that the pan weighed seven pounds and was made of cast iron. We might pluck those facts from a police report. They add rich detail to the story. Good writers use specific details in their stories not just to convey information but also to convey emotion (and viewers will remember what they feel longer than what they know).

When writers lean on worn-out adjective clichés to describe a scene, viewers get the sense this is not a unique or singularly important story. It is a generic tale. When we tell viewers, "Here is a story you have to see to believe," the seed of doubt is planted in their minds: There may be a good reason not to believe it.

Recently I heard a newscaster describe a shooting as a "tragic murder," as if some murders are not tragic. Nobody needs to call a murder or fire "tragic"; we all know it is. (Although where I grew up in Kentucky, people would say of particularly ornery cusses, "He just needs killin'.")

Other adjective clichés include "fantastic" and "unbelievable." These words show up most often in the second or third day of coverage following an event. It is as though journalists feel a need to pump oxygen into a dying story, so we use these inflated words. Viewers know these words are hyperbole. Worse, the words reveal the journalists' biases.

Media lawyers cringe when they hear journalists using subjective adjectives. When a public figure sues a TV station for libel, that public figure has to prove two main things: that the journalist acted with reckless disregard for the truth and that the journalist acted with malice. Subjective adjectives can be just what the plaintiff uses to prove the journalist had malice.

Imagine sitting on the witness stand trying to answer why you wrote, "The city councilman flashed an evil look as he voted in favor of the contract."

It may be true and objective that he smiled; it may be true that he waived at his friend the contractor who kicked $2 million into the councilman's re-election fund. But it would be purely a reporter's opinion that the smile was "evil." And if you say he had an evil look on his face, it could be evidence that you didn't like the guy—in fact, you held malice toward him.

Watch your lawyer cringe as you say such things as "The deal was one big rip-off," "The car dealer was a scam artist," "The sleazy doctor was back in court."

Just stick to the facts. Use objective adjectives in your copy.

For example, there is a famous story from KATU-TV in Portland, Oregon. The story is so unusual that there are five Internet websites devoted to it.

On November 12, 1970, reporter (later anchor) Paul Linnman was a witness to a whale of a problem.

An 8-ton, 45-foot sperm whale washed up on the central Oregon coast, south of Florence. Linnman said it had been dead for quite some time and was starting to get a bit foul. The state highway workers called on the Department of the Navy for some advice. The workers soon made a plan. Since they couldn't bury the whale (the ocean tides would soon uncover it), and cutting it up and burning it was out of the question (nobody wanted that job), they settled on simply using some dynamite.

They planned to blow up the whale into pieces small enough for the crabs and seagulls to take care of.

They didn't know how much of the explosives to use. Nobody had ever done anything like this before. They took an educated guess and packed a half-ton of dynamite around the carcass, backed up onlookers a quarter of a mile away and counted down to the explosion.

Not only did the blast pulverize just a portion of the whale, but the wind blew particles of smelly, rotten, whale flesh in the direction of the spectators, which came down on them like a spring rain.

There were large chunks spewed all over the beach including a 3-foot by 5-foot hunk that landed a direct hit on the roof of a brand-new Buick parked a quarter-mile away.

Thankfully, nobody was injured, except maybe the pride of the Oregon State Highway Division. In the end, workers buried the larger remains of the whale in the sand.

As Linnman said, "The Oregon State Highway Division learned a valuable, but messy, lesson not so much about what to do, but as what *not* to do if they ever faced a situation like this again."

On rare occasions, I play Linnman's story for reporters and producers at seminars. I ask them to think of words that describe the video of the exploding whale. They often use such words as "unbelievable" and "amazing." Once in a while somebody will say "disgusting" or "sick." A couple of years ago, while doing a seminar in Oregon, I played the story and one producer said she thought what those cleanup workers did was "disrespectful." I asked why she felt that way, and she said she always felt close to whales and hated to see anything bad happen to them.

I grew up in Kentucky. I thought the exploding whale video was at least amusing, if not outright funny. The only whales I ever saw were in books or in movies.

That producer taught me a lot that day. She taught me that the descriptions we use in our stories directly reflect who we are. The main lesson we should take from the "exploding whale" story is that if we claim to write with precision in our news stories, we should limit the adjectives, especially the subjective adjectives, we use.

NOTES

1. David Ogilvy, *Confessions of an Advertising Man* (New York: Ballantine Books, 1971), 99.
2. *NBC Nightly News,* May 31, 2001.
3. Interview with the author, December 2001.
4. Charles Kuralt, *Charles Kuralt's America* (New York: G. P. Putnam's Sons, 1995), 27.
5. "It's No Accident: Advocates Speak of Car 'Crashes' Instead," *New York Times,* May 23, 2016, http://www.nytimes.com/2016/05/23/science/its-no-accident-advocates-want-to-speak-of-car-crashes-instead.html?emc=edit_th_20160523&nl=todaysheadlines&nlid=16911953&_r=0.

CHAPTER 6

The Art of the Interview

> *The most basic of all human needs is the need to understand and be understood. The best way to understand people is to listen to them.*
>
> —Ralph Nichols,
> Researcher and author of *Are You Listening?*[1]

My wife, Sidney, is a minister and psychotherapist, and sometimes she conducts relationships workshops for couples. The one-day workshop is designed to jump-start relationships that lose their juice or slide off track. Sidney puts the couples through one exercise about listening—an exercise I have adopted (she says "stole") for use in my journalism seminars. She asks the partners to think about something critically important that they want to tell their spouse. She asks them to imagine in some detail how they will say what they have to say and how excited they will be to say it. She assigns one of the partners to be the speaker, and the other is the listener. Then she tells the listener to send clear signals that he or she is not interested in what the speaker has to say. Then she shouts, "Go." Instantly, the person whose job is to not listen begins looking away or reading a magazine; some even get out of their chairs and walk off.

My wife tells me that in more than 20 years of doing those workshops, she has never had one single person ask, "How do I show someone that I am not interested?" We all are experts at that. We have spent lifetimes perfecting the fine art of tuning out others. But learning to listen, *that* is a skill that is so rare that when we find somebody who really listens, we open up and say things we might never tell another soul. Great journalists learn to listen.

In this chapter we will cover the following:

- How to ask questions that allow the other person to talk more and allow you to deeply listen to their answers
- How to focus your questions to get more focused answers
- Strategies for handling difficult interviews
- Guidelines for tough ethical issues that come up while interviewing sources, especially when the interviews involve juveniles and vulnerable people
- Interviewing "don'ts"

LEARNING TO LISTEN: USING YOUR EARS MORE THAN YOUR MOUTH

From the moment babies are born, people start coaxing them to talk. Adults celebrate a child's first words. Then what happens? As soon as kids start talking, adults insist they be quiet. How odd!

The same thing happens in journalism schools. Professors spend so much time training students to report and write that they miss the most important part of reporting: listening. Listening is the essence of journalism. Every journalism school should have a formal course in how to listen to other people.

How many times in an interview do you find yourself doing the following:

- Thinking that the subject is uninteresting
- Criticizing the speaker or the speaker's delivery
- Listening only for facts or sound bites (bottom line)
- Not taking notes
- Faking attention

- Tolerating or even creating distractions during the interview
- Tuning out difficult material rather than trying to understand it
- Letting emotional words block the message
- Wasting the time difference between speed of speech and speed of thought, not processing what is being said during the pauses
- Interrupting the speaker when the conversation slows
- Making statements rather than asking questions[2]

I teach a workshop on how to be a better listener. I usually ask people to write down the name of a person they would consider a great listener. Then I ask them to write down a few characteristics that show others how this person is a good listener.

The list often includes the following:

- They do not interrupt me.
- They make time for me, no matter what they are doing.
- They focus on me; they don't keep typing on the computer or reading the newspaper while I talk.
- They don't try to give me the answer; they don't tell me what to do. They just listen and help me think through the situation for myself.
- They ask questions to let me know they are really listening and that they are focused on my story.
- They don't judge. They just want to help.

Listening skills are central to great news interviews. The key is to listen more than you talk. You are interviewing to learn. If you are talking, you are not learning anything. Use your ears more than your mouth.

Journalists must learn what those in the healing arts have known for centuries; much of our job is to listen. Here is a quote I found in a magazine for nurse midwives about the importance of listening. I am struck by how much journalists can learn from it.

Listening is noting what, when, and how something is being said. Listening is distinguishing what is not being said from what is silence. Listening is not acting like you're in a hurry, even if you are. Listening is eye contact, a hand placed gently upon an arm. Sometimes, listening is taking careful notes in the person's own words. Listening involves suspension of judgment. It is neither analyzing nor racking your brain for labels, diagnoses, or remedies before the person is done relating her symptoms. Listening, like labor assisting, creates a safe space where whatever needs to happen or be said can come.[3]

■ ■ ■ REMEMBER

Listen more than you talk. Listening is essential in conducting interviews.

Asking Better Questions

Before you head out for any interview, you need to be prepared to ask your questions. Here are some tips to help focus your thinking.

THINK ABOUT THE PURPOSE OF THE INTERVIEW

If your goal is to gather facts, use objective questions. If you are trying to elicit sound bites or opinions, ask subjective questions. Subjective questions usually begin with such phrases as "Why," "Tell me more about," or "Would you explain." Objective questions get information that will end up in your voice-over copy: "How much money did they get away with?" "Did the victim die?" "How many protestors did you count?"

ASK OPEN-ENDED QUESTIONS

Open-ended questions cannot be answered with a "yes" or a "no." Open-ended questions do not offer a choice, such as "Do you feel X or Y?" Great conversation starters include "How did," "What if," "Why do." Questions that stop conversations include "Do you deny" and "Will you."

MIRROR WHAT YOU HEAR

Tell the person you are interviewing what you hear him or her saying and then ask, "Did I get that right? Is there more?" Remember not to interrupt or disagree; that blocks your ability to listen. Mirroring checks your understanding.

WHY SHORTER QUESTIONS
PRODUCE BETTER ANSWERS

Let's look at a news conference to see if we can discover what kinds of questions produce the most insightful answers.

During President Barack Obama's joint news conference with Canadian Prime Minister Justin Trudeau in March 2016, journalists asked some crazy-long questions.[4]

Julie Davis, a White House correspondent for *The New York Times*, opened the question-and-answer session with a 224-word inquiry. Davis' question at the news conference contains several examples of practices journalists should generally avoid. It includes four queries for Obama, two for Trudeau, several observations and one example of editorializing. I've annotated each instance with a number before the sentence or question.

> Thank you, Mr. President. I want to ask you about the Supreme Court. (1) You've already said you're looking for a highly qualified nominee with impeccable credentials. (2) Can you give us a sense of what other factors you're considering in making your final choice? (3) How much of this comes down to a gut feeling for you? (4) And does it affect your decision to know that your nominee is very likely to hang out in the public eye without hearings or a vote for a long time, or maybe ever? (5) And, frankly, shouldn't that be driving your decision if you're asking someone to put themselves forward for this position as this point?
>
> For Prime Minister Trudeau, I wanted to ask you — (6) we know you've been following our presidential campaign here in the U.S. (7) As the president alluded to, you've even made a joke about welcoming Americans who might be frightened

of a Donald Trump presidency to your country. (8) What do you think the stakes are for you and for the relationship between Canada and the United States if Donald Trump or Ted Cruz were to win the presidency and to succeed President Obama? (9) You obviously see eye-to-eye with him on a lot of issues. (10) What do you think — how would it affect the relationship if one of them were to succeed President Obama?

1. A bit of obvious background here that nobody really needs.

2. "Can you give us a sense" starts a closed-ended question. Closed-ended questions give the subject a choice to answer yes or no without supplying the information you really want. An open-ended way of asking the question might be, "What factors do you consider when choosing a Supreme Court nominee?" As my colleague Chip Scanlan has written for Poynter.org, "The best questions are open-ended. They begin with 'How?' 'What?' 'Where?' 'When?' 'Why?' They're conversations starters and encourage expansive answers that produce an abundance of information needed to produce a complete and accurate story."

3. This is really a follow-up question, and it is not likely to produce an answer anyway. No presidential decision with the gravity of a Supreme Court nomination is a gut feeling. It is a calculation.

4. Another closed-ended question. I really like where the question is going if we just sharpen it. "How does the GOP's plan to stall a vote on a nominee affect who you choose?"

5. We are wandering into an opinion on this question. The journalist seems to be saying that is the way the president should see things.

6. Ok, just ask.

7. Instead of asking questions, we're telling the subject what he said.

8. The best question she asked. She asks an open-ended question, "What do you think the stakes are?" It would have been even sharper if she had stuck to the Trump question, however. She sets up the scenario with the premise that some people threaten to leave the U.S. if Trump is elected, then lumps Cruz in with her question. Some who see a conspiracy behind every question may ask why the journalist asks about Cruz and Trump but not the rest of the pack.

9. This is an observation not a question, and if it is so obvious why ask it?

10. It's a repeat of point eight.

There was so much to choose from in these questions. Obama said nothing new, and Trudeau didn't even address the question about Trump and Cruz except to say, "I have tremendous confidence in the American people, and look forward to working with whomever they choose to send to this White House later this year."

At the same conference, the president noted the length of another question from respected journalist Margaret Brennan of CBS News when she asked three queries at once:

Brennan: Thank you, Mr. President. (1) Some of your critics have pointed to the incredibly polarized political climate under your administration as contributing to the rise of someone as provocative as Donald Trump. (2) Do you feel responsibility for that, or even some of the protectionist rhetoric from some Democratic candidates? (3) Do you have a timeline for when you might make a presidential endorsement? (4) And to follow on my colleague's question here, do you feel political heat is constraining your pool of viable Supreme Court nominees? Thank you.

Obama: That's a three-fer.

1. This is background that is widely known. Why include it?

2. This is a closed-ended question. An open-ended version would be, "How much responsibility do you take for the polarized climate of this election season?"

3. Another closed question. An open-ended way to ask the question might be, "How will you decide when or whether to endorse a candidate?"

4. "Do you feel political heat?" is a closed-ended question. "How much heat are you taking?" is another way to ask the question. But the more important question might be to what extent he is "constraining" his nomination.

WHY DO THEY ASK SUCH LONG QUESTIONS?

White House reporters have told me that their questions have to be different from the questions other reporters might ask a mayor or a police chief.

"When a foreign leader comes to the White House, they use a two-and-two format for questions," Davis told me. "You get two questions from American journalists and two from foreign journalists, and you can ask a question of each leader."

The reporters who get to ask a question feel some pressure to pry as much out of each leader as they can on a wide variety of topics, Davis said.

"Everybody is depending on you," she said. "I knew for my own purposes that the Supreme Court nomination was a big thing that we all wanted to know about, we just had a big upset on primary election night, and another debate and primary election day was coming, plus you have other sorts of world events going on."

And, Davis explained, White House journalists have restricted access to the president. So when they do have an opportunity to ask a question, they cast a wider net than they would if it they were granted a sit-down interview or routine access that allows reporters to drill down on issues.

This wide-ranging strategy was also on display in November 2015 when *Los Angeles Times* reporter Michael Memoli asked Obama and Trudeau a 283-word question when they appeared before reporters.

In an email to me, Memoli also attributed his lengthy question to Obama's limited availability.

"Because the president has not done more regular full-blown news conferences, reporters enter these limited one-and-one or two-and-two format press availabilities with foreign leaders feeling the need to ask more elaborate, multi-part questions to cover various news developments that he has not commented publicly on," Memoli said. "In my case last November we knew there would be only one chance to ask him a question that day and a few developments overnight that we wanted to hear from him on."

Davis said reporters who covered Obama learned that if they ask foreign leaders a question that is particularly interesting, Obama will often jump in and respond to that question even after he's already given an answer.

WHEN TO USE A CLOSED-ENDED QUESTION

But closed-ended questions do have a purpose. Davis showed us how a good reporter sometimes uses closed-ended questions in October 2015 when Vice President Joe Biden was toying with a White House run, peppering him with questions aimed at eliciting a "yes" or "no" answer.

> **"Mr. Vice President, are you running for president?"**
>
> **"Have you made your decision yet?"**
>
> **"Is there still [an] opening in the race for you, sir?"**[5]

READY FOR MY CLOSE-UP

Televised news conferences present an opportunity for network correspondents to appear smart, connected and confrontational. If their questions are short, punchy and pointed enough, networks may even include them in newscasts to show that their journalists are getting answers for viewers.

One recent example of this tactic is from CNN's Jim Acosta, who asked President Obama, "Why can't we take out these bastards?" in reference to ISIS in November after the 2015 Paris terrorist attacks. But he got no useful response from that question because it was preceded by such a long run-up:

> This is an organization that you once described as a JV team that evolved into a now occupied territory in Iraq and Syria and is now able to use that safe haven to launch attacks in other parts of the world. How is that not underestimating their capabilities? And how is that contained, quite frankly? And I think a lot of Americans have this frustration that they see that the United States has the greatest military in the world, it has the backing of nearly every other country in the world when it comes to taking on ISIS. I guess the question is, and if you'll forgive the language, is why can't we take out these bastards?[6]

Imagine if he had just asked, "Mr. President, why can't we take out these bastards?" I am not sure I would use that language in a presidential news conference, but it would have been a difficult question to ignore.

In that same news conference, NBC's Ron Allen asked a series of short but closed-ended questions:

> Were you aware that they had the capability of pulling off the kind of attack that they did in Paris? Are you concerned? And do you think they have that same capability to strike in the United States?
>
> And do you think that given all you've learned about ISIS over the past year or so, and given all the criticism about your underestimating them, do you think you really understand this enemy well enough to defeat them and to protect the homeland?

The closed-ended nature of the questions prevented Obama from offering much insight. His answers were, essentially, "sure, yes, they might, we're trying."

FIND FOCUS

In an October 2015 news conference, Reuters' Julia Edwards asked four questions rolled into one.

> Thank you, Mr. President. You just said that you reject President Putin's approach to Syria and his attacks on moderate opposition forces. You said it was a recipe for disaster. (1) But

what are you willing to do to stop President Putin and protect moderate opposition fighters? (2) Would you consider imposing sanctions against Russia? Would you go so far as to equip moderate rebels with anti-aircraft weapons to protect them from Russian air attacks? (3) And how do you respond to critics who say Putin is outsmarting you, that he took a measure of you in Ukraine and he felt he could get away with it?[7]

1. What a great question! It is pointed, open-ended and likely to produce some news.

2. These closed-ended questions elaborate on the open-ended question before them, but they may allow the president to duck the first question.

3. This is a punchy open-ended question, but the answer will overwhelm the substance of what came before it.

Obama laughed at the last question and launched into a long answer about Putin. The rambling answer even included the president asking, "So what was the question again?" He did not answer her key first question or either of her second questions. He does focus on the pithy last question to say Putin is leading Russia into economic decline. Not much news there.

In October 2015, CBS' Major Garrett asked a short but dense four-part question on three topics at a White House news conference:

(1) Mr. President, I wonder if you could tell the country to what degree you were changed or moved by what you discussed in private with Pope Francis? (2) What do you think his visit might have meant for the country long-term? (3) And for Democrats who might already be wondering, is it too late for Joe Biden to decide whether or not to run for president? (4) And lastly, just to clarify, to what degree did Hillary Clinton's endorsement just yesterday of a no-fly zone put her in a category of embracing a half-baked answer on Syria that borders on mumbo jumbo?[8]

1. What a nice question. It would have been even better without the "to what degree" premise. Perhaps, "How did your private meeting with Pope Francis change or move you?"

2. The question is short and specific. The phrase long-term is an interesting choice — as if there is a difference between what it means short-term and long-term.

3. This closed-ended question isn't really what we want to know the answer to. We really wanted to know whether Obama would back Biden and whether he was encouraging Biden to run.

4. There's that "to what degree" question again. It also suggests that Garrett believes Clinton's position is half-baked.

FOCUS ON ONE ISSUE AT A TIME

After the 2008 presidential campaign, a reporter asked vice presidential candidate Sarah Palin this 85-word question. Read it out loud to see if you can figure out where the question is heading:

> **Reporter: One more question about the election that just ended yesterday. If you look at some of the polls and you talk to some of the people who are really crunching the numbers, and specifically who voted what way, who was swayed one way or the other, Independent voters, suburban voters, women, people who the campaign thought you would be able to help, actually, saw your presence on the ticket and said I am going to vote the other way. What do you make of that?**

> **Palin: I don't think anybody should give Sarah Palin that much credit, that I would trump an economic woeful time in this nation, that occurred two months ago, that my presence on the ticket would trump the economic crisis that America found itself in a couple of months ago, and attribute John McCain's loss to me.**

The reporter could have asked one strong question:

"The Republicans counted on you to deliver women, suburban voters and Independent voters. Why didn't those groups vote for you?"

One of Canada's premier investigative journalists, author John Sawatsky, says if you offer a double-barrel question, you may not know which part of the question the interviewee is answering. Here is a famous exchange between *60 Minutes* correspondent Steve Kroft and candidate Bill Clinton who, at the time was facing allegations that he had carried on a long affair with a woman named Gennifer Flowers.

> **Kroft: Who is Gennifer Flowers? You know her.**
>
> **Bill Clinton: Oh, yes.**
>
> **Kroft: How do you know her? How would you describe your relationship?**
>
> **Bill Clinton: Very limited, but until this, you know, friendly but limited . . .**
>
> **Kroft: Was she a friend, an acquaintance? Does your wife know her?**
>
> **Hillary Clinton: Oh, sure.**
>
> **Bill Clinton: Yes. She was an acquaintance, I would say a friendly acquaintance . . .**
>
> **Kroft: She is alleging and has described in some detail in the supermarket tabloid what she calls a 12-year affair with you.**
>
> **Bill Clinton: That allegation is false.[9]**

The complexity of the questions leads to unclear answers, which is exactly what a politician in trouble prefers. Is the allegation that there was an affair false or is it that the affair was only 10 years? That they were lovers or that the relationship lasted 12 years? Diffuse questions lead to vague answers. Start by asking, "Was Gennifer Flowers your lover?" Follow up with the open-ended question, "How long did the relationship last?"

BE NAÏVE

A great question is, "Nah, really?" when someone tells you something surprising. It leads the person to tell you more. Former NBC correspondent Bob Dotson calls this technique the "non-question question." Dotson says, "When you ask your subject a question, they are going to give you the answer they think you want to hear. Then, they stare at you without you saying a word. Then, they give you the deeper, more heartfelt answer. In other words, people hate silence; let them fill it in."

Edward R. Murrow liked to share his interviewing secrets with his younger colleagues. He told new correspondents, "If you put a direct question, the interviewee will answer it as he has probably answered the same question dozens of times before. Then begins the waiting game. He thinks he has given you the definitive answer. You manage a slightly uncomprehending, puzzled expression, and you can watch his mind work. 'You stupid oaf, if you didn't comprehend that, I'll put it in language you can understand,' and proceeds to do so. Then, in the course of editing, you throw out the first answer and use the second one."[10]

AVOID EDITORIALIZING

Resist the impulse to make any statements in your questions and never editorialize or anticipate the response. Let the subject do the work.

Sawatsky says that people, by nature, are either "inputters" or "outputters." TV journalists, for instance, tend to leave their dial on output. Inputters are straight men, allowing sources to crack wise and showcase personality. "I can go into any newsroom and usually tell you who gets the best stories in the paper. It's usually the reporters with the blander personality. They're not the life of the party. They're amazingly consistent if you eavesdrop on them during interviews: You'll hear plain, neutral, bland questions. Colorless questions usually provide colorful answers."

The best questions are like clean windows, Sawatsky says. "When we ask a question, we want to get a window into the source. When you put values into your questions, it's like putting dirt on the window. It obscures the view of the lake beyond. People shouldn't notice the question in an interview, just like they shouldn't notice the windows. They should be looking at the lake."[11]

SETTING MATTERS

Where you interview people often makes a big difference in how they act and what they say. Interviewing a pro football player in a press center after a game is very different from interviewing him in the end zone the day after he missed the field goal. Interviewing a mother in her missing child's bedroom will produce different emotions than interviewing her while standing in the front yard.

Interviewing people where they are comfortable and confident can produce big returns. I once interviewed a truck driver about rising fuel prices while standing in a parking lot. He was stiff and emotionless. I followed him into his rig, and once he climbed behind the wheel, he became confident and funny. I realized that there, behind the wheel, he was the CEO, he was in charge, he was in the office. The setting made all the difference.

BE TOUGH

You don't do an interview subject any favors by not asking tough questions. Ask the questions the public wants to know the answers to, or the story will lose credibility with the audience.

However, Sawatsky urges reporters to "Ask tough questions; don't just ask tough-sounding questions." Asking a subject, "Are you a racist?" is an easy question that sounds tough. The answer most certainly will be no. Instead, ask focused, open-ended questions about evidence that suggests the source is a racist.

The order of your questions matters. Don't lead off with: "Well, why *did* you embezzle all that money?" Ask more innocuous questions to get the subject talking before you go for the hard stuff.

If you are going to ask difficult questions in a confrontational interview, it is dishonest to lead the person to believe it is going to be a softball conversation. While setting up the meeting, I would say, "Look, I have some tough questions to ask, but I think it would be unfair to write a story without asking you to speak to these questions." That open-minded approach to a tough interview helps to prove you do not have malicious intent and that you are not recklessly disregarding the truth, which are key components to a successful libel or defamation case. It is the sort of forewarning that you would like to be able to tell a jury if you had to defend yourself in a lawsuit.

It is also honest and fair and shows the subject that you want to hear his or her side of the story. Just as important, if the subject arrives at the interview unprepared to give you the information you want or need to know, the forewarning gives you license to press harder than you might have if you had not told the subject you needed some precise answers.

PUT THE BURDEN OF PROOF ON THE SOURCE

If a source insists, "There was no crime," ask, "How do you know that?" If a source says, "I can't remember," ask, "Why can't you remember?"[12]

Pick a key phrase and repeat it in an open-ended question. If a politician is caught having an affair with an intern, and then, in an interview, says of his marriage, "We've had difficult times," you might respond, "What do you mean by 'difficult times'?" or ask, "What was difficult about those times?" When a source offers you a key word like "difficult" or "remember," I have found it useful to use that key word in the follow-up question. It is a way of demonstrating that you heard the person, and using his or her words helps force the source to own the answer because it is based on the person's own words.

EMPATHIZE

This is different from sympathy. Try to put yourself in the other person's shoes to understand how he or she must feel. Allow your subjects to define what they are saying. Former *Dateline NBC* correspondent John Larson says, "When interviewing someone about an emotional experience, do not interview about the emotion. Let emotion show naturally. Remember, don't do interviews; have conversations. If your story is about an empty factory, find someone—a janitor or the person who has to close it down. Ask that person to tell you about the 'ghosts,' the people who once worked there."

GETTING STARTED

The best interviews are not interviews at all. Rather than asking for an interview, just say, "I would like to talk with you" or "Let's chat about" or "Could you help me understand this?" An "interview" sounds so imposing, as though the journalist is the boss and the interview subject is the job applicant.

Dotson tells reporters and photojournalists to spend a few minutes getting to know the person before turning on the camera. But Dotson says, "Don't talk to them about the subject you really want to know about at first." Once you start the conversation, try the non-question question, "Now that looks like a fine mobile home you used to live in." The person is more likely to tell you what they lost and why the home was important.

If you are standing near a grieving relative, just saying something such as "It's a sad day" might open the conversation by letting the person know you are empathetic.

■ ■ ■ REMEMBER

Focus your questions. Short questions, which focus on one point, are better than long double-barrel questions. Ask tough questions, not just tough-sounding questions.

PRACTICE INTERVIEWING

No matter how experienced you are, practice the questions you want answered. Record your interviews. Transcribe them to examine how you ask questions and to see which questions elicit the most useful answers. After *Roots* was published in 1976, I interviewed author Alex Haley, and that conversation has shaped the way I ask questions. I asked, "How did you know this story would resonate?" "What did you do to capture what Kunta Kinte must have felt?" and "How did you know you were a writer?" The answers were so rich and personal that we ran out of film.

I find that closed-ended questions usually work best if I have asked an open-ended question first. The open questions expose the news and the closed ones nail it down. Know what you're looking for before you ask the question. Are you seeking a fact, a plan, an emotion?

There is nothing unprofessional about writing out your questions before an interview. Use them as a guide and allow the conversation to fill in between your questions, but as you have seen, the sharpness of your questions may determine the quality of the answers you land.

CBS' Steve Kroft wrote out his questions for one of the biggest interviews of his career, an interview he did with Barack Obama after the raid that killed Osama bin Laden.

Kroft told me that when he sat down with the president, he had a list of 62 questions that he might ask. He said he consulted with others before drafting a list of questions. Then "I got up at 5 o'clock Wednesday morning and went through all of them again."[13]

"We wanted to do the interview in three sections: the raid and the planning, the Situation Room and Pakistan. I knew I was not going to get through all of the questions."

Kroft kept the questions short and constantly mixed up the types of questions he asked to alternately seek facts, emotion and insight. Because he knew he would only get limited time with the president, he said, "I was very cognizant of eliminating questions that would lead to long answers."

The story opened quickly, no Flintstoning. The piece began assuming any reasonable person watching would be familiar with the basic facts of bin Laden's death that had dominated the news that week. That was a great decision.

Kroft gets right to the interview with, interestingly, an objective (or closed-ended) question. Not what journalists might expect.

> **Steve Kroft: Mr. President, was this the most satisfying week of your presidency?**
>
> **President Barack Obama: Well, it was certainly one of the most satisfying weeks not only for my presidency but I think for the United States since I've been president. Obviously, bin Laden had been not only a symbol of terrorism but a mass murderer who had eluded justice for so long, and so many families who have been affected I think had given up hope. And for us to be able to definitively say, "We got the man who caused thousands of deaths here in the United States" was something that I think all of us were profoundly grateful to be a part of.**

I would have expected a subjective question to work best at the beginning of the interview. I might have asked the question, "How satisfying was this week?" But Kroft's question was better than mine. His question would reveal any hint of gloating.

Kroft told me he carefully chose the word "satisfying" for the first question. "I played around with a couple of other words—'happy,' for example—but it brought up 'celebration,' which didn't seem right to me, so I settled on 'satisfying.'"

Kroft's second question was also closed-ended:

> **Kroft: Was the decision to launch this attack the most difficult decision that you've made as commander-in-chief?**

A little later, Kroft asked a "double-barreled" question, two questions at once that can allow the interviewee to escape the first question and choose the second one.

> **Kroft: How much of it was gut instinct? Did you have personal feelings about whether . . . he was there?**

Notice that the first part of that question, the subjective part, produced a quote, a sound bite when the president responded:

> **Obama: The thing about gut instinct is if it works, then you think, "Boy, I had good instincts." If it doesn't, then you're gonna be running back in your mind all the things that told you maybe you shouldn't have done it. Obviously I had enough of an instinct that we could be right, that it was worth doing.**

Kroft used several other double-barreled questions, some a bit indirect that could have been more direct:

> **Kroft: When the CIA first brought this information to you . . .**
>
> **Obama: Right.**
>
> **Kroft: . . . what was your reaction? Was there a sense of excitement? Did this look promising from the very beginning?**

The last part of the question is the useful part. I would have asked, "When the CIA first approached you with information, how promising did that information seem to be?"

Then, I would have followed up with, "What was your reaction when you saw what the CIA had?"

Here is another example of how a double-barreled question allowed the president to escape without a direct answer.

> **Kroft: Did you have to suppress the urge to tell someone? Did you wanna tell somebody? Did you wanna tell Michelle? Did you tell Michelle?**

But the president never said whether he told his wife. The president chose to respond to the first question over the more interesting last one, a danger when asking multiple questions at once.

Kroft followed with single, direct questions, all in the perfect order to build our understanding of the sequence of events:

> **Kroft: When was that, when you set that plan in motion?**

> **Kroft: How actively were you involved in that process?**

> **Kroft: Were you surprised when they came to you with this compound right in the middle of sort of the military center of Pakistan?**

The objective questions were the right tool because Kroft was trying to get facts, not opinions, in this part of the interview. This information will not generate a quote or sound bite in anybody's story but will be important copy or narrative text:

> **Kroft: Do you have any idea how long he was there?**

> **Obama: We know he was there at least five years.**

> **Kroft: Five years?**

> **Obama: Yeah.**

THE VALUE OF SHORT QUESTIONS

Even when he asks double-barreled questions, Kroft keeps his questions short, 15 words or less.

That brevity makes this interview so watchable.

"I probably wrote the questions longer, but the good thing about writing your own questions is you know the material," Kroft told me. "I had to keep moving. I was so cognizant of the clock."

Kroft also knows the interview is not about him. Less confident interviewers have a habit of asking long-winded questions to make themselves look informed and commanding. Kroft is authoritative.

Look at this quick, open-ended question. It produced an answer that made its way into newscasts around the world.

> **Kroft: This was your decision whether to proceed or not and how to proceed. What was the most difficult part of that decision?**
>
> **Obama: The most difficult part is always the fact that you're sending guys into harm's way. And there are a lot of things that could go wrong. I mean there're a lot of moving parts here. So my biggest concern was if I'm sending those guys in and Murphy's Law applies and something happens, can we still get our guys out?**
>
> **So that's point number one. These guys are going in, you know, the darkness of night. And they don't know what they're gonna find there. They don't know if the building is rigged. They don't know if, you know, there are explosives that are triggered by a particular door opening. So huge risks that these guys are taking. And so my number one concern was, if I send them in, can I get them out?**

Not every question is perfect. This one missed the mark:

> **Kroft: It's been reported that there was some resistance from advisers and planners who disagreed with the commando raid approach. Was it difficult for you to overcome that?**

Of course, the president is going to say no. Anything but a "no" would make it appear he has a divided circle of advisers.

A different question might have elicited better information, such as "What did you say to your closest advisers who told you they didn't want you to approve this raid?" Or an open-ended question could have worked: "Your closest advisers were reported to be divided about this raid. How important was it to have unanimous agreement on something so important?"

Kroft asked a great question about how past failures shaped this mission without providing long background in the question.

> **Kroft: How much did some of the past failures, like the Iran hostage rescue attempt, how did that weigh on you?**

He had to assume that people watching this interview knew something about history. It could be a risky assumption in some cases, so journalists have to know their audience.

By using short, punchy questions, Kroft added an urgency to the part of the interview in which the president talks about watching and listening to the actual raid. Look at the length of these questions:

> **Kroft: I want to go to the Situation Room. What was the mood?**
>
> **Kroft: Were you nervous?**
>
> **Kroft: What could you see?**
>
> **Kroft: Right. And that went on for a long time? Could you hear gunfire?**
>
> **Kroft: Flashes?**

It's a nice mixture of objective and subjective questions, facts and feelings.

Kroft didn't restate the debate about the release of those bin Laden death photos. He just asked the question that people wanted answered:

> **Kroft: Why haven't you released them?**

Later, Kroft tried a non-question question.

> **Kroft: There are people in Pakistan, for example, who say, "Look, this is all a lie. This is another American trick. Osama's not dead."**

Kroft needed to gather another fact about the burial. So he used a closed-ended question:

Kroft: Was it your decision to bury him at sea?

One of Kroft's craftiest questions came late in the piece. It sounds innocent enough, but the answer could have generated headlines:

Kroft: Is this the first time that you've ever ordered someone killed?

The direct question gets at a key issue about the raid: Was this a "kill mission" or could it have been a "capture mission"? It was the most sobering moment of the piece, set up by a simply worded question.

President Obama: Well, keep in mind that, you know, every time I make a decision about launching a missile, every time I make a decision about sending troops into battle, you know, I understand that this will result in people being killed. And that is a sobering fact. But it is one that comes with the job.

While I spend a lot of time talking with journalists about how they open their stories, the *60 Minutes* interview is more remarkable for the way the piece ended.

Kroft moved toward the final sound bite with a statement, so the president was not backed into a corner, and offered a remarkable ending:

Kroft: This was one man. This is somebody who has cast a shadow, has been cast a shadow in this place, in the White House for almost . . . a decade.

Obama: As nervous as I was about this whole process, the one thing I didn't lose sleep over was the possibility of taking bin Laden out. Justice was done. And I think that anyone who would question that the perpetrator of mass murder on American soil didn't deserve what he got needs to have their head examined.

"We put that at the end because I thought it had a real sense of finality. I thought it was the strongest answer," Kroft told me. "I was interested in whether he had moral thoughts about it."

Again, the subjective answer proves to be the most memorable answer in the interview.

The *60 Minutes* interview was laser-focused. Kroft didn't swerve off into politics and only lightly treaded into international affairs regarding Pakistan. Those issues will find their place in other shows at other times. This interview was about the decision-making process that led to a historic capture.

■ ■ ■ REMEMBER

Map out your questions in advance of your interview. Know what you're looking for in your interview and with each question. Study your interviews so you know which questions generate the kinds of answers you are looking for.

INTERVIEWING RELUCTANT SOURCES: EXPLAIN THE RATIONALE

Journalists often encounter people at the worst moment in their lives. A person may have lost a loved one in an accident or lost a house and everything he or she owns in a fire, or someone might have been the victim of a horrible crime. The journalist's job is to find ways to tell the story without causing more undue harm. Despite what the public might think, most journalists I know hate to approach people who are in pain and ask for an interview.

But Sue Carter, a journalism professor who coordinated the Michigan State University Victims and the Media Program, says, "It is sometimes the *duty* of the reporter to offer the person the chance to say yes or no to an interview. Many people will not want to be interviewed—some may well scream or even become abusive when approached by a reporter. But your goal should be to provide those who want to talk the opportunity to do so, and that means explaining to them the mission or rationale for talking with you."

Carter says the mission includes the following:

Warning the community of the danger. Victims, family and friends may be willing to be interviewed when they understand that this provides an opportunity to help others avoid victimization.

Telling their side. There are times when a victim may want to put his or her version on the record—the warning light wasn't flashing, the attacker threatened to kill her if she called police. Many victims complain that initial articles contained glaring errors of fact that they were not given the opportunity to correct at the time.

Illustrating an important issue. As the culture tries to grapple with issues of violence—on the street, in homes and at the workplace—the stories of victims help us understand the dynamics that allow such problems to persist. Remember, however, that victims of violence often feel guilty. Domestic violence victims feel shame because they didn't leave. Rape victims think they should have known that the person they were dating would turn violent. You are not violating your oath of objectivity to assure such victims that it was the perpetrator and not the victim who was at fault.

The best storytellers I know are tough and smart, but they also show caring compassion in their work. They show sensitivity for people who have been affected adversely by news coverage. They use special care when they interview children or others who are inexperienced in dealing with the media.

Some reporters and photojournalists seem to have a knack for landing interviews with people who tell others they don't want to talk to the media. There are plenty of tactics great reporters use to gather information from reluctant sources.

KNOW WHAT YOU ARE GOING TO SAY

Before you pick up the telephone or knock on the door, make a mental note of the points you want to make and words or issues to avoid. Be direct in your approach, especially if the potential source is impatient or wants to leave. Practice your pitch in the shower and on the way to the interview. This is a skill, just as writing and photojournalism are skills you can develop with practice. Develop contingency plans if sources turn away from you. Try appealing to their senses of fairness. Convince them that this is their opportunity to set the record straight. For example, you might say:

"I just want to get your side of the story." Or "I know there may be an explanation for what looks pretty damning here." You can appeal to their sense of public duty by saying, "If nobody speaks out or helps get the real truth out there, more people may be harmed."

IDENTIFY YOURSELF

Be sure the source knows right away that you are a journalist. This is not the time to be tricky or sneaky. Establish trust from the start, and it will serve you later when you start pressing for answers to tough questions. Make sure those you are interviewing know the purpose of your questions. Do not offer favors or gifts to families to gain access. I especially dislike the practice of sending flowers or food baskets to reluctant sources you want to interview. It gets dangerously close to paying for interviews, which most thoughtful newsrooms forbid.

HAVE A BUSINESS CARD READY

When you leave the card, include a short note explaining who you are, what you want and how to contact you at your office, by cell and at home. You will need this note and card if a source flatly says he or she is unwilling to talk or if nobody is at the location. Notes can be especially helpful when you are seeking information or an interview from somebody who is in deep pain at the moment. Sources may not want to talk to you, and you don't want to disturb them. But well-written notes can open doors. It is difficult to write such a note standing on the steps with the door closed in your face. Write it beforehand and have it ready if you need it.

MAKING FIRST IMPRESSIONS

If you are dealing with a reluctant source, it is often best to leave the microphone, camera and lights in the car at first. Talk to the person first without a camera. If appropriate, wear casual clothes. Keep your notebook in your pocket for a little while so you don't scare the person. Then, when you start writing notes, explain that you are just writing down some details you don't want to forget when you get back to the office. I used to say something like "I am getting too old to trust my memory, so I need to write things down—does that ever happen to you, you forget names or numbers?" Often the subject would say "yes," see that I am human and warm up. You might offer a business card and assure the person that you can be reached if he or she needs to correct any factual mistakes made while talking with you or needs to talk more later. You are not handing over editorial control of the story. The source must be clear that you and your colleagues, not the source, will edit the story. If a person allowed me into his or her home or told me important private details, I usually gave out my cell phone, my direct line at the TV station and often my home phone number. I have never had an unlisted phone number because I always wanted sources to be able to reach me. Reluctant sources need to know you are after the truth, not just a "gotcha" sound bite.

DISCUSS GROUND RULES

After you explain the purpose of the story, provide your honest estimate of the time required for the interview. If appropriate, offer a suggestion about the place, and ask for other suggestions. Tell sources how to let you know if they need a break, if they want the lights turned off or how to talk about what remarks they want to avoid making. Journalists should be sure their sources understand that the reporter wants as much information as possible on the record. Everybody should be clear about the meaning of the terms "on background" or "not for attribution." Depending on how experienced the source is in dealing with the media, the reporter may have an obligation to help the source understand the potential outcomes of participation, including being fired from his or her job, making others angry or becoming well-known by viewers.

Journalists who have these discussions at the front end, before the interview, avoid haggling over whether they can or can't use part of an interview after the source says something newsworthy and then wants to be left out of the story. Make sure that victims know you are there as a reporter, not as their friend, but that your goal is to help them tell their stories—and tell them the way that they want to. Do all you can to avoid a dual relationship as a friend and a journalist. The best thing journalists can do to help people in trouble is to tell the story honestly and clearly.

PROTECT SOURCES, ESPECIALLY CONFIDENTIAL OR RELUCTANT SOURCES

This is a legal as well as an ethical issue. Be careful about inadvertently burning a confidential source by carelessly giving out the source's name or business card. Don't leave the information lying on your desk or visible to others in your notes.

BE BETTER THAN YOURSELF

Former *Los Angeles Times* investigative reporter Victor Merina says reporters should "be themselves." "If being themselves is not very nice," Merina says, "be nicer than yourself." Sources see through insincerity and can spot a fake a mile away. In the end most sources will talk with you because they like you or because they believe you can help them.

TRY THE "YOU'RE NOT ALONE" APPROACH

Merina says one of the most powerful tools a reporter has is if he or she can honestly say, "I am talking with other people about this, too." Without revealing names of other sources, unless you have permission, indicate to the reluctant source that you are getting only a portion of the story from this source. With the help of this person and others, you can piece the entire story together, but without them the story might lack context and not be fair.

MAKE SURE THE FAMILY HAS BEEN NOTIFIED

The one assignment I hated above all others was when I would be told to go out to talk with family members who had lost a loved one in an accident, a war or some other tragedy. Even when you have official assurances that notification of death or serious injury already has taken place, remember that in today's world of fractured families you might inadvertently be the bearer of this news to someone who has not yet been told. Always plan in advance what you will say and do if that happens. Have a plan for follow-up verification and try to make sure that the person is not left alone while you help sort out what happened.

ASK FAMILIES HOW THEY WANT LOVED ONES TO BE REMEMBERED

Sometimes families welcome the opportunity to take control over which photographs are used. Ensure that any photographs you receive are returned to the family as quickly as possible and in good condition. Be cautious when considering whether to include biographical information about a victim that might cast that person in a negative light. Ask yourself whether that information is essential and relevant to the story. How public was the person? How widely known is the potentially negative information? Why does the public need to know that detail of the person's life?

CONSIDER ALTERNATIVES AND OTHER SOURCES

Who (other than a reporter) could act as an intermediary with grieving families to ask whether family members would be willing to do interviews or supply background information and photographs of the victims?

If the source is unwilling to talk, ask if there are other family members, clergy, friends, neighbors or co-workers who could talk knowledgeably. Even if the source you wanted grants an interview, don't forget to ask for a list of others who should speak as well.

THANK PEOPLE FOR THEIR TIME AND EFFORT

Reliving a trauma takes a toll. Tell victims how much you appreciate their willingness to share their stories with you. ABC's Byron Pitts sends thank-you notes to everyone he interviews. Pitts told me that he carries postcards and postage stamps in his briefcase at all times. He usually writes the notes in the taxi on the way to the airport after filing his story. He says he sometimes finds he is the only network correspondent whom people are actually glad to see come back to their town. Sources you have carefully nurtured don't want to feel abandoned or used by you. Call up every now and then to see how they are doing. Get to know the names of family members and important dates in their lives. Send an anniversary or birthday card if it is appropriate. Take time to get to know the "whole person," not just the part of the person who can help you in your job.

Go slowly and gently with reluctant sources. Consider several approaches when trying to interview reluctant sources. Find a way to tell the story without causing more undue harm.

INTERVIEWING JUVENILES AND OTHER VULNERABLE PEOPLE

I have seen the toughest, most experienced journalists struggle when they have to interview children. Every TV reporter has tried to interview children who are far more interested in how microphones and cameras work than in answering a journalist's questions. Kids don't care that you are smart, famous and aggressive. Kids focus most on how they think you feel about them.

Journalists should talk with and interview children more often. Some of the nation's most vital stories revolve around kids:

- 16.4 million American children lived in poverty in 2016.[14]

- 1.2 million American schoolchildren are homeless.[15]

- 54,000 young people are locked up in juvenile jails.[16]

- 60 percent of all fourth- and eighth-grade public school students and more than 80 percent of black and 75 percent of Hispanic students in these grades could not read or compute at grade level in 2014.[17]

- Nearly one in ten 12- to 17-year-olds in the U.S. have experienced binge-drinking.[18]

Plenty of lobbying groups say they work for kids. Every politician tells prospective voters, "Our kids come first." But you can re-read the bullet points and know that is just not true. Journalists who do not find ways to interview and understand children overlook the single most vulnerable group of people living in their viewing area.

But there are lots of reasons journalists don't interview kids. It's not just an issue of knowing how to ask questions in a way that a child will answer. Journalists must develop protocols for interviewing and identifying children. Those guidelines can free journalists to pursue stories they might otherwise avoid. But interviewing young people raises some of the most challenging questions faced by journalists.

Especially in breaking-news situations, juveniles may not be able to recognize the ramifications of what they say to others. Journalists should be especially careful in interviewing juveniles live because such live coverage is more difficult to control and edit. Juveniles should be given greater privacy protection than you give adults.

Journalists must weigh the journalistic duty of "seeking truth and reporting it as fully as possible" against the need to minimize any harm that might come to a juvenile in the collection of information. When interviewing juveniles, journalists should consider several points.

THE JOURNALISTIC PURPOSE

- In what light will this person be shown? What is his or her understanding or ability to understand how viewers or listeners might perceive the interview? How mature is this juvenile? How aware is the young person of the ramifications of his or her comments?

- What motivations does the juvenile have in cooperating with this interview?

- How do you know whether what this young person says is true? How much of what this young person says does he or she know firsthand? How able is he or she to put the information into context? Do others, including adults, know the same information? How can you corroborate the juvenile's information?

- How clearly have you identified yourself as a reporter to the juvenile?

WAYS TO MINIMIZE HARM

- What harm might you cause by asking questions or taking pictures of the juvenile even if you never include the interview or pictures in a story?

- How would you react if you were the parent of this child? What would be your concerns and how would you want to be included in the decision about whether the child is included in a news story?

- How can you include a parent or guardian in the decision to interview a juvenile? What effort have you made to secure parental permission for the child to be included in a news story? Is it possible to have the parent/guardian present during the interview? What are the parents' motivations for allowing the child to be interviewed? Are there legal issues you should consider, such as the legal age of consent in your state?

If you conclude that parental consent is not required, at least give the child your business card so the parents can contact you if they have an objection to the interview being used.

OTHER CONSIDERATIONS

- What alternatives can you use instead of interviewing a child on camera?

- What are the potential consequences of this person's comments, short term and long term?

- What rules or guidelines does your news organization have about interviewing juveniles? Do those guidelines change if the juvenile is a suspect in a crime and not a victim? What protocols should your newsroom consider for live coverage that could involve juveniles?

- How would you justify your decision to include this juvenile in your story to your newsroom, to viewers or listeners, to the juvenile's parents?

THE "GOLDEN RULE" FOR INTERVIEWING CHILDREN

Do unto other people's kids as you would have them do unto your kids.

■ ■ ■ REMEMBER

Show special sensitivity toward juveniles, crime victims and other vulnerable sources, but do not avoid them as potential interviews.

A Few Interviewing Don'ts

Avoid any hint of blackmail or coercion. Victims often report being acutely aware of undue pressure. Never say, "Tell me about your daughter or I will be forced to get my information elsewhere."

Avoid talking about other sources or bad-mouthing people. Merina warns, "You don't know where this source's loyalties lie. If you start bad-mouthing other people, the source will wonder if you will do the same thing when the source is not around."

Watch what you say and do at the scene. Reporters, like other first responders such as police and emergency medical personnel, sometimes indulge in dark humor to cope with their own trauma. The danger, of course, is that family and friends could overhear those insensitive remarks and that could easily cost you an interview (and the witnesses' respect for you and your news organization). It is particularly distasteful when journalists snap selfies of themselves at crime scenes or tragic events.

I have seen reporters smiling and posting that they are covering a murder or flood. Just don't. If you would not do it, say it or show it on the air, think carefully about whether you should do it, say it or show it online or on social media.

■ ■ ■ REMEMBER

Watch your words. Especially in difficult situations, you want to make sure your intentions are not misunderstood.

Notes

1. R. G. Nichols and L. A. Stevens, *Are You Listening?* (New York: McGraw-Hill, 1957).
2. Adapted from ibid.
3. Alison Para Bastien, "The Healing Art of Listening," *Midwifery Today* 1, no. 50 (Dec. 10, 1999).
4. "Why You Shouldn't Ask Questions Like a White House Reporter," March 11, 2016, Poynter.org, http://www.poynter.org/2016/why-you-shouldnt-ask-questions-like-a-white-house-reporter/401061/.

5. Source: http://www.businessinsider.com/joe-biden-2016-plans-nyt-reporter-2015-10.

6. Transcript, The White House, https://www.whitehouse.gov/photos-and-video/video/2015/11/16/president-holds-press-conference-turkey.

7. Source: https://www.whitehouse.gov/the-press-office/2015/10/02/press-conference-president.

8. Source: https://www.whitehouse.gov/the-press-office/2015/10/02/press-conference-president.

9. Source: http://www.washingtonpost.com/wp-srv/politics/special/clinton/stories/flowers012792.htm, Jan. 26, 1992.

10. Joseph E. Persico, *Edward R. Murrow: An American Original* (New York: Dell Publishing, 1988).

11. John Sawatsky, "The Question Man," *American Journalism Review* (Oct. 2000), 56.

12. Ibid., 53.

13. Telephone interview with the author, May 9, 2011. Original version of this interview was published on Poynter.org.

14. Anne E. Casey Foundation, 2016.

15. Children's Defense Fund, 2014.

16. Source: http://datacenter.kidscount.org/, 2016.

17. Children's Defense Fund State of America's Children annual report, http://www.childrensdefense.org/library/data/state-data-repository/children-in-the-states.html, 2015

18. Source: http://datacenter.kidscount.org/, 2016.

CHAPTER 7

Why Pictures Are So Powerful

If I could tell a story in words, I wouldn't have to lug a camera.

—Lewis Hine,
Investigative photographer (1874–1940) best known for his
photos of immigrants at Ellis Island and for pictures of children
being forced to work, which led to new labor laws.

We assume that "seeing is believing." It would be logical to assume that the brain accurately records the scene that the eye observes. And yet that is not true. Eyewitnesses to violent crime are notoriously unreliable when it comes to giving descriptions of the criminals, and yet there is no doubt they saw something. Former WCPO-TV, Cincinnati, investigative reporter Laure Quinlivan produced a remarkable story about misidentification of criminal suspects. She said that about half of all eyewitness reports prove to be false. And she reported that when a weapon is involved in a crime, witnesses are able to give a far more accurate description of the weapon than of the person holding the weapon. Experts told her that if the victim is of a different race or ethnicity than the criminal, the reliability of the eyewitnesses' accounts gets shakier still. So, *seeing* is not to be believed.

Ann Marie Seward Barry, associate professor of communication at Boston College, cites a study by the Educational Foundation of the American Association of Advertising Agencies that shows that even when we see images on television, we usually don't understand them. Barry writes, "Even when we watch television, *we misunderstand approximately 30 percent of what is shown to us.* Our emotional state, our mindset at the time and our experience all seem to conspire against our seeing things as they really are. We go about our lives, however, mostly assuming that what we see really 'is,' as if there were no intermediary process—in other words, as if the map were indeed the territory."[1]

There is no doubt, Barry says, that visual communication dominates verbal communication. It is a powerful notion for television journalists to consider. Pictures overwhelm the words they cover.

In this chapter we will cover the following:

- How human minds process and make sense of images
- How viewers see images before they hear words
- Why images are so powerful
- Ways to make words, sounds and pictures work together, rather than compete for the viewer's attention
- See how powerful video and the words that air with it can shape public attitudes

A Little Bit of Visual Theory

How do viewers misunderstand a third of what they see on TV? The answer may lie in how they process the images they see. Once you understand the theory behind how we process images, you can begin to form your own ideas about how to more effectively tell stories through pictures and graphics.

Gestalt psychology, a term derived from the German term *gestalten* or "organized wholes," is a theory of perception. This short exploration of visual perception will help you understand the power and potential for television visuals, including photographic images, graphics and animation.

Look at this Gestalt illustration. What do you see?

Some people see two faces in silhouette. Some see a vase or chalice.

Gestalt theory maintains that the mind has innate organizational abilities that allow us to deconstruct a whole image into various components without having to actively analyze them. So you can see one, then the other—the faces, then the vase—without much thought about either.

Vision goes on between the eye and the brain, but perception is a process entirely within the mind.

WE SEE THE BIG PICTURE FIRST

The guiding principle of Gestalt psychology is that the larger picture will be seen before its component parts. This has particular relevance for television news and is effectively the psychological equivalent of the old saying "The whole is bigger than the sum of its parts." Break a story into component parts (using different focal lengths and angles) and viewers begin to understand the scene more fully. By varying shots, you allow the brain to analyze the story from many points of view.

Probably the most important Gestalt concept is the theory that in any visual display there is always one element that will be perceived as the object. Everything else is perceived as background. In television we clutter our screens with information we think will appeal to viewers. In fact the brain is not able to process so much information.

Gestalt theory probably would suggest that CNN *Headline News'* complex design of box upon box of information, coupled with changing headlines and throbbing music, is too much for viewers to comprehend. Viewers, Gestalt theory might hold, would focus on one main object and put everything else in the background.

WE SEE WHAT WE WANT TO SEE

Another guiding principle of Gestalt psychology is that when there are a number of possible interpretations, we automatically choose the one for which we need the least amount of additional information. We associate visual images with personal experiences. It is a way of saying, "The viewer will see what he or she wants to see." If a newscast aired a story in which demonstrators were chanting anti-government slogans, my father might see that story as being "anti-American." I might see the same story as being a demonstration of the power of protected free speech. We filter stories through our own experiences, and we turn first to the interpretation we understand most. We choose the interpretation that is the most obvious to our own eyes and brain.

The images we choose to tell our stories shape how viewers understand them. Stories about same-sex marriage, for example, often include images of gay couples kissing, embracing or holding hands. Gay-rights stories often include images from gay-pride parades. All of those pictures are all part of life, to be sure. But gay couples also prepare dinner, watch TV, attend PTA meetings and work in offices. The images you choose may say as much about you as the people you are portraying in your stories.

In the first version of this textbook, I wrote, "Video photography, unlike the visual media of painting or sculpture, does not rely on a person to interpret a setting in order to capture it. To be sure, the photojournalist can influence our understanding or reaction to an image in a myriad of ways, but what he or she records is an unaltered truth. It is up to the viewer to interpret it."

But I realize now how subjective the role of the journalist, especially the photojournalist, can be. What we record is one version of the truth, seen from our lens and heard through our microphone. But turn the lens in a different direction, change the focal length, adjust the lighting or exposure, and you may see a different truth.

Seeing, for many viewers, is believing. But to really "understand" requires explanation and context. That is a key role journalists fill.

■ ■ ■ REMEMBER

Perception is a process beyond what goes on between the eye and the brain. It is entirely within the mind. The eye sees one main object in any picture or image before it looks at component parts or secondary images. When there are a number of possible interpretations of an image, viewers automatically choose the one that requires the least new information.

THE POWER OF THE PICTURE

Photojournalism has the power to influence foreign policy and even military actions.

A few minutes after I picked my daughter up from day care one January night in 1991, the Allied bombing of Baghdad began. I sat in my newsroom office in Nashville, watching as CNN's Bernard Shaw, Peter Arnett and John Holliman described the stunning pictures of missiles exploding and Iraqi guns throwing up flack. At the same moment, British Prime Minister Margaret Thatcher watched the coverage in Britain, Russian President Boris Yeltsin watched in Moscow and U.S. President George H. W. Bush watched the war he had just ordered unfold on his television set. In her book *Lights, Camera, War,* Johanna Neuman writes, "Even Libya's Muammar al-Qadhafi watched the CNN coverage from his tent in Tripoli, calling CNN's control room in the days before the war to say he had a plan to resolve the conflict peacefully. Staffers assumed he was a crackpot and hung up. There simply was no precedent for this experience. This was real-time war."[2]

Sometimes a single still photographic image holds the most power over human emotion. *The Washington Post* media critic Tom Shales concluded, "Shocking and heartbreaking TV pictures of starving children in Somalia helped motivate the American response to send troops to that country."[3]

For 10 years viewers in the United States barely noticed as more than a million Somalis died of starvation, disease and civil war. In 1991 and 1992, CNN aired 14 separate stories on the growing desperation in Somalia and Sudan.[4] It was not until TV and newspapers showed the image of a baby girl dying of starvation while a vulture sat a few feet away that Americans put a face on starvation and intervened with what the administration called a "humanitarian effort." In late December 1992, 10,000 American soldiers were on their way to Somalia.

But the mission that started with humanitarian intentions turned ugly less than a year later. On October 3, 1993, 75 U.S. Army Rangers and 40 Delta Force troops in 17 helicopters began searching for lieutenants to Somali "warlord" Gen. Mohamed Farah Aidid. The search went bad, and Somalis shot two Army Blackhawk helicopters out of the sky. The Somalis captured one soldier, a Blackhawk pilot, who was part of the 160th U.S. Army Division, the secret special operations regiment known as the Nightstalkers. The regiment was based at Fort Campbell, Kentucky, an hour's drive from our television station in Nashville.

A WSMV-TV reporter, Annette Nole, confirmed that the captive soldier was Michael Durant. We learned that his wife and 11-month-old son lived in our viewing area.

By the next day the Somalis had released a videotape of Durant. His face was swollen and bloody. He could barely speak. "You kill people innocent," the interviewer insisted. "Innocent people being killed is not good" is all Durant would mutter in return.

The power of that short videotape set the nation on edge. CNN, then the only 24-hour cable network, played the tape endlessly. Then television delivered the next round of pictures. *The Toronto Star* photojournalist/reporter Paul Watson saw Somalis mutilating soldiers' bodies. Television networks picked up the newspaper's still pictures of Somalis dragging one of the bodies through the streets of Mogadishu and jubilant Somalis jumping on the downed helicopter's rotor blades. This is the story behind the book and movie *Black Hawk Down*.

The heartbreaking and gruesome photos of the dead and of Durant covered newspapers and newsmagazines, and ran endlessly on television. U.S. Rep. Luis Gutierrez spoke for many when he said that he turned against the U.S. intervention in Somalia because "[t]he pictures caused me great pain and consternation, as I'm sure they did to every American."

On October 14, 1993, the Somalis released Durant after 11 hellish days. The pictures of his release signaled the beginning of the end of

U.S. involvement in Somalia. Americans could not get out of there fast enough. On Christmas Eve, only a few weeks later, I stood on a Fort Campbell tarmac, the same place where Durant had come home to a hero's welcome a few weeks earlier. I was covering the arrival of one of the last airlifts of soldiers who served in Somalia. (See "Soldier Comes Home," Chapter 1.) U.S. involvement started when photographs of starving children pierced the hearts of viewers who felt they could not stand by and watch a nation starve. A year later, photographs of U.S. servicemen battered, imprisoned and dead led to the end of the mission.

Professor David Perlmutter called this power of news photography on foreign policy "the CNN effect."[5]

VISUAL VERSUS VERBAL: THE EYE WINS

Pictures, sounds and graphic images hold great power. In his book *On Bended Knee: The Press and the Reagan Presidency*, writer Mark Hertsgaard quoted ABC News' Sam Donaldson as saying, "A simple truism about television: The eye always dominates the ear when there is a fundamental clash between the two."[6]

That simple truism explains why men watching NFL football can't hear their wives trying to talk to them, why my son can't hear me while his eyes are radar-locked on SpongeBob cartoons and why the news viewer can't hear the reporter explain the long history of safety about an airliner when the station is showing photographs of a plane crash.

Politicians who show up on the news know the power of images. They often stand in front of American flags, surround themselves with children or make certain that decorated war veterans are at their side as they speak at political rallies. CBS *60 Minutes* correspondent Lesley Stahl talked about this in a Bill Moyers documentary for PBS, *Illusions of News.*[7]

Stahl said, "We just didn't get the enormity of the visual impact over the verbal. It was a White House official who finally told me. . . . I did a piece where I was quite negative about [President] Reagan, yet the pictures were terrific—and I thought they'd be mad at me. But they weren't. They loved it and the official outright said to me, 'They didn't hear you. They didn't hear what you said. They only saw those pictures.' And what he really meant was it's the visual impact that overrides the verbal."

"Researchers tell us that negative images wipe out what viewers hear in the audio track of a TV story," says Deborah Potter, executive director of NewsLab, a news laboratory based in Washington, D.C., that helps local stations tell more effective stories. "If a viewer is watching an emotional and negative piece of video like a plane bursting into flames and crashing, they are not listening much. They are processing the image."

POYNTER NEWSU E-LEARNING COURSE

Learn more about using words to explain images at www.newsu.org/heart.

USE WORDS TO EXPLAIN IMAGES, NOT TO MATCH IMAGES

Pictures and words should not match. Some of my reporter and photographer friends will see this statement and wonder whether I have lost my marbles. For decades reporters have been taught that words and pictures should match. I thought so too, until my photojournalist partner Pat Slattery, chief of photography at WSMV-TV in Nashville, taught me not to "say dog, see dog." It took me a while to understand his well-placed point.

He meant that we shouldn't mention a dog if we are showing a picture of him. Talk about the dog being man's best friend, talk about the dog saving a child's life, give the dog's name or something about him, but don't tell viewers it is a dog. They can see that.

Slattery taught me that words should explain the pictures. The words should tell viewers something they would not know about the pictures, even if they were standing next to the photojournalist when the pictures were taken. When words and pictures compete, the pictures win. But when they work together, the images do not overwhelm the words; the words make the pictures even more powerful and meaningful.

Think about how an expert would lead you on a tour through an art museum. She would not point to a famous picture and tell you, "That picture has a gold frame." You could see that.

If the art expert wanted to be helpful, she might tell you, "The painter was angry when he painted this picture, which is why he used short, choppy strokes." Now you might understand something you would not have known even if you and the expert were standing side by side looking at the same picture. A journalist, like an art expert, should add meaning to the viewers' understanding of what they see.

CBS correspondent Steve Hartman told me, "I never write a sentence without knowing what pictures go along with it." Hartman becomes a guide for the viewers to understand not just what they are seeing in his stories but also to understand what they do not see. Writing to the pictures is just telling the viewer "what" is on the screen. Jill Geisler, a former colleague at The Poynter Institute, says, "Words and pictures should hold hands." They should not compete with each other, and they should not be redundant.

In the "1030 Morgan" story (see Chapter 2), Boyd Huppert did not "narrate" the pictures. The words and pictures held hands. For example, when a fire hose that was showering the dust of the demolition created a rainbow, Huppert *did not* write, "Then, a fire hose sprayed water to keep down the dust. The sunlight hit the water and formed a rainbow, and several people noticed it."

That would have been say-dog, see-dog writing. Instead, Huppert wrote:

Huppert: Yet out of that sun came a symbol.

Neighbor Number Five: Do you see the rainbow? Yea.

Huppert: A sign of hope.

Huppert allows the viewer to understand the pictures by experiencing them. He tells viewers something about the rainbow; it is a sign of hope. The pictures tell viewers "what." The copy tells viewers "what about that."

Former NBC correspondent and anchor Linda Ellerbee wrote about her discovery that writers should write "*with* television, letting pictures tell the story. To explain, let me suggest an experiment. Turn on the newscast and go into the next room. Now, listen to any story on the newscast—from beginning to end. If the story is perfectly clear to you at all times, it is a normal newscast. There is a name for this manner of

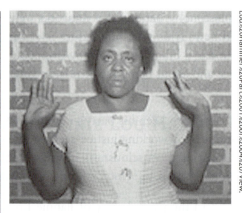

https://vault.fbi.gov/fannie-lou-hammer/Fannie%20Lou%20Hammer%20Part%2001%20of%2004%20/view.

to live as decent human beings—in America?

In the end, Johnson's attempt to keep the public from seeing her testimony backfired. Hamer became an icon for the voting rights movement. Such is the power of a powerful image.

This 1963 FBI photo Fannie Lou Hamer showed the injuries she suffered being beaten while in jail. She suffered eye, leg, kidney and back injuries that lasted the rest of her life.

■■■ REMEMBER

Images have great power over viewers. People see the images before they hear the words. When words and images compete, people remember the images, not the words. Use words to guide viewers through the visuals, not to duplicate visuals or compete with visuals.

NOTES

1. Ann Marie Seward Barry, *Visual Intelligence* (Albany: State University of New York Press, 1997), 16.
2. Johanna Neuman, *Lights, Camera, War* (New York: St. Martin's Press, 1996), 212.
3. Tom Shales, "Looking Forward, Looking Back," *The Washington Post*, Dec. 27, 1992.
4. Neuman, *Lights, Camera, War*, 229.
5. David Perlmutter, *Photojournalism and Foreign Policy: Icons of Outrage in International Crises*, Praeger Series in Political Communication (Westport, CT: Praeger, 1998), 5.
6. Mark Hertsgaard, *On Bended Knee: The Press and the Reagan Presidency* (New York: Farrar, Straus and Giroux, 1988), 25.
7. Bill Moyers, "The Public Mind: Image and Reality," PBS broadcast, 1989.
8. Linda Ellerbee, *And So It Goes* (New York: G. P. Putnam's Sons, 1986), 85.

CHAPTER 8

The Vital Role of Lighting

> *And God said, "Let there be light," and there was light. God saw that the light was good, and He separated the light from the darkness.*
>
> —Genesis 1:3–4

If God Himself thought that lighting was the second most important thing to do, after creating Earth and the Heavens, maybe we as journalists should pay attention to it, too. Lighting and shadows are as important to video as sound is to radio.

Professionals don't just use "available light." They control the light, they maximize the effect of shadows, they understand the subtle editorial messages that light or darkness signal to the viewer.

In this chapter we will cover the following:

- Why photographers should always put the camera on the "shadow side" of the subject
- How to construct effective lighting
- How to work in bright light

LIGHTING SETS AN EDITORIAL TONE

Almost nothing can change the editorial tone of an image more than the lighting. Photojournalists who blast their subjects with bright Frezzi lights, or "sun guns," may make the subject look guilty. Bright light often makes men look unshaven or skin appear to be spotted or splotchy. Dark light or shadows on the face can make an interview subject appear shady, evil or untrustworthy. But shadows are important tools for giving images texture and definition.

In this book I have prescribed lots of guidelines but very few rules. This is one of the rare rules: Keep the shadow side of the subject to the camera.

The image of a Gettysburg statue shows you what it looks like to keep the shadow side to the camera.[1] The sun is acting as a key light. It lights the right side of the statue's face, and it adds a nice shadow that gives the image depth and texture. You would light an interview exactly the same way.

Statue at Gettysburg.

CONSTRUCT THE LIGHT AND GO FOR THE SHADOW SIDE

The technical word for using the shadow side is "modeling." In addition to adding dimension to an image, shadows also hide acne scars and turkey necks, and they can take away pounds from a person's face. To hide a turkey neck, raise the key light even higher than normal and you will see the shadow fall from the chin to the collar.

The camera and the eye look for the brightest part of an image. No wonder the great photographer Ansel Adams worked in stark whites and deep blacks. Make the light side of the subject's face the brightest part of the image. When the subject is wearing bright clothing, such as a white shirt, the camera wants to make the shirt, not the face, the brightest part of the image. If you expose for the face, the shirt will be "blown out" or overexposed.

Warm, even light can make interview subjects appear soft and friendly. CBS photojournalist Les Rose told me, "If you want to light well, you have to first remove existing lights. Often that means getting rid of all of the light you did not construct yourself, such as lamps, overhead lights and window light, so that you can construct the photographic light."

Rose seats the reporter between the main key light and the camera. That puts the camera on the same side as the shadow on the subject's face. (Keep the camera on the shadow side.) A second, lesser light should be on the other side of the camera, filling in a bit of the shadow on the subject's face. A third light would highlight the person's hair and shoulders from the back, giving separation from the background. If a fourth light can be added, use it to light the physical background to give it definition, texture or color.

Let's see what this would look like. First, we remove all existing light in the room.[2]

Photos used with permission from Larry Hatteberg, KAKE-TV, Witchita.

No light.

This backlight should not be so bright that it becomes a center of our attention, but it should create separation between the subject and the background. It also fills just a little of the shadow on the side of her face. The back of her head no longer just fades into the black background. We can see there is space between her head and the bank of monitors.

Be careful not to let the fill light overpower the key. The fill should not erase the shadows, just fill in some of them to add definition and texture.

This is the classic three-light, triangulated setup. But you may be surprised to see the lights that photojournalist Larry Hatteberg used. They are not expensive studio lights. They are battery-operated work lights, just like you can buy at the local hardware store.

Light placement.

Hatteberg, who often works as a one-man-band, has used all sorts of flashlights, book lights and other gadgets when TV lights are not practical to light his stories.

Even when you use great lighting, most subjects need at least a touch of makeup to remove the shine. When you apply make-up to a man, don't call it "makeup"—just call it "something to cut the shine." You will earn their appreciation. Use as little makeup as you can. We don't want viewers to notice the shine, and we don't want them to notice the makeup either.

In Bright Sunlight Add Light

Now let's see what happens when we go outside, in the bright sunlight.

Here the sunlight behind the reporter is so bright that Hatteberg has had to open his camera's iris wide to compensate. The shot is washed out, and the light on top of the reporter's head is so powerful you can barely see her face. It looks just awful. The answer, believe it or not, is to add light.

Photos used with permission from Larry Hatteberg, KAKE-TV, Witchita.

Daylight.

Hatteberg added a powerful outdoor light called an hydrargyrum medium-arc iodide (HMI). It emits light that is the color of sunlight and is often used to accent sunlight. But the problem is the overhead sunlight. Hatteberg set up a reflector to go above the reporter's head to block the sunlight. Once again, just as he did inside, he is "controlling" the light outdoors.

If you don't have HMI lights, and in smaller markets you probably won't (the bulbs alone can cost several hundred dollars), use a high-wattage

Outside light.

tungsten light and put a blue gel over it to produce daylight color. If you have no lights, use a reflector to fill the reporter's face with light. You don't have to buy expensive TV reflectors from video supply stores. Just go to the auto parts store and buy the kind of reflectors people put in the front windows of their cars in the summer to keep the sun from beating down on the car's interior. I have used aluminum foil over a piece of cardboard. I have used an aluminum trash can lid. Be creative and resourceful, but you must cut the overhead sun and fill the shadows.

Just look at the difference an added light and an overhead reflector make.

Outside light comparison.

Photographers often refer to the hour before sunrise and the hour before sunset as the "golden hours." The colors you capture outside often are richer and warmer. But remember to "white balance" often during those times because the color temperature changes frequently as the sun rises and sets.

The main difference between professional photography and home movies is the quality of the lighting.

Rose says if the photojournalist is in a hurry and can string only two lights, "Use the key light and the hair light." You can use lights you find around the person's house or office to help out, too. House lamps can be great as background lights, adding separation between the subject and the background.

The best lighting is when viewers do not even notice the interview was lit. The lighting should never be more memorable than the subject. You want viewers to enjoy the story, not the lighting.

Be Careful

NBC correspondent Kerry Sanders posted a note on Twitter in March 2014 that he would be off the air for a while because he received serious eye injuries while covering a trial.[3] Sanders told me a story that should be a warning for all reporters and photojournalists.

In an interview after he was hurt, Sanders said that the injuries were caused by a malfunctioning HMI light that slowly damaged his corneas while he reported live on the *Today* show, MSNBC and NBC *Nightly News*.

Sanders said that the light fried the skin on his face. "Not only could I not see, but my eyes burned in pain as if two hot coals smoldered in my sockets," he said. "The darkness lasted a frightening 36 hours. I still see foggy halos and out-of-focus views."

Sanders said when he got to the hospital, doctors told him his corneas were "fried."

"The anesthetic eye-drops to ease the pain lasted only about 15 minutes and then the agony returned. The biggest problem: Those powerful drops could cause permanent injury, so I would get only four per eye and no more."

It took weeks for his sight and skin to return to normal.

Networks and high-end production companies use HMI lights because the lights are color balanced for outdoor use. The light they put out is about the same color as sunlight. But the lights are dangerous if used incorrectly.

Every HMI should have ultraviolet (UV) safety glass covering it. When the UV filter fails, injuries like the one Sanders suffered can result. Usually HMI lights have a safety switch that shuts off the light globe if the UV filter lens door is broken or open. We don't know how the filter failed in Sanders' case.

On the local news level, you probably will use lower-cost tungsten or LED lights and put color gels over the lights to achieve about the same color temperatures as the HMI lights. LEDs are replacing other lights because they are durable, energy efficient, last longer and don't have the safety issues that HMI lights do. LEDs are great for interviews because they provide a light that is easy to mute in a softbox.

■ ■ ■ REMEMBER

Lighting sets an editorial tone. Put the camera to the "shadow side" to give a richer image of your subject. Build light so that viewers notice the subject, not the effect of your lighting. Be aware of the dangers that lights can cause.

NOTES

1. Photo © Al Tompkins. Used by permission of the author.
2. Photos used with permission from Larry Hatteberg, KAKE-TV, Wichita.
3. Interview with the author March 6, 2014.

CHAPTER 9

Video and Visual Techniques

> *It is important for the photojournalist to think first as a journalist, second as a photographer.*
>
> —*J. Bruce Baumann,*
> Photojournalist

Some people, I am convinced, are naturally more artistic than others. I have worked with many photojournalists who have a flair, a grace about their movements and composition. I am also convinced that photography is a learnable craft. You can learn the essential skills that will help you shoot better video.

In this chapter we will cover the following:

- What's the difference between compelling video and amateur quality video?
- What is "photographic objectivity" and should it be our goal?
- The importance of backgrounds and settings
- Why special effects need special care

LET'S GET VISUAL: CAPTURING COMPELLING VIDEO

Pictures tell stories. Cavemen told stories—elaborate stories—about the day's hunt or an encounter with a bear, without ever scratching down a word. They drew pictures on cave walls that told stories so clearly a grade-school child centuries later can decipher the tale. But television photojournalism takes those pictures and adds sound, sequencing and movement. The cave drawings told stories one frame at a time. TV tells stories 30 frames per second.

The best television stories get *up close* to help viewers feel, taste, hear, smell and see the story. And they get *wide* to give viewers context and perspective. Wide shots give viewers a sense of place, visual breathing room. The wide shot is to video what a rest is to music.

Mark Anderson, former chief photojournalist at KSTP-TV, Minneapolis, and a National Press Photographers Association (NPPA) Photojournalist of the Year, says part of his success could be found in how he pressured himself to include a variety of shots and visual sequences in his stories. "I want every story to have wide, medium, close-up and super-close-up shots," he says.

As we discussed in Chapter 3, great photojournalism and great writing include a sequence: wide, medium, close-up and super-close-up. By editing the individual shots into these sequences, one action leading to another, the story gets a flow.

Anderson's visual storytelling guide is rooted in a solid journalistic concept. The wide shot is the context for the story. The close-up is the detail and, often, the emotion. Imagine that the city council is going to vote on a controversial issue. The wide shot of the crowded council meeting tells viewers how many people packed the room. The close-up of the angry faces or clapping hands details the tension in the meeting.

It would be possible to make a nearly empty council chamber look crowded by capturing only close-ups and images from far away that were zoomed in with a narrow depth of field. The images would be accurate but not a true representation of the meeting. Truth requires both accuracy and context.

AN ACTION WITHOUT A
REACTION IS ONLY HALF AN ACTION

Every journalist understands what I mean when I say I have been relieved to arrive on the scene of a tragedy to find the building was still burning or the ambulances were still on the scene. It is the feeling of "I am sorry for the people this happened to, but at least I didn't miss the action." Action captivates photojournalists and reporters. When we arrive on the scene of a breaking news story, of course we capture the images of the flames and chaos in front of us. A good rule of thumb when covering breaking news is to record what will go away first. In other words, immediately shoot the fire, shoot the rescue work, shoot the action. But Anderson says it is also important for photojournalists to "turn your back on the action to see the *reaction* to the action."

"That is where you will see the faces of the firemen, the scenes of horror and fright of the people who are losing their homes to the fire," Anderson says. "You will never see the emotional reaction to anything if you only face the action. Turn your back on it." His advice sounds simple enough, but it goes against every instinct when the story is breaking and the flames are leaping. But anybody can capture a fire. YouTube is full of amateur videos of such things. But it is a rare amateur who will capture the reaction to the action. More often, you hear the reaction sound in the background and you wish the camera would move to see who is reacting.

Les Rose, who for a couple of decades was the photojournalist for the popular CBS News series *Everybody Has a Story* with correspondent Steve Hartman, says TV photojournalists should "always be thinking about the person editing the video. While I am shooting, I try to give ourselves as many options as possible once we get into the edit booth. I think, 'If there were five cameras shooting this live, what camera shot would a director punch up next?' I ask myself constantly, 'Am I capturing the moment?'"

Rose says, "We are merchants of moments. There is nothing more valuable in video storytelling than a real human interaction. You have to put yourself in people's shoes, in their hospital beds, in their lives," he said. "Don't just shoot a picture of a child struggling on crutches to take his first steps at a rehab center. Imagine what a struggle that kid has gone through. Think of the therapist's reaction; think about the parents who are holding back tears and cheering silently. When you think this way, you will anticipate moments and plan your next shot. Be ready not only to record what is in front of you but also anticipate what is to come. You can't do that if you don't shoot with your heart."[1]

Rose says, "A big part of my job is to predict what people will do. If you are just shooting the moment, you will miss what comes next. If, for example, you are photographing a child eating an ice-cream cone on a summer day, you should be alert to the idea that the ice cream might melt and fall out of the cone. When it begins to fall, you would get in close. Then you would anticipate that the child might start crying, so you would not wait until she yells to move in on her face. If you wait until she yells, you have missed the shot. Once the scream leaves her mouth, be alert to the parent who will come to her rescue with a napkin and a hug."

Some photojournalists would shoot the sequence of events as one long action. Great photojournalists would see the dropping ice cream as an action followed by a series of reactions: surprise, crying and compassion. Rose sees the shots not just as a sequence but also as an unfolding story—a drama. Photojournalists who do not *anticipate* reaction have little influence over their images; they just shoot what is before them. But photojournalists who anticipate action and reaction can make crucial decisions about framing, focal length and background before the shot even presents itself.

Reporters can help photojournalists anticipate what action will come next by being an extra set of eyes and ears. This "lookout" function can be especially important if the action is about to take place on the right side of the camera. TV photographers have one blind spot, and it is on the right side. While a photojournalist is looking through a viewfinder, the camera blocks the right side. The reporter should protect that side and be alert to images and action the photojournalist can't see without looking away from the viewfinder.

Get on the same level as the action. I am 6 feet 4 inches tall. If I were photographing a young child, the kids would be 3 feet below my shoulder, where most photographers keep the camera.

Walk with the camera. Zoom with your feet. To get smoother action as you walk, move heel to toe, not with big steps. If you walk backward, it helps to have somebody guiding you, or at least keep both eyes open and look sideways often. I have tripped over a lot of shrubs and steps walking backward while photographing suspects in perp walks or politicians who are avoiding reporters' questions.

SHOOTING MORE THAN AN INTERVIEW: B-ROLL AND OTHER WAYS TO ADD CONTEXT

Rose also taught me a valuable lesson that I wish I had known when I was a street reporter. Normally, I would interview a person, then capture video of that person doing whatever he or she normally does. But Rose says I had it backward. He says it is a lot more productive to capture as much video of a person as you can before you interview her. The more you know about what she is like, the more productive the interview will be. And the person will be more relaxed in the interview if she has spent time showing you whatever it is that makes her newsworthy.

If you can, capture two interviews. Conduct an informal conversation while the person is doing whatever she is doing in the b-roll (the video that is not an interview).[2]

Then conduct a more formal, sit-down conversation that includes great lighting and perfect sound. Rose doesn't call it an interview but a conversation. An interview, he says, can feel like an interrogation, a stiff back and forth. But a conversation leads to understanding and often includes empathy.

I know that most journalists are desperately pressed for time when they are shooting stories. That fact makes it all the more important that when they start shooting, they know they need the main characters to be in more than one physical scene. I urge you to capture the main subject of your story in at least two settings. One setting is a more formal sit-down using a tripod-steadied shot. This setting is particularly good for those questions that require deep thinking and analysis. The second main interview is "off the shoulder" with the camera moving as the subject is in a more relaxed setting. The off-the-shoulder interview is more informal, may not include the distraction of a lot of light stands and other TV gear and often elicits the most heartfelt sound bites, the emotional part of the story.

If you cut between these interviews and the b-roll, it gives viewers the idea that you have spent a lot of time with the person because they experience her in more than one setting.

For example if you are doing a story on the rising divorce rate in your state, you may get video of a marriage license clerk as she types marriage licenses or files papers. As she digs through the files, ask her about what she sees flowing through her office every day. Then, in a more formal sit-down, get the facts and data. You will probably find that you will use a lot less of the sit-down than the informal b-roll interview where she explains how quickly her files are growing and how sad she is every time she adds another divorce file to the cabinet.

This word of caution: If you ask a story subject to do something in front of the camera, be sure the viewer knows you asked the person to do that. Let's suppose we are telling the story of an old Army veteran who did something heroic on this day 50 years ago. We have very little time to shoot the story, very little file tape and no time to go get other war buddies. It is just him, and we have to have this piece on in a few hours. How can we make the story look full and seem as though we spent some time with the subject?

It is completely acceptable to say, "We asked him to show us the yellowing photographs of his Army life. He keeps those memories stuffed in a cardboard box on the third shelf of his hall closet. The old photos are starting to fade with time, but his memories of Charlie Company are as clear as the day he snapped this picture."

To maximize the moment, don't ask your subject to gather some pictures before you get there. Go with the subject to the hallway closet, rolling on everything. Get a close-up on the door handle as he opens the door. Get him turning on the light switch to the closet and grunting as he reaches into the closet. Get the pictures and sound of him bringing down the box and opening the cardboard lid. Capture those first seconds of him shuffling through the photos looking for just the right one. You know he will say something like, "Oh, here is one I won't forget." This is *great* video and sound that would cover a couple of paragraphs of track easily. Just as important, it gives viewers a sense that you spent some time with this guy and that you know him. The feel of the story will be far different than if you just interview him on the sofa and cut to some static still pictures.

Even in news conferences, try to get with the main subject before she begins an official speech. Ask her what would make this a really good day, a really useful news conference? Press for the subjective reasons for even holding this news conference. What were the arguments in favor of or against making an announcement here and now? During the news conference look for symbols that time has passed. People getting tired, people checking their watches, the speaker's water glass emptying,

TV crews packing up and going away, the banners and bunting coming down, the janitors moving in. Keep shooting when others stop because they assume that if the event has ended, the story must be over.

Always get to news conferences early to get the best spot for your tripod. Don't get pushed to the outside where you will be capturing only a profile of the person who is speaking.

GET YOUR SUBJECTS COMFORTABLE WITH THE CAMERA

The best photojournalists I have worked with are stealthy in big crowds. They move quickly and quietly around their subjects. They do all they can to make the camera, microphone and lights as invisible as possible. They know that the less attention they draw to the camera, the more natural the subjects are likely to be in front of it. Great photojournalists show children how the camera gear works, to demystify it. Most kids get tired of it all and soon go back to being their normal selves.

In interviews, great photojournalists do all they can to make their subjects bored with the camera and other gear. They try to make it all just seem mechanical, uninteresting and part of the woodwork. The first pictures that great photojournalists usually take are of the subject doing some mundane activity, not usually the most important photographic moment they anticipate happening that day. There is a reason. They want the subject to be comfortable with the camera before the big moments, the "money shots," unfold.

Try to be comfortable when you are in another person's home. If he offers you a glass of tea, take it. Be gracious and allow others to be as well. Reporters must give the photojournalist an opportunity to become fully human to the subject. Rose laminated his kids' photos to his press credentials so he could flip them over and show them to people as a way of warming up to them. It is not unusual for interview subjects to talk more freely to the photojournalist, the "regular Joe in blue jeans," than to the reporter who is wearing a suit and tie.

You won't always have time to do this, but when you can, leave the gear in the car when you first arrive at a subject's house. Pay attention to the small things in the house that give you clues and insights. If you came into my home, you would see lots of family photos, kids' trophies and Asian antiques. All of these details give clues about my life. (My wife lived and worked in Korea before we met, and she fell in love with Asian culture. It may explain why two of our three adopted kids are Asian.)

The best photojournalists I have worked with helped shape the stories they were working on; they were not content to just shoot the pictures. They offered ideas to develop the story, and they offered questions to ask the people we interviewed. After reporters ask the who, what, when, where and why questions, great photojournalists can sometimes ask the "heart and soul" questions that the subject might answer. Photojournalists are journalists who use a camera instead of a notebook or laptop.

■ ■ ■ REMEMBER

The most powerful and memorable images on television often are not action shots but images in which people are reacting to the action. Extra visual dimensions give viewers the feeling that they have spent more time with a person or give them a more complete sense of the story. You will capture better video when the person is comfortable with the presence of a camera.

PRINCIPLES AND TECHNIQUES FOR PHOTOGRAPHIC OBJECTIVITY

There is no such thing as an objective photograph or graphic. Before we record, produce or edit any image, the photojournalist, reporter and producer make many decisions that affect the outcome. The nature of the news process edits out information. So every decision a photojournalist, producer, editor or reporter makes is subjective, based on his or her own opinions, experience and judgment about what is newsworthy and important. Decisions you make can affect viewers' perceptions.

GUIDE VIEWERS WITH CROPPING AND FRAMING

Depending on how the photojournalist frames a picture, scenes may appear close or far away, almost touching or separated by great space.

Extremely close cropping of a picture may be wonderfully intimate or have the effect of a Turkish prison inquisition.

Think of the frame in thirds. There is a top third, a middle third and a bottom third. Then think of the frame vertically: There is a right third, a middle and a left third.

It is safe but boring to plunk the image smack in the middle of the frame. As TV screens grow larger, the photographer must drag the viewer's eye around the frame with content from one corner to the other. Fill the frame with all sorts of interesting things to see.

Here is an example. I took this shot of Benjamin Franklin's desk at Independence Hall in Philadelphia.[3]

There is something interesting in every third of the frame except for the dead center. Your eye moves across the entire frame to see the pipe, the quill, the journal, the doodling, the walking stick and the journal entries. The stick is what photojournalists call "a leading line," which guides your eye to another part of the image. Leading lines can be anything from sidewalks to stadium seats to farm fences or interstate highways.

Let's look at the photo of the statue and the cannon.

The statue is more interesting because of the cannon, and the cannon has context thanks to the statue. I shot

Benjamin Franklin's desk, shot in thirds.

the image with a 55 mm lens standing a few feet from the cannon. I wanted the background to be in focus this time and I wanted the foreground to be slightly out of focus. I liked the light that fell between the two subjects because it added separation.

I shot this next photo in the field where Pickett's Charge took place during the Battle of Gettysburg. More than 12,500 Confederate infantry ran across an open field on July 3, 1863. It happened that I took this photograph on July 3, 2008. Within 50 minutes of the beginning of

Gettysburg statue with background in focus.

Gettysburg statue from ground perspective.

that charge in 1863, half of the charging Confederates were dead or wounded.[4]

I imagined their last image of this earth might well have been the blood-soaked field and the pale Pennsylvania summer sky.

So I put my camera down in the grass and allowed the statue of the running soldier to fall slightly out of focus, appearing as a ghostly image. I shot the photo with a 55 mm lens because I wanted some depth of field. Notice how the bottom third of the image is grass, the solider in the statue appears in the top third and there is nothing remarkable in the center. I wanted the viewers' eyes to be in the grassy field where the soldiers died.

BACKGROUND IMAGES ADD MEANING TO YOUR STORY

Rose makes the point clearly. "If I am giving a speech and the nine U.S. Supreme Court justices are standing behind me, the speech certainly has one meaning. But if I am giving the same speech and the nine people standing behind me are Elvis impersonators, then the speech takes on a different meaning. That is how important the background is to an image."[5]

Political image-makers drape their candidate's stage with the American flag or enormous campaign banners bearing the candidate's name or likeness. Donald Trump would often wear a red tie with a white shirt and a blue jacket adorned with an American flag lapel pin while standing in front of a display of American flags and delivering his "Make America Great Again" message. Some 2016 candidates started placing supporters behind them while they spoke, which gave the impression they were speaking to huge crowds even when they weren't. In March 2016, a few days after he dropped out of the Republican presidential primary race and endorsed Donald Trump, Chris Christie stood behind Trump with what NBC News called a "befuddled-looking stare."[6] The background image overtook the Trump speech and even was the idea behind a *Saturday Night Live* sketch.

In 2008, photojournalist Scott Jensen was covering an appearance at a turkey farm by Alaska Governor Sarah Palin, who was fresh off her defeat in the 2008 presidential election. The governor was scheduled to issue the ceremonial "pardon" to a turkey just before Thanksgiving. Jensen, who was working for Anchorage, Alaska, station KTUU-TV, told me that just as Palin was about to speak, he noticed there was a guy in the background who was actually killing turkeys, something that turkey processors do but not usually on TV. Jensen said he told the governor what was going on in the background to which she responded, "No problem." Jensen rightfully went on with the event and when the video hit online sites, it became a video sensation with more than 2 million views in a few days.[7]

CAMERA ANGLES CAN INDICATE AUTHORITY, POWER

Ann Marie Seward Barry, associate professor of communication at Boston College, writes, "The language of camera angles is also highly manipulative emotionally and is perhaps one of the simplest and easiest to understand examples of visual language grounded in perceptual experience."[8]

When your subject and the viewer are at the same level, they are on neutral territory in terms of power. But by shooting a subject from a low angle, the person takes on an image of power. This works the opposite way also. On occasion, news directors have asked me why their anchors seem to lack "on-camera authority." Sometimes I find the anchor is actually looking up to the camera lens, making him or her appear weak.

Barry observes, "In Nazi propaganda posters, for example, the Aryan family, the Nazi soldier, the worker in the field, the Hitler youth: all are always shown from low angle and bathed in light and color. Likewise in the National Socialist Democratic Party children's books, German workers and officers are depicted in high angle and bright colors; Jews, however, are shown caricatured with dark complexions, ill-shaven and scowling, inevitably from a high angle, and predominately in black and white."[9]

When setting up an interview, be aware of the subtle signals you send to viewers with the camera angle.

USE CAMERA MOVEMENT, PANS AND ZOOMS AS TOOLS, NOT CRUTCHES

Intentional camera movement gives a feeling of urgency and "being there." The movement provides viewers with a sense that this scene is not rehearsed. The scene unfolding in front of you may be too unpredictable to set the camera on a tripod and get steady. However, too much camera movement, or movement that is not inspired by on-the-screen action, leaves viewers feeling that the photojournalist is on a visual ride to nowhere. Viewers begin to focus more on the movement than on the visual and editorial content of the story.

Unnecessary camera movement is the hallmark of amateur photography. Just watch what inexperienced photographers do with a new camera or smartphone as they test out their new device. They pan and zoom and pan and zoom endlessly like a firefighter spraying spreading flames. Camera movement should be a photographic tool, not a crutch. Movement should be driven by content not because you are bored with a static shot.

Generally, use pans only when you are following movement or if the pan shows context. Zooms work best when the movement is motivated. If a man walked into a classroom holding a gun, your eye would zoom past your classmates and zoom in on the man and the gun. It is a motivated, focused movement.

Photojournalist Pat Slattery explains, "The camera can extend your vision and understanding by revealing what the eye can't."[10]

KEEP PROPORTIONS HONEST IN YOUR IMAGES

Another reason to zoom in on an image is to alter the focal length and depth of field of the scene. It is possible for a photojournalist to shoot a room with five people in it and make the room appear crowded. By standing far away from the people and shooting them in a shallow depth of field, the image is compressed and the people seem to be crowded together.

Sometimes you want the background to go away. Here is an image I captured at the Gettysburg National Cemetery in Pennsylvania. I used a 200 mm zoom lens, which made the background fall out of focus. If I had moved closer and used a shorter lens, the monuments in the background would be more clear. They would have distracted you from the main part of the image: the bug that is about to become the bird's lunch.

Use depth of field to focus attention on the main part of the image, the bird and the bug.

By zooming in and compressing the background to the foreground, even a beginning photographer can make a puddle look like a lake or turn a burning bush into a virtual forest fire.

You can also achieve the "compressed look" by using exposure. Your camera may include a "density filter" switch. If so, just expose the image properly and flip on the density filter. You will see the background begin to fall out of focus as the filter crushes the exposure. Experiment with the filter to find the setting that keeps the most perfect exposure while achieving the best possible background.

Use this photographic tool ethically to keep proportions truthful.

■ ■ ■ REMEMBER

Remember: Journalists have a responsibility to ensure that they honestly and accurately present images in the context of what happened. Resist visual effects that might skew the viewer's understanding or perception of an event or issue. Cropping, framing, background, camera angles, and camera movement all may reflect your biases about the subject. Recognize your biases and find ways to report around them.

Special Effects Are "Special": Use With Care

Effects such as slow motion can influence viewers' understanding and feelings. I believe that when TV stations show slow-motion images of someone in handcuffs, it can make that person look even more sinister.

One researcher found that TV viewers commonly believe that slow motion reveals the truth of what happened. And why not? We used slow-motion replays in sports to see if a foul really occurred or if a baseball player was really out at home plate. But slow motion can also change reality. Arthur Shimamura, professor of psychology and faculty member of the Helen Wills Neuroscience Institute, University of California, Berkeley, writes in his book *Psychocinematics: Exploring Cognition at the Movies* that slow-motion can change the basic understanding of what happened by changing the speed of the action. He uses as an example the 1991 video of Rodney King being beaten by Los Angeles police. The police said King was resisting arrest so they hit him with repeated stun-gun shots and beat him more than 50 times with steel nightsticks. Doctors treated King for 11 fractures and other injuries. Four officers were charged in connection with the beating, which was captured on videotape. Lawyers for the officers broke the video of the incident into individual frames, slowing the action down. Jurors, who acquitted the officers, said the slowed-down and still images did not make it appear that the beating was nearly as severe as King claimed.[11]

Shimamura said his own laboratory experiments show that viewers perceive the impact of a movement to be softer when the video is slower. In the case of King, the slow-motion playback altered the truth that the jurors used to decide their case. Another study by the University of Chicago School of Business showed that when people see action in slow motion, they tend to think it is intentional and lasts longer than the event actually lasted. The slow-motion video of a crash, for example, can exaggerate the amount of time a driver had to avoid the crash.[12] That same study examined a 2010 NFL helmet-to-helmet collision between Pittsburgh Steelers player James Harrison and Cleveland Browns player Mohamed Massaquoi. Massaquoi suffered a concussion and was carried off the field. Harrison was fined $75,000. The researchers found that the hit looks intentional and avoidable in slow motion, but at regular speed it is not nearly so clear.

The reliability of the effects from slow-motion video even reached into the court system when John "Jordan" Lewis was on trial for killing a Philadelphia police officer in a 2007 robbery. Lewis' lawyer said his client panicked when the officer confronted him. But surveillance video, in slow motion, convinced a jury that Lewis meant to shoot the officer.[13]

The worst reason to use slow motion is because you need the shot to be longer to cover a voice track. It is easy to use the "fit-to-fill" function in a video editing program that would make a shot as short or long as you wish. You could effortlessly and seamlessly make it appear that somebody is scurrying away from the camera when the person didn't hurry at all, or traffic could appear to be moving faster than it actually did. I remember once seeing a story about sailboats that racers glide across frozen lakes in the winter. When I asked if the boats go as fast as the story made it appear, I learned the editor sped the video up to make them look more interesting.

The only way to ethically change the speed of those shots is to disclose the method to the viewer or make the change so obvious that anybody could recognize it as altered.

SHUTTER AND FRAME RATE

Photojournalists also use the camera's shutter setting to capture details viewers might not see. For example, a shutter setting allows the camera to capture individual flakes falling in a snowstorm. Shutter speed refers to the amount of time each frame is exposed—the length of time a camera shutter is open. In video, the shutter speed you use will almost always be a fraction of a second. If you set the camera's shutter speed at 60, it means each frame is exposed for 1/60th of a second. Shutter speed affects how much motion blur is in each frame of your video.

The shutter speed is different from the frame rate, even though the two are often confused. The frame rate is the number of individual frames that make up one second of video. Thirty frames is the most commonly used frame rate for TV news. (Actually, the frame rate is 29.97 frames per second, but we round up to 30.) The European rate is commonly 25 frames per second.

So, confusing as it may sound at first, you could capture an image at a shutter speed of 60 and a frame rate of 30. So each individual frame would be exposed for 1/60th of a second while you are capturing 30 frames per second. And generally, that is a normal ratio: The shutter speed should be about twice the frame rate. If you moved to a faster shutter speed, say 1/400th of a second, you could capture less smooth but more detailed images of raindrops or snowflakes. Slow the shutter to say 1/30th and the snowflakes will appear blurred and may even appear to be falling harder than they are. At 1/30th a turning fan blade would be a blur. But move the shutter speed to 1/1500, for example, and you would see the individual blades turning even if they are moving quickly.

■ ■ ■ REMEMBER

Any time you alter the reality of what actually happened, you may change the viewer's understanding of the truth. We should not impose a ban on such techniques such as slow-motion or increasing camera shutter speeds or compressing depth of field but use these techniques thoughtfully, not just as an artistic expression. Ask yourself if what you are showing on video is what you saw through your viewfinder. If it is not, consider telling the viewer how you altered the image and why.

NOTES

1. Interview with the author, June 4, 2009.
2. B-roll sometimes is called "cover video" because it covers narration and sometimes it covers sound bites. The term comes from the old film days when there were two film chain projectors rolling in the control room at the same time. The director would cut to the "A" projector for the interview portions of the story and would cut to the "B" projector for the video that would roll over the announcer's voice. Even now, 40 years after the last film aired on most TV stations, we have kept the term "b-roll" to mean "cover video."
3. All photos © Al Tompkins. Used by permission of the author.
4. "The Fame of Pickett's Charge," National Park Service, https://www.nps.gov/gett/learn/education/upload/Pickett-s_Charge_Guide.pdf.
5. Interview with the author, Nov. 2, 2001.
6. Source: http://www.nbcnews.com/politics/2016-election/christie-trump-press-conference-flap-no-i-was-not-being-n531166.
7. Interview with the author Nov. 26, 2008, and https://mudflats.wordpress.com/2008/11/22/turkey-gate-the-fiasco-that-wouldnt-die/.
8. Ann Marie Seward Barry, *Visual Intelligence* (Albany: State University of New York Press, 1997), 135.
9. Ibid., 136.
10. Interview with the author, Apr. 26, 2009.
11. Arthur Shimamura, ed., *Psychocinematics: Exploring Cognition at the Movies* (Oxford: Oxford University Press, 2013), 155.
12. Zachary Burns and Eugene Caruso, "It All Happened So Slow" (Chicago: University of Chicago Booth School of Business, 2012) http://www.sjdm.org/archive/burns2012.pdf.
13. Source: http://www.philly.com/philly/blogs/206188281.html.

CHAPTER 10

Caution, This May Get Graphic: Thinking Visually

> *Graphics are not decorations. Graphics are an important part of visual journalism and should be as carefully designed and fact-checked as every other part of the story.*
>
> —Sara Quinn,
> R.M. Seaton Endowed Chair and
> Instructor, Kansas State University

W hen I was a news director, there were few comments that could draw my ire as quickly as when someone said, "That is not a TV story; that is a story for newspapers."

It was as if some stories were so complex that they could not be told clearly and interestingly on television. It seems to me that what the person usually meant was, "We don't have any visual way of telling that story well on television."

I want to spend a few pages helping you think through what makes graphics work effectively for television. The goal is not to make you a graphics expert or graphic artist but to give you a language and appreciation for the power and potential of graphics in stories.

In this chapter we will cover the following:

- How to think visually when designing graphics for television
- Why context is key in graphic design
- Why precision matters for graphics

THINK "SHAPES": A CHECKLIST FOR EFFECTIVE GRAPHICS

Think about all of the shapes we respond to without a second thought. In airplanes people of many languages and cultures understand the "no-smoking" and "fasten seat belt" signs. If a stop sign didn't include the word "stop" on it, we would still recognize it. Drivers know they should slow down when they see a yellow sign with an image of school-children on it. When I was working in South Africa, I saw this sign and marveled at how little explanation I needed to understand that I should be very careful driving on this road.[1]

South African "Hippo Crossing" road sign.

The sign served as fair warning that unless I drove carefully I might have a hippo bouncing off my car's front grill.

My big breakthrough in thinking about graphics came from a one-sentence utterance from a special projects executive producer at KYW-TV, Philadelphia. Teresa Nazario said the secret to great graphics is "to think shapes, not numbers or words." It makes so much sense. With that great line of thinking as a launch pad, I drafted a checklist for reporters and producers to consider when they ask for or design television graphics.

UNDERSTAND FIRST; THEN BE UNDERSTOOD

How clearly do you understand this story? Does the information make sense? Is it logical, believable and reliable? Do you know the source or motivation the source has for supplying the information? Understand the story completely before you try to design a graphic. Vague understanding produces vague or, worse, confusing news graphics.

KNOW THE CONTEXT OF THE GRAPHIC

If the story is about a rise in crime, for example, ask these questions:

- Where is the rise occurring?
- How does this rise compare with the total crime pattern?
- What are the possible reasons for it?
- Who is most affected?
- Who is not at all affected?
- Who has the power to keep the system as it is?
- Who profits from the system staying as it is?

Nazario used examples like these:

- Nicetown records 50 murders this year.
- Pleasantville records 25 murders this year.
- Is Nicetown twice as dangerous as Pleasantville?

You would need more information, such as:

- Nicetown has a population of 200,000 people.
- Pleasantville has a population of 25,000 people.

So, you should ask, what is the ratio of murders to population?

- Nicetown's murder rate is 50 per 200,000 (or 1 in 4,000 people is murdered).

- Pleasantville's murder rate is 25 per 25,000 (or 1 in 1,000 people is murdered).

In fact, Pleasantville's murder rate is *four times higher* than Nicetown's.

ASK MORE SOPHISTICATED
QUESTIONS TO GET BETTER GRAPHICS

Is a 100 percent increase in murder the result of one mass murder or many acts in separate areas of town? Does the increase represent a significant increase in crime, or has the murder rate gone from one person killed per year to two killed this year? How could you show where crimes occur in your town? Most cities have crime pockets, not random crime that occurs everywhere.

With graphics and stronger information we could make the story much clearer. By asking *where* the robberies occurred, not just how many robberies occurred, we could learn that 48 of the 50 robberies occurred in Nicetown's upper northeast side in a 10-block area.

Our graphic could be a map showing where the robberies occurred.

Then we could ask *what* the robbers are hitting most often. We learn that 45 of the 48 robberies involve liquor stores, and most of Nicetown's liquor stores are in the upper northeast side. Suddenly, we understand the root of the city's robbery wave. Nicetown's police department needs to get more patrols around the liquor stores.

GO LIGHTLY ON NUMBERS

Consider these numbers:

2000: 54

2010: 63

2017: 71

The numbers are simple but not effective as graphics. Your eye is trying to make mental calculations bouncing around the relative differences of the years first. The years and robberies represent different things (time and criminal incidents), yet they are represented by the same symbols—numbers. The eye sees and the brain decodes the difference in the second set of numbers. Back and forth, back and forth as many as 12 times to absorb the entire graphic. It all gets so complex, and the graphic is on the screen for only a matter of seconds. Remember, few viewers sit silently staring at the news like deer staring at car headlights. They are trying to take in this information while doing other things. No wonder viewers understand only a third of what they see on TV!

BE SYMBOLIC

It is difficult to see the relative nature of numbers when they are presented quickly on the TV screen, but it is easy to understand that a budget is growing when the bag of money on the screen is growing. Imagine you have no words: The graphic should be visual information that needs little or no verbal interpretation. How clearly would viewers understand what you are trying to show? Remember that numbers can be hard to read on a television from across the room. Symbols that replace numbers might be clearer.

Viewers have even more trouble visualizing big numbers. Kokogiak Media (www.Kokogiak.com) developed a website called the MegaPenny Project to help the public understand big numbers by using simple, familiar objects. For example, if I asked you to imagine 1,000 pennies you could probably come up with a fairly accurate image.

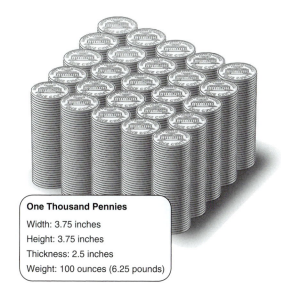

One Thousand Pennies
Width: 3.75 inches
Height: 3.75 inches
Thickness: 2.5 inches
Weight: 100 ounces (6.25 pounds)

But what would 100,000 pennies look like?

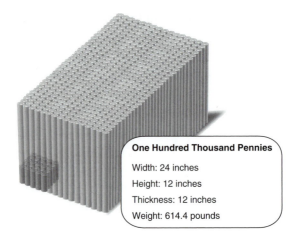

One Hundred Thousand Pennies

Width: 24 inches

Height: 12 inches

Thickness: 12 inches

Weight: 614.4 pounds

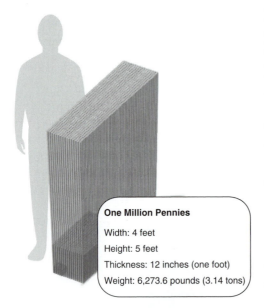

One Million Pennies

Width: 4 feet

Height: 5 feet

Thickness: 12 inches (one foot)

Weight: 6,273.6 pounds (3.14 tons)

Now, try to imagine 1,000,000 pennies. What if I told you it was a stack measuring 5 feet high by 1 foot thick. It might still be difficult for you to get an image in your mind. But when you see the image, you understand right away how big a stack of 1 million pennies would be.

Now that we know what a million pennies look like, let's move into the billions. This is where we really start to lose our viewers. Think about it: Does an interstate bridge cost a million dollars, or is it a billion dollars? What would be a reasonable guess? Most of us would not know where to begin. Seeing the difference between these two numbers might help. Here is a stack of 1 billion pennies. Each block of pennies is the size of a school bus. If you were to stack these pennies in a single pile, the stack would reach 1,000 miles.

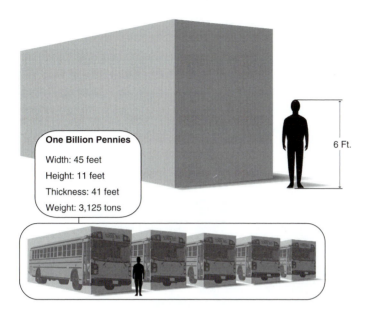

One Billion Pennies

Width: 45 feet
Height: 11 feet
Thickness: 41 feet
Weight: 3,125 tons

6 Ft.

Now let's move to the numbers of a mind-boggling size, the kinds that journalists toss around when they speak of state and federal budgets. How much space would 10 billion pennies fill?

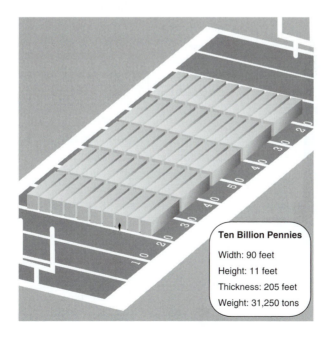

Ten Billion Pennies

Width: 90 feet
Height: 11 feet
Thickness: 205 feet
Weight: 31,250 tons

Without the football field, the 10 billion figure becomes too difficult to imagine.

Remember, viewers learn more quickly and deeply when they can relate the information to their own experiences. Take a look at why this next illustration does not mean as much; then let's see if we can find a way to make it more meaningful. Here is a pile of 1 trillion pennies.

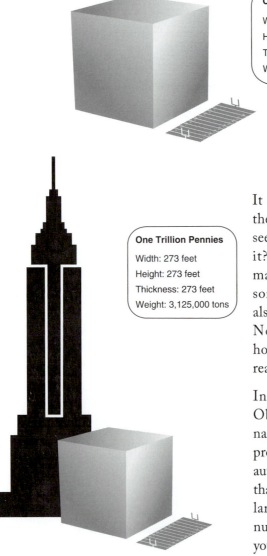

One Trillion Pennies

Width: 273 feet
Height: 273 feet
Thickness: 273 feet
Weight: 3,125,000 tons

One Trillion Pennies

Width: 273 feet
Height: 273 feet
Thickness: 273 feet
Weight: 3,125,000 tons

It is difficult to get a fix on the size of the cube. We can see its length, but how tall is it? To understand its real mass, let's compare it with something familiar that is also large and block-shaped. Now, you can imagine how big the 1 trillion stack really is.

In the early days of the Obama administration, the nation started hearing about proposals to bail out banks, automakers and homeowners that involved trillions of dollars. It is a mind-boggling number. From right to left you see the football field, then the cube of 1 trillion pennies, then the Empire State Building. By the way, 1 trillion pennies is worth 10 billion dollars.

But often in local television there is not time for the graphics department to produce a graphic for your story. On weekends and early-morning shifts, many newsrooms have no graphics support at all. At such times think graphically. How could you find something of similar size or shape to the image you are trying to create in the viewer's mind?

When ABC News's *20/20* program investigated how inaccurate some lab results were when reading PAP smear results, the network explained the work of the cytotechnologist, the person who uses a microscope to look at cells that have been smeared onto a glass slide. The technician is looking for abnormal cells. Then Diane Sawyer makes the difficulty of the job clear by showing an aerial image of a crowded parking lot and explaining, "Here is a sense of what it's like. Imagine every car in this parking lot is a cell under the microscope. Now imagine that all of the four-door cars in the parking lot are benign noncancerous cells but the two-door models are cancer and any two-door vehicle you fail to spot could cost a woman her life."[2]

Parking lot image used to demonstrate the ratio of cancer-causing and noncancerous cells on ABC News's program, *20/20*.

Another good example of visual imagery appears in a CBS *60 Minutes* piece on "honeybee colony collapse disorder":

Story Intro: If you want to grow fruits, vegetables or nuts in the United States on a commercial basis you have to have soil, sun, seeds, water and honeybees—millions and millions of honeybees brought in from all over the country to pollinate the crops. As correspondent Steve Kroft explains, honeybees are the unsung heroes of the food chain, crucial to the production of one-third of the foods we eat. So when billions of bees began to mysteriously disappear last year, there was plenty of concern and no shortage of theories, blaming everything from cell phones to divine rapture. None of the usual explanations seemed to fit. Some of the nation's top scientists are trying to understand this phenomenon, but no one is more immersed in the mystery than the man who is widely credited with discovering it.

Kroft: Lewisburg, Pennsylvania, has a population of 6,000 people and 88 million bees—enough to sting every resident of New York, California and Texas combined.[3]

What a great job of turning a number, "88 million," into a shape, "enough to sting every resident of New York, California and Texas combined." I especially like that the analogy includes a "bee" reference. He could have said 88 million is the same as the population of those three states, but when he says it is enough to "sting" every resident, the analogy comes together.

USE MOVEMENT WITH CAUTION

The Nicetown robberies graphic could be effective if the line grows as you reveal the numbers. But be careful with movement. Make things grow or disappear in accurate proportion. For example, if lawmakers voted for a series of budget cuts for the police department over several years, you might show a fever line moving slowly south. (A fever line is used in a chart; it shows a rising-and-falling line with points over time joined by a line.) But if the number of crimes rose at the same time, be careful not to make the upward arrow shoot up too quickly. The movement may make an inaccurate editorial statement. Make the growth proportional to the years that passed.

Movement near or behind the main information of the graphic is lost on the viewer. Even worse, the movement may draw attention to itself and away from the information you are trying to convey.

WRITE AFTER YOU MAKE THE GRAPHIC

Don't do this the other way around. If you write after the graphic is made, it ensures that the copy and graphic match exactly.

ASK OTHERS TO LOOK AT
THE COMPLETED GRAPHIC

Have others tell you what they think the graphic is communicating. This process is no different and certainly no less important than copyediting.

■ ■ ■ REMEMBER

Be certain you understand the information before you try to display it graphically. Think shapes, not numbers. Compare big numbers to something viewers can visualize. Use motion with care.

GET IT RIGHT: GRAPHICS ARE PRECISION WORK

Demand the same level of accuracy in your graphics that you demand for your news copy and photojournalism. Because visuals can communicate in ways the spoken word cannot, there is a special need for numerical and graphic accuracy. So if you want to show that crime has doubled in five years, your graphic should show a doubling by proportional growth. Graphic representation should be precision work, just as news writing should be precision work.

The gun control debate of 2016 often included charts and graphics of the number of gun deaths in the United States. The chart would make a different point depending on which year the journalist chooses as the first year to display in the graphic.

Look at these two graphics that explore the same data. This first graphic shows that gun-related deaths now exceed auto fatalities in the United States. The graphic gives some useful historic context however, showing that even with the uptick in firearms deaths, the current gun death count is below the peaks of the 1990s.

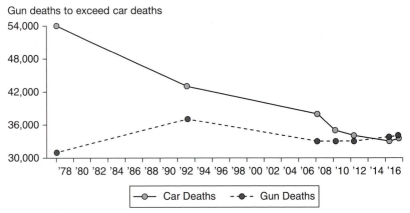

Note: Data based on Centers for Disease Control estimates.

Now let's use the same data but start the chart at 2012, not 1978. The rise in gun deaths appears more ominous.

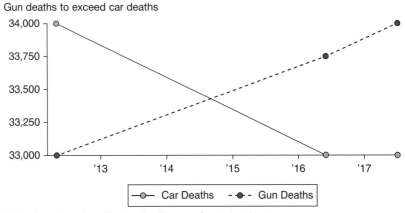

Note: Data based on Centers for Disease Control estimates.

Neither chart alone tells key facts about why one number is falling and the other is rising. Could the drop in auto deaths be related to the 2008 recession that altered driving habits? Remember that firearm deaths include suicides, which are the majority of gun-related deaths in the United States. And in the same period, car travel got significantly safer with airbags and mandatory child restraints. It would be right to ask whether the charts tell us anything useful at all. Is there any relation between gun deaths and car deaths? If the per capita consumption of butter fell at the same time that divorces rose, we would not assume one is related to the other without some proof.

Let's examine another graphic that made big news in mid-2016 when the United Kingdom voted to exit the European Union. (Media called it Brexit.) One popular theme on social media after the vote was that Brits didn't know what they were voting for. As proof, they pointed to this post from Google Trends an hour or so after that it was becoming clear that the UK would vote to "Brexit":

The post ignited headlines saying,

Google search spike suggests people don't know why they Brexited

Could one Google Trends graphic tell us that UK voters were having second thoughts?

That is a fundamental misunderstanding of what Google Trends displays. Google Trends is not a raw display of searches but an index showing relative interest in a topic. So the 250 percent increase could be a jump from very little interest to a new spike of interest in a topic. It happens every day when something unexpected makes news and people Google the word or name to find out what is happening. Google explains the tool:

Google Trends adjusts search data to make comparisons between terms easier. Otherwise, places with the most search volume would always be ranked highest. To do this, each data point is divided by the total searches of the geography and

time range it represents, to compare relative popularity. The resulting numbers are then scaled to a range of 0 to 100.

The chart below shows how the Google Trends line looked for the question, "What happens if we leave/remain in the EU?" for the one year before the vote. The top line is the "leave" question; the bottom is "stay." This chart, taken by itself, might indicate Brits were not paying attention to the EU question until after they voted. Then they hopped on Google to learn about it.

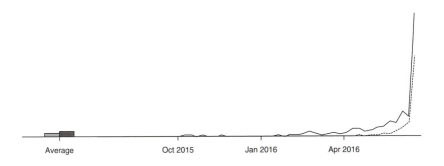

And what if we just look at the Google Trends for the week of the vote? It shows people were searching in the days before the balloting and searched even more on the day of the vote. Again, the biggest search phrase on this topic is, "What happens if we leave the EU?" It makes sense because they voted to leave, and the chart shows four times more people searched for that phrase than, "What happens if we stay in the EU." But that's all it shows. It does not prove that people didn't know why they voted as they did. It didn't prove any panic or urgency. In fact, the chart might show the opposite. The day after the vote, Google searches returned to the same level they were in the days before the vote.

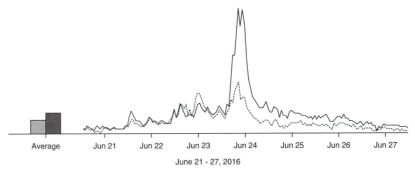

June 21 - 27, 2016

AIM FOR THE HEART

The key is to remember what the visual tells us as well as what it does not. The Google Trends graphic tells us that there was a spike of interest in the question "What happens if we leave the EU?" And once again, context matters.

Monica Moses, an expert in visual journalism and graphic design says, "Never illustrate what you do not know to be true." Journalists would not attempt to tell stories in copy that they do not know to be true. The principle is no different in visual journalism.

"It is easier for writers to write around ambiguities and holes in their stories," Moses said. "Writers use vague words like 'some,' 'many' and 'often' when they do not have hard facts. But it is almost impossible to draw around what you don't know. That's why news graphics require journalistic precision."

If an animator tried to illustrate the assassination of President John Kennedy, for example, she would show how bullets entered and exited the president's body. The illustration would show the trajectory of the shots. Those issues are subjects of heated political and historical debate even today. Besides issues of accuracy, there are questions about whether news consumers can handle the cold dissection of tragic events emotionally, even if such examination improves the public's understanding of important events.

Mario Garcia, an online and print visual communication expert, has advice that translates well for television journalists who are trying to learn how to more effectively use graphics in their stories. "Visual journalists wear the hats of the writer and editor as they move through the progression of an assignment. Something that looks good but is difficult to comprehend fails to communicate information quickly and deters from the story. Graphics can be as complicated as stories. A good visual journalist knows that simplicity and elegance work best."

According to Garcia, here is what the public is saying:

- "Please uncomplicate those graphics. I don't have all day to analyze statistics that you have to be an MBA recipient from Harvard to understand."

- "Put in those little touches that tell me if this is a happy or sad story. Show me mood."

- "Calculate that my time is reduced these days." Don't waste the viewer's time with graphics just for the sake of graphics. Just because your station bought a fancy new switcher or animation package does not mean your stories need to include graphics with images flying around in them. Ask yourself, "What is the best way to make this story clearer and more useful for the viewer?"

- "Be aware that I am a visual animal, not by choice but by conditioning. I like to see things—the face of the politician or the corner intersection near my house where two cars collided. Show me."

■ ■ ■ REMEMBER

Newsrooms should have the same standards for accuracy and context in graphics that they have for writing and photojournalism. If you do not capture a truthful story that is worth telling, you have wasted the time of your viewers, and they won't be back for more.

NOTES

1. Photo © Al Tompkins. Used by permission of the author.
2. Photo from ABC's *20/20 "Rush to Read,"* Sept. 1, 1994.
3. CBS *60 Minutes.* This segment was originally broadcast on Oct. 28, 2007. It was updated on Feb. 21, 2008.

CHAPTER 11

The Sound of the Story

> *Sound is fifty percent of the movie-going experience, and I've always believed audiences are moved and excited by what they hear in my movies at least as much as by what they see.*
>
> —George Lucas,
> Director of *Star Wars*

One of the fastest ways to improve your storytelling is to dramatically increase the amount and quality of meaningful sound in your stories. Great stories about fires and firefighters include breaks to allow viewers to hear the water rushing out of the hoses or the crackle of the fire. Great stories allow viewers to listen as a roof caves in or as a firefighter yells frantically for more water pressure.

Sound helps viewers experience the story, not just understand it. Consider these two sentences:

- Sixty million gallons of water rushed through the building (sound of water swooshing).
- Sixty million gallons of water (sound of water swooshing) rushed through the building (sound of water swooshing).

The second example gives viewers twice as much water swooshing. More important, the sound of the water is near the first mention of the water. The sound authenticates the picture. It lets viewers know exactly how close to the water we are standing.

Sound is best used when the sound is closest to the action. KTUU-TV photojournalist Scott Jensen captured a breathtaking story about the grizzly bears of Alaska by trudging deep into the McNeil River sanctuary, an area so protected that only 10 visitors are allowed into the area at a time. A bald eagle perched on a hillside watched Jensen's entry into the wilderness. Jenson recorded the squishing sounds of his own rubber boots slopping through a muddy bog as he sunk ankle deep into the muck. Jensen inched close enough to capture the sloppy sound of the bears sloshing through the mud, too. He hiked down to a shallow lagoon and captured crisp sounds of bears gorging themselves on sockeye salmon as the great fish leaped in the air in a life-and-death struggle trying to make it upstream to their spawning grounds. Years after I first watched that story, I still remember the moment when I could hear the sound of the bears crunching down on the fishes' writhing bodies. This clearly was a close-up encounter. Jensen didn't have to tell viewers that. The sound said it all.

In this chapter you will learn the following:

- How to capture sound that lets viewers experience the story
- The ethical use of music to news stories
- The ethics of editing and rearranging sound bites
- The ethics of adding or altering sounds

CAPTURING POWERFUL SOUND

If you want to tell great stories with video, you must become fanatical about great sound.

Three-time National Press Photographers Association Photographer of the Year Darren Durlach loads his stories with natural sound. He says sound takes you closer to the story; it draws viewers in. He also has found that listening for sound in the field draws him to the most memorable action. "Great sound has a short shelf life, so the very first thing I do is shoot anything that makes noise."

Durlach says, "If it is firefighters yelling at each other, if it is people twisting hoses or parents desperately searching for somebody, any moment, any sound I immediately start shooting."

SOUNDS THAT "TAKE YOU THERE": GET CLOSE TO THE ACTION

Photojournalist Mark Anderson once put a microphone on a dog that was having a great time running out on a frozen lake chasing a stick tossed by his owner. You can hear the dog's joyful panting, the kind of noise a dog makes when he is having a really good day. You can hear his claws dig into the ice as he slides to a stop, and you can hear his teeth close around the stick. A zoom lens can point me to the story, but the sound takes me to right out there on the frozen lake with that dog.

Ken Speake, who retired from KARE-TV in Minneapolis, made a career of telling sound-rich stories. I have seen him strap a wireless microphone on a bird feeder when he wanted to capture the flutter of a sparrow's wings. I have seen him plant a microphone inside a bucket to capture the dripping sound of maple sap. "The secret to great sound," Speake says matter-of-factly, "is to put the microphone closer to where the action is."

Speake often went to great lengths to get the microphone closer.

"I think of naturally occurring sound as the spice that makes the meat and potatoes of the story more palatable, more interesting and more attractive," Speake says. "I find that little, quieter things are frequently more punctuating than are noises, because folks have learned to ignore noise.

"And I generally merely ask viewers to notice the little things. Of course, it's important to put the little things front and center so they're there to be noticed and appreciated, but it's a tool, or gimmick, if you'd prefer, that gets the viewer involved. Sound draws the viewers in and grabs their attention. Once we have the viewers' active participation, it's easier to get them to remember the important stuff."

One of Speake's best-known stories was one about some barn swallows who had taken up residence in a Home Depot store. The swallows learned how to open the automatic doors at the store. The birds built nests inside the store, and Speake showed the tiny fliers swoop by the door sensors, then dart inside before the doors closed.

"The swallow nest was high near the ceiling of the 'big-box' store. And the store noises were loud enough so we couldn't hear the chicks clearly," Speake said. "It seemed only natural to me that we had to get a mic

nothing wrong with unplugging the appliance while you do the interview. You can do the same thing if you are interviewing a person in a cubicle at work and a nearby copy machine is drowning out the interview or a nearby fan is creating wind noise.

You cross an ethical line, however, when you take what is true and make it false. For example, if you were shooting a piece about a peaceful beach and to make it appear and sound peaceful you asked 100 swimmers to leave the area, that is a problem. A general guideline with environmental sound is to control the environment as you would control the ambient light. Just be sure you have not changed the surroundings so radically that the story is no longer true.

Microphones usually work best when they are close to the source of the sound that you want to record. For interviews it's essential that you move the mic as close as you can without intimidating the subject.

Wireless microphones can be a godsend, especially if the subject of your story is unfamiliar with mics. Wireless mics have two parts, a transmitter and a receiver, which allows you to put the microphone close to the source while working farther away. If you were doing a story about a kindergarten teacher, for example, you could record the teacher while she works with the little children hanging their coats in their cubbies. You would be able to hear the chalk pecking on the chalkboard; you would hear her sighs of frustration or joy while standing across the room from her. You will find that people just seem to act more naturally when they are wearing a wireless microphone; they often forget you are recording them.

You can hook virtually any kind of microphone into a wireless transmitter. Most often we use lavalier microphones (usually cardioid or multi-directional in pattern) for interviews. That mic will pick up sounds from many directions. You may need a windscreen on the lav mic to cut down on the popping sounds that people make when they say words that begin with the letters "P," "T" and "B"—called the "implosive" letters.

At news conferences, for example, there is no substitute for getting to a news conference a little early to be sure that multiline distribution boxes (mult boxes) work when you plug into them. (A mult box enables a single line of audio, from a lectern or sound system, to be fed to multiple lines out so journalists can capture clean audio without stringing their own cables and microphones.) If you are placing a mic on a speaker's stand, get the microphone close to the speaker's mouth. I have worked with plenty of photojournalists who insist we can get great sound by just sticking a mic near a loudspeaker. But try to avoid that technique. The sound is overdriven, muffled, tinny or, worse, full of feedback. It is a lazy and unprofessional way of gathering sound. There may be times, especially when you are working alone, that micing a loudspeaker is the only option. But don't make it your first choice.

When you're capturing natural sound, get the mic close to the source. If you were trying to record the clicking sounds of my computer keyboard while I pecked out this sentence, you would need to move that mic a few inches from my computer to get the best sound. If you shot the sound from across my office, you would get muffled "clunks" but not the crisp sound of my fingers pressing the keys, which is the sound I hear when I type.

You can zoom in with a long lens to capture the images, but close-up sound puts the viewer right in the middle of the action. If you are shooting a story about horse racing, put a microphone on the ground to hear the pounding of the hoofs as the horses gallop by. If you are doing a story on a rural mail carrier, your viewers will experience the story when they hear the sound of his car tires crunching through the gravel on the rural road.

Les Rose, a former CBS news photojournalist, says when you use a mic in an unusual way, remember that microphones are to be heard, not seen. If viewers start noticing the mechanics of the story, including the editing and equipment, they start "watching TV," not "watching a story." There is a big difference.

BUILD IN SILENCE

Musicians use "rests" in their melodies to add drama. When you rest in music, the music that follows becomes more meaningful.

Think of these two sentences:

"He died after having a heart attack."

"He had a heart attack . . . and died."

A pause in the second sentence adds drama. Silence does that, even when it is a tiny pause. Great television writing is not a gabfest. It is not wall-to-wall talking and sound bites. Take a few seconds to allow the story to breathe. Write in some silence.

This is a powerful tool because silence is increasingly rare. The world quite clearly is becoming a louder place. Recently Congress tried to pass legislation to make national parks quieter. In one study more than 90 percent of the people questioned said they visited the Grand Canyon, in part, to experience the silence of nature and escape the noise made by people.[2]

Viewers rarely experience silence on television. To many television journalists it may sound odd to include silence in stories, but it is a technique as old as the first motion pictures. Silence builds suspense, creates space and pulls viewers deeper into the scene. Edward R. Murrow's "Christmas in Korea" opened with the sound of a shovel pinging against the frozen ground. But there was a second or so delay between the pings—a frozen, lonely silence that was not filled with other soldiers talking or laughing. We knew that soldier was out there alone, digging. We could see the shovel hit the ground, but the sound told us the tundra was impossibly frozen. Sound and silence work together to authenticate the pictures.

In stories that are dense with copy or in newscasts in which one 15-second story follows another, a short break in the reading to allow a voice-over story to breathe can be so stark that it draws viewers back to the screen. Viewers are busy while they watch TV. They are helping their kids with homework, they are cooking dinner, they are talking on the phone while the news is on. When the news goes silent, even for a couple of seconds, it breaks the pattern of noise and asks viewers to come back to the story with their full attention.

This principle of building in silence is just as important for 20-second voice-overs that the anchors read with video as it is to longer stories full of drama and tension. In fact, a few seconds of well-placed silence builds drama and tension in what are otherwise flat, ordinary stories. Allow the viewer to wait a second or two while a judge prepares to read a verdict. Allow an ambulance to rush through the screen. Write an anchor pause into the script; allow the story to take a breath.

But don't add silence where it did not occur. Former network anchor Katie Couric produced a documentary film in 2016 about gun violence. In one scene of *Under the Gun*, Couric asks, "If there are no background checks for gun purchasers, how do you prevent felons or terrorists from purchasing a gun?" For eight seconds, the documentary shows the citizens she is interviewing silently looking at one another, seemingly at a loss for answer to her question. But an unedited audio version of the conversation emerged without the nine-second pause. The people responded immediately to Couric's question. The film's producer added silence for drama, perhaps to imply that there was no good answer and that everyone should undergo a background check to buy a gun.

The film's director and producer Stephanie Soechtig tried to explain the edit saying, "My intention was to provide a pause for the viewer to have a moment to consider this important question before presenting the facts on Americans' opinions on background checks. I never intended to make anyone look bad and I apologize if anyone felt that way."[3] The apology misses the point. It is not that the edit makes the subjects look bad. The edit makes the documentary untrustworthy.

To test the power of silence, start talking to someone, stop for a couple of seconds and then start again. You will see the listener pay closer attention after the pause.

■ ■ ■ REMEMBER

Sound allows viewers to experience the story, so make sure you've captured quality sound. It takes discipline to allow stories to unfold in pictures and sound, as well as words. Silence can be a powerful storytelling tool. It can draw viewers back into a story, give them time to digest information before you move on to the next point and even add suspense and drama to a story.

ETHICAL CONCERNS WITH ADDING MUSIC AND SOUND EFFECTS

I usually oppose the use of music in news stories. Notice that I didn't say, "Never use music" in your stories. I would say, however, use it sparingly and carefully.

I learned a painful lesson about this when I was a reporter in Nashville. WSMV-TV photojournalist Lyle Jackson and I had produced a powerful series of stories about the number of aging convicts who were piling up in prisons around the country. Inmates as old as 75 and 80 years old showed us their knee and hip replacements, and one inmate showed us his scars from a recent bypass surgery. We watched prison-run physical therapy sessions for convicts whose shoulders and elbows were getting too stiff. Some of these inmates needed special soft food because they had no teeth. A large percentage of them could not have escaped from prison if you left the front gate wide open. They could barely walk. We wanted to raise the question of whether it made any sense to keep these seniors in prison at all. Wouldn't it be cheaper to open low-security nursing homes for these old men?

One of the stories we produced focused on the inmate who had served more years in prison than anyone else in Tennessee. The old guy was moaning and groaning as he strolled across the prison yard, which was framed by dew-coated razor wire. You could hear him wheezing the early morning air into his lungs as his prison-issued hard-soled leather shoes crunched on the gravel path. A mockingbird perched on the prison fence tweeted off a subtle tune. It was as beautiful a sight as a maximum-security prison yard can be at dawn's first light. For a little extra dramatic flair, Jackson and I added a lonely, low piano score to the scene. It was slow and soft as the prisoner's scratchy voice rose above it, talking about all of his years at hard labor working in a prison cotton field. He had murdered another man in a barroom fight and escaped after he was sent to prison for that crime. After he got out of prison, he killed his wife by holding a pillow over her face. Now he was a pitiful old man.

My own mother, who was watching the news that night, called me to complain. "Don't try to make me feel sorry for those convicts," she scolded me. "He is a murderer, and murderers should be in prison," she ranted. I realized that the music added a tone of sympathy to the story that the words and pictures did not convey.

Music is a powerful tool that stirs emotions, moods and memories. My friend Ken Speake in Minneapolis once produced a story on a harp player who softly plays for restless babies in a hospital intensive care unit (ICU). Speake showed how from the very moment the harp music filled the ICU, the babies stopped crying. He even showed that when the harpist played, the babies stopped tossing restlessly, heartbeats slowed and, one by one, the infants drifted off to sleep.

Music is so powerful that scientists are trying to find ways to use it to tap into such brain disorders as autism.[4] Researchers have found that when they played pieces of music to people who have been isolated from the world, the same piece of music can stimulate similar responses. It may suggest that all humans are linked, in some way, by musical stimuli. Now *that* is powerful![5] So you must handle music carefully.

If you record music that occurred at the scene of the story, then that is ambient sound that might ethically be edited into the story. But if the music is a sound track audio recording, you must ask whether the music adds an editorial tone to the story that would not be present without the music.

As difficult as it can be to defend the ethical use of music in news stories, it is even more difficult to use sound effects ethically. Viewers probably would recognize that you added music to a spectacular sunset over the ocean. But let's say that while you were shooting, you forgot to plug in your microphone, so you didn't capture the sounds of the waves and sea gulls. Then you go to an online site and download those sounds from a sound-effect library and add them. You, my friend, have a big ethical problem. You have added sound to a story viewers believe is real. You are misleading viewers. Yes, you heard birds, but they were not the birds the viewers heard. That is deception. How comfortable would you be explaining your methods to the public?

■ ■ ■ REMEMBER

If you choose to add music to your story, do so carefully and thoughtfully. Realize that you may stir viewers' emotions and inappropriately change their understanding of the story.

Do Not Rearrange Audio or Sound Bites

In their book *The Elements of Journalism,* Bill Kovach and Tom Rosenstiel suggest one of the principles of journalism should be,

"Do not add." That means do not add something to the story that did not happen. Kovach and Rosenstiel write, "This goes further than never invent or make things up, for it also encompasses rearranging events in time or place or conflating (combining into one composite) characters or events. If a siren rang out during a TV story, and for dramatic effect it is moved from one scene to another, it has been added to that second place. What was once fact has become fiction."[6]

This kind of "audio sliding" has become both easy and common in television news, and it is a kind of deception that is invisible to the viewer. With the advent of digital editing, I have noticed a lot of television editors, photojournalists and reporters "sliding audio" in stories. The editor takes a sound that occurred in one scene and edits it into a scene in which it did not exist in reality. Here are some examples of this technique:

The photojournalist is taking pictures of a storm. He gets great sound of the wind howling and rain pelting the street. A few minutes later the photojournalist gets a great picture of trees bending in the wind, but the sound is no good; for instance, somebody nearby is hollering or a truck is passing by behind him. He decides to marry the great sound with the great picture in the edit booth.

This is an acceptable editing technique in some newsrooms. But don't "reconstitute the truth" in editing. When journalists reassemble reality, they have to take great care not to distort or mislead the viewers about what happened. For example, it would be unacceptable for the editor to borrow sound of a howling wind from a story he shot during a storm six months ago.

I think that viewers understand and accept that television, and all video storytelling, is a process of editing out. They are more confused about what we choose to leave in stories.

On the evening of President Barack Obama's inauguration, January 20, 2009, the British Broadcasting Corporation's *Newsnight* show opened with what seemed like a single sound bite from the newly sworn-in president's speech. But on closer examination, the blog Harmless Sky found that the BBC used three different parts of the inauguration speech and edited them together to create the sound bite. If anyone were to listen to the audio, it would not be clear to that person that it had been edited.

Here is a transcript of the audio:

> **We will restore science to its rightful place, roll back the specter of a warming planet. We will harness the sun and the winds and the soil to fuel our cars and run our factories.**[7]

When I heard the sound bite, I wondered if I had somehow missed that quote in the speech. I didn't see how I could have because I had spent a good part of the day writing about the speech and the inauguration. Then I discovered that Obama never said it.

Let's go to the official transcript of the president's speech to see what he actually said. I will highlight the parts of the paragraphs the BBC used.

PARAGRAPH 13 OF THE SPEECH:

"For everywhere we look, there is work to be done. The state of our economy calls for action, bold and swift. And we will act, not only to create new jobs, but to lay a new foundation for growth. We will build the roads and bridges, the electric grids and digital lines that feed our commerce and bind us together. **We will restore science to its rightful place,** and wield technology's wonders to raise health care's quality and lower its cost. **We will harness the sun and the winds and the soil to fuel our cars and run our factories.** And we will transform our schools and colleges and universities to meet the demands of a new age. All this we can do. All this we will do."

PARAGRAPH 20 OF THE SPEECH:

"We are the keepers of this legacy. Guided by these principles once more we can meet those new threats that demand even greater effort, even greater cooperation and understanding between nations. We will begin to responsibly leave Iraq to its people and forge a hard-earned peace in Afghanistan. With old friends and former foes, we'll work tirelessly to lessen the nuclear threat, and **roll back the specter of a warming planet.**"

Rosenstiel and Kovach say, "Journalists should not deceive [the viewer]. Fooling people is a form of lying and mocks the idea that journalism is committed to truthfulness." This principle is closely related to "Do not add."

A good question to ask while editing is, "What would the viewer say if he or she knew the truth about how this story was gathered and edited? Would the viewer feel deceived or tricked?" When adding any sound or effect, it should be obvious and apparent to the viewer that the journalist has chosen to alter the scene or sound.

■ ■ ■ REMEMBER

When you edit, be careful not to change the essential truth and context of what the subject says. Don't mislead viewers about what happened by the choices you make in editing.

NOTES

1. Interview with the author, Feb. 16, 2007.
2. National Park Service, *Report on Effects of Aircraft Overflights on the National Park System: Executive Summary, Report to Congress, Appendixes* (Washington, DC: U.S. Department of the Interior, 1995).
3. "Manipulative Editing Reflects Poorly on Katie Couric, Gun Commentary," National Public Radio, May 26, 2016.
4. Mark Wheeler, "Study Uses Music to Explore the Autistic Brain's Emotion Processing" (UCLA Office of Media Relations May 7, 2008).
5. Dave Munger, "Even Isolated Cultures Understand Emotions Conveyed by Western Music," *Cognitive Daily* (Apr. 8, 2009).
6. Bill Kovach and Tom Rosenstiel, *Elements of Journalism* (New York: Crown, 2001), 79.
7. The BBC show, "Obama's First 100 Days: The Environment," aired Jan. 21, 2009.
8. "BBC's Edit of Obama's Inauguration Speech Raises Important Ethical Questions," article on Poynter Online, Jan. 27, 2009.

CHAPTER 12

What Every Journalist Should Know About Guns, Ammunition and Armed Violence

> *A well regulated Militia, being necessary to the security of a free State, the right of the people to keep and bear Arms, shall not be infringed.*
>
> —*The Second Amendment of the United States Constitution*

In this third edition of *Aim for the Heart*, I decided to add this chapter about a topic that experience tells me journalists cover a lot, yet they have little personal knowledge of: guns.

Since we published the last edition, I have taught hundreds of journalists about guns and gun-control issues. I even participated in taking dozens of journalists out to gun ranges to help them learn to fire handguns, rifles and shotguns.

I am a gun owner and have been since I was 13. When I do journalism workshops around the country, I often ask journalists how many of them own guns. Even in such places as Texas and Oklahoma, a tiny percentage of the journalists I talk to own a gun or say they know much about them, but they cover stories all the time that involve guns.

My goal in this chapter is not to make journalists gun enthusiasts or even gun-rights supporters but to help you get smarter about such a hotly debated topic.

In this chapter we will cover the following:

- Ammo, gauge and caliber, a primer for journalists
- Differences among pistols, shotguns, rifles and assault rifles
- Differences between automatic and semi-automatic weapons
- How to think critically about gun and crime statistics
- Background about gun sales and gun control legislation

WHAT IS A CALIBER/GAUGE AND WHY DOES IT MATTER?

For starters, a *bullet* is what comes out of the barrel of a gun.

A *cartridge* includes the bullet, the casing, the propellant (gunpowder) and the primer. The cartridge casing usually is made of brass. That is what police often find at the crime scene. At the end of the casing is the primer. When you pull the trigger, it drops a hammer on the primer and the primer ignites the gunpowder in the shell casing, which forces a rapid expansion of gasses that pushes the projectile out the barrel.

The *caliber* of a gun is the measure of the inside diameter of the gun's barrel. It is expressed either in inches or millimeters. These three factors determine how lethal a weapon is: the caliber, the amount of power behind it, and how close the weapon is to the target.

So a .45 caliber is a firearm with 0.45-inch diameter projectiles. The most common calibers, in order of size are .22, .25, .308, .32, .357, .38, .380, .40, .44, .45 and .50. You sometimes hear the word "magnum" included. That means the cartridge attached to the projectile contains more powder, which creates more velocity.

Shotguns usually come in 10 gauge, 12 gauge, 16 gauge, 20 gauge and .410 gauge. (Technically a .410 shotgun is actually expressed as a caliber, but owners commonly call it a .410 gauge.) Shotguns fire shells loaded with shot. Unlike caliber, the higher the shotgun gauge, the less powerful the shot.

https://www.atf.gov.

From left to right: .22 short, .22 long rifle, .22 magnum, 9 mm, .357, .44 magnum, .30-30, .270, .30-06, .444, 12-gauge shotgun shell with buckshot.

The two tallest ammunition rounds are common big-game loads, which a hunter might use to hunt deer. The round on the extreme left is the sort of thing you might use to plink soda cans. The 9 mm round is what police commonly carry. The .357 and .44 rounds are serious stopping power ammo.

https://www.atf.gov.

Property of
The Bureau of Alcohol, Tobacco, Firearms and Explosives

The tip of this "hollow-point" round flattens out when it hits a target. That adds to the ammo's stopping power.

Property of
The Bureau of Alcohol, Tobacco, Firearms and Explosives

The AR-15 may be one of the most vilified and controversial weapons of our time. It is widely used in competitive shooting sports and sometimes shows up at high-profile crime scenes, but it is not the most widely owned or used weapon despite its reputation in media reports.

This is an AR-15 rifle. It fires a .223 caliber round. Sports shooters love these because they are highly accurate, have a long range and don't have much "recoil," meaning when you fire a round the weapon doesn't jar the shooter.

AR does not stand for "automatic rifle." It stands for Armalite rifle, after the company that developed it in the 1950s.

In 1994, with the passage of the Public Safety and Recreational Firearms Use Protection Act, the United States banned the importation and manufacturing of AR-15s and similar "assault weapons" and banned magazines that would hold more than 10 rounds. But there were so many already in circulation that they were not hard to find, even while the ban was in effect.

Ten years later, in 2004, the ban expired.

Gun opponents often say AR-15s are "made for only one purpose, to kill people." It's not a fair description. Lots of AR-15 owners use them for target shooting, hunting and, yes, home protection, but handguns are far more practical for home protection because they are not so bulky.

Assault rifles may have flash suppressors, bayonet mounts, adjustable or folding stocks, and they may use high-capacity magazines. Even though these rifles show up in a lot of news stories and gun-control groups focus on them, AR-15 type weapons are not the leading weapon used in gun crimes—handguns are.

Just because a gun can accept an ammo magazine does not mean it is an assault weapon. Magazines feed cartridges into a gun, rather than the gun handler using a cocking or pumping action to feed the gun's chamber. Even small-caliber guns can be built to use magazines. Gun-control groups would like to limit the number of rounds a magazine can hold. Gun advocates say it does nothing to control crime because a bad guy can just eject a spent magazine and slap another one in place in a second or two.

The AR-15 is the civilian version of the fully automatic M16 military rifle. Journalists sometimes confuse the two and wrongly call AR-15s military weapons. They may look similar, but they are very different. The M16 is the workhorse that can be switched to semiautomatic or fully automatic. The photo is from a workshop I organized for journalists who want to learn how to cover gun issues. She is firing a fully automatic M16.

This journalist is attending a "Covering Guns" seminar I organized at the University of Maryland. She is firing a fully automatic M16 military assault rifle. With one pull of the trigger, the rifle fires a burst of rounds. Fully automatic weapons are heavily regulated.

THE DIFFERENCE BETWEEN AUTOMATIC AND SEMI-AUTOMATIC WEAPONS

We are talking about AR-15s and M16s so this is a good time to clear up the difference between automatic and semi-automatic weapons. This is a mistake I hear journalists make fairly often, and it is something that gun owners laugh about. When journalists mistake the two weapons, it is a signal to the gun-owning world that the journalist has no idea what he or she is talking about.

- **Automatic weapons** fire when you pull the trigger and keep firing until you release the trigger or you fire all the ammo. A machine gun is an automatic weapon. Automatic weapons are highly regulated and you need a special permit to own one legally.

- **A semi-automatic weapon** requires you to pull the trigger for each shot. The spent casing is ejected and a new round loads in a fraction of a second. Semi-automatic weapons may be pistols, rifles or shotguns. AR-15s are semi-automatic rifles.

- **A single-shot weapon** requires you to reload, cock or pump the new load each time. A single-shot firearm must be reloaded by hand after each shot.

- **Lever guns, pump guns or bolt-action guns** require some action by the shooter to put another round into the chamber.

The use of the phrase "semi-automatic" when talking about guns is like using the phrase "gasoline cars." You could be describing a pistol, a rifle or a shotgun. It could be one of many calibers. Journalists should use model numbers, calibers/gauges and manufacturers if you want to be precise.

https://www.atf.gov.

Property of
The Bureau of Alcohol, Tobacco, Firearms and Explosives

This pump shotgun is the kind routinely used in hunting waterfowl. The hunter pulls the shorter tube below the barrel. The hunter would fill the magazine, typically with three rounds in addition to the round in the chamber. The fore-end, which is the handle that slides back and forth, is the mechanism that unloads the spent shell and loads the new round. It makes a distinctive sound that movies often use to demonstrate an attacker is in big trouble.

Shotguns like this 12-gauge use "shells" rather than cartridges. A shotgun shell may contain pellets or a slug. Shotguns are generally used to hunt birds such as geese or pheasants or to shoot skeet/trap as sport. Shotgun loads do not travel nearly as far and are not as lethal at a distance as rifle bullets. At close range, shotguns can be highly lethal.

Shotgun shells are different from the rounds that rifles and pistols fire. Shotgun shells can be loaded with two kinds of projectiles. Duck or pheasant hunters, for example, use "bird shot," which is a shotgun shell packed with small lead balls. But a big-game hunter might use a shotgun slug, a weighty projectile that also loads into the shell. Shotgun slugs are the most damaging of all of the shotgun rounds; they would obliterate smaller game. Hunters use smaller shot that forms a "pattern" spreading out and increasing the chances of hitting a fast-moving target such as a bird or a rabbit.

Shotgun gauges are measured in a way that, in my experience, even most hunters don't fully understand. Here's how it works. Shotgun gauges are determined by the number of balls of a given diameter required to make one pound of a ball that size. For a 12-gauge shotgun, it would take a dozen 12-gauge balls to make one pound. It is an odd measurement because shotgun shells hold less than two ounces of shot, but the measurement was adopted at a time when hunters loaded their own shells and purchased shot by the pound. Shotgun shells used to use lead shot, but now, because of concerns that the lead was contaminating waterways, they use steel or tungsten-nickel-iron.

https://www.atf.gov.

Typically a .22 caliber rifle is for shooting soda cans or small rodents. They can be single-shot bolt action rifles, level-action rifles, or semi-automatic weapons that can store multiple rounds. These rifles also can be manufactured to accept magazines. Many young shooters learn how to aim a rifle using a .22 caliber rifle because it has such little kickback and the ammo is inexpensive.

Rifles are a large category that can include a range of weapons, from the more powerful ones to smaller .22-caliber rifle (shown in the photograph) used by young shooters because they have so little kickback or by farmers who might use them to shoot rodents. Rifles have long barrels and can be single shot or semi-automatic, lever action, pump action or bolt action.

Property of
The Bureau of Alcohol, Tobacco, Firearms and Explosives

This handgun is a revolver. The cylinder revolves each time the weapon is fired to place a fresh round in front of the hammer.

Pistols are handguns. They can range from cheap .22 caliber guns to the hefty "Dirty Harry" Smith & Wesson Model 29 revolver, chambered for a .44 Magnum cartridge. Police commonly carry semi-automatic pistols rather than the revolvers like Dirty Harry used.

The weapon in the photograph is a revolver. See the cylinder that revolves as the shooter fires each round. Revolvers generally hold six rounds, but not always. That's why cowboy movies sometimes referred to the handgun on the sheriff's hip as a six-shooter. When the sheriff was really angry, he would carry a shotgun. The cowboys called it a "scatter gun," maybe because the shot scattered into a pattern or maybe because people scattered when the sheriff pulled it out and started hollering.

Revolvers are reliable because they are mechanically simple. In old cowboy movies you would often see the gunman pull back the hammer as if to threaten, "I'm going to shoot." Pulling back the hammer makes the gun ready to fire with a light squeeze of the trigger, but you can also discharge the weapon without pulling the hammer back. Pulling the trigger just a tad harder will pull the hammer back and

The number one rule of gun ownership is to treat every weapon as if it is loaded. The only sure way to know if a gun IS loaded is to inspect the open chamber.

discharge the round. Pulling the hammer back is just a way to make the trigger more sensitive. One confusing term you may hear is "double-action" or "single-action," which originally applied to revolvers. Now it also applies to semi-automatic weapons. A single-action weapon would require the gun to be manually "cocked" before firing by pulling back the hammer. A double-action weapon allows the shooter to fire by making a longer stronger pull on the trigger, which cocks the hammer, rotates the cylinder and fires. A key difference in these weapons is how the shooter loads the ammo. In a single-action weapon, the cylinder is fixed but in a double-action weapon, the cylinder tilts open for ejecting spent rounds and loading new ones. It is much faster and easier.

The pistol shown next is a 9mm semi-automatic pistol. The handle holds a magazine that feeds rounds into the chamber as the shooter fires the weapon. The top slide recoils after each shot and ejects the spent cartridge. One big mistake new owners make is to allow their hand to ride too high on the grip. The slide moves back after the shooter fires a round and (ouch!) slices the shooter's hand. Newbies might drop the pistol then, and dropping a loaded pistol is a bad idea.

The most widely sold gun in America today, the semi-automatic pistol. The top of the gun slides back and ejects the spent round while loading the new round. Shooters have to be careful not to allow their hands to ride too high on the grip or the slide will hit their hands. It hurts a lot!

■ ■ ■ REMEMBER

When people tell you they heard automatic gunfire, remember, they probably didn't. They may have heard rapid shots squeezed off from a revolver or more likely from a semi-automatic weapon. A scope or a laser sight does not make the weapon more lethal any more than a lot of chrome makes a car faster. When you arrive at a crime scene, look around on the ground. Lots of spent cartridges may tell you something about the weapons that were involved. Calibers and gauges measure the size of the ammo a weapon uses. Caliber measures the width of the base of the bullet. Remember for caliber, the higher the number the bigger the round. For shotguns, the lower the gauge, the more powerful the round.

GUNS IN CRIME

For decades the weapon used most often in crimes was the .38 revolver, according to the Bureau of Alcohol, Tobacco, Firearms and Explosives (ATF).[1] But today, the .38 ranks fourth on the ATF's crime-guns list. The most commonly used weapon in crimes today is the semi-automatic 9 mm pistol.[2]

https://www.atf.gov.

9 mm pistol photo from ATF.gov.

They can cost as little as a few hundred dollars new and commonly accept between 8 and 16 rounds. Second on the AFT's most-used list is the cheap, small .22 caliber pistol sometime called the "Saturday Night Special." The AR-15, the so-called "assault rifle" that gets so much media attention, is not in the top-10 weapons most used in crimes. Gun experts have told me the AR-15 is simply too large for criminals to carry and hide.[3] That said, the AR-15 was used in some high-profile killings including the mass killings in the Aurora, Colorado, movie theater (July 2012); Sandy Hook Elementary School, Newtown, Connecticut (December 2012); Inland Regional Medical Center, San Bernardino, California (December 2015); the Pulse nightclub shooting in Orlando, Florida (June 2016); and the police shootings in Dallas, Texas (July 2016).

In early 2016, *The Washington Post* tracked 125 shootings in which four or more people were killed by a single shooter. The *Post* found these important facts:

- Shooters brought an average of three weapons to each shooting. One killer brought seven weapons.
- Of the 128 shooters studied, all of the mass killers were men, most were 20 to 29 years old, half died at the scene and many of their deaths were suicide.
- 27 percent of mass shootings occurred in workplaces.

- Public mass killings that get the most press coverage make up less than 1 percent of all gun deaths. In fact, half of all gun-related deaths in the United States are suicides.

USA Today found that one mass killing occurs in the United States about every two weeks.

The paper also reported the following:

- Breakups and family arguments are at the center of most mass killings. In fact, family killings make up 53 percent of all mass killings.[4]
- 57 percent of the victims knew their killer.
- Three of four mass killings involved a handgun.
- Half of the handguns used in mass killings were semi-automatic.
- Semi-automatic "assault-style" rifles were used in fewer than 10 percent of all mass killings, about the same as shotguns.[5]

QUESTIONING CONVENTIONAL WISDOM: A LOOK AT WHY STUDENTS KILL

Conventional wisdom once said that the Earth was flat, that humans would never fly or that an African American would never be elected president of the United States.

When you begin to think critically, you will question conventional wisdom. Following a series of deadly school shootings around the country, including the 1999 attack at Columbine High School in Colorado, journalists needed to know why students kill.

There were assumptions that school shooters are loners, feel bullied, avoid school activities, must be poor students, have a violent history, have no close friends and come from broken homes—and that right before the shooting they must have "just snapped."

But when the U.S. Secret Service and Department of Education extensively studied 37 school shootings and attacks, virtually every preconceived notion about who these killers were and what led up to the shootings proved false.

Here is what the study found:

- Almost two-thirds of the attackers came from two-parent families (63 percent), living either with both biological parents (44 percent) or with one biological parent and one stepparent (19 percent). Only 5 percent lived with a foster parent or legal guardian.

- Incidents of targeted violence at school rarely were sudden, impulsive acts. They were planned attacks, sometimes involving highly detailed plans. Some attackers conceived of the attack as few as one or two days before launching that attack; other attackers had held the idea of the attack for as long as a year before carrying it out.

- Before most incidents, other people knew about the attacker's idea or plan to attack.

- 41 percent of the attackers were doing well in school at the time of the attack, generally receiving A's and B's in their courses (some were even taking Advanced Placement courses at the time of the incident or had been on the honor roll repeatedly). Fewer (15 percent) of the attackers were receiving B's and C's, and only one in five of the attackers (22 percent) were making C's or D's at the time of the attack. Only 5 percent of the attackers were failing classes at the times of the attacks.

- The largest group (41 percent) of attackers for whom this information was available appeared to socialize with mainstream students or were considered mainstream students themselves. One-quarter of the attackers (27 percent) socialized with fellow students who were disliked by most mainstream students or were considered part of a "fringe" group. Few attackers (12 percent) had no close friends.

- One-third of attackers had been characterized by others as "loners" or considered themselves loners.

- Nearly half (44 percent) of the attackers were involved in some organized social activities in or outside of school. These activities included sports teams, school clubs, extracurricular activities and mainstream religious groups.

- Most attackers did not threaten their targets directly before the attack. Fewer than one-third (31 percent) of the attackers were known to have acted violently toward others at some point before the incident. Very few (12 percent) of the attackers were known to have harmed or killed an animal at any time before the incident. Only one-quarter (27 percent) of the attackers had a prior history of arrest.

- Most attackers engaged in some behavior before the incident that caused others' concern or indicated a need for help. This goes against the commonly held theory that these kinds of attacks simply cannot be prevented.

- Many attackers felt bullied, persecuted or injured by others before the attack.

- In many cases, other students were involved in some capacity. This point disproves the "nobody knew it was coming" notion.

- Despite prompt law enforcement responses, most shooting incidents were stopped by means other than law enforcement intervention. This goes against the popularly held "more police will keep us safe" notion. Almost half (47 percent) of the incidents lasted minutes or less from the beginning of the shooting to the time the attacker was apprehended, surrendered or stopped shooting. One-quarter of the incidents were over within five minutes after they began. Police simply did not have time to respond.[6]

■ ■ ■ REMEMBER

Question conventional wisdom. Statistics challenge the assumptions about gun deaths. Myth busting can make for great news stories because it teaches and informs the audience at the same time. Journalists may unintentionally shape public policy by constantly reporting widely believed but misleading information about violent crime. Challenge simplistic solutions to complex societal problems.

Buying and Selling Guns

The debate about gun control sometimes focuses on where guns come from. In study after study, the majority of guns used in crimes do not come from the criminal purchasing the weapon from a licensed firearms dealer.[7] Data from the ATF says three of four guns purchased in the United States are purchased in the buyer's home state. But states with stricter gun laws do export fewer weapons (per capita) than do gun-friendly states such as West Virginia and Alaska.[8]

The ATF estimates about 10 to 15 percent of guns used in crimes are stolen. But not all gun sales are tracked or even recorded. The state and federal governments are involved in two parts of the life of most guns, especially pistols. When an individual goes to a retailer to purchase a firearm, the retailer contacts the FBI to run a background check on each gun purchaser. The FBI checks the National Instant Criminal Background Check System (NICS) to see whether the person is a prohibited purchaser. In some states, a state agency helps in the background check system. Prohibited purchasers include felons, fugitives, domestic abusers and the dangerously mentally ill.

The ATF says the average background check is completed in a matter of a few minutes.[9] If the quick check turns up potential issues that need deeper investigation, the background check laws give the government three business days to conduct and finish the background investigation. Under federal law, if a firearms dealer who has initiated a background check has not been notified within three business days that the sale would violate federal or state laws, the sale may proceed by default. Advocates for stronger gun laws say the law should change to allow the FBI more time to investigate, and a handful of states have passed such legislation.[10]

By federal law, the FBI cannot keep a record of "successful" background checks that clear the buyer. The FBI is required to destroy any record of a successful background check within 24 hours as a way to preserve the buyer's privacy.

Several states and the District of Columbia require background checks for rifles and shotguns (California, Colorado, Connecticut, Delaware, Hawaii, Illinois, Massachusetts, New Jersey, New York and Rhode Island).[11]

The Brady Campaign to Prevent Gun Violence, a gun-control advocate group, says about 40 percent of all gun sales involve no background checks because they are private sales from unlicensed (but legal) sellers. A growing number of states, but still a minority, have adopted background checks for guns whether or not they are purchased from a licensed retailer.[12]

Since the passage of the Gun Control Act of 1968, licensed gun dealers—called FFLs or Federal Firearms License holders—are required by the ATF to have gun purchasers fill out a federal Form 4473, which allows law enforcement officials to trace guns to their original purchaser. The retailer does not return that form to the ATF; the retailer holds on to it for 20 years to give to law enforcement if the cops recover a weapon and want to know who originally purchased it. The record is considered private, and it is not subject to open records requests until it ends up as part of the public record in a lawsuit or criminal case.[13] But if the buyer sells the gun or gives it to a relative, there would be no record of that. If the gun is stolen and there is no police report, it would be hard to trace, too.

WHAT'S LEGAL?

As the National Rifle Association (NRA) points out, "While federal legislation receives the most media attention, state legislatures and city councils make many more decisions regarding [the] right to own and carry firearms."

In Florida, where I live, one would not need to register a handgun, but in other states residents must register. In some states it is against the law to ever carry a loaded firearm; in others you can get a permit to do so. In Kentucky, where I grew up, it is perfectly legal to carry a gun in the open where anybody can see it, though workplaces and other businesses may still restrict weapons.

Some states, including Connecticut, Massachusetts, New Jersey and New York, ban assault weapons. Hawaii and Maryland ban "assault pistols," and some cities in Ohio have an assault weapon ban. California bans some large-caliber pistols and assault weapons.

The hodge-podge of laws reflects the complexity of political and even regional sensitivities to this issue.

In addition to state laws, the federal government requires some types of weapons to be registered. The ATF designates the following types of firearms as those that must be registered:

- Machine guns

- The frames or receivers of machine guns

- Any combination of parts designed and intended for use in converting weapons into machine guns

- Any part designed and intended solely and exclusively for converting a weapon into a machine gun

- Any combination of parts from which a machine gun can be assembled if the parts are in the possession or under the control of a person

- Silencers and any part designed and intended for fabricating a silencer

- Short-barreled rifles

- Short-barreled shotguns

A QUICK HISTORY OF GUN CONTROL

In 1791, the Second Amendment to the U.S. Constitution gave citizens the right to bear arms in 1791. Forty years later, the Supreme Court opened the possibility that states could regulate gun rights.[14]

Congress passed legislation in the late 1800s to control pistol sales, especially through the mail. Despite granting specific constitutional protection, the Second Amendment is not blanket permission for anybody to own a gun. The Supreme Court has repeatedly ruled that like every other right granted in the Constitution, the Second Amendment allows for some regulation. Free speech, for example, has its limits when the speech endangers or imposes harm on others. So it is with gun ownership.

In 1934, Congress passed the National Firearms Act, which imposed a $200 tax on shotguns and rifles having barrels less than 18 inches in length, certain firearms described as "any other weapons," machine guns, and firearm mufflers and silencers. Those guns were thought back then to be especially dangerous after being used in the St. Valentine's Day massacre.

In 1968, after the assassinations of John and Robert Kennedy and Martin Luther King Jr., Congress passed gun control laws that prohibited felons, those under indictment, fugitives, undocumented immigrants, drug users, those dishonorably discharged from the military and those in mental institutions from owning guns. The Gun Control Act of 1968 also made it harder to import cheap handguns commonly called Saturday Night Specials and placed a limit on automatic weapons and kits that would convert semi-automatic guns into fully automatic weapons.

In 1986, Congress passed the Firearm Owners' Protection Act, which outlawed the sale or possession of machine guns without an ATF-issued permit.

In 1994, Congress banned the sale of assault rifles. The Violent Crime Control and Law Enforcement Act focused on guns that had "flash suppressors," folding stocks and magazines that held more than 10 rounds. Gun supporters said the ban did nothing to lower crime rates because these weapons were so seldom used in crimes. Anti-assault-weapon groups said the reason the law was ineffective is because it had so many loopholes.

In *District of Columbia v. Heller*, decided in 2008, the Supreme Court ruled that individuals in Washington, D.C., have the right to own guns. It was a strong affirmation of the Second Amendment rights that pro-gun groups hoped for.

The Supreme Course extended the ruling to the rest of the country in a 2010 case, *McDonald v. City of Chicago*. Until this ruling, Chicago effectively banned residential handgun ownership by private citizens. As *The Washington Post* explained, "The 5 to 4 decision does not strike down any gun-control laws, nor does it elaborate on what kind of laws would offend the Constitution."

Justice Samuel A. Alito Jr., who wrote the opinion for the court's dominant conservatives, said, "It is clear that the Framers . . . counted the right to keep and bear arms among those fundamental rights necessary to our system of ordered liberty."

That decision will be the lightning rod for any future lawsuits that challenge the Second Amendment protections to own firearms in the United States.

COMPARISONS WITH OTHER COUNTRIES

Gun opponents sometimes compare U.S. gun laws to those in Canada. Canada records far fewer gun deaths in both raw numbers and per capita and has much more strict gun ownership laws than the United States has. Canada requires gun owners to be at least 18 years old, undergo a background check and take a public safety course. But the kinds of guns they may own varies significantly from the United States. Canada has a federal gun registration program that is exactly the sort of thing American gun owners strongly oppose.[15]

Canada treats firearms differently:

- Nonrestricted: rifles and shotguns (since 2012 no federal registration required)

- Restricted: handguns, semi-automatic rifles/shotguns (requires federal registration)

- Prohibited: automatic weapons

As in the United States, where cities and states sometimes impose their own gun control laws, in Canada, provinces, territories or municipalities may impose additional restrictions on gun ownership. For example, they may restrict what caliber of weapon may be used in hunting in a province. The federal license gives the owner the right to own a gun. The registration is for each individual gun a person owns.

Canada also limits the number of rounds a magazine may house. Long guns may use five round magazines, and handguns may use magazines with a maximum of 10 rounds.

Great Britain, Norway and Japan have much more restrictive gun laws. In Norway, the buyer has to prove a "valid reason" to want to own a gun. Japan, which has an extremely low gun murder rate of one in 10 million people, also makes it illegal to own practically all guns except for shotguns. Even to own a shotgun, the applicant has to pass a mental evaluation, drug test and more. The owner also has to present the weapon for annual inspection to government authorities.

In Britain, Ireland, Norway, New Zealand and Japan, the police do not routinely carry weapons on patrol.[16]

A DIVISIVE ISSUE

I want you to learn about the hot topic of guns so you can be sensitive to the nuances of the story.

Almost exactly half of the population says it is more important to control gun ownership, while the other half tells researchers at the Pew Research Center it is more important to protect gun ownership.

And no wonder. Fifty-four percent of Americans surveyed told Pew that they thought gun ownership does more "to protect people from becoming victims" compared with 40 percent who said gun ownership puts people's safety at risk. Whites are far more likely to say gun ownership keeps the owner safe.[17]

Gun lobby groups, including the NRA, donate 15 times as much as gun opponents do to national elections.[18]

But it's not the money that makes the difference. It is the devotion of NRA members that frightens politicians into falling in line against expanding gun control laws. The Center for Public Integrity reported, "Among the 46 senators who voted to prevent any expansion of background checks, 43 have received help—either direct campaign contributions or independent expenditures—from pro-gun interests since 2000; in aggregate about $8.5 million." That vote came only four months after Adam Lanza killed 26 people at the Sandy Hook Elementary School in Newtown, Connecticut.

■ ■ ■ REMEMBER

Although the Second Amendment broadly protects gun ownership, states and cities may impose some restrictions. Gun registration varies from state to state. Most states do not require registration for rifles or shotguns. Background checks often miss gun sales when the sale is between private individuals. Most criminals get their guns without going through background checks.

Notes

1. Source: https://www.atf.gov/resource-center/docs/ycgii-report-2000 -highlightspdf-0/download.
2. Alcohol Tobacco and Firearms 2015 Trace Data, https://www.atf.gov/ about/firearms-trace-data-2015.
3. ATF Firearms Trace Data, https://www.atf.gov/about/firearms-trace -data-2015.
4. Source: http://www.gannett-cdn.com/GDContent/mass-killings/index .html#triggers.
5. "Behind the Bloodshed," *USA Today* (October 1, 2015), http://www .gannett-cdn.com/GDContent/mass-killings/index.html.
6. Bryan Vossekuil, *The Final Report and Findings of the Safe School Initiative for the Prevention of School Attacks in the United States* (Washington, DC: U.S. Secret Service, May 2002), 11–12, 19–21, 24, 28.
7. Source: https://www.atf.gov/resource-center/docs/ycgii-report-2000- highlightspdf-0/download.
8. "Where Guns Used in Crimes Come From," *The Washington Post*, December 29, 2015.
9. Source: https://www.fbi.gov/services/cjis/nics.
10. Source: http://smartgunlaws.org/background-check-procedures-policy -summary/.
11. Source: http://www.mayorsagainstillegalguns.com.
12. Source: http://www.bradycampaign.org/our-impact/campaigns/back ground-checks.
13. Source: https://www.fbi.gov/about-us/cjis/nics.
14. *Barron v. Baltimore*, 32 U.S. (7 Pet.) 243 (1833).
15. Source: Royal Canadian Mounted Police website, http://www.rcmp-grc .gc.ca/cfp-pcaf/faq/index-eng.htm.
16. Mohammed Abbas, "British Police Still Shun Guns Despite Paris Attack," Agence France-Press (AFP), Nov. 20, 2015.
17. Source: http://www.people-press.org/2015/08/13/continued-bipartisan -support-for-expanded-background-checks-on-gun-sales/.
18. James Surowiecki, "Taking on the N.R.A.," *The New Yorker*, Oct. 19, 2015.

- Get the action and sounds that are going to go away quickly. If the building is falling down, shoot it and then turn around and get people's reaction to that.

- Get well-composed shots from your tripod.

- Get close-ups and extreme wide shots.

- Look for other elements that might fill out the story.

Durlach adds, "You always have to be prepared for the story to change." Don't lock into your story focus too quickly; stay open to new facts and developments. You never know when a great character will appear and change everything.

Durlach says that, especially when he is working alone, he pays attention to the quality of the sound he is capturing. "Great sound makes memorable stories. The camera brings the scene into your living room, but the microphone brings the viewer to the scene. My microphone is hands-down my most valuable tool to letting viewers experience the story for themselves," Durlach said.

It can be tempting when you are working alone in the field to pay more attention to the video you are capturing than the audio that goes with it. But sometimes the difference between a good story and great piece is the sound, so you may have to pause and clip a wireless mic on your subject (something a reporter might do in a two-person crew). But the effort to get quality sound is worth it. Durlach says, "Seeing a kid who has never walked in his life walk for the first time across a stage to accept his high school diploma is very powerful, but add a mic and you realize that under his breath he's scared to death that he'll fall. Without the mic, the viewer is feeling proud for the boy. But add the mic and you add suspense, which is invaluable to storytelling. With suspense viewers feel that they must continue watching to see if the boy makes it. All that simply by adding a mic. It adds a new level of emotions for the viewer to experience."

DON'T LIMIT YOURSELF TO TRADITIONAL VIDEO CAMERAS

One of my fears in writing a book about video storytelling is that technology changes so quickly that something I mention here may be quickly outdated. But GoPro cameras seem to have staying power among TV journalists. These high-def cameras can be attached nearly anywhere by suction cups or on a helmet, the hood of a car, bicycle handlebars or on a pole. Some photojournalists now attach them to the top of their TV cameras and use them to capture wide shots while the photojournalist is zoomed in for a closer shot. The on-air effect is to have a two-camera angle that you can edit between. It is also a sure way not to miss a magic moment in breaking news; keep the GoPro running even while you are turning the TV camera on and off.

In addition to video journalists who work with small video cameras, a growing number of traditional still photographers are making high-quality videos using digital single-lens reflex (DSLR) cameras. These remarkable cameras look just like still cameras, but they record high-definition video as well as stills.

Photojournalist Ami Vitale, who has shot for *National Geographic*, *Newsweek* and other prestigious magazines, also shoots video on his still camera when in far-flung spots around the globe.

"I was surprised by how it opens the possibilities for powerful storytelling. I think I was heavily influenced by TV video news shows, and I am now realizing that this is nothing like that," Vitale said. "We have a whole new medium here with unimaginable opportunities. I can tell compelling stories with more tools, and these tools can be used artfully, poetically and in a compelling way.

The biggest downside to DSLR video is the number of things you have to attach to the camera to capture professional quality sound. I have used an attached four-channel audio mixer, a shotgun microphone, a wireless mic receiver and attached an eyepiece to the LED screen so I could see the image in the bright daylight. I needed a small LED top light to fill in shadows. By the time you put the whole rig together you may as well be using a full-sized TV camera.

THE STUFF YOU NEED IN YOUR BAG

Travel as light as you can but if you do not have the gear you need, you are wasting your time and the subject's time. Plus, you may not have this opportunity again. Professional gear usually isn't cheap. Based on a lot of experience, let me tell you cheap microphones, lenses, tripods, lights and batteries break. And they break right when you need them most. Get the best you can afford.

Here is a shopping list beyond the camera:

- **A camera-mounted shotgun microphone.** You will pay at least a few hundred dollars for this. Don't scrimp on this. It is vital to your sound quality.

- **A "curly cord" to connect your microphone to your camera.** The cord looks like an old-style phone cord that retracts when you are not using it. The curly cord allows you to pull the microphone off the camera and stick it closer to the subject in noisy environments. Get a heavy one, not a cheap thin one. This will be the best $40 you spend, trust me.

- **Two wireless lavalier microphones, transmitters and receivers.** Depending on your budget, these can range from $300 each to more than $1,000 each. These will be among the most useful tools you own, so get the best you can afford. You will be coordinating the frequencies you use with other journalists in your area. Each station should have a chief photographer who communicates with the other stations.

- **A wireless "block" that can turn any handheld microphone into a wireless using your wireless receiver.** You will use this constantly in news conferences, in city council meetings and in spot news. The block can run from $200 to $400, depending on which wireless system you buy. You will use this just about every day.

- **Spare batteries for your wireless mics.** Buy them by the dozens. Don't wait for them to die to toss them. You cannot afford for a wireless mic to die in the middle of an interview or news event.

- **A tripod.** This is a key piece of gear. Buy the best you can afford. Make sure the tripod uses a "fluid" head. It will ensure smooth movement. The tripod legs need solid locking devices. Cheap tripod legs collapse, and your camera will go crashing to the ground. Lightweight tripods may not be able to bear the weight of a pro camera, batteries, wireless attachments and a device to connect your camera to live signal that you send back to the station.

- **A dimmable light that you can mount on your camera.** The best top lights also allow you to "focus" the beam from wide to narrow. The top light allows you to "fill" eyes and small shadows without overwhelming the scene. Daily news photojournalists, video journalists and mobile journalists use the top light daily. The best setup is for the light to be powered by a big rechargeable battery attached to your camera. LED (light-emitting diode) lights are efficient. Make sure the head tilts. Some LEDs now have a blend of both LED and tungsten color-balanced lights in the same little light head. That allows you to adjust the light to match the color of nearly any incandescent light that might surround you. You can even match daylight color if you are filling shadows while shooting near a window or outside.

- **External camera battery for extended shooting life.** We sometimes call these "bricks" because they are about the size of a brick and weigh a couple of pounds. Protect the connectors. I put fat rubber bands on mine to keep them from getting beat up when they are not attached to a camera. Not all cameras will accept the large, extended-life batteries.

- **An external hard drive.** I carry two 2 terabyte (TB) hard drives. Video hogs storage and you don't want to be caught short. A 2 TB hard drive will cost around $100.

- **Headphones (not the noise-canceling type).** This is a real personal issue with some photographers. Some insist on in-ear headphones, others over the ear. The key here is to get something durable and comfortable that is high enough quality that you can hear what you are recording and that you can wear while you are editing. An iPhone headphone doesn't get the job done for me. I also leave my left ear uncovered so I can hear the natural sound around me. I can also hear approaching cars and angry people around me. When you are staring into an eyepiece and your ears are only hearing the amplified sound from a wireless mic 20 feet away, you can find yourself detached from your surroundings, which can be dangerous.

- **Spare connectors and audio in case something comes undone.** Keep at least one long cable with you for when you cannot use a wireless and need to cover events such as news conferences and need to wire your microphone to your camera.

- **A GPS device that is not your phone.** If your phone battery goes dead, you still want to be able to get home. Don't forget to update your GPS map data once in a while. Roads change.

FIELD TIPS FOR COVERING ROUGH WEATHER

- **Take cash.** Lots of cash. ATMs will be out of power, and credit card machines won't work. Cash is the ticket out of a lot of tight spots. Estimate how long you might be gone and take at least $200 per person per day.

- **Be self-sufficient.** You won't be able to buy food, water, ice or other things you will need. Even if you could, the locals need it more than you do. Take enough food and water to feed your crew for 48 hours.

- **Every chance you get, top off your gas tank.** You never know when gas pumps will stop running.

- **Carry several cans of Fix-A-Flat.** You will have flat tires in hurricanes. You will run over debris. Be sure you have a spare (or two) and be sure you have a jack that works.

- **Buy expensive professional rain gear.** Do not try to save money on this. If your station won't buy good rain gear, it may say something about how serious they are about covering this story. Forget ponchos; they are terrible in the wind. Wear tight-fitting rain gear. Hip waders are the best at keeping you as dry as possible. The key is to keep your socks dry. Squishy socks make for a miserable day.

- **Have an up-to-date tetanus shot.** If you cover a storm aftermath long enough, you will step on something sharp. Wear boots. Nails are everywhere after a storm.

- **Do not take safety risks.** Even if you are willing to do something stupid for a picture, you will force rescue crews to risk their lives to save you. The problem is not the wind or the rain, even though being pelted by 100 mile per hour rain hurts—it hurts a *lot*. The problem is flying debris. Photojournalists can't see it coming when they are staring into a viewfinder.

- **Block the wind.** Use building walls and other things to block the wind. Make sure your truck is parked against a building and away from the wind as much as possible. Former CNN photojournalist Andre Jones advises, "Look for an overhead shelter. Sometimes photojournalists can shoot from a hallway that leads to the beach. Put the reporter out in the wind and rain while the photographer stands in the sheltered area. I tell my reporters, 'Look, we can have one shot in the rain or we can cover the whole storm if I stay dry. Which do you want?'" Jones says shooting out the window of the news car is safer than walking around during the storm. He also says if you have a hotel room, it is a good idea to fill the bathtub with water. In case you lose power, you will still have water to flush toilets or wash up.

- **If the camera gets wet, you are done.** Take along a blow dryer that you can operate with a cigarette lighter. You'll need to dry out the electronics occasionally. Rich Murphy, veteran storm photographer says, "Baby her. Talk nice to her and she'll treat you right. My camera's name was Cecilia. Wrap it tight, especially around the viewfinder and battery. Water will find those little openings. Take off your clear lens filter. Condensation builds up in that small space between that and your lens. Wrap your wireless cube with a balloon up past where your mic connects. Don't run the air conditioner in your car. Your camera hates to go from extreme cold to wet and humid. Try to keep the environment stable for your camera."

- **Protect your equipment.** If you don't have a customized rain jacket for your camera, try using a garbage bag and gaffer tape. Cut the plastic bag into long strips and place them over any and all connections on your camera. Wrap the viewfinder completely and cover all cracks and seams. Make sure you tape the strips down and on the smallest cracks. Jones says he used condoms on his shotgun microphone, then covered the latex with the windscreen. The key is to keep the electronics of the mic dry and the condom will not block much sound. (It can be a challenge explaining the expense to the accounting department, however.)

Richard Adkins, chief photojournalist at WRAL-TV in Raleigh, North Carolina, says his crews carry what became known in the business as the "Jack Pack," named after a veteran photographer at his station who covered many hurricanes. The Jack Pack became standard issue for crews covering storms.

the limits of the drone's ability to operate safely, and it must be flown in a manner that ensures the safety of the public.

- *Sanctity of law and public spaces:* A drone operator must abide by the regulations that apply to the airspace where the drone is operated whenever possible. An exception to this is provided in instances where journalists are unfairly blocked from using drones to provide critical information in accordance with their duties as members of the fourth estate. The drone must be operated in a manner that is least disruptive to the general population in a public setting.

- *Privacy:* The drone must be operated in a fashion that does not needlessly compromise the privacy of non-public figures. If at all possible, record only images of activities in public spaces, and censor or redact images of private individuals in private spaces that occur beyond the scope of the investigation.

- *Traditional ethics:* As outlined by professional codes of conduct for journalists.

■ ■ ■ REMEMBER

Even on the toughest days there are ways to manage the work. Make sure you have the gear and supplies you need to do the job and stay safe in rough weather. Protect your gear. Wet electronics die fast. If you risk your safety to get a story, you may put somebody else at risk when he or she has to come to rescue you.

STORY IDEAS

Here are some of my favorite story angles in a big storm and afterward.

- **Look for heroes.** After Hurricane Andrew, I met some Miami business owners who took it upon themselves to set up a huge relief center in front of a blown-out liquor store. They were amazing in their efficiency and tireless work. Home Depot, some drug stores and pizza chains were big heroes after Andrew for their unselfish service to the community in time of crisis. The pizza places just started shoveling free pies out the window of makeshift stores.

- **The rolling kitchens.** The Baptists, Methodists, Lutherans, and Mormons all have impressive emergency relief efforts after major events. Never underestimate the value of a hot meal to restore a person's spirit. It is not unusual to see these folks, who respond to emergency after emergency, set up and cooking within hours of the storm.

- **Shadow the adjusters.** Follow the story of an insurance adjuster on the day after a storm. What does she see and hear? The key will be to find a great insurance agent *before* the storm hits.

- **Follow the water.** Before the storm, keep an eye on low-lying areas that you know will flood. Be alert to cars that will be flooded, then resold. WRAL-TV consumer reporter Monica Laliberte landed an Edward R. Murrow Award for her coverage of flooded cars. She said, "I came up with it when we were out covering Hurricane Floyd's floods. Seeing all those cars floating, I realized it was an incredible opportunity to find out what really happens to 'flood cars.' In those first few days, we gathered the Vehicle Identification Numbers and took video of every late model 'flood car' we could find. Then we spent the next year tracking the cars through insurance records, DMV offices and computer databases to find out where they landed. We found they went all over the country and even out of the country. Many ended up with so-called 'clean' titles, which would make it almost impossible for future buyers to find out about the vehicle's flood history. Our story was instrumental in convincing Sen. John Edwards to co-sponsor federal legislation aimed at making it easier for consumers to find out about that history. Among other things, it also prompted the attorney general's office to post on its website the VIN numbers of more than 10,000 vehicles known to be flooded during Floyd. The AG also took action against the dealers who knowingly sold 'flood cars' to two families featured in our stories. Most of all, the stories greatly increased public awareness of the issue."

- **Find kids.** After Hurricane Andrew, we interviewed a child who rode out the storm in a big plastic trash can. She thought the storm was a person named Andrew who was going to come back. Talk to kids. They are always great.

- **Old folks run out of medicine.** Often pharmacies can't help because they have no power.

- **The scams.** Watch for them. For example, roofers move in after every disaster knowing that homeowners have insurance checks in their hands and are desperate to get their roofs patched up. The roofers come in and do a lousy job or leave the work unfinished.

- **Price gouging.** While covering disasters I have done stories on people trying to sell chain saws for twice the retail price. Same for ice, water and windows.

- **What worked?** Assess whether police radios, evacuation plans, building codes, insurance regulations, contractor licensing and fraud investigations worked. What new planning and zoning regulations are needed to keep people from building in flood zones that are persistent problems?

- **Set up a time-lapse before the storm hits.** Use a tower camera or just set up a small camera outside the newsroom and record the storm as it arrives and develops. So often we think of this after the storm arrives. Do it before the storm. The best time lapses that I have seen involve an iconic image, a landmark that the community loves.

- **Ride with emergency workers**. Any time there is a measurable amount of snow, the work of emergency workers becomes anything but routine. In addition to responding to a heart attack, workers also have to battle their way through snow. Sometimes they cannot find the house because house numbers are blocked. Doors won't open. They can't get into driveways or side streets. The battle to get to the patient can be a great obstacle.

- **Go to the impound lot.** Consider hanging a wireless mic on the person working at the impound lot who has to suffer the abuse of people whose cars have been towed because they parked on snow routes. The people who show up to claim their cars have had to find a way to get to the lot. In Minneapolis, they have to pay nearly $175 in penalties and towing charges. On top of that, there could be impound fees. The people who pay these fees are not happy. Some people just do not hear about approaching storms, despite extensive media coverage, so they don't move their cars from snow plow routes.

- **Look for the beauty.** Often journalists report only the emergency story and miss the other moments around them. Don't run the beauty pieces next to the emergency stories in your newscasts, but don't ignore the fact that kids love snow, dogs love snow, ski runs open and lots of people have fun.

■ ■ ■ REMEMBER

Beyond the breaking news, you can find stories that give your viewers greater context. The story will pretty quickly change from "what happened" to "what's next?" Ask, "What do people need?" "What problems are people having?" "How did the system that is supposed to protect and help people work?"

ASSESSING THREATS AND STAYING SAFE

On August 26, 2015, a disgruntled former employee of WDBJ-TV in Roanoke waited for two of his former colleagues to go live on the air before he pulled a gun and shot the photojournalist, a reporter and the guest they were interviewing on live TV.

A couple of weeks later, the president and general manager of WDBJ told me he hopes the murders of those two employees don't scare journalists away from doing their jobs. "The job of a journalist is to investigate," Jeffrey Marks said. "It requires brave people, whether you're going out into the fields of Afghanistan or into city hall. And that is what we need. It's not about being on television. It's not about being on radio. It's not about getting that byline. It's about the responsibility of the Fourth Estate. . . . Make sure to align your goals with the tradition of investigation, finding out the truth and helping people understand the world as a result."

Marks went on the air to announce his staff members' deaths. Marks, a journalist with decades of experience, said before he went on the air that morning he recalled a sad day when NBC anchor Tim Russert died. The network called on Tom Brokaw to deliver the news.

"Brokaw went on air and his first few words were, 'It's my sad duty to report . . .' Those are the words I started with," Marks said.

WDBJ morning anchor Kim McBroom was on the air when the former employee gunned down reporter Alison Parker and photojournalist Adam Ward. McBroom was caught startled when the director cut away from the live shot to the studio.

"In that moment, I did not realize that my friends had been shot," she said. "I did not think that at all. . . . All these different scenarios were playing in my head. That was not one of them."

Viewers and journalists have asked how she could stay on the air, coolly reporting the events of the day and anchoring as usual the next morning.

"It's something that you hope you never have to deal with, but like with any traumatic situation, you've got to dig down deep and do your job," McBroom said.

Marks told me that, just weeks before the shooting, the station had undergone safety training including "situational awareness training" taught by local police. Because of that training, in the moments after the shooting, Marks said the newsroom staff moved away from the station's windows and journalists working alone in bureaus were told to come to the station because the shooter was still on the loose and nobody knew whether there would be more violence.

Kelly Zuber, the WDBJ news director when the shooting occurred, said the shooting changed the way the station thinks about "going live." The station, she said, has received many disturbing online threats since the killings, and there was even a disturbing online conversation that claimed the whole incident was a big hoax.

In the days after the shootings, WDBJ staff learned to be hypervigilant about safety.

"We had photographers out there shooting at the same time and the rest of the media was coming up very close behind them, and that was unnerving," Zuber said. "And that was just because of what we'd been through."

Normally we think about journalists facing danger in war zones, not Norfolk. But that has changed. In November 2013, WDAZ reporter Adam Ladwig was attacked by two people while covering a fire. A month earlier, a woman attacked a WUSA-TV crew in Washington, D.C. In a six-week period in 2015, thieves attacked journalists six times, targeting cameras, computers and tripods and taking gear at gunpoint in at least one case.

I turned to seasoned reporters and photojournalists and to the Dart Center for Journalism and Trauma for advice on how to stay safe and still get your job done.

I asked my questions of

- Byron Pitts, ABC News correspondent
- Lynn French, former photojournalist and visuals editor and coach for the Arizona Republic/KPNX-TV Phoenix/azcentral.com
- Richard Adkins, chief photojournalist for WRAL-TV Raleigh
- Bruce Shapiro, executive director of the Dart Center for Journalism and Trauma

What advice do you have about how to stay safe and still get the job done?

Lynn French

Lynn French, former KPNX photojournalist: Even though it feels a little "Mother may I?," I always let the assignment desk or someone in my department know where I am going and when I should be back. It sounds simple, but journalists are independent by nature and have to fight the urge to just run out the door and hope for the best. No matter where I am going, I have my phone on me and location services turned on so if worst came to worst the newsroom could track my phone for evidence. If I am going into a tense situation, especially a door knock, I will call someone at the station to stay on the phone with me and I will tuck my phone somewhere where they can hear me (Arizona is a one-party state). And they know the exact address I am at so if things turn bad they can call the police and I can concentrate on getting to safety.

Bruce Shapiro

Bruce Shapiro, Dart Center for Trauma and Journalism: Even local journalists need to be aware of a potentially hostile environment, and pay attention both to the vulnerabilities we share with other citizens and the special risks which may be involved in our work. Anyone should worry, for instance, about being alone on a dark street. On the other hand, a journalist may also need to worry about being mistaken for law enforcement or some other unwanted presence, may be knocking on doors or taking photos in a community that has felt badly treated by media in the past, or may be displaying technology that makes us a target.

Richard Adkins

Richard Adkins, WRAL-TV Raleigh: Knowledge is more than power—knowledge is armor. Know your surroundings and your way around. In the rush to the scene of breaking news, pay attention to how you got there. What was the road/intersection where you parked your vehicle? Remember the street names. If you need to call 911 on your cell, could you give your exact location? I'm amazed at how often a reporter turns to me and asks, "Where are we?" If I'm working with a reporter at an active scene, the first thing I do is give the reporter my wireless microphone and turn it on—that way while I'm shooting video I can keep track of the reporter, who may go knocking on doors or talking with gathering crowds. This not only helps with safety but also lets me come running if the reporter finds a great interview.

Byron Pitts

Byron Pitts, ABC News: Pack the best first-aid kit possible. Get certified in basic first aid and CPR. I always carry a bandana, flashlights, local map and contact numbers. I also have a get-out-of-jail card—either a note or phone number from the most important person in that part of the world I know. A colleague asked me once, "How much blood are you bringing?" There are places in the world where that is a legitimate question. Read, read, read. And always pray, pray, pray. But at the end of the day none of that may be enough. Sometimes the best reporting is not going and telling the story another way.

What are the key things to never do and always do?

French: The number one thing to never do is play the "Don't you know who I am?" card. I have watched reporters do this time and time again in heated situations and not once has the other party stepped back and said, "Oh, I love your newscast, by all means proceed." The desperation behind their motives is far greater than the stature you believe your organization has in the community. Something I learned from wildfire training is to always have an escape route. I try to stay close to my vehicle or have a place to flee to where someone can call for help. I am always looking for security cameras on buildings and ATMs, so that if something is going to happen, at least it is caught on someone else's camera. And even though it is a competitive environment, when it comes to some situations there's safety in numbers.

Pitts: The "ugly American" thing never works. Be kind. Be kind. Be kind to all you meet.

Adkins: Probably the most important advice I can give is for people to speak up. Don't be afraid to tell the assignment desk when you have concerns for your safety—especially if you are working alone. The desk may give you an address that's just a street with numbers to them, but you may know it's an area with issues. Speak up. Tell them that's not a safe area. In the field, get out if you feel threatened—don't wait for the situation to escalate. Always have an escape plan.

French: I just try to stay calm and aware, which is much tougher to do than it sounds. If someone asks why I'm there shooting video—especially if they have an edge of contention about them—I'm honest but don't give any details other than the headline of the story. A little perceived ignorance can go a long way toward keeping the situation calm. If someone prods for more details on the story and it's not apparent how they are attached to it, I'm apt to shrug my shoulders and say, "I was just told to get some shots of this building, I think it's for tonight's newscast. Do you know what goes on here that might help me understand why I'm here?" If someone asks me how much my gear is worth, again I play ignorant: "This stuff? It's pretty old. It's like cars—the value decreases really fast. We're really the last ones using this old format."

If you are working alone, does that change things?

Adkins: I often work alone. Awhile back I was shooting video along Oregon Inlet, North Carolina. I stepped wrong and one leg went into a hole up to my waist while the other leg went 90 degrees out to my left, a gymnastic move I had never practiced. I was stuck, couldn't free myself and could feel blood running down my leg. Luckily a couple of guys fishing nearby saw me and came to help. While I was being stitched up at the local Urgent Care, I knew that from now on someone needed to keep tabs on me while I was out. The assignment desk is too busy, so we enabled my phone for my wife to keep up with me via GPS. I also text her where I am and where I'm going. If too long passes without her hearing from me, she will call and check on me.

French: Working alone absolutely changes things. Other than your camera, there are no witnesses who have your back. When I am working alone, I roll tape on every interaction and whenever my Spidey sense tingles. While nothing may come of the interaction in the moment, it has helped me prove my conduct was proper when someone has called the news director after the fact to say I was trespassing or being unprofessional. If a situation feels bad, I trust my gut and treat it as a dangerous situation. That may include not advancing into the scene as fast as I normally would, calling the desk to alert them that my safety is in question or finding an alternative way to cover the story.

What do you wish your reporter/photojournalist partner would or would not do to lower the temperature out there?

Pitts: My checklist: Get the latest security intel from the government, local law enforcement, private security and any reliable source on the ground. Make sure I'm aware of local customs, weapon systems and the proper threat assessment. What's the biggest threat: kidnapping, murder, violence, intimidation, robbery? I make sure I pack the proper clothes to fit in or not fit in. I make sure I'm in the best physical shape I can possibly be in. In many parts of the world size matters—if you look like someone not to be fooled with, people will usually leave you alone. Have an exit strategy. I usually travel with a team, and here are the rules: Let someone in the home office know your schedule, then stay on schedule. We travel most often in daylight. We know in advance (as best we can) who must get paid on the trip—local drivers, interpreters, etc. Avoid negotiating prices on the ground and never flash money. We make all safety decisions as a group, and unanimous votes are the only ones that count. If anyone votes to stop, we stop—no questions asked.

Adkins: Door knocks are one of the most difficult things we do, and most of us don't want to be there. Recently I was with a reporter on a door knock, and when we got back to the car he turned to me and thanked me for being beside him on the stoop. He said, "You're the only photog I work with that gets out of the car on these things." I told him it's a safety-in-numbers thing, so I always go to the door with the reporter. Some reporters like to sit in the car while I may be out shooting B-roll. In some situations, I'll ask them to get out of the car with me. Again, safety in numbers—and while my eye is glued to the viewfinder, their eyes can be open to our surroundings.

French: Read the situation and consider how the camera will change the dynamic. Cameras are a lot like alcohol, they intensify people's personalities and intentions. If people are happy, they become happier around the camera; if they are angry, they become angrier at the camera and the person using it. Everyone is trying to hit a deadline, but remembering the people we are covering have to live with a situation long after our deadline has passed will hopefully help us be more respectful of the emotional temperature. Finally, keep an eye on each other and help if needed. Yes, we are competitors but at the end of the day our goal is the same.

Do newsrooms train journalists to handle this sort of thing? What would such training include?

Shapiro: No—and they should. Assessing threats and staying safe—whether that means being smart about physical threats, understanding basic cybersecurity, being able to deliver routine first aid, or basic awareness of psychological trauma is part of the training news organizations should provide. This isn't just something for correspondents covering exotic conflicts. Even local journalists may contend with mass shootings, disasters, civil unrest or simply dangerous streets, disturbed individuals, traumatic assignments or the risk of mugging, sexual assault or being targeted because of our work. It's an occupational health risk, just like repetitive strain injury. If a news company would invest in ergonomic chairs, why not invest in a safety briefing, first-aid course or trauma-awareness session?

Pitts: The first time I went to Afghanistan for CBS News, Dan Rather called me into his office. "Here are the rules of the road," he said. "Don't eat the meat, don't drink the water and never look at the women."

- How to ethically use social media websites
- Why learning online and social media skills will be key to your career

Why Online and Social Media Are Important to Local TV

Online journalism is more than just an extension of what you are putting on the air; it is an important part of a station's business that will gain importance in the years ahead. Successful stations don't just slap stories online that they have aired. They break stories online before they air the stories. They think of the online audience as the day unfolds.

When it comes to the business side of local television, what goes over the air or out on cable makes a heck of a lot more money than what goes online.

But online revenue represents a significant chunk of a TV station's revenue, for some local stations about 10 percent, and social media sites are the number one referral to those websites. Social media, especially Facebook, is the number one referral to local news websites. In the second edition of *Aim for the Heart*, the number one referral was search engines. Before that, users would bookmark websites or manually enter the URL into the search engine toolbar.

The Pew Research Center found in 2016 that nearly two-thirds of American adults—62 percent—got news from a social media site. But only 18 percent said they used social media "often" to get news. Only four years earlier, less than half of Americans surveyed said they used social media for news.[1] In every demographic category, social media use has grown since 2010.

In addition, the Pew study found that people who watch local TV for news also make the most use of social media for news. People who read print newspapers make the least use of social media for news. People who get most of their news from news websites also make the most use of Twitter for news.

Demographic Profile of Social Networking Site News Users

% of news users of each site who are . . .

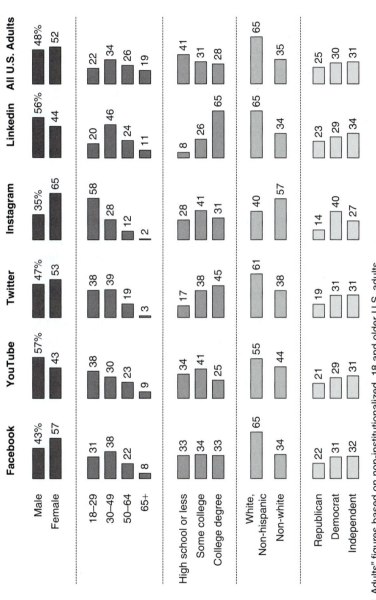

Note: "All U.S. Adults" figures based on non-institutionalized, 18 and older U.S. adults.

Source: "News Use Across Social Media Platforms 2016." Pew Research Center, Washington, DC (May, 2016). Retrieved from http://www.journalism.org/2016/05/05/news-use-across-social-media-platforms-2016.

Pew Research found that two-thirds of Facebook users get news while on the social site. But other social media sites including YouTube, Vine and Snapchat were not used much for news.

Bloomberg columnist Rani Molla says that although Twitter's audience is not as large as Facebook's, it is popular among politicians, journalists and other thought leaders. Twitter's audience is richer, better educated and more urban than Facebook.[2]

News apps are also growing in popularity, and TV stations find that app users tend to be the most loyal online users of all. Still, news apps don't drive nearly as much traffic to the station's site as social media, especially Facebook.

The key takeaway from all of this is that news consumers are on the move. They don't use any single source or even any single medium to get their information. They are constantly snacking on information and they want it quickly. And social media users don't necessarily want their social media sites to solve all of their needs. They seem willing to move from app to app to accomplish specific tasks like chatting, photo sharing or searching for interesting information.

Depending on the market, significantly more than half (and I have seen markets like Los Angeles where more than 9 in 10) of online users are coming to stations' websites on mobile devices.

Successful newsrooms have adopted a "digital first" mentality, which is to say they aim to serve the online and social media and social media audiences first. They don't wait until the next TV newscast rolls around to put the information in front of the public. The audiences for online and broadcast audiences overlap, but online audiences are so on-the-move that there is not much danger of harming broadcast viewership by reporting the story first online. Newspapers are finding that online and newspaper audiences are so different that the papers including *The Washington Post* and *The Tampa Bay Times* sometimes publish their biggest stories online days ahead of publishing them in print. *The Tampa Bay Times'* Pulitzer Prize–winning investigation into local schools, for example, published online on a Thursday but published the newspaper print version on a Sunday. The online version was not a lighter edition teasing the print version. It was a complete interactive package.

DRIVE TO THE MOTHERSHIP

In my view, there are three key reasons to post on social media, whether it is Facebook, Twitter, Instagram or any other.

- **Drive traffic to the Mothership.** I consider the Mothership to be anything that your station monetizes, whether it is your website, your app or your air. That means linking what you post to work you are doing on the platforms that you make money from. A post without a link is not without value, but your company is not realizing the income—the social media company is. In the coming years, no doubt, TV stations will form new alliances with social media to share revenue, and the social media sites will push TV stations to place their content directly on the social media site rather than hosting the content on the TV station site.

- **Break news, help the public.** There will be times when you will post content online that you do not currently have available on the Mothership website or air. If you can help the public by posting that information, do so. And, as quickly as you can, get the Mothership up to speed so you can monetize the effort.

- **Build your street credibility.** There will be times when you can connect the public with useful and reliable information that isn't available on the Mothership but viewers may still want to see and would not find without your help. It is fine to use social media to guide them toward content they might love even if the only benefit to you is that the public will love you for thinking of them. The same goes for posts that give the public a glimpse of who you are and what you know. Be careful to reflect your station's brand image and not say anything on social media that you would not be comfortable revealing on the air. Online posts last forever.

WHAT YOUR NEWSROOM NEEDS FROM YOU

When you are out reporting a story, here is a simple checklist of what your newsroom needs from you for online posting in order of priority:

- **100 to 150 words of information.** The number one thing that web editors, social media editors, assignment editors and producers need from people working in the field is information.

couple to a few minutes on a news site per visit. There are exceptions where stations hold readers for rich package stories or lively interactions with important information. For example, CNN online users spend just more than three minutes on the site. The online sports website Bleacher Report is one of the leaders in time spent on site with 3.5 minutes per visit according to comScore Media Metrix. But mostly, online users dive in, find what they want and move on.

■ ■ ■ REMEMBER

Social media consumed on mobile devices are increasingly important ways your audience gets its news. No matter what tools you use to tell the story, make sure you always drive to the Mothership and are able to measure how effective you are.

REPORTING AND WRITING FOR ONLINE

Online news delivery is a different experience. It can make broadcast journalism even better by helping the viewer understand, localize and participate in the story.

BROADCAST THINKING	ONLINE THINKING
We tell you what we know.	You decide what you want. You contribute to content. You generate content.
We serve viewers.	We engage with viewers, listeners, podcast consumers, wireless consumers, online readers, RSS feeds, aggregators and even send signals to taxis, buses, subways, tunnels, gas pumps—you name it.
We seek a mass audience.	We share news wherever the audience consumes it. We use multiple channels that reach smaller audiences. We build dominance through many smaller audiences by providing unique services.
We publish or broadcast on our timeframe.	We refresh news nonstop on our website, blogs and social networks. Publishing is the first step to telling the story instead of the last step.

BROADCAST THINKING	ONLINE THINKING
I am a TV journalist.	I appreciate the power of many media platforms. I can adapt to how the public wants the information, the platform on which they want it and the platform through which I can tell the most effective story. I can shoot, edit and post video and still photos, and I can report using whatever tools I need to help me share the news the public needs quickly.
We can slap the print/TV version on the web.	We can produce web-exclusive content that clarifies and enhances understanding and adds context. We can use raw video and uncut moments to help tell the authentic story.
We inform you.	We involve and engage you.
We use video and sound.	We use video, sound, text, live interaction, chats, conversations, blogs, interactive maps, mobile applications, searchable databases and any other tools available.
We control access.	We distribute content using RSS, free access and archives, with a minimum of registration hassle.
Make the advertiser pay.	We find a variety of funding, including user micropayments, advertisers paying for targeted ads, and "for pay" premium unique content. Ethical partnerships, sponsorships and grant funding can be part of the picture.
Lone Wolf: It's about us.	We consider lots of media partners who can deliver unique value. We collaborate with those who may seem to be competitors. We aggregate information even from competitors if it helps the public get the information it needs.
It's OK to be boring. This is serious stuff we are doing here.	News can honor traditional journalism values while still embracing new ones by being fun, interactive and visually appealing. It is serious sometimes but never boring.

SO WHAT WORKS ONLINE?

First, without question, breaking news attracts online traffic. Online and social media deliver the "what happened" version of the story. That allows television to focus more on the significant questions of "Why?" "What does this mean?" and "What will happen next?"

Social media works best when you include an image or a graphic. It is almost a requirement to break through the page clutter.

Video can be a hit but not just any video. Fully edited television packages seldom generate much online traffic. There are exceptions, including remarkable feature stories or complex investigations that turn up something significant, but day-in and day-out natural sound, lightly edited or even raw action-packed videos will attract the most online and social media traffic.

There are reasons for this:

- **Connectivity:** Remember that not everybody has high-speed internet access. Lots of people don't want to pay for the data to download video when they are not using a free wireless connection. And glitch buffering makes watching video a hassle.

- **Commercials:** When you make the user wait to see a video by using pre-roll commercials, you start seeing a rising number of people click away. It is a fact of online life that we want to monetize our work by selling commercials, and pre-rolls are one way to do that. But there is a cost.

- **Online users watch silently:** There is a reason social media sites default to silent video. People don't want to get busted for watching kitten videos while they are sitting in class, church or some staff meeting. So social media sites defaulted their video players to silent. You have to assume that a significant portion of your viewers will not listen to your video. So you should add graphics to the page to make the stories easier to consume. Think of all the people who might be watching your video while they are in a noisy setting. Think how hard it is to hear anything from a phone speaker.

MAKE IT INTERACTIVE: USERS CHOOSE

When I was an impressionable youngster in 1967, a racy film called *The Graduate*, starring Dustin Hoffman became one of the hottest films in American history, landing number seven on the American Film Institute's Top 100 list of Greatest American Films.[4] Hoffman's character, 21-year-old Benjamin Braddock had just graduated college and had no real plans for life. As his family threw a graduation party for him, he is met by the know-it-all Mr. McGuire who offered the young man some advice about the future. Even if you don't know this passage I promise you your parents do!

Mr. Mcguire: I want to say one word to you. Just one word.

Benjamin: Yes, sir.

Mr. Mcguire: Are you listening?

Benjamin: Yes, I am.

Mr. Mcguire: Plastics.

Benjamin: Just how do you mean that, sir?

If I could whisper one magic word of advice to every broadcast journalist about the future of the internet, it would be "interaction."

You may say, "How do you mean that, sir?"

We cannot be certain of many things when it comes to the future of media consumption, but the one thing that I am absolutely certain of is that, however people get their information in the future, the delivery system must include the ability to interact with it. Allow users to decide what they want to know more about. Interaction promotes a deeper understanding of the story.

News consumers want what they want, how they want it and when they want it. It is true for the fast-food business, it is true for the coffee business, and it stands to reason that it would be true in the information delivery business, too.

If the user wants a completely packaged story, we should offer that. If the user wants a short text brief, we should offer that. If the user wants just the video with no narration, let's give it to him or her. Let users decide and let them interact with the information. They choose what they want to know, when and how they want to get it.

Interactivity comes in many forms. For an investigative story the interaction may include giving the reader the ability to click on the government documents on which the investigation is based. It may also include unedited versions of the key interviews in the story, especially if the subject claims he or she has been misquoted or taken "out of context." Interactivity may include searchable databases that allow users to localize the story by keying in on the part of the story nearest them, such as an unsafe child-care center, a substandard bridge or a toxic waste site near their home.

KCNC-TV in Denver investigated the company that administered tests to certify the workers who de-ice aircraft. Investigative reporter Brian Maas found that the testing company actually read the answers aloud during the test to be sure everyone passed. KCNC went undercover to record four different tests. Not only did the station report the story, but also it put the raw, unedited video of the tests online. It assured viewers that the video was as outrageous as it seemed to be on TV.[5]

I don't want to see our online producers posting raw video just because they think it will get them out of reporting for the day because there's no editing involved. Whoever is posting the video needs to be even *more diligent* as a reporter because you have to make sure viewers get the available facts and information in a very small, easy-to-find place. That's usually the title, but it may be a video summary or a text slide. In any case it should tell me as much as possible.

FIND WAYS TO MEANINGFULLY INVOLVE THE PUBLIC

Lots of news websites offer lame polls under the guise of public involvement. That's not enough. Give the public chances for real involvement. How easy is it for your online users to contribute video and photos or report details of spot-news stories, parades, holidays and weather?

In the 2016 presidential election, Washington Post reporter David Fahrenthold investigated Donald Trump's family foundation, partly by looking for items the foundation had purchased with charitable income. He found a painting that Trump had purchased by looking on TripAdvisor.com, a travel website where vacationers post pictures of their favorite destinations. Fahrenthold took to Twitter asking for help finding other items.[6]

NPR's Radiolab asked listeners to help track the return of the 17-year cicada swarms by monitoring 600 sensors planted in the ground on the Eastern Seaboard.[7]

When *The New York Times* investigated the cost of medical care in the United States, reporter Elisabeth Rosenthal invited readers to share their stories, asking, "Have you had a hip replacement? Tell us about your costs and bills." Hundreds of readers responded to that question and others that followed about their experiences giving birth and other medical procedures. Thousands more joined a Facebook group to keep sharing stories with the journalist and with each other.[8]

WNYC radio asked readers to help map which New York streets had been plowed after a monster snowstorm blanketed the city.[9]

Globally, crowd-sourced websites are turning to the very people they serve for content:

- Ipaidabribe.com in India tracks reports of people who say they paid government workers for everything from passport services to tax collectors.

- The New York Civil Liberties Union launched the Stop and Frisk app and asked the public to capture short videos when police conduct a frisk and send the videos as a way to build a body of evidence to stop the controversial New York law.[10]

- Newzulu.com uses 100,000 largely nonprofessional "journalists" to collect stories and photos around the world.

The Tow Center for Digital Journalism saw crowdsourced journalism fall into six groups:[11]

- **Voting**—prioritizing which stories reporters should tackle.

- **Witnessing**—sharing what you saw during a news event.

- **Sharing personal experiences**—telling what you know about your life experience.

- **Tapping specialized expertise**—contributing data or unique knowledge.

- **Completing a task**—volunteering time or skills to help create a news story.

- **Engaging audiences**—joining in call-outs that can range from informative to playful.

Journalists sometimes find online is a great way to explain how they found the story, how they investigated the story, how they wrestled with ethical questions while nailing down the story. The online version also can invite reader feedback on how fair the story was, what is still missing and how to follow up on the story.

I do not recommend opening every news story to comments. Some stories lend themselves to comments, and some don't. If you open your news site to public comments, be prepared to monitor discussions about news stories. You should consider whom you will allow to post. Will those who comment remain anonymous? Do you require registration before a reader can post a comment to your site? When will you screen (or will you screen) or even delete a comment? How will you make your "terms of service" clear to readers?

MAP DATA TO CONNECT VIEWERS TO THE STORY

Interactive maps are a great way to allow the public to interact with information. Maps add context by showing the user where something happened, and they can add context to trends. WTHR-TV in Indianapolis discovered that communities around that city were depending on tornado sirens that were broken to warn of oncoming storms. The station discovered the sirens failed to work properly 4,689 times over six years; therefore it built maps that allowed viewers to go online and see whether the siren nearest to them worked. It was a great way to take a "broadcast" story and make it highly personal and as local as the viewer's city block.

When journalists map violent crimes, they sometimes find trends that show which neighborhoods are the most and least safe. They can compare those findings with police patrolling patterns and ask why more cops are not working in high-crime areas. My friend, reporter Ted Oberg at KTRK-TV in Houston, noticed that patrol cars were equipped with GPS devices showing police dispatchers where the squad cars were at any given time. Oberg requested several days' worth of that data and put together a map showing where the police were, hour by hour, compared with where the most crimes occur hour by hour. By mapping his findings, Oberg learned, "There is an average of 268 officers available for 911 calls citywide any time of the day; not many when you consider a Houstonian calls 911 every 30 seconds. The highest number of on-duty units is at 3 p.m., when there are 395. But at that hour, more than a third of them are parked at police substations. The lowest number of units is at 2 a.m., when just 186 officers are available to answer your call for help. It's also when the Crime Tracker map shows violent crime is near its daily peak."

Just by mapping the data, Oberg learned that the time of day when the most officers are on duty is the time of day when crime is at or near its lowest. But the time of day when the fewest cops are on patrol is the time of day when crime is highest.

SAVE ELABORATE PRESENTATIONS FOR PROJECTS WITH LONG LEGS

Don't be afraid to build coverage over time. When a high-profile crime occurs, for example, build a special section of your site to become the home of continuing coverage that could last years as the case moves through the system. For major investigative projects, include reactions, follow-ups, legislative action and resolutions that flow from the stories. Put your biggest multimedia efforts in those parts of the site that will have a long life. A great hurricane resource page could be useful for years. There are topics and stories that occur over and over in your community. Save your big efforts for those kinds of projects.

SOCIAL MEDIA POSTS

When you post on social media, remember the first goal is to drive to the Mothership, so you need a link and a graphic or image. The second goal is for the user to interact with the content. You want them to "like" it, comment on it and share it with others. The "open rate" goes way up when people you trust send you content. If somebody you don't know posts an item, you might or might not open it. But if your best friend says it's great, you trust your friend so you might open the link.

Any post that generates comments is a post that people have judged to be worth their time. Others follow. And the social media algorithms will notice and promote that interaction figuring it must be interesting content if people are taking the time to comment on it.

Beyond that what should we write? Facebook frowns on anything that seems like a commercial. Those posts will get buried. Readers don't respond well to teases on social media. So what's left? Real content, that's what.

The best social media posts are those that have some value even if I don't click to the link you are offering. You will teach me, inform me, alert me, entertain me and pique my curiosity. It is a bit like a candy store offering its best samples. Every interaction I have with you should be high quality and not a hard sell.

WRITE TIGHT

Online news consumers are not coming to you for a literary experience. They want to know what is going on. You will lose online readers if you bury the lead.

Remember how your readers are consuming your material. They are on mobile devices, so the sentences may run several lines on a small screen. If they miss key information it is a pain to have to scroll up to understand a longer sentence. So keep your sentences short. Try reading your online writing aloud. If you run out of breath before the end of the sentence, the sentence may be too long.

An inverted pyramid style works best for most online writing. Don't bury important information.

Let's imagine we were reporting on floods in Texas that killed some people. You would NOT say,

> *The rain finally stopped last night, and now, the long hard cleanup begins. Texas has not seen floods like this in more than forty years and the governor will arrive today to survey the damage.*

Tell me something I don't know. CNN.com got right to the story, no Flintstoning, when it reported,

> *Six people have died in flood-related incidents in southeast Texas after the region was inundated with rain, authorities said. Four were killed in Washington County, about 75 miles west of Houston, an area hammered with 17 inches of rain Thursday. One was killed in Travis County and another died in Kendall County.*[12]

Let's compare several versions of the same story, a tractor-trailer that overturned on a New York City bridge. Which of these opening lines would a New York reader find valuable and interesting? Remember the reader most likely would be on a mobile device. I will comment on each one.

NY 1 reported:

"It was a scary scene Monday in the Bronx as an overturned tractor-trailer dangled over the Sheridan Expressway." *(You don't have to tell me a truck dangling off a bridge is scary. I can guess that. Tell me what I don't know.)*

WABC reported:

"An accident on the Cross Bronx Expressway left a tractor-trailer precariously hanging over the Sheridan Parkway in the Bronx Monday." *(WABC gives me good location information, not just which bridge the truck crashed on but what highway it is dangling over.)*

WCBS reported:

"A tractor-trailer dangling over the Sheridan Expressway backed up drivers in all directions for hours." *(I think WCBS is more in-tune with the public's needs. The public would want to know that this crash is making a mess of traffic all over that section of town. That is how this story affects most people.)*

Fox 5 reported:

"A tractor-trailer was left hanging over the Sheridan Parkway after a crash on the Cross Bronx Expressway." *(It is factual, but the opening line does not say when the story happened or if the situation is still unfolding. It misses the key motivators of how this affects me, the audience.)*

Pix 11 reported:

"Three people were injured when a tractor-trailer overturned on a Bronx expressway Monday." *(This opening line makes this sound like just another run-of-the-mill crash. It does not establish why anybody would care.)*

WNBC reported:

"A tractor-trailer truck was left dangling from on overpass on the Cross Bronx Expressway after it overturned Monday afternoon, snarling traffic for hours on Memorial Day, authorities said." *(This gets to the traffic problems and the precarious nature of the crash.)*

New York Daily News reported:

"A tractor-trailer was hanging off a Bronx overpass after crashing into multiple cars and through a guardrail Monday afternoon—seriously injuring two people, officials said." (*This is the most descriptive writing of all of the versions. I would be happier if the sentence used active verbs.*)

I would recommend, "A tractor-trailer plowed through cars and a guardrail then hung off the Cross Bronx Expressway Bridge snarling Sheridan Expressway traffic below."

WRITE IN CHUNKS

In May 2016, Pew Research delivered some good news to online writers. Mobile users are learning to navigate longer stories, even stories that are 1,000 words or longer.[13]

U.S. Public Show Signs of Engaging With Long-Form Articles on Cellphones

 Within cellphone news habits . . .

Long-form articles get more than **twice** the engaged time of short-form articles

Average engaged time across complete interactions

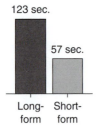

And they get **about the same number** of visitors

Average number of complete interactions per article

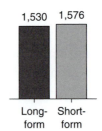

Note: A complete interaction represents all of a unique visitor's sessions with one article on a cellphone.

Source: "Long-Form Reading Shows Signs of life in Our Mobile News World" Pew Reseearch Center, Washington, DC (May, 2016). Retrrieved from http://www.journalism.org/2016/05/05/long-form-reading-shows-signs-of-life-in-our-mobile-news-world/pj_2016-05-05_long-form-02

Until now, the common belief has been that online has to be short writing and that the move from desktop to mobile means stories will need to be shorter still.

Even though online readers have shown that they will read longer, well-told stories, you should avoid big blocks of text that intimidate readers. If you are writing a long and complex online story, offer it in "chunks" that users can select or ignore. Each chunk should be limited to a single thought.

For example, a story about a murder trial might include a short copy story explaining what happened in court that day. Then the presentation might include a video of the defense's opening argument, the prosecution's opening statement, a profile of the jury and judge and a map of where the murder took place. The coverage might include a section on the victim and another on the evidence. Another link might take me to stories about other high-profile murders in this county. Online readers can select what they want to know without plowing through a 2,000-word story.

Online readers scan as much as they read word-for-word, so sub-headlines serve as navigation guideposts. Shorter sentences are easier to scan than long, complex ones. Online, the ideal paragraph length is between three and four lines. When most readers were desktop users, five or six lines were fine, but smaller screens make longer paragraphs difficult to consume. Break them up.

Block quotes, bulleted lists and single-line quotes also stand out online, especially on mobile.

LINK TO YOUR SOURCES, BUT VERIFY THEM FIRST

It is perfectly acceptable for journalists to build links to other sources of information. A story about the U.S. trade deficit, for example, might link to the Office of Management and Budget for details on how the government calculates the deficit. A story about fracking (a natural gas exploration that involves drilling into the earth, then shooting high pressure steams of water into the underlying rock. The water pressure fractures the rock and releases the natural gas that was trapped below ground) for oil might link to the Environmental Protection Agency, to the U.S. Geological Survey and to the National Earthquake Center. The links also might take readers to other stories your newsroom has written.

- **Is the website current?** Old information is a tip-off that the site may not be legitimate or actively managed.

- **Have others cited this website as a source?** Websites such as www.linkpopularity.com can help you.

COPYRIGHT AND "FAIR USE" GUIDELINES

Even if the copyright notice does not appear prominently, someone wrote, or is responsible for, the creation of a document, graphic, sound or image, and therefore the material falls under the copyright conventions. "Fair use" applies to short, cited excerpts, usually as an example for commentary or research. Materials are in the public domain if this is explicitly stated. Internet users, as users of print media, must respect copyright.

Generally, journalists should use a four-part test in determining what copyrighted material they may use online:

- Is the existence of the copyrighted work bona fide news? For example, let's say a guy kills his wife and publishes a photograph of himself on his Facebook site. The photograph shows him holding a gun in each hand and a knife in his teeth. The woman is shot with the same caliber gun and is stabbed. The photograph would be news. The mere existence of the photograph is news. (Now to be sure, we don't know if the picture is real, but that is a different issue.)

- Is it open to fair use? Generally this has to do with how much of a copyrighted work you use, why you use it and for how long you use it. One way to mitigate the damage of fair use is to keep the work in its original form. Rather than pulling a photograph from a newspaper story and using it full-screen on TV, take a picture of the newspaper. Keep it in its original form and you cause much less intrusion.

- In what way have you harmed the copyright holder's ability to earn a living from his or her work? That is the real damage that you can wind up paying. Was the person attempting to sell the information, photograph or music?

- Did the person have a reasonable expectation of privacy? You cause more legal problems for yourself when you pose as somebody you are not and go behind privacy walls to obtain information online.

Journalism today is a process, not a product. At the beginning of the process, think of different ways you can tell the story online, engage your online audience with the story and update the story through the day.

ETHICS AND SOCIAL NETWORKS

Some years ago, I sat down with a handful of news directors, a media lawyer and an online editor to draft what we consider to be guidelines for the ethical use of social media. (These guidelines were written by Al Tompkins, Kevin Benz, Stacey Woelfel, Ryan Murphy, Richard Goehler, Carol Knopes and Kathleen Graham, and were adopted by the Radio Television Digital News Association [RTDNA] in 2010.)

RTDNA'S SOCIAL MEDIA AND BLOGGING GUIDELINES

Social media and blogs are important elements of journalism. They narrow the distance between journalists and the public. They encourage lively, immediate and spirited discussion. They can be vital newsgathering and news-delivery tools. As a journalist you should uphold the same professional and ethical standards of fairness, accuracy, truthfulness, transparency and independence when using social media as you do on air and on all digital news platforms.

Truth and Fairness

- Information gleaned online should be confirmed just as you must confirm scanner traffic or phone tips before reporting them. If you cannot independently confirm critical information, reveal your sources; tell the public how you know what you know and what you cannot confirm. Don't stop there. Keep seeking confirmation. This guideline is the same for covering breaking news on station websites as on the air. You should not leave the public "hanging." Lead the public to completeness and understanding.

- Twitter's character limits and immediacy are not excuses for inaccuracy and unfairness.

- Remember that social media postings live on as online archives. Correct and clarify mistakes, whether they are factual mistakes or mistakes of omission.

- When using content from blogs or social media, ask critical questions such as these:

  1. What is the source of the video or photograph? Who wrote the comment and what was the motivation for posting it?

  2. Does the source have the legal right to the material posted? Did that person take the photograph or capture the video?

  3. Has the photograph or video been manipulated? Have we checked to see if the metadata attached to the image reveals that it has been altered?

Social networks typically offer a "privacy" setting, so users can choose not to have their photographs or thoughts in front of the uninvited public. Capturing material from a public Facebook site is different from prying behind a password-protected wall posing as a friend. When considering whether to access "private" content, journalists should apply the same RTDNA guidelines recommended for undercover journalism. Ask,

- Does the poster have a "reasonable expectation" of privacy?

- Is this a story of great significance?

- Is there any other way to get the information?

- Are you willing to disclose your methods and reasoning?

- What are your journalistic motivations?

- What protocols does your newsroom have to correct mistakes on social media sites such as Twitter and Facebook?

- Does your newsroom have a process for copyediting and oversight of the content posted on social media sites? What decision-making process do you go through before you post?

- What protocols do you have for checking the truthfulness of photographs or video that you find on Facebook, YouTube or photo-sharing sites? Have you contacted the photographer?

Can you see the unedited video or raw photograph file? Does the image or video make sense when compared with the facts of the story?

- Who in the newsroom is charged with confirming information gleaned from social media sites?

Accountability and Transparency

- You should not write anonymously or use an avatar or username that cloaks your real identity on newsroom or personal websites. You are responsible for everything you say. Commenting or blogging anonymously compromises this core principle.

- Be especially careful when you are writing, Tweeting or blogging about a topic that you or your newsroom covers. Editorializing about a topic or person can reveal your personal feelings. Biased comments could be used in a court of law to demonstrate a predisposition, or even malicious intent, in a libel action against the news organization, even for an unrelated story.

- Just as you keep distance between your station's advertising and journalism divisions, you should not use social media to promote business or personal interests without disclosing that relationship to the public. Sponsored links should be clearly labeled, not cloaked as journalistic content.

Image and Reputation

- Remember that what's posted online is open to the public (even if you consider it private). Personal and professional lives merge online. Newsroom employees should recognize that even though their comments may seem to be in their "private space," their words become direct extensions of their news organizations. Search engines and social mapping sites can locate their posts and link the writers' names to their employers.

- There are journalistic reasons to connect with people online, even if you cover them, but consider whom you "friend" or "follow" on such sites as Facebook and Twitter. You may believe that online friends are different from other friends in your life, but the public may not always see it that way. For example, be prepared to explain publicly why you show up as a friend on a politician's website.

CHAPTER 15

Ethics and Broadcast Journalists: Seek Truth and Report It as Fully as Possible

And ye shall know the truth, and the truth shall make you free.

—John 8:32

One day I was teaching an all-day ethics seminar in South Carolina. I presented a series of case studies in which journalists had made tough and sometimes controversial decisions in stories that involved juveniles and sexual abuse. One student journalist marched up to me when we took a break in the class and demanded to know, "Are you saying there is no right or wrong answer? Is there no truth? Are you saying that every journalist has to make his or her own decision without any rules to go by?"

Then I had what for me became an important insight. We should have standards, guidelines and protocols to go by. The participant in South Carolina was demanding inflexible and rigid *rules* for coverage. I want to make an argument that journalists should establish thoughtful guidelines for coverage but resist the temptation to write a lot of rules that may limit their ability to report important stories.

So in this and the next two chapters I will offer some guidelines that your newsroom might adopt, amend or improve. Many of the guidelines I wrote in collaboration with Bob Steele, whom I consider one of the nation's leading thinkers on media ethics issues. I can't prove it, but I suspect I would not be challenged when I suggest that Steele has taught more ethics seminars to more professional journalists than anyone else in the United States during the last decade and a half. The Society of Professional Journalists (SPJ) and the Radio Television Digital News Association (RTDNA) adopted a considerable amount of Steele's thinking and writing into their national codes of ethics.

Steele teaches three main concepts as "guiding principles" for ethical decision making:

- Seek truth and report it as fully as possible.
- Act independently.
- Minimize harm.

We will address these guiding principles in this and next two chapters, starting with seeking truth. In this chapter we will cover the following:

- Guidelines for conducting honest, vigorous reporting that seeks multiple truths
- Guidelines for journalists to evaluate the sources they use
- Criteria for when and how confidential sources should be included in coverage

SEEK TRUTH AND REPORT IT AS FULLY AS POSSIBLE

Where should journalists go to find truths? Every decision a journalist makes while reporting influences the truth he or she might find. I suggest the following guidelines.

BE THOROUGH

How do you choose to whom you talk, or not talk? How many voices and points of view should you include in your reporting? What was your motivation for talking to some people and excluding others? What truths could others have given you that might have added perspective to your investigation?

In the workshops and seminars I teach around the country, many journalists tell me that they consider it their job to "tell both sides of a story." I urge them to find more voices than "both sides." I struggle to find even one story that has only two sides. Let's look at the issue of the death penalty. Here is a partial list of those who have a stake or interest in this issue:

- The condemned prisoner
- The victim(s)
- The family of the victim(s)
- The prisoner's family
- Anti-death penalty groups
- Pro-death penalty groups
- Prosecutors
- Defense attorneys
- Lawmakers/politicians
- Judges
- Juries
- The warden
- All other death-row prisoners
- All other inmates
- All other crime victims
- Society at large

What a rich list of stakeholders, and it is just the beginning. Yet we have to admit that few of these stakeholders ever make it into the news. Great journalists seek truths through many voices with many points of view, especially those whose voices are seldom heard.

BE ACCOUNTABLE TO THE PUBLIC

This does not mean that the public's views should guide journalists. We should be guided by the principles of our news organization, principles that should include seeking the truth and telling it as fully as possible. But we should be *informed* by the views, morals and values of our community. If you were doing a story about segregation, for example, it would be crucial to know how various parts of your community feel about the issue. But even if the majority favored legal segregation, your journalism should not be swayed by that. Your journalism should be guided by the need to seek the views of as many voices as possible, including those in the minority who are being discriminated against.

SET THE STORY IN CONTEXT

Great stories include both intimate examples and wider content to show the size of the issue. It is possible to be "accurate" but not true. If you have no context for the action, you still have not captured the truth.

For example, let's suppose you went undercover investigating "dirty restaurants" and found a food worker touching his or her hair then preparing food. You also record undercover images of food workers touching raw meat, then not washing their hands before touching other food they are preparing. You notice some dented cans in the pantry, and you see that the refrigerator thermometer is broken. Do you have the proof you need to expose this restaurant as unhealthy and dangerous? What if, on closer inspection, you found that the restaurant had a long history of excellent inspections? Not one person is known to have ever gotten sick at that restaurant. In fact, the restaurant owner was one of the first organizers of a voluntary food workers' education program sponsored by the local restaurant association.

The pictures you recorded were true, but they do not accurately reflect how seriously the restaurant tries to comply with health rules.

Journalists should provide context in their stories. They should go beyond the question of "what" and explain "why," "how often" and "who is responsible."

USE UNDERCOVER TECHNIQUES CAREFULLY

At various town meetings I show a hard-hitting investigative story about a Cincinnati road supervisor who had taken repeated taxpayer-financed trips to Las Vegas to attend trade shows. WCPO-TV, Cincinnati, a station well respected for its outstanding investigative work, used undercover techniques to document how the supervisor and two of his assistants never attended one minute of the convention but spent days at gambling tables and restaurants. Then the station confronted the supervisor and even showed him the under-cover tape of him hanging out and placing bets at the casino. As a result of the investigation, the supervisor lost his job and his two underlings had to pay the county government thousands of dollars in travel expenses.

The journalists in a town meeting in New Orleans loved the story and roared their approval. But viewers reacted differently. They began to feel sorry for the road supervisor, they wondered whether the journalist was being "too rough" on him, and some said they wished he had not lost his job over it. An elementary school teacher in one town meeting asked, "Shouldn't you have to get permission from someone before you take pictures of a person without them knowing it?" When I asked who, for example, journalists should ask for permission to go undercover, she said, "Maybe the police." But the same station, WCPO-TV, also has used undercover tactics to expose police brutality.

A Baltimore focus group took the issue further, saying that undercover tactics should be used only for stories with overwhelming public impor-tance. They said that most often TV stations use undercover cameras to target "little guys," not big violators. They said if TV stations are going to use undercover investigation techniques, they should invest more time to be sure that what is shown on TV is part of an ongoing pattern, not just a one-time occurrence.

As you work on a story, ask yourself: Does this story warrant undercover techniques? Are there any other ways of gaining the information? Is the station willing to invest the time and effort to be sure what it discovers undercover is part of a pattern and not a single incident? What motives does the station have for going undercover? Stations should use under-cover investigations only when the technique will uncover important truths that otherwise would go unreported.

GUIDELINES FOR INTERVIEWING
CONFIDENTIAL SOURCES: WHO, WHEN, WHY

I recommend that we set the bar high for when we use unnamed sources. It should not be impossibly high, just tough enough that it does not become a default position for journalists who don't make the effort to find a named source that will add gravity to their reporting. So, before you use a confidential source, I suggest you fulfill all of these criteria:

- A story that uses confidential sources should be of overwhelming public concern.

- Before using an unnamed source, you must be convinced there is no other way to get the essential information *on the record.*

- The unnamed source must have verifiable and firsthand knowledge of the story. Even if the source cannot be named, the information must be proven true. If you are unsure the information is true, admit it to the public. A promise of confidentiality may protect a liar or a manipulator, and the promise may make it difficult or even impossible for the journalist to ever set the record straight.

- You should be willing to reveal to the public why the source cannot be named and what, if any, promises the news organization made to get the information.

- Only in the rarest cases of all should a journalist allow a confidential source to assert something damaging to an individual, particularly a private individual. It should be a nearly absolute rule that confidential sources not be allowed to attack someone else and remain nameless.

Questions to consider:

- What does the use of a confidential source mean to the factual accuracy and contextual authenticity of your story?

- Does this source deserve the protection of his or her identity?

- What legal obligations do you incur by promising not to reveal this source's name? If you are sued, are you willing to go to jail to protect this source? If you are sued, will the source come forward and be named? Is the reluctance justifiable?

- How would viewers evaluate the same information if they knew the source's name and motivations?

- What have you done to help the source understand the risks he or she is taking by giving you information?

- If you promised to protect a source's identity, are you using production techniques that will ensure the protection you promised? What if a lawyer subpoenas the raw tapes? Would the person be identifiable in the tape outtakes? You should understand your newsroom's policy on confidentiality before you promise it to sources. You may need the consent of an editor or you may have to, by policy, reveal a source's identity to a supervisor. Your source should be told you might have to identity him or her to others in your newsroom.

BIDDING FOR NEWS: THE CHALLENGE OF "CHECKBOOK JOURNALISM"

Be wary of sources offering information for favors or money. Journalists should not pay for interviews. When journalists pay sources for information, it creates a motive for the sources to provide information that they do not know to be true. The source might be motivated by a paycheck to fabricate information, obtain documents and information illegally, violate confidences or alter photographs, videotape or documents.

"Checkbook journalism" also might motivate amateur photographers or stringers to take unwarranted risks to capture images they can sell. It should be acceptable for journalists to pay a reasonable "stringer fee" for pictures of videotape of newsworthy events if they can verify the pictures to be true and accurate. When journalists air pictures they have purchased from someone, that business arrangement should be disclosed to the public.

When I was a news director, a call came into the WSMV-TV newsroom one day that two Black Hawk helicopters had crashed into each other while on a routine training mission at Fort Campbell, 60 miles away. We initially heard "there were multiple fatalities and no survivors." In what I recall to be minutes after the crash, a freelance photographer who had been taking pictures of the mission for families of the soldiers involved called to say he had "very good" video of the crash that he wanted to sell. I told him I wanted the video, and we agreed on a price. (I recall the price to be $500.) A few minutes later he called to say somebody else had offered more. I told him I would pay $1,000 but that I would not go further. We agreed to the price again and agreed on a deal to deliver the tape. The transaction never took place.

Networks launched into a bidding war over the tape and within a couple of hours, CBS had secured the rights to the crash video for what was reported to be more than $20,000. I purchased still pictures of the crash from a freelance photographer who was standing next to the video photographer. The still photographer asked me to make a $1,000 donation to a fund for the dead soldiers' families. To me, the lower price seemed to be a fee for photographic services, but the higher number seemed to be profiteering over somebody else's misfortune.

While trying to decide how much to pay for valuable video, journalists should consider whether the person who shot the video was acting in a journalistic capacity or was a participant in the story. Newsrooms pay for journalistic content; they should not pay for interviews.

A personal confession: I have to admit that if our network (NBC) had bought the pictures, I am sure we would have run the video, which showed what happened more clearly than anyone could describe.

Checkbook journalism takes other forms. Some newsrooms hire consultants to be readily available to talk on the record about such issues as defense, aviation safety and medicine. Those paid consultant relationships should be disclosed to the public, especially when the consultant is a former government employee such as a military general or political strategist for a campaign or administration. Of course, there is the danger that the consultant might be more willing to speculate about matters if she is afraid that, by not speculating, she might lose a paycheck.

■ ■ ■ REMEMBER

Constantly evaluate the sources you use in stories. What motives do your sources have to provide you information? How can you verify the information they give you?

Be Honest With Viewers About Your Reporting and Your Mistakes

While he was running for president, Donald Trump pounded journalists as being "among the most dishonest people that I have ever met." He repeatedly turned crowds against journalists. He accused journalists of deliberately not showing how big his crowds were, and he screamed at photojournalists and urged crowds to do the same. The crowds loved it.[3] But why did it resonate with the public, and what can journalists do about that?

In a December 2015 Gallup poll, only 27 percent of Americans rated journalists as "high" or "very high" when it comes to honesty and ethical standards. That's about on par with bankers and building contractors. It was, by the way, three times higher than members of Congress. Only a matter of months earlier, Pew researchers found that only 19 percent of Americans trust the government, a nearly all-time low. But despite what you might think, Gallup's polling shows the public's opinion of "the press" has always been tepid. In the post-Watergate days of 1976, 33 percent rated journalists' ethics and honesty high or very high. In 1988, the figures dropped to the level they have remained, only fluctuating a couple of points each year.[4] Gallup finds that "trust" in "the media" declines during election years as it did in 2004, 2008 and 2012. Younger audiences, those under age 50, trust media less than their parents do. In fact, they trust media a *lot* less.[5]

National Public Radio (NPR)'s Code of Ethics includes this passage about honesty that inspires me:

> Journalists who conduct themselves honestly prove themselves worthy of trust. In the course of our work, we are genuine and candid. We attribute information we receive from others, making perfectly clear to our audience what information comes from which source. We avoid hyperbole and sensational conjecture. We may sometimes construct hypotheticals to help explain issues and events, but we reveal any fabrication, and do not otherwise mix fiction with our news reporting. We edit and present information honestly, without deception, and we identify ourselves as NPR journalists when we report. Only in the rarest of instances—such as when public safety is at issue, or

In the next five minutes and 26 seconds of the news story, Williams used the word "we" 19 times, the word "us" eight times and "our" twice.

That is the foundation of the complaints that some soldiers raised. Williams took stories about others and made them reflect a story about himself as a compassionate, brave, worldly and "on the scene" anchor.

That image is the foundation of the anniversary promos NBC aired. The advertisement ends with a line, "He's been there, he'll be there."

Williams used first-person phrasing again in 2008 when he blogged on NBC News' site:

> I was with **my** friend and NBC News Military Analyst Wayne Downing, a retired 4-Star Army General. Wayne and I were riding along as part of an Army mission to deliver bridge components to the Euphrates River, so that the invading forces of the 3rd Infantry could cross the river on their way to Baghdad. **We** came under fire by what appeared to be Iraqi farmers with RPGs and AK-47s. The Chinook helicopter flying in front of **ours** (from the 101st Airborne) took an RPG to the rear rotor, as all four of our low-flying Chinooks took fire. **We** were forced down and stayed down — for the better (or worse) part of 3 days and 2 nights.

On March 23, 2013, Williams told David Letterman, "Two of **our** four helicopters were hit by ground-fire, including the one **I** was in, RPG and AK-47."

Williams delivered this passage in the story about how he took a veteran to a New York Rangers' hockey game. Williams said on *Nightly News*, "The story actually started with a terrible moment a dozen years back during the invasion of Iraq when the helicopter **we** were traveling in was forced down after being hit by an RPG. **Our** traveling NBC News team was rescued, surrounded and kept alive by an armor mechanized platoon from the U.S. Army 3rd Infantry."

The feel-good story that followed was as much about Williams being a good guy as it was about a soldier who risked his life serving in Iraq. Officials from Madison Square Garden and NBC refused to answer Poynter's questions about who pitched the story idea to the Rangers' public address announcers, who supplied the copy that the announcer read saying Williams had been in a military helicopter that was crippled by gunfire, and who told Madison Square Garden officials that the anchorman would be at the game with a veteran in tow.

Even in retracting the story, Williams couldn't break his first-person reference addiction. He said, "On this broadcast last week in an effort to honor and thank a veteran who protected **me** and so many others following a ground-fire incident in the desert during the Iraq War ..."

Nobody would argue Williams' use of first-person when he owned the whole stinking mess, saying, "**I** want to apologize."

Williams' other recollections under attack are also first-person references. His memory of watching a man jump to his death in the New Orleans Super Dome after Hurricane Katrina, for example, included this passage:

> We **watched, all of** us **watched, as one man committed suicide.**

The problems that Williams faced largely had to do with what he said about himself, what he experienced, not what he said about others. Television reporters everywhere may be able to relate to this pressure to promote themselves as a franchise, be pithy and visible online and in social media, show some personality on the air, appear to be empathetic and informed and relate what they saw, not what others experienced. Williams' case may just be the poster child for what happens when journalists forget that the story they are covering shouldn't be about them.

That is not to say that first-person reporting has no place in journalism. In 1887, Nellie Bly, that crusading journalist, had herself admitted to a New York asylum to uncover the deplorable conditions of "Mad-Houses" warehousing the mentally ill. But she has no photos, video or audio to prove her story. Bly's first-person accounts told readers how she knew what she knew:

> The insane asylum on Blackwell's Island is a human rat-trap. It is easy to get in, but once there it is impossible to get out. I had intended to have myself committed to the violent wards, the Lodge and Retreat, but when I got the testimony of two

**sane women and could give it, I decided not to risk my health—
and hair—so I did not get violent.**

Similarly, when Edward R. Murrow reported on the liberation of the Buchenwald concentration camp in World War II, Murrow described in first person the events that transpired. Keep in mind, Murrow was reporting for radio. He had no images to illustrate the story. Murrow must have known his reputation for honesty and accuracy would add to the report.

Murrow said, "I pray you to believe about what I have said about Buchenwald. I have reported what I saw and heard. But only part of it. For most of it, I have no words." Murrow didn't need to use first-person reporting to prove he had credibility. That first-person reporting gave the story credibility because Murrow had credibility.

First-person reporting is most effective when the reporter has so much credibility that his or her reporting makes a hard-to-believe set of facts more believable. When Murrow said he saw something, there was good reason to believe him because of his years of credible reporting. Journalists get in trouble when they use a story to make themselves look bigger at the expense of the people they should be covering.

In June 2015, four months after Williams was suspended from his anchor job, he attempted to explain himself to the *Today* show's Matt Lauer. But because Williams didn't come clean about what happened and why, the apology didn't explain anything. And one reason his mea culpa rang hollow is because Williams did what children and criminals do; he used passive verbs when he should have used active verbs.

Williams said,

> I would like to take this opportunity to say that what **has** happened in the past **has** been identified and torn apart by me and **has** been fixed. **Has** been dealt with. And going forward there **are** going to be different rules of the road.

He did not say *what* had been identified or *what* had happened. He did not say *how* those mistakes had been fixed, and he did not say what the new rules of the road would be.

I wish he had said something like this:

> I exaggerated or fabricated 10 stories that I told on late night talk shows and speeches. (Then name them.) In each case, I apologized to the people who were harmed. In the future I will stick to doing the news.

Williams said,

> I am sorry for what happened here.

Something didn't just happen. Somebody caused it to happen.

He should have said,

> I hurt my news organization, I hurt my colleagues, I hurt my family and I have made a wreck of my career. I am truly and deeply sorry for what I did. I am solely responsible for what I said. I am deeply grateful to NBC that I have a job. Most of all, I apologize to the viewers of NBC *Nightly News* for having squandered their trust in me. I will now spend the rest of my career trying to gain that trust back.

He said,

> It had to have been my ego that made me think I had to be sharper, funnier, quicker than anybody else. I put myself closer to the action—having been at the action in the beginning.

He should have said,

> I tried to be sharper and funnier and quicker than anybody else, so I put myself closer to the action than I really was. I was feeding my ego.

There is no need to remind us your stories were partly true. Now is the time to own mistakes, not justify them. Everybody has exaggerated some experience to make himself or herself look more accomplished or heroic. Just own it. (Full disclosure here: To all whom I have led to believe I was a football star in high school, I was not. It must have been my ego that made me think that.)

Williams also spoke about his statements as if someone else were inside his body. He blamed the misstatements, exaggerations and some call them lies on "a bad place," "a bad urge inside me." And he said, "What happened is the fault of a whole host of other sins. What happened is clearly part of my ego getting the better of me."

In a follow-up question, Lauer tried again to pry some ownership out of Williams. Did he mean to mislead? Williams went back to that spirit inside of him:

> No, it came from a bad place. It came from a sloppy choice of words. I told stories that were not true over the years. Looking back, it is very clear that I never intended to, it got mixed up, it got turned around in my mind.

There's that passive ownership again. *It* came from a bad place. *It* got mixed up. *It* got turned around. Own the mistake by saying, "I exaggerated the facts to make myself look better."

"It came from a bad place" is like saying, "The devil made me do it."

Amazingly, even in the *Today* interview, he still got facts wrong. About the helicopter story that touched off this whole mess, Williams said on *Today*,

> I told the story correctly for years before I told it incorrectly. That, to me, is a huge difference here. After that incident I tried and failed as others have tried and failed—and why is it that when we're trying to say "I'm sorry," that we can't come out and say, "I'm sorry"?

Nope. Wrong. The problem here is that the helicopter story was wrong from the first time he told it on *Dateline*. In that report he said the formation he was flying in came under fire. It didn't. So he told the story incorrectly from the first and kept getting it wrong. Now, in his apology interview he got it wrong again. And the second part of that statement is one any parent identifies as the "others do it" cop-out. He said he tried and failed as others try and fail to say they are sorry.

The whole mess cost Williams his anchor job. By the fall of 2015, he was relegated to anchoring breaking news occasionally on MSNBC. A contrite detailed apology when the mistakes first surfaced might have saved his career, saved NBC months of embarrassment and become an example of how to salvage the public's trust in broadcast journalism.

If only Fox News had learned from Brian Williams' mistakes. September 6, 2016, Fox announced, but did not immediately report on its own air, that it agreed to pay a former anchor, Gretchen Carlson, $20 million to settle her sexual harassment lawsuit against the network and its CEO Roger Ailes. The network posted a one-paragraph statement:

> **21st Century Fox is pleased to announce that it has settled Gretchen Carlson's lawsuit. During her tenure at Fox News, Gretchen exhibited the highest standards of journalism and professionalism. She developed a loyal audience and was a daily source of information for many Americans. We are proud that she was part of the Fox News team. We sincerely regret and apologize for the fact that Gretchen was not treated with the respect and dignity that she and all of our colleagues deserve.**

The statement failed in the same way many half-hearted apologies do. Note the careful omission of any guilty party: "Gretchen was not treated with the respect . . ." The statement does not say who failed to respect her. It holds no individual accountable.

The public has a long history of forgiving high-profile people and companies who fall short but make a heartfelt, sincerely apologize and follow up with a high-profile and measureable course correction. Journalists demand that from others and the public has every reason to expect that in return.

■ ■ ■ REMEMBER

Be honest with your viewers about how you obtained video or information. Be honest enough to admit when you make mistakes in your stories and correct those mistakes as quickly as possible. The correction should get the same on-air prominence and emphasis as the mistaken information received.

Attack Dogs, Watchdogs and Guide Dogs: A Journalist's Commitment to Seeking Truth

In a Baltimore town meeting I asked the viewers what they thought about the idea that journalists have a certain "watchdog" function—holding the powerful accountable and giving voice to the voiceless.

The Baltimore residents and those of many other focus groups in New Orleans, Philadelphia, Oklahoma City, Atlanta and more have said they are not sure journalists can or do fulfill such a watchdog function. I asked the Baltimore group, "OK, if you don't want journalists to be 'watchdogs,' what kind of dogs do you want them to be?"

One man spoke up. "I want you to be golden retrievers."

I was already sorry I had started down this line of questioning, but I asked him to explain his answer anyway.

"Golden retrievers are versatile," he said. "They can be guide dogs, they can be guard dogs, they sniff out drugs from airport baggage, they are great companions. They are smart, good looking and don't go around barking at every little noise. I think newspeople are like those little yap dogs that some people have. They yap at everything, they get up on your furniture, and they pee on everything." By now, the whole room was laughing, except the journalists.

With his dog metaphor this man, an ordinary viewer, put his finger on a central problem. The viewers we met that night in Baltimore were trying to tell us that they believed journalism served an important function, but that journalists had given up their role as truth seekers and truth tellers in favor of self-promotion and profiteering.

Starting with that evening in Baltimore, I moderated 26 town hall meetings over 11 years, listening to viewers from coast to coast. In every single conversation the public confirmed to me that they believe powerful advertisers, business leaders and politicians have great influence on news content. How could your coverage confirm or dispel such notions? Does your news reporting, for example, go after the biggest polluters or just the little garage owner who spills a barrel of oil on the ground? How are the wealthy and powerful people in your community held accountable on your newscasts compared with coverage of the power-less and poor?

Great investigations don't just pick on little guys; great investigations hold the powerful accountable and give voice to the voiceless. Be vigilant and courageous in seeking and telling truths.

■ ■ ■ REMEMBER

Be courageous. Hold the powerful accountable and give voice to those who are seldom heard. The overarching principle for journalists is to seek truths and tell them as fully as possible.

FILE TAPE: TRUTHFUL REPORTING OR LAZY JOURNALISM?

When jetliners crash, it is unquestionably "news" that journalists should air, print and post online as the story was breaking and developing. The pictures help us to understand the size, the response to and sometimes the causes of the accidents.

But when journalists continuously air or print pictures of such catastrophes, the public becomes concerned about the wrong things, said Barry Glassner, a University of Southern California sociologist.

In his book *The Culture of Fear*, Glassner wrote, "Upon landing at the Baltimore airport, as he taxied to the terminal, the pilot of my flight from Los Angeles announced, 'The safest part of your journey is over. Drive home safely.'" It is true, of course, that far more people die in car crashes every year in the United States than have died in airplane crashes in the last century. But dramatic images of plane crashes can play for days on end.[8]

"When television news departments show those [file tapes] of disasters, it is lazy production," Glassner said.

Even considering the number of people who died on airlines in the September 11, 2001, al-Qaida attacks, air travel is far safer, per mile, than any other means of travel. Contrary to what you might believe based on what you see on the news, 7 out of 10 people who die in airplane crashes die in small general aviation planes, not commercial airliners.[9] According to the National Safety Council, you're more likely to die as a pedestrian, on a motorcycle, in a car, on a bus or on a bicycle than flying in an airplane.[10]

The International Business Times quoted Harvard researcher David Ropeik saying the risk of dying in a plane crash are about 1 in 11 million. By comparison, the odds of dying from a shark attack are about 1 in 3 million. The odds of dying in a car crash are about 1 in 5,000, he says.[11] Yet file footage of airplane accidents can make us feel far less safe than these statistics show.

Newsrooms should limit the use of file tape for other reasons, according to Deborah Potter, executive director of NewsLab, a Washington, D.C.–based news laboratory that helps local stations tell more effective stories. Potter says audience researchers find that viewers see file tape as a signal that there is nothing new about the story, that they are seeing old news, even if the audio accompanying the file tape contains new information.

"One reason these pictures are so overused is that there is a desperation in TV newsrooms, a feeling we have to have a picture because we are TV. The research I have seen does not support the common newsroom rule that any video is better than none," Potter said.

Here are some guidelines to help newsrooms make ethical decisions about how, when and how often to use file tape:

- What is the journalistic purpose for using file tape? Ask each time you use an image, "What truths does this image tell that would not be told if we didn't use the picture?"

- How does the truth of the file picture measure up to the potential harm the continued use of the image might cause to others who were involved in the story?

- How clear is the viewer that the file tape is, in fact, historic, not shot today?

- What "harm" could the use of file video cause to the viewer by repeatedly showing disturbing pictures?

- What discussion does your newsroom have about how long graphic images remain "news" and when they become "file"?

- What obligation do you have to notify the people who are shown in file tape that you intend to use their images again, sometimes weeks or months after an incident?

- What guidelines does your newsroom have about the use of file tape in promotions?

■ ■ ■ REMEMBER

Consider your journalistic purpose in using file tape. Be clear with your viewers about your reasons for using it to seek and report truth as fully as possible.

NOTES

1. Jack Fuller, *News Values* (Chicago: University of Chicago Press, 1996), 58.
2. Ibid., 60.
3. "Trump's Favorite Target: Photojournalists," Al Tompkins, February 26, 2016, Poynter.org.
4. "Honesty/Ethics in Professions," Gallup Research, December 2–6, 2015, http://www.gallup.com/poll/1654/honesty-ethics-professions.aspx.
5. "Americans' Trust in Media Remains at Historical Low," Gallup Research, September 28, 2015, http://www.gallup.com/poll/185927/americans-trust-media-remains-historical-low.aspx.
6. "Honesty," *National Public Radio Ethics Handbook*, http://ethics.npr.org/category/d-honesty/.
7. Christine Urban, *Examining Our Credibility: Perspectives of the Public and the Press* (Reston, VA: American Society of Newspaper Editors, 1999).
8. Barry Glassner, *The Culture of Fear* (New York: Basic Books, 1999), 183.
9. "Aviation Accident Statistics 1983–1999," National Transportation Safety Board, http://www.ntsb.gov/investigations/data/pages/aviation_stats.aspx.
10. Source: http://www.nsc.org/news_resources/Documents/nscInjuryFacts 2011_037.pdf.
11. "After Air Algerie AH5017 Incident, A Statistical Look at the Probability and Chances of Dying in an Air Crash" *International Business Times*, July 24, 2015, http://www.ibtimes.com/after-air-algerie-ah5017-incident-statistical-look-probability-chances-dying-plane-crash-1638206.

and offer alternatives that go beyond the typical "Do we cover . . . ?" conversations that arise with a heated ethics issue. The thoughtful journalist presses the conversation toward "How do we cover this story?"

Journalistic independence begins with accepting personal accountability for our own biases, decisions and actions. No boss can force you to act unethically. You may choose to follow an order because you don't want to lose your job, or you may choose not to fight over this particular issue at this time. But those are choices. There are far more choices journalists must make on their own to be independent in their journalism.

In this chapter we will cover the following:

- Guidelines for avoiding, or disclosing, conflicts of interest
- Refusing freebies and favors
- How to respect the business side of your company while protecting the journalism

Avoid Conflicts of Interest

Journalists should avoid conflicts of interest, whether the conflicts are real or perceived. It is impossible for any of us to be "objective" in our reporting. For example, I am

- A gun owner
- Divorced and remarried
- A pickup truck owner
- A United Methodist
- A parent of internationally adopted children
- White
- A registered Democrat
- Male

Does this mean I, as a reporter, should not be allowed to report on issues of gun control, truck safety, politics or adoption, or on those involving divorce? Of course not. In fact, one might argue that I am more qualified to cover gun issues because I actually own a gun. I might be very good at reporting about pickup trucks because I drive one.

The main test is whether causes I support profit in some way by my journalism. Imagine the conflicts that arise when a journalist's spouse decides to run for public office or if a journalist is married to a politically or socially active spouse. For example, before we met, my wife, a psychotherapist, often appeared in the media commenting on issues about relationships, stress and family. But once we married, we decided it would be inappropriate for her to appear on newscasts at the station where I was the news director. We didn't want reporters to wonder whether they had to treat her with kid gloves in an interview. We didn't want the public to wonder whether she was appearing on TV as a way of promoting her family therapy practice.

If journalists have unavoidable conflicts that compromise their independence, they should disclose those conflicts. We can't control and often can't even influence the actions of others. Family members run for political office, make controversial public statements, can be victims of crimes and can even become criminals. Journalists must do all they can to distance themselves from stories about those people.

The public has a need to know about personal conflicts that compromise a journalist's independence. If an automotive reporter, for example, owned stock in a car company, wouldn't the public want or need to know about that conflict while reading a glowing report on the newest model the company just built? If a reporter is a member of the local Republican Women's Club, wouldn't the public need to know that the reporter also covers politics? Merely disclosing the conflicts does not absolve the journalist, but the disclosure gives viewers a filter through which they can see and sort the information in the story.

Our job as journalists requires us to admit our biases and find ways to report around them. That is part of showing journalistic independence.

The Society of Professional Journalists Code of Ethics says, "Journalists should remain free of associations and activities that may compromise integrity or damage credibility. Journalists should shun secondary employment, political involvement, public office and service in community organizations if the outside work compromises journalistic integrity."

This point can be a tough one for some journalists. It means resisting the temptation to join groups, foundations and associations that are now or might someday become newsworthy. The journalist's first obligation is to the viewing public. This also means journalists should avoid public displays of support for or against political causes. It means journalists should avoid putting bumper stickers on their cars or signs in their yards favoring or opposing issues that their station is covering or might cover as news stories. This point can become particularly difficult when spouses or family members are involved in high-profile issues or causes.

Station management often encourages or even demands that news anchors "get plugged in" to the community by serving on charitable boards or committees for everything from the United Way to charitable hospitals. Although that kind of worthy work can benefit the community and help the journalist gain public stature and visibility, charities often find themselves at the center of pointed news stories, and hospitals could easily find themselves as the target of lawsuits alleging malpractice or financial irregularities. The journalist should remain free to aggressively report on such matters without fear or favor.

Journalists should also avoid taking any freelance jobs if they have the potential to compromise their independence. For example, a journalist should not cover a story about a factory opening and then write a story for that same company's newsletter.

This issue arose in my newsroom when a movie company came to town and wanted journalists to play reporters and anchors in the movies. I was against the idea, but several of my staff wanted to be in the film. I allowed it but banned them from covering any story about the movie. I think now that was the wrong decision. The public already is confused about the difference between reality and fantasy. The movie business made news in our town a few times. Once a script was stolen from an actor's hotel room. Another time a Teamsters' strike held up production. Journalists shouldn't be actors; they should be the real thing. Journalists have no business being paid by movie companies that might become the focus of news coverage.

A good "sniff test" is to ask, "What would my viewers say if they knew what I was doing?"

I have a few friends in journalism who carry this canon to an extreme. They do not vote in elections because they fear the act of voting will legitimize the public's notion that they are "biased." Of course, they are biased; we all are. Journalists need only to find ways to report around those biases.

Jack Fuller, former Tribune Company Publishing president and former editor and publisher of *The Chicago Tribune*, once said,

> Journalists often end up in close relationships with people who make news. Now that some journalists themselves have become celebrities, and newspapers are covering each other as a beat, even within the cloister it is not possible to avoid such situations. The best approach to the problem of the conflict between friendship and craft combines sensitivity to the reasonable expectations of the person one is dealing with and openness about the conflicting loyalties in play. For example, if an editor is having dinner with a friend in a family setting and the friend tells the editor that he has been nervous lately because the prominent company of which he is an executive is in financial difficulty, the editor might explain at that point that he assumes his friend does not mean for this to be made public and it would make the editor uncomfortable to learn any more about the matter because this is something his newspaper would print if it learned of it under other circumstances.[1]

A journalist's primary loyalty is to the public. Nothing else comes first.

REFUSE GIFTS, FOOD AND SPECIAL TREATMENT

When Bob Selwyn hired me as a reporter at WSMV-TV in 1984, he explained the newsroom's guidelines for accepting food and gifts, saying, "We have a 'stand and snack' rule. If you can eat or drink it standing up, it is fine. If it is a sit-down dinner, then take a pass."

That commonsense guideline might allow reporters to drink a cup of coffee and down a doughnut, but it would not allow them to eat a prime rib dinner on somebody else's dime. Selwyn also sent out an annual memo near the holiday season reminding journalists not to accept invitations to parties from people who might seek to influence coverage. WSMV reporters and photojournalists understood, for example, that we were not to attend the governor's Christmas party at the mansion. The event was purely social, not a news briefing or news event. More than once, in fact, our newsroom did news stories about reporters from newspapers, radio and other TV stations eating lunch on the governor's dime.

If holiday cocktails with the governor are off-limits, then free tickets to theme parks, circuses and sporting events are off the charts of acceptable behavior.

Journalists should never use their press privileges to gain access to events or areas to which any other member of the public does not have access. For example, they should not use press credentials to watch a football game from the sidelines or go backstage at a concert that they are not covering.

Off duty or on the job, journalists should resist VIP treatment from those who might seek preferential news coverage in the future. The key question for journalists is *not* whether there is a conflict of interest. Journalists should avoid even the *appearance* of a conflict of interest. Business reporters, for example, should not buy or sell stock based on information they gather in the course of their reporting.

DISCLOSE UNAVOIDABLE CONFLICTS

Politicians in most states are required by law to disclose potential personal or financial conflicts of interest they might have with legislation that comes before them. Newsrooms should establish similar standards for journalists to disclose potential conflicts to their newsroom supervisors so the decision makers can determine whether another journalist should take over the story.

If a member of your news staff finds himself or herself in legal trouble, the station should ask, "If this person were anyone other than a station employee, would it be news?" In fact, a good case can be made for reporting some stories involving journalists that might not be reported otherwise, such as a drunken driving or domestic violence arrest involving a journalist. The more high profile the journalist the higher the responsibility of the newsroom to report the story.

A former editor of the *St. Petersburg Times* (now the *Tampa Bay Times*), Eugene Patterson, set a standard for this kind of public disclosure.[2] In July 1976, while editor, he was arrested for driving under the influence of alcohol. According to Bob Haiman, who was the newspaper's managing editor at the time, "Gene had been to a cocktail party at a friend's house. As he was driving home from an American bicentennial party with his wife, he pulled up alongside another car at a stop light, was a bit too close and the cars' doors 'kissed' slightly side to side with almost no visible damage. Cops came, asked Gene if he had anything to drink and he said yes. They gave him the breath test and he came in barely over the limit, by a few thousandths of a point. Although he seemed sober, he failed the test."

Editor Patterson called his newsroom. He ordered Haiman to write a story about the arrest. Haiman protested, "I told him we almost never published stories about simple DWIs, unless there was a big accident, a spectacular crash, injuries, death, high-speed chase, somebody who was falling down drunk at the wheel, and none of these was the case here. But he insisted. So we wrote a four- or five-paragraph story."

When Patterson insisted that the story play on the front page, Haiman said, "I *really* protested then, saying the *Times* was a strictly departmentalized paper with national and international news on Page A-1 and the big local stories on Page B-1. 'Hell, Gene,' I said, 'If it was the city manager we'd probably only put it on 3-B, so why the hell isn't B-1 enough play for Gene Patterson, the editor?'"

Haiman said Patterson replied, "It's precisely because I am the editor, Bob." And Haiman recalls Patterson saying, "As a good and honest newspaper, we are always printing embarrassing news that somebody wishes we wouldn't print—so we can never go easy on ourselves. In fact, we have to bend over backward to be tough on ourselves. We should hold ourselves to a notch above the very highest standard we'd ever use to judge anyone else."

The paper published the arrest in the lower right-hand column of Page A-1. Haiman says the reaction from the community, in letters, phone calls and talk on the street was overwhelmingly positive and complimentary that the *Times* would report on its own editor's troubles. Patterson says, "Not all of the feedback was positive. For years afterward, when the *Times* would run a liberal editorial, I would get mail from conservatives saying, 'Well, I see the editor's drunk again.' All you could do is laugh, which is what they were doing."

Haiman told me, "A few years later, what Gene had sown so well at his own expense, I reaped: A politician who'd been arrested for DWI called me to try to keep the story out of the paper. I said we couldn't do that. He got furious and shouted, 'Well, I bet if it was Gene Patterson, you Goddamn well would not print it!' I smiled and said, 'As a matter of fact, commissioner, we would, and did, and put it on Page A-1. So you have no cause at all to object to the story about you being in the B section, do you?'"

Reporting such stories says to the viewer that you hold your own profession to the same high standards to which you hold others. Of course, just reporting the story does not erase the damage that journalists cause when they commit an illegal or immoral act. But when stations report their own dirty laundry, it can be a signal to the public that the station's coverage knows no sacred cows.

We also should be willing to expose the unethical practices of other journalists. We hold others to a high standard, and we should expect no less of our own craft. When journalists show they are capable and willing to self-regulate their profession, it presents a stronger defense against those on the outside who would seek to curb press freedoms.

RESPECT THE BUSINESS SIDE, BUT DON'T COMPROMISE NEWS COVERAGE

Hofstra University's Annual Survey of local news shows local news departments consistently have produced profits since the survey began in 2000.[3] News departments have been the profit engine of local TV, accounting for at least half of a station's income.[4]

In fact, local news is so profitable that stations nationwide have added hour upon hour of newscasts per day rather than paying for syndicated programming. Hofstra's study found that the amount of local news in TV hit a record high in 2016. "The average amount of weekday news tied the all-time high set in 2012 of 5.5 hours." The largest local newsrooms produce more than 11 hours of news a day.[5]

And in years when hotly contested political races dump millions of dollars into TV advertising, the stations rake in the money.[6]

But new competition from cable and online have cut into what was once a business that produced remarkable profits. A Federal Communications Commission study reported, "In comments filed with the Future of Media project, the National Association of Broadcasters said local TV news pre-tax profits declined 56.3 percent from 1998 to 2008—and that the drop was even sharper, 62.9 percent, in smaller cities (media markets number 150–210). But many local TV stations remain highly profitable. According to survey data compiled by the National Association of Broadcasters, a local TV station in 2009 with average net revenues and cash flow would have a cash flow margin of nearly 23 percent of revenues."[7]

To add to the pressure, newsrooms are right to be concerned that advertisers and newsmakers have learned to use social media to deliver their message directly to the viewers. In 2016, TV stations saw the rise of "sponsored content" and "native advertising," which companies use to deliver useful or entertaining information to the user. Dick's Sporting Goods, for example, built a webpage that shows the most popular NFL jerseys sold week to week as a reflection of who the most popular players are around the country. The reader can buy a jersey right there, online.[8]

In the 2016 presidential campaign Donald Trump made especially powerful use of Twitter to deliver jabs to his opponents and media.

The New York Police Department began writing stories for Facebook about itself and even wrote the story in the same voice a journalist would use including words such as cop, gun-toting and left-for-dead:

> A rookie Bronx cop on a footpost this morning chased down and arrested a gun-toting 17-year-old who, moments earlier, fired four shots into another man and left him for dead on a Mount Eden street.[9]

The New York Police Department didn't send the release to newsrooms. It published the statement on Facebook.

So advertisers who once depended on television, radio, newspapers and magazines to deliver their messages now are in a stronger position to make demands.

Even before broadcasters went from turning a 24 percent profit to single- or low double-digit profits, journalists were feeling the heat from advertisers to compromise their once strict standard against allowing advertisers to influence what and how journalists covered. As far back as 2001, the Pew Research Center's Project for Excellence in Journalism surveyed 188 news directors and found that 47 percent said they have felt pressure from advertisers to provide positive coverage of the advertiser's businesses. Almost one out of five news directors (18 percent) said an advertiser had tried to kill a story or prevent negative coverage; about half of all stations surveyed said they include advertising logos on the screen during newscasts. In smaller markets (those with fewer than 376,000 households), the pressure to bow to advertisers is even more intense. Two-thirds of news directors in the smallest markets said they felt pressure to provide positive coverage to sponsors.

The study found that car dealerships and restaurants were particularly interested in stopping negative stories. Some news directors say they no longer go after stories about car dealers; one said a car dealer was successful in killing a story the newsroom wanted to air. Two stations said restaurants had the power to kill negative stories. The report quoted news directors as saying, "The pressure to do puff pieces about sponsors occurs 'constantly,' 'all the time,' 'every day,' 'routinely' and 'every time a sales person opened his/her mouth.'" Another news manager said, "It is getting harder every year to maintain the wall between sales and news."

An FCC study on the state of local TV news said, "For TV news veterans and the audience as well, one of the most worrisome developments in local TV journalism is the rise of "pay-for-play" business deals in which news coverage is directly shaped by advertisers." The study documents the stories I hear from colleagues in markets big and small. Station groups make deals with hospitals and push reporters to only interview doctors from those hospitals when they are doing health-related stories.

In a 2010 Pew Research survey one-fourth of local TV news executives reported "a blurring of lines between advertising and news." Pew reported,

Sponsored segments have in some cases become paid content that looks like news. One executive described "news time paid for by a local hospital with hospital having approval over content." Another station executive, similarly, mentioned a daily paid interview with the local hospital. One broadcast executive described how "ask-the-expert segments" are sold by sales people and then the news department is strongly encouraged to validate the expertise of these people by interviewing them for legitimate news stories. Others described the same thing. "We have an interview format newscast. Our sale staff has 'sold' some interviews to our online experts. They don't always offer great content, but a guest appearance is part of their sales package." Said another news executive, "Our sales department comes to the newsroom with story ideas they've already 'sold.' They just need a reporter to do the story."

Los Angeles Times reporter James Rainey wrote about how a "toy expert" named Elizabeth Werner appeared on newscasts in 10 big cities in 2010. The *Times* reported,

Werner whipped through pitches for seven toys in just a few minutes. Perky and positive-plus, Werner seemed to wow morning news people in towns like Detroit, Atlanta and Phoenix. They oohed and aahed as they smelled Play-Doh, poked at mechanical bugs and strummed an electronic guitar she brought to the studio.

Though parents might have welcomed the advice, and even bought some of the toys, they probably would have liked to know that Werner serves as a spokeswoman for hire, not an independent consumer advocate. She touted only products from companies that forked over $11,000 (the initial asking price, anyway) to be part of her back-to-school television "tour."[10]

Rainey says the problem of "pay for play" is growing worse as TV producers feel pressure to fill more half hours of newscasts, "and advertisers, fearful of being blocked by viewers with video recorders and mute buttons, don't mind paying for promotional appearances that make them more visible and credible."

The public has detected this trend of advertisers pressuring television news coverage for some time. Over the last 20 years, I have led more than two-dozen focus groups with everyday TV news viewers in 25 cities. Almost all the participants in a Baltimore focus group said they believe that people who buy commercials on a TV or radio station get more favorable coverage than those who don't. I asked these focus groups the question, "If a car dealer in this town bought a quarter of a million dollars' worth of ads at a TV station, do you think the car dealer could expect some positive news coverage of its dealership?" The overwhelming majority of residents said yes. They usually said it should not be that way, but they suspect that in reality, it is.

Reporters, producers and photojournalists sometimes feel powerless in this struggle. But even nonmanagers can be powerful and influential when they raise thoughtful questions about the newsroom's position on the separation of business and journalism.

Bob Steele and I drafted these guidelines for balancing the sometimes-competing pressures of journalism and business:

- Do not let the pressure for profits undermine your obligation to produce high quality, ethically sound journalism. **News coverage should not be for sale.**
- Build and sustain a high degree of communication and trust among station leadership and staff members in all departments.
- Don't show favoritism to advertisers.
- Don't generate news content just to provide a vehicle for advertising.
- Journalists are in the business of telling news, not selling products.
- A journalist's most important public service is to report the news; everything else comes second.
- Avoid real or perceived conflicts that arise when commercialism underwrites journalism.
- Don't allow commercialism to buy a higher profile in your reporting than is journalistically justified. Use caution in covering sponsored events.

- Don't run promotional material that viewers/listeners could confuse with news.

- Avoid "tie-in" stories to prime-time, entertainment programming that has no journalistic value. Do not allow your news judgment to be skewed by the pressures to hold or attract audiences.

- Journalists should remain independent of the business associations that stations legitimately have with advertisers. Don't trade on the good name of your organization by accepting favors or gifts not available to the general public.

- Make sure your online product is consistent with the high journalistic and ethical standards of your on-air product.

■ ■ ■ REMEMBER

Journalists must remain independent. Find ways to report around your own biases and avoid conflicts of interests or even the appearance of conflicts of interests with those you cover. Where unavoidable conflicts arise, disclose them to the public. Refuse gifts, favors and special treatment from those who might be the subject of news coverage or who might seek to influence news coverage. Respect the business side but don't allow news content to be for sale and don't compromise with businesses that might seek to buy coverage.

NOTES

1. Jack Fuller, *News Values* (Chicago: University of Chicago Press, 1996), 61.
2. "Times Editor Arrested," *St. Petersburg Times,* July 6, 1976, A-1.
3. Bob Papper, "RTDNA Research 2015: The Business of News," June 1, 2015, http://www.rtdna.org/article/the_business_of_news.
4. "Television," Federal Communications Commission, https://transition .fcc.gov/osp/inc-report/INoC-3-TV.pdf.
5. Bob Papper, "RTDNA Research: News by the Numbers," http://www .rtdna.org/article/rtdna_research_local_news_by_the_numbers#sthash .ZtT1zFLk.dpuf.
6. "Local TV News Factsheet," Pew Research Center, June 15, 2016, http:// www.journalism.org/2016/06/15/local-tv-news-fact-sheet/.

7. "Television," Federal Communications Commission, https://transition
.fcc.gov/osp/inc-report/INoC-3-TV.pdf.

8. "Dick's Sporting Goods Jersey Report," http://www.dsg.com/jerseyreport/
football.

9. NYPD Facebook page, https://m.facebook.com/notes/nypd/rookie
-nypd-officer-chases-down-shooter-loaded-gun-recovered/
666228496787269.

10. James Rainey, "The News Is, That Pitch Was Paid For," *Los Angeles Times*,
September 15, 2010.

CHAPTER 17

Ethics and Broadcast Journalists: Minimize Harm

> *When a dog bites a man that is not news, but when a man bites a dog that is news.*
>
> —Charles Anderson Dana,
> Journalist (1819–1897)

Take special notice that the minimize harm guideline is third on Bob Steele's list of guiding principles, not first. It is that way for a reason. If we start our decision making by asking, "How can we cause the least harm?" we won't report many important stories.

Journalism is a messy business. Sometimes journalists invade privacy, take pictures of people who don't want to be photographed and ask probing questions of people who don't want to talk or be held accountable. The job of a journalist is to seek truths. However, as the Society of Professional Journalists Code of Ethics puts it, "Pursuit of the news is not a license for arrogance."

Journalists should be aggressive and show respect. As Steele says, "The journalist's guideline should not be 'never invade privacy'; it should be to 'respect privacy.'"

Many professions require their practitioners to ask pressing questions. When I visited my doctor last year for my annual physical, I was a little bit surprised when she asked me, "Do you need to take an AIDS test this year?" I told her I was surprised at the question, and she responded, "Al, I'm your doctor; I am supposed to ask good questions." Our professions have similar demands. We both are to ask tough and detailed questions. But journalists, like doctors, should invade privacy only when they can justify their actions.

Trish Van Pilsum started as a reporter at WCCO-TV in Minneapolis and covered the police beat for many years. "They used to call me Trish and Tragedy," she once told a Poynter Institute class while talking about her early years in reporting on the "death and destruction beat." She said she would sometimes approach tragic stories knowing that, "I can't make the situation any better by reporting on it, but I can do my best not to make it any worse." It is no wonder Van Pilsum often landed interviews with vulnerable people who would not speak with other journalists.

In this chapter we will cover the following:

- How privacy is different for private people and public officials
- Should we withhold the names of criminals, especially mass killers to deny them publicity?
- The choices in tone and degree of coverage for graphic images and language
- How and when to identify suspects and juveniles accused of crimes
- The hazards of covering "breaking news" live

RIGHTS TO PRIVACY FOR PRIVATE PEOPLE AND PUBLIC OFFICIALS

Recognize that private people have a greater right to control information about themselves than do public officials and others who seek power, influence or attention. Only an overriding public need can justify intrusion into anyone's privacy.

Since 1890, nearly every state has enacted some form of privacy rights. Generally, if you are a public official, candidate for office, sports figure, entertainer or celebrity your privacy rights are limited. But people who have not thrust themselves into the spotlight have a right, albeit limited, to be left alone.

The two most common privacy violations that journalists get accused of are "intrusion" and "false light."

Intrusion is when a journalist goes into a place that a person would reasonably consider to be private such as peeking over a fenced-in back yard or reporting private facts that are not in the public record.

In a 1998 California case, the state Supreme Court said that a recording of victims on the side of the road in a car wreck would not be an intrusion on the person's privacy. It happened on a public road. But once the person is moved to a rescue helicopter or ambulance, he or she has more privacy rights. The person is in a space where he would expect not to be recorded by a TV camera.[1]

False light usually involves some kind of fraud in obtaining or reporting information or portraying an individual in an untruthful way. Generally journalists are protected from false light claims if they can prove the information to be true or if the information exists in a public record such as an arrest record, autopsy report, court filing or license.[2]

But when, if ever, should journalists report on the private information about private people? Sometimes people by fate or circumstances become publicly known even if they want to stay out of the limelight. Consider, for example, how you would handle information that a winner of a multimillion-dollar lottery had a criminal background. The crimes were years ago. What if that same person's crimes were all financial crimes in which he bilked small investors out of millions of dollars?

At issue is how the lottery win relates to the criminal past. Clearly if the lottery winner chooses to hold big news conferences and to portray himself as a philanthropic angel, the journalist has more license and maybe even more of an obligation to set the record straight. How would your decisions change if the financial crimes involved a few thousand dollars? What if he had repaid all of the victims 20 years ago?

WHEN PUBLIC RECORDS
SHOULD REMAIN PRIVATE

A couple of weeks after a lone killer entered Sandy Hook Elementary School in Newtown, Connecticut, *The Journal News* in Westchester, New York, wanted to hold gun owners accountable for owning weapons. The paper published the names and home addresses of people who had been issued pistol permits in two counties the paper served. The information was freely available through open records. Publishing them was clearly legal. And readers were furious, as they should have been.

The problem is not that *The Journal News* was too aggressive. The problem is that the paper was *not aggressive enough* in its reporting to justify invading the privacy of people who legally own handguns.

Janet Hasson, publisher of *The Journal News* at the time, told me that she felt publishing the information was "important," in the aftermath of the Sandy Hook shootings. But she did not say why.

Timeliness is not reason enough to publish this information, though there are important reasons—including public safety—that journalists regularly invade people's privacy. But when we publish private information we should weigh the public's right to know against the potential harm publishing could cause.

My former colleague Bob Steele used to compare the journalist's role in this situation to a doctor who had to decide whether to perform surgery, knowing she would have to cut through healthy tissue to get to a tumor. The damage caused to the skin is outweighed by the good that comes from removing the tumor. But, as Steele used to say, the surgeon uses great care and years of training to cause only the damage that is justifiable—and no more.

Journalistic invasions of privacy ought to produce outstanding insights into an issue or problem, as *The Washington Post* did in "The Hidden Life of Guns."[3] The package included reporting about the National Rifle Association's influence over politicians and "time to crime" data from the Bureau of Alcohol, Tobacco, Firearms and Explosives showing how guns from one store move quickly to the streets to be used in crimes. That story links specific stores to a huge number of crimes. Yes, name the stores, and find out why they are so popular among criminals.

WRAL-TV in Raleigh, North Carolina, stirred up a hornet's nest by investigating concealed-carry permits. The station went well beyond the controversial database to examine the questionable claims that concealed weapons alone lower crime.

Those are the kinds of stories that make public records data vitally important, the kind of stories that opportunistic lawmakers and anti-media pundits would have a harder time attacking.

Alternatives The Journal News Could Have Considered

Here are some stories any newsroom could explore as part of publishing some version of a gun permit database.

If journalists could show flaws in the gun permitting system, that would be newsworthy. Or, for example, if gun owners were exempted from permits because of political connections, then journalists could better justify the privacy invasion.

If the data showed the relationship between the number of permits issued and the crime rates, that serves a public purpose. You would have to also look at income, population density, housing patterns, policing policies and more to really understand what is going on and why.

If a news organization compared permit owners with a database of felony offenders in local counties, that could be a public service. Years ago I recall WCCO-TV in Minneapolis doing this and they found the state was issuing hunting licenses to felons.

But none of those stories would require the journalist to identify the names and home addresses of every permit holder. The mapping might be done by ZIP code or even by street.

I am not a big fan of the maps that show sex offenders, but at least there is a logical reason for posting them, even though the offenders often no longer live where the maps show them to be. And even when they do, how much risk do they pose? The maps can't know that. The difference between the sex offender maps and the gun permit maps is that sex offenders have been convicted of a crime. The permit holders are accused of nothing.

Counterarguments

After I took on *The Journal News'* publication of gun owner names and addresses in an article for Poynter.org, some readers contacted me to say the database is the kind of thing parents can use to learn whether their kids are safe at a friend's house. I disagree. I am a gun owner. When my kids were growing up, my pistol was locked in a safe at a friend's house on the other side of town. A permit map would have shown it at my house.

The Journal News database didn't show shotguns, rifles, even the much discussed "assault weapons." The data could give a parent a false sense of security. It might be more useful to ask the parents of your child's friends about guns in the house, rather than rely on a database that might not provide a clear picture.

The Journal News says it was flooded with criticism that publishing the maps makes the permit owners targets for thieves. I understand the concern but am not sure I buy it. I wonder if the homes *without* permits are bigger targets—there may be no guns there to fight back. In any case, I have seen nothing yet that leads me to believe publishing such data results in a higher incidence of burglaries.

One argument for publishing the database might go something like this: "We are not implying anything by publishing this data. We are not vilifying anybody. It is a public record. The public is smart enough to figure that out. Trust the public to make good decisions if we supply them with information." I accept that argument if the data has some context. Don't just show us numbers. Tell us what they mean or we draw our own conclusions based on our own biases, which is dangerous.

What's the Journalistic Purpose?

If publishing the data because it is public and the public seems to be interested in the topic right now is reason enough, then there are endless databases to exploit.

If your county required dog and cat licenses, would you publish that interactive map if the licenses were public? I sure would like to know whether three dogs were living behind me before I moved in.

I have seen news organizations publish the salaries of local and state government employees for no reason other than that they can. Why? Did we think they all worked for free? If somebody is playing the system, expose that person. But use the surgeon's tools, not a chainsaw approach.[4]

CRIME VICTIMS AND PRIVACY

Journalists should usually give crime victims more privacy than they give to criminals. Crime victims generally are caught in the vortex of a news story by circumstance and bad luck. Van Pilsum's guideline to try to cause no further harm is a good one. But that does not mean that crime victims should always be shielded from the public. Although journalists do not name every victim of spousal abuse, they might if the victim is the spouse of the mayor or the police chief.

Do not "shoot now and ask questions later." Journalists can cause harm just by asking questions, taking pictures or obtaining information, even if they do not air what they record or find. Think how you would feel if someone started asking questions of your family and friends about your past, your finances or your business.

Steele says journalists should ask, "How can I better understand this person's vulnerability and desire for privacy? Can I make a better decision by talking with this person? What alternative approaches can I take in my reporting and my storytelling to minimize the harm of privacy invasion while still fulfilling my journalistic duty to inform the public? For instance, can I leave out some 'private' matters while still accurately and fairly reporting the story? Or can I focus more on a system failure issue rather than reporting intensely on one individual?"

COVERING CRIMINALS AND CRIMINAL ACTS

On April 16, 2007, Virginia Tech student Seung-Hui Cho went on a shooting rampage at the university. He killed 32 people and wounded 20 more before taking his own life in Norris Hall, an engineering classroom building. At that time, it was the deadliest shooting incident ever committed by a single gunman in the United States.[5]

Just as the country absorbed the horror of the violence, NBC News in New York received a package, a manifesto that Cho mailed to the newsroom on the day that he opened fire. In fact, he already had killed two people by the time he mailed the package, which contained 43 photographs of himself, a series of rambling videos and an 1,800-word statement.

"You had a hundred billion chances and ways to have avoided today," Cho said. "But you decided to spill my blood. You forced me into a corner and gave me only one option. The decision was yours. Now you have blood on your hands that will never wash off."

NBC News aired excerpts of the video on NBC *Nightly News.* Then on its cable channel MSNBC, the network repeatedly re-aired the videos and some of the disturbing still photos, including Cho holding two pistols. Another showed him holding a knife, and some showed hollow-point bullets lined up on a table.

The network put an "NBC Exclusive" logo on copies that it released to other networks. It appeared that NBC was attempting to cash in on a world exclusive.

Victims' families howled in protest and cancelled media interviews. Meredith Vieira, co-host of NBC's *Today* program, said, "We had planned to speak to some family members of victims this morning, but they cancelled their appearances because they were very upset with NBC for airing the images."[6]

Steven Capus, who was NBC News president at the time, explained his network's decision to air the video and photos in an email to Poynter Online. Capus said,

> Prior to the release, we worked very closely with law enforcement authorities. They asked us to remain silent about the material until they had a chance to review the content. We naturally abided by that request. We handed over to the FBI all of the original documents in a quick manner with the expressed desire to do anything to help investigators. Indeed, we appreciated the acknowledgment by the Virginia State

Police during their press briefing yesterday, of our handling of this incident.

Some 7 and 1/2 hours passed before we aired the first video from the material, and again it was done in an extremely limited manner. Our Standards and Policies chief reviewed all material before it was released. One of our most experienced correspondents, Pete Williams, handled the reporting. We believe it provides some answers to the critical question, "WHY did this man carry out these awful murders?" The same decision to run this video was reached by virtually every news organization in the world, as evidenced by their coverage on television, on websites and in newspapers.

The pain suffered by the Virginia Tech community and indeed the country is real and will last forever. I believe our coverage to date has been handled with great sensitivity. We are committed to nothing less.[7]

I believe that NBC was right to air the video and photos. However, the network showed great insensitivity by showing the images repeatedly and showed even worse judgment by including an NBC logo over the video that it shared with other news outlets.

This decision to air Cho's words and images is an example of how difficult it can be to balance the journalist's obligation to publish or air what he or she knows versus the harm that publishing those images might cause to families or to the public. Newsrooms around the world had to make choices about what they would publish on the air or in print and how they might make different decisions for their online publications. Some newsrooms used the images sparingly in print, where the public has less of a choice about what it sees, and used the images more liberally online, where online readers can choose what they want to see or ignore.

Some critics of NBC's decision said using the images caused damage to the families and friends of Cho's victims and gave Cho precisely what he wanted, a voice from beyond the grave that condemned his enemies. They worried that airing Cho's images and words would encourage others to commit violence.

There are reasons not to use some parts of the video. Poynter vice president and ethicist Kelly McBride says, "If the person in the video was naming people, blaming them, it could cause them harm. You could withhold airing at least until you talk to those people." And if you air disturbing images, she says, "You explain it. You tell the public this is why and how we made this decision and you also open up a line of communication from the audience so you can hear from them."[8]

"You have to be responsible as a journalist," McBride says. "But that said, I am uncomfortable with the journalist not publishing something out of a paternalistic desire to protect the audience from something that might make them uncomfortable, because as a society we have to deal with this. There are other people out there like this guy, and we have to recognize it and figure out a way to deal with it."

■ ■ ■ REMEMBER

Only an overriding public need can justify intrusion into anyone's privacy. Treat sources, subjects and colleagues as human beings deserving of respect, not merely as the means to any journalistic ends. Balance your obligation to air what you know with the harm it might cause to the subject, those affected by the news and the public.

WOULD WITHHOLDING SHOOTERS' NAMES AND PHOTOS REDUCE VIOLENCE?

Caren Teves wants journalists to remember her 24-year-old son, Alex, the next time you write a story about a mass shooting. Alex was one of the 11 people murdered when a gunman opened fired in a movie theater in Aurora, Colorado, July 20, 2012.

She wants you to feel free to name her son, to use his photo if you like. But she is asking journalists not to use the name or photos of the accused shooter over and over. Teves and the organization she is a part of, Moms Demand Action for Gun Sense in America, are *not* asking for a prohibition against the photos or using the name. In an interview for a story I wrote for Poynter.org, she told me, "If you are practicing serious journalism, if the name or the image are really important to the story, then of course you should use it. But every day, it seems, I see these images of these criminals I see or hear their names, and they are being used just for shock value or to get web clicks."[9]

Teves says she is constantly in touch with other families who have suffered from mass tragedies. The families launched a petition drive to try to convince networks to dial back their use of mass killers' names and pictures. "These families talk about the pain that the repeated use of the killers' names and pictures. It is a big issue."

In June 2014, *Sun News* in Canada agreed with Moms Demand Action and decided not to name the person accused of killing three Royal Canadian Mounted Police officers and wounding two others in Moncton, New Brunswick. The network explained its decision:

> When it comes to mass murderers, too often, it is attention and infamy they crave. Luckily, shootings of this nature are rare in Canada.
>
> And, in the U.S. they account for less than one percent of all gun-related deaths. Far more people have been killed in the bad neighborhoods of Chicago than were killed in all of the mass shootings combined. But these rare incidents are never forgotten. And with the rise of social media, they have become a spectacle.[10]

In my view, the policy sets up a false dichotomy. Either be irresponsible and speculate or don't report at all. It ignores the possibility that full, thoughtful reporting might lead to understanding and even prevention.

And Teves makes a point that journalists should consider. Beyond the pain, news coverage of high-profile crimes does contribute to a killer's celebrity, and celebrities generate followers.

Investigators found that the shooter who killed children at Sandy Hook Elementary School in Newtown, Connecticut, kept detailed records of mass shootings. He was preoccupied with the killings at Columbine High School in Colorado. He is not the first. Around the globe, killers and attempted killers said they wanted to commit a Columbine-like attack. Other high-profile cases involve Columbine killer devotees who took their own lives in sympathy with the Columbine shooters.[11]

After the shooting at the Aurora, Colorado, movie theater where Caren Teves' son died, police noted three specific cases in which copycats directly mentioned the theater shooting as they threatened others. *The Denver Post* said that after the shootings at Columbine High School, there were at least 3,000 copycat threats made at high schools around America. And the man who carried out the shootings at Virginia Tech compared himself to what he called the Columbine "martyrs."[12]

The Washington Post once noted, "Marilyn Monroe's suicide in 1962 allegedly triggered a spike in suicide among young women. Shootings by disgruntled workers at U.S. Postal Service facilities during the 1980s became so relatively common that the phrase "going postal" entered the language. The snipers who terrorized the Washington area in 2002 may have touched off imitators in Ohio, Florida, Britain and Spain shortly thereafter.[13]

Sun News, in explaining why it was withholding the shooter's name in that Canadian case, correctly pointed out that sometimes news events inspire copycats. To be fair, sometimes people see others doing good, charitable things and they copy those acts, too. But who among us would suggest journalists should not have identified and investigated everything there was to know about the hijackers in the September 11, 2001, attacks on the World Trade Center and the Pentagon? The wall-to-wall coverage of the Boston Marathon bombing has not led to copycat bombings; the coverage of the horrific Oklahoma City federal courthouse bombing didn't lead to similar terrorism.

In an attempt to do something to stop senseless killings, well-meaning families of victims press journalists to withhold the names of suspects in mass shooting cases even for weeks after a killing. They say journalists shouldn't report specific facts about a shooting or show photos of the suspect at all. The same line of thinking says journalists shouldn't report on possible motives for the shootings.

I don't agree. It is too simplistic to draw such a hard line between news reporting and homicidal acts. One does not necessarily lead to the other without adding other complicated ingredients such as mental illness, addictions and easy access to weapons.

I understand the line of thinking that withholding details of a horrific shooting might spare families more pain. Families are stakeholders in tragic events. Emergency workers, communities and, yes, all citizens have a stake in these awful events. It is right for journalists to find out and report who did it, who knew about it and who enabled it, and find ways it could have been stopped.

After the September 11, 2001, attacks, it was clear the nation needed to know the names of the attackers and their supporters. We needed to find out how they slipped through airport security and how to fix it. As *The Washington Post* pointed out, the extensive reporting about the man who carried out the 2007 Virginia Tech shooting "helped expose flaws in Virginia's mental health system, leading to reforms." And the *Post* said extensive reporting on the Columbine shooting focused new attention on troubled teens.

The problem I have with Caren Teves' petition is its specific wording, not in the spirit in which it is offered. The petition asks journalists to abide by these requests:

- Do not use the name of the shooter, except when necessary in initial identification or to aid in apprehension of a suspect still at large.

- Do not publish photos that glamorize or aggrandize the shooter.

- Do not air self-serving statements made by the shooter.

The requests are too broad. When the shooter is the focus of actual news developments, like a trial, or if police discover new insights about how they carried out their crime, certainly journalists should use the suspect's name. It is a matter of clarity. What if multiple suspects are involved, as in the Boston Marathon bombing case? Would the petitioners be more satisfied if journalists called the suspects Bomber Number One and Bomber Number Two? It is too confusing, and journalists should be in the clarity business. But on the other end of the scale, I think of the overly dramatic reporting about Depression Era thugs coupled with headline-grabbing names such as "Machine Gun Kelly" that turned criminals into household names. We should be looking for ground that lies somewhere between anonymity and celebrity.

Whether a photo glamorizes or aggrandizes a killer may be in the eye of the beholder. Even staged images like those of the Virginia Tech shooter that I discussed earlier in this chapter may give us insight into the brazenness and rage of the killer. Some criminals crave publicity. Bonnie Parker and Clyde Barrow grabbed headlines and built their legend by mugging with guns. Just as damaging as photos may be the monikers that journalists apply to suspected killers such as "mysterious," "ruthless" or "dark." We should ask how we display images of accused killers. Journalists repeatedly use the photo of the Aurora shooter appearing with strangely bright-colored hair, adding to his celebrity aura.

Journalists have struggled with what to do about self-serving statements from suspected criminals for decades. In 1995, the terrorist known as the Unabomber threatened to continue his bombing attacks unless national media published his 35,000-word manifesto against science and technology. *The New York Times* and *The Washington Post* published it. Journalists repeatedly had to make decisions about whether to publish or air statements released by Osama bin Laden, giving him a world stage to spew his thoughts.

QUICK FIXES FEEL GOOD AND SOLVE NOTHING

When we understand the problem, we avoid quick-fix solutions that don't work. The surest solution to any problem begins with the free flow of reliable information. I generally default to "report," not "withhold."

Caren Teves told me, "I feel the pain of losing Alex every day." Although she and I have some disagreement on the details of her proposal for more sensitive news coverage of mass tragedy, generally, I think she is making a reasonable request: that journalists more carefully consider how they report the news.

I tried, in my article about Teves, to honor her wishes and wrote the whole piece without using the name of any recent mass killer. We could have decorated the story with file photos of the man who shot her son, but it would have served no journalistic purpose. Still, while complying with her request, I don't think I meaningfully compromised any important truth or clarity.

So I tried to create my own version of her request to move toward the same general outcome she wants while not giving away important journalistic duties:

- Journalists should consider how their coverage will affect victims and their families. The journalist's first obligation is to seek truth and tell it as fully as possible, while seeking ways to minimize the harm that coverage will cause.

- Journalists should avoid the repeated and unjustified use of images that could glamorize criminals and their actions. Journalists should avoid using monikers or nicknames for criminals that minimize the harm they have caused.

- It is not the journalist's job to vilify a suspect who has not been convicted. Be careful to use accurate images of the suspect that are as current as possible. Pay special attention to the adjectives you use to describe the subject, sticking to objective factual adjectives rather than opinion-laden subjective adjectives.

- Use extra caution when deciding whether to air or publish statements from the accused criminal, especially if the accuser attempts to blame others for his or her actions. Be especially circumspect about whether to allow the accused to name others for blame. If you do broadcast such statements, attempt to put them into context, testing the statements for accuracy and truth.

- One way to justify the use of a suspect's name and image would be if the identification were part of a meaningful exploration of complex angles of the incident.

For example, the *St. Louis Post-Dispatch* produced a spectacular investigation into how James Holmes, the man convicted in the Aurora theater shooting, got the ammunition he used. The *Post-Dispatch* showed how Holmes legally purchased thousands of rounds of ammo and tear gas canisters online.

PBS' *Frontline* and the *Hartford Courant* deeply and responsibly reported on who Sandy Hook killer Adam Lanza was, how he grew up and what we could learn about him that could help us understand what led to the Sandy Hook shooting.

When we explore who the killers are, we come to more clearly understand their motives. As *The Washington Post* pointed out, the extensive reporting on the man who carried out the 2007 Virginia Tech shooting "helped expose flaws in Virginia's mental health system, leading to reforms." The Virginia Tech shooting led to campus security reforms. Emails from Seung-Hui Cho to his professors revealed valuable insight into the mind of a troubled young man.

It is easy to report on the life of the killer, to scour his Facebook page and to speculate about motive, but doing so could actually encourage the perception that his heinous acts are somehow justified.

The public has a need and a desire to know who has been accused of a crime, the evidence that supports criminal charges and how the crime happened. Some countries, including Canada, subscribe to the idea that the public has no right to know details of the case until trial. But when it might take years for a case to come to trial, the details of a system that failed to protect the public could stay broken far too long.

The tension is always between the pressures of reporting news and not wanting to reward terrorists with publicity. The safe decision may be to claim some imaginary ethical high ground saying you won't give terrorists or killers the airtime or ink they crave. It sounds good. But I dread the day when journalists turn timid about reporting and important truth just to appear to be sensitive and avoid criticism.

USING GRAPHIC OR VIOLENT IMAGES AND LANGUAGE

A second-grade teacher in a Baltimore focus group said she used to tell her students to watch the evening news and report back to the class what they learned. "I can't do that anymore," she said, noting that violence and graphic images pervade newscasts and make them too disturbing for her students.

I asked the focus group to watch two different television stations' stories from the same night. The stories were about a man who had climbed to the top of a radio tower. After several hours on the tower, the man fell to his death in full view of a gathered crowd.

Focus group members said they were disturbed by how the local newscasts "got so excited about the story." They wondered whether the story should have any place in a newscast. The group did not seem to be telling journalists to never show violent images. They said we broadcast those images when, too often, they were not really news.

A Radio Television Digital News Association (RTDNA) study of local TV viewers asked whether reporters are insensitive to people's pain when they report on victims of accidents or crime. Thirty-four percent of the general public said it was a "major problem." Only 15 percent of news directors, half as many, saw journalists' insensitivity as a "major problem." That is a sizable disconnect.

On April 21, 1994, a middle school student was shot and killed in Nashville, Tennessee. The teacher was treating the class to a movie, *Beauty and the Beast*. It was to have been a light and fun afternoon for the kids. But one young boy carried a gun to school that day. In the darkened classroom he fired the gun and killed another middle-school student.

We responded to the shooting with wall-to-wall live coverage. One of WSMV's best spot-news photojournalists, Toney Cook, arrived on the scene quickly, as he often did in breaking news situations. He walked beside paramedics as they wheeled the young shooting victim on a gurney toward a waiting ambulance. One paramedic pumped the injured boy's chest. We were jarred by the image Cook sent back to the station. Cook told me he felt fairly certain the boy would die before he made it to the hospital.

My first instinct was to not run this graphic video. Not ever. After a few minutes I decided to call some people I trusted on such matters. One of them was Nashville child psychologist Warren Thompson, who had served as an adviser to the city schools on issues of violence. I described the scene to Thompson and asked him what arguments he would make in favor of running the pictures. I intentionally framed the question that way because I knew all of the reasons I might not run the video. I needed to know whether there were reasons I might consider running pictures of a young boy dying on an EMT's gurney.

Thompson surprised me when he said, "Oh yes, I think you should run it." He said he thought it was important for young people and for their community to see that guns in school hurt people. He explained that young people see a lot of violence, but usually it is "happy violence," such as Rambo killing the bad guys or Bruce Willis enduring all manner of shooting and fighting and, just before the closing credits roll, escaping from the bad guys and establishing justice.

Thompson recommended I adopt a few guidelines for using the video. He said he would not run the pictures in headlines or teases; he would not use the video over and over, just that day. And he said, "You need to warn the viewers that they are going to see some pretty disturbing stuff." It was excellent advice. We invited Thompson to be with us on the set that night to explain how parents should talk with their kids about the images they were seeing on the news that night.

The shooting at John Trotwood Moore Middle School became a far more significant event than we anticipated. Over the next few years, our newsroom would respond to more shootings inside schools. On November 15, 1995, a student killed a teacher and fellow student and wounded another teacher at Richland High School, Lynnville, Tennessee. A little over two years later, on December 1, 1997, a student opened fire at Heath High School near Paducah, Kentucky. The 14-year-old boy killed three students and wounded seven others. On May 19, 1998, our news crews were on the scene of a fourth school shooting in four years. Two days before his graduation, an honor student opened fire in a parking lot of the Lincoln County High School in Fayetteville, Tennessee. The next year the nation gasped at the unspeakable horrors that unfolded at Columbine High School in Colorado.

The lessons from the 1994 shooting guided how we covered the others. Looking back I see that we used the same principles Steele recommends:

- **Seek truth and tell it as fully as possible:** Find ways to show the pictures so the viewers can fully understand what happened and how this can be prevented in the future.

- **Act independently:** We tried to be independent of the pressures we felt for ratings and public approval, and to recognize our own biases about the images. Several of us in the newsroom were parents of young children. I had a middle-school-aged child at the time. I believe that one of my gut reactions was to want to protect kids like her from the graphic images we intended to show on TV. In the end, showing those images may have been a caring act.

- **Minimize harm:** We warned the viewers about what they were going to see and explained why we chose to use the images. Sometimes TV stations call these "disclaimers." I wish we would call them "claimers," in which we would claim responsibility for our decision to show the video. We also limited the tone of our writing and the number of times we showed the images.

WHEN IT'S UNFAIR NOT TO SHOW THE GRAPHIC VIDEO

The lead image on the front of *The New York Times'* website April 6, 2015, was graphic raw video of a white North Charleston, South Carolina, police officer shooting an apparently unarmed black man who was running away after a traffic stop Saturday.

Within 24 hours the officer was charged with murder in the case.

Why would the *Times* show such a graphic video of officer Michael T. Slager shooting Walter L. Scott eight times? Is this just an example of gratuitous violence that will attract online clicks and sharing, or are there solid journalistic reasons to let the public see this video? Let me pose some questions that might lead us to a reasoned decision on how or whether to use this video:

> **What do we know; what do we need to know?** The *Times* says a lawyer for the Scott family provided the video, which was captured by an unnamed bystander. We do not know why the bystander was capturing the video. We do not know whether the video was altered or edited. It does not appear to be, and nobody so far has made such a claim.

The *Times* says, seconds after he fired his weapon, Officer Slager radioed, "Shots fired and the subject is down. He took my Taser." But the video seemed to tell a different story.

The video showed the officer yanking something away from Scott, then Scott runs away and the officer begins firing.

The *Times* says it appears Scott had been hit by the stun gun and still had wires attached when he began to run. The video does not clearly show how much of a tussle the two had before the shooting. It does not show if Scott ever had possession of the stun gun.

Under the Supreme Court's 1985 "fleeing suspect" ruling,[14] an officer must believe he or she is in danger. In that ruling Justice Byron White said, "We conclude that such force may not be used unless it is necessary to prevent the escape and the officer has probable cause to believe that the suspect poses a significant threat of death or serious physical injury to the officer or others." Before that ruling, police, in some states, had the legal authority to shoot fleeing felony suspects.

The video appears to show Scott is nearly 20 feet away from the officer when the shooting begins. The *Times* also points out, "The officer then runs back toward where the initial scuffle occurred and picks something up off the ground. Moments later, he drops an object near Mr. Scott's body, the video shows."

But we have to admit, we do not know what happened in the moments before Scott broke away and ran. We do not know for certain why the officer picked something up then dropped it next to the body. It sure looks like he is picking up his stun gun and dropping it close to Scott, but the video does not prove that.

The *Times* said police reports claimed the officers performed CPR on Scott. The video shows no such effort. Scott died on the scene, hands cuffed behind his back.

The video does not show whether Scott was violent. Local newspaper reports said Scott had a long criminal history with at least one arrest for assault but most of his crimes were nonviolent.

Why is this video newsworthy? What is the journalistic reason for making it public? One question I ask in cases like this is, "If the main function of journalism is to 'seek truth and report it as fully as possible,' then how would you explain why you withheld the video?" Remember, the lawyer for the shooting victim's family provided the video, so presumably the family wanted the video to go public, which mitigates concerns you might have about being sensitive to the family by showing the video.

A key reason to show video, even graphic video, is that it reveals facts that are counter to official reports. The officer said his life was in danger; the video appears to show otherwise. The officer said Scott took his stun gun; the video questions that.

Some TV reports only used the shooting video but not what happened next. There may be a reason to show the disturbing images of Scott lying on the ground. The *Times* said the officer claimed, in police reports, to have provided CPR on Scott, but the video does not show that to be the case.

Given the recent history of questionable police shootings in the United States, if this shooting had been justified, if the officer had been in danger and the video proved that, the video should have been shown out of fairness to the officer. So it is fair to show the video when the video casts the officer in a bad light too.

What is the right tone and degree of coverage? Tone and degree are two words that ethicist Steele said often when he taught ethics at Poynter. Steele would often ask journalists about the tone of their coverage and the degree to which they would use the graphic video. Would they use it over and over, in slow motion, in promotions, teases or as file video days later? Would they use subjective adjectives to describe the video or narrate it factually without the hype?

What are the alternatives? "Alternatives" is another great Steele word. What alternatives could you consider if you chose not to show the graphic video? Still frames might have showed the story accurately but less completely than the video. You cannot see how quickly Scott ran away in a still frame sequence. Still frames would not show how slowly the officer walked around after the shooting. Still frames would not have proven whether the officer attempted CPR. It would be possible to attempt to describe the video with text only, but that is one step away from witnessing it with your own eyes.

It's justified. This video goes well beyond its shock value. The public has a need to know that police are acting within the law and this video draws that truth into question.

Journalists are in the truth-telling business. Sometimes the truth is hard to watch. But the public has to be able to trust that when police make mistakes, journalists will hold them accountable, just as when the police shoot a suspect out of legitimate fear for their safety, journalists will report that fairly and aggressively, too.[15]

AIRING GRAPHIC VIDEO FOR THE WRONG REASON

Sometimes television stations decide to air stories not because they affect many people but just because the story contains "great pictures."

Identifying Suspects, Covering "Off-Limits" Stories and Other Tough Ethics Calls

September 18, 2016, a bomb exploded in the Chelsea neighborhood of New York City. By the next morning, police named a "suspect" they were looking for, 28-year-old Ahmad Khan Rahami. The FBI published photos of him, every major news outlet aired and published his name and image. But at the moment, he had not been charged with a crime.

FBI Most Wanted ✔
@FBIMostWanted

⟳ Follow

Help the #FBI locate Ahmad Khan Rahami for questioning related to Chelsea, NY explosion: fbi.gov/wanted/seeking…

7:44 AM - 19 Sep 2016

↩   ⟲ 2,437   ♥ 1,282

It is a tough call to name a "suspect" or as police sometimes characterize a person they want to talk to as "a person of interest." In Rahami's case, neighbors spotted him because of all of the publicity and police nabbed him quickly. But what if he had been found to have nothing to do with the bombings. What if he had never been charged? How would he ever gain his reputation back after being suspected of such a crime?

Usually, journalists do not name suspects until they have been charged. But in this case, journalists had a duty to help connect law enforcement with the person who they said they believed was involved in at least one bombing and could still pose a danger. One way to think about whether to report a suspect's name is to consider how you would explain to the public why you withheld the information.

In 2012, police named a Minnesota man, Ryan Larson, as a person they were investigating in the murder of a police officer. Journalists followed suit with the cops and named him too. Some incorrectly reported he had been charged. He was not. Police said they didn't have enough evidence. Larson filed three lawsuits against media seeking damages.[16] The case serves as a tough lesson for journalists who want to help solve a terrible crime, but can cause undo harm in the process. Minnesota Public Radio summarized the issue, "The police were in a big hurry to find the guy who killed their colleague and the news media didn't raise the standard for naming suspects, given the lowering of theirs."[17]

A year later, in the same community, police named a father as their "primary suspect" in the death of the man's 10-year-old son, Barway Collins. Again, most, but not all local media named the man and quoted police as saying he had not been "cooperative" but he was also not immediately charged. The boy had been missing, the community was on edge. The stories that police had a pretty good idea of who was responsible may have calmed tensions. Four months later, the father confessed to the killing.[18]

Eighty-nine percent of the people whom RTDNA questioned in its survey said local news stations should wait until a suspect is charged before naming the person. Seventy percent of news directors in the survey agreed that stations should wait for formal charges before releasing a suspect's name. Before naming suspects who have not been charged, ask yourself these questions:

- How likely is it that the charges will "stick?"
- What is the strength of the evidence?
- What is missing from the evidence, and how likely are police to gather those missing parts?
- Who might be harmed if you name the suspect?
- Who might be harmed if you do not name the suspect? Could somebody else be implicated?

IDENTIFYING JUVENILES

Gut decisions to identify juveniles can cause unjustified harm. Strict policies against identifying juveniles can prevent the public from understanding important issues. Newsrooms should not enact a universal ban on naming juveniles because sometimes the public has a legitimate need to know as much as possible about a juvenile who is charged with a serious crime. Yet juveniles, especially those in their preteen years, deserve a special level of privacy protection because of their vulnerability.

Journalists can find ways to tell stories involving juveniles that go beyond the daily news event to gather a deeper understanding of the context of a story. But they need to ask themselves some questions before deciding how to go about it. Journalists should consider these:

- **Identification:** Who is served by identifying this juvenile? Why does the public need to know the identity? What is the journalistic purpose in identifying the juvenile?

- **Charges:** If the juvenile is charged with a crime, how strong is the evidence? Have formal charges been filed? Is the juvenile only a suspect? How likely are the charges to stick and the juvenile to be prosecuted? If the juvenile is charged with a crime, will she be tried as an adult?

- **Harm:** What is the severity of the crime and the nature of the crime, and how much harm was done in the process of the crime?

- **Implication:** If you do not name the juvenile, who else could be implicated by rumor or confusion about who is charged?

- **Record:** What is this juvenile's record? What is his history? How would shielding his identification and history expose the public to potential harm? What if you don't name the juvenile? What harm could occur?

- **Exposure:** What is the level of public knowledge? Is the juvenile's identification widely known already? How public was the juvenile's arrest or apprehension or the incident that landed the person in the public eye?

- **Family:** How does the juvenile's family feel about identifying the young person? Has the family granted interviews or provided information to the media? Has the juvenile talked publicly?

- **Damage:** Once a juvenile is identified, some damage is done to him or her that can never be completely reversed. If charges against the juvenile are dropped or proven untrue, you may prevent further damage by no longer identifying the juvenile. The journalist should continuously evaluate the decision to name a juvenile, always testing the value of the information against the harm caused to the minor.

- **Depth:** How does naming the juvenile allow the journalist to take the story into a deeper, more contextual level of reporting? What would identifying the juvenile allow the journalist to tell a viewer that the audience could not understand otherwise? Perhaps a deeper understanding of this minor allows us to understand the circumstances of a crime or incident.

- **Tone:** What is the tone and degree of your coverage? How often would the juvenile be identified? How big is the coverage? How will the juvenile be characterized in the coverage? What guidelines do you have about the use of her picture or name in follow-up stories or continuing coverage?

- **Timing:** When would the identification occur? Minutes, hours, days or even years after an incident, identification would have different impacts on the juvenile.

- **Legality:** What are the legal implications of your decisions? What laws apply about juvenile identification? What is the position of the presiding court?

- **Understanding:** How old is this juvenile? What is he capable of understanding about the situation in which he is involved?

- **Impact:** Who, besides the juvenile, will be affected by your decision? Other juveniles? Parents? Families? Victims? Officials? Investigators? Courts?

- **Advocate:** In the absence of a parent or guardian, can the journalist find someone who can act in an unofficial capacity to raise concerns on behalf of the juvenile so that her interests do not get lost in the journalist's quest to tell a story?

- **Alternatives:** What alternatives have you considered to identifying the juvenile?

- What is the potential harm that could come from not reporting the story? For example, if a teenager kills himself, other young people are likely to hear about the death. But parents might not know about the death of the young person without media coverage. Parents would not know that they should be especially alert to changes in the behavior of their children, who might be in shock. News coverage can alert parents to be open with their kids about this sensitive topic.

- What guidelines does your newsroom have about how to minimize the danger of a story about suicide, especially the suicide of a juvenile, triggering copycat deaths? How could your newsroom include, as a matter of policy, the phone number of a local crisis line any time you run a suicide story?

- How well does the newsroom understand the underlying warning signs and motivations of suicide? What experts does your newsroom have contact with who can advise the newsroom on deadline about how to handle suicide stories.

The following are some guidelines and warning signs published by the American Association of Suicidology:

- To discourage copycat suicides, avoid or minimize reporting specific details of the method the victim used in taking his or her life. Avoid descriptions of a suicide as "unexplainable," such as "he had everything going for him." Avoid reporting romanticized versions of the reasons for the suicide, such as "they wanted to be together for all eternity." And avoid reporting simplistic reasons for suicides such as "the boy committed suicide because he has to wear braces on his teeth." The rationale for suicidal thoughts is much deeper.

- Consider how you play the story. Consider minimizing harm by not playing the story in headlines. Consider not using the photo of the person. It will make the suicide less glamorous to someone who might consider imitating the act.

- Report suicide in a straightforward manner so suicide does not appear to be exciting. Reports should not make the suicidal person appear admirable nor should they seem to approve of suicide.

- Present alternatives to suicide such as calling a suicide hotline or getting counseling.
- Whenever possible, present examples of positive outcomes of people in suicidal crisis.

COVERING BOMB THREATS

Well-intentioned journalists often fall back on old newsroom rules not to cover bomb threats. The theory is that coverage will only spawn more threats and that the media should not "feed" the panic.

But journalists are in the business of telling the news, not withholding it. Journalists should use a thoughtful tone while covering such stories. The stories should focus more on the underlying issues than on the threatening calls themselves.

Before covering bomb threats or other threats to public safety, answer the following questions:

- What do you know? What do you need to know?
- What do your viewers want to know? What do they need to know?
- What is the real threat to life or property?
- What are the consequences of the event? Reporting a false threat could lead to copycat threats. Conversely, reporting arrests might discourage such threats. Other consequences might include raising the public's level of insecurity when it is not warranted. Repeated broadcasting of bomb hoaxes can make the public less responsive when actual danger arises. But reporting on the volume and range of threats could inform viewers about the pressures under which police and school officials labor. It could be important for the public to understand why officials react as they do.
- How significant is the evacuation and the interruption of normal life in your community?
- What effect does this event have on law enforcement or emergency crews' ability to respond to other calls?
- What else is the story about? What is the story behind the story? What thought are you giving to the bigger issues

involved in this story? How easy is it for schools, the phone company or the police to track down a threatening caller? How seriously are violators treated? Have you ever followed one of these cases through the legal system to find out what happens? How many bomb/biological threats did the police handle last year? How many resulted in prosecution? How many of those prosecuted went to jail or were actually punished? What was the extent of the punishment? Do your schools have caller ID systems in place? Do they or should they record incoming phone calls?

- Who could help you understand the short-term and long-term consequences of your coverage? Keep an up-to-date list of experts who can help educate you about the stories you cover. These experts might never be named in your coverage, but they can inform your thinking and reporting.

- How do you explain your decision to your staff and your viewers? How could you justify your decisions about where and how you play stories about bomb threats? How much discussion have you had in your newsroom about your coverage?

- Encourage others to be the voice of the contrarian in your decision-making conversations. Who might offer different perspectives and diverse ideas in the decision-making process?

- What alternatives can you consider to maximize your truth telling but minimize the sensationalism for your coverage, including: not going live, playing the story deeper in the newscast, or not teasing the story in preshow opens or promotions? How can you justify the positioning of your coverage?

Avoid words such as "chaos," "terror" and "mayhem." They are subjective words. Play it straight, especially at a time when your community or, depending on the gravity of the story, even the nation is tense. Tone down your teases, leads and graphics. The tone of what you report should not contradict the careful reporting of facts.

Think carefully before going live in covering these stories. You have less editorial control in live situations. The emphasis on live coverage may deflect the attention these stories deserve.

COVERING RAPE AND OTHER "UNSPEAKABLE" STORIES

In the early 1980s my newsroom in rural Kentucky knew about but barely covered the story of a virus that seemed to be mainly confined to gay males. We didn't have the vocabulary or the awareness of how many people were infected; we were uncomfortable talking on television about sexuality, sexual orientation and sexual acts. For newsrooms like the ones I worked for in the Bible Belt, any suggestion that same-sex relationships might be normal would set the phones ringing with viewer complaints. "Safe sex" meant abstinence, and condoms were still hidden behind drugstore counters.

I thought about our early ham-handed coverage of AIDS as I listened one night at a Poynter Institute conference to the heartrending stories of three women who had been raped. They told journalists that not covering rape could be more harmful than covering it.

One woman, 21, was raped as a child. An unknown attacker raped her again just months before I heard her speak. She was assaulted in her sleep. She said that when journalists wrote about her case, they never spoke with her. She said she felt powerless over her own victimization.

"I'm not saying use people's names without their permission, but if a reporter had come to me and asked to use my name, I would have said, 'Please, put my name in big print.'"

She said that when journalists ignore the victims, even if the journalists are trying to protect them, the victims may feel they are losing control over yet another part of life. "When you have been raped, the last thing you want to do is feel the loss of control again."

She says that if journalists will cover the issue of rape, beyond the daily crime reporting of individual attacks, the public will begin to understand the root causes and lasting effects of this crime. Just as years of coverage of the AIDS epidemic began to put innocent faces and names on a disease, protracted and consistent coverage of rape will help the public to understand that victims "didn't ask for it." But for the public to deeply connect with stories about rape, the viewer needs to see the survivor's face, know her or his name and experience that person's story.

Rape survivor Nobuko Oyabu, a news photographer who has talked and written extensively about the issue of rape, says, "It's like it's always the victim's fault. What kind of clothes were they wearing? The woman hears that so often, they can forget an actual crime happens here."

Newsrooms generally withhold the names of sexual assault victims so they don't cause further harm. As Helen Benedict wrote in her 1992 book *Virgin or Vamp: How the Press Covers Sex Crimes,* "To name a rape victim is to guarantee that whenever somebody hears her name, that somebody will picture her in the act of being sexually tortured. To expose a rape victim to this without her consent is nothing short of punitive."

Journalists have the unique opportunity to shape the public's understanding of this issue. In all news coverage it is the small story that lends clarity to such larger issues as these:

- We don't understand war until we sit in the foxhole with the lowly soldier or huddle with the frightened refugee.

- We don't understand civil rights struggles until we see the injustice of a kindergartner who is denied an education because of the color of her skin.

- When we have the names of the criminals, we can learn their life patterns and habits, which lead to their crimes.

It stands to reason, then, that to understand rape, we do what we can to see the faces of rape. Respect privacy but drive toward truth telling when the victims will allow it. When we see the faces and names of victims, we see their innocence, their resolve and their loss.

To understand the whole, we have to examine the parts. To get to the parts, journalists must get off the sidelines of the story and move in close-up. Move in carefully, with great skill and empathy. *But move in.*

Here is a framework of stories and ideas for a newsroom's deeper coverage of rape and sexual abuse:

Educate journalists

- Listen to victims, hear their stories, enrich our understanding.

- Listen to experts, to cops, to therapists, to social workers who see the stories.
- Begin to understand the contexts of race, ethnicity, age and social mores that shape our societal attitudes.

Educate the public

- Write stories and columns.
- Regularize/normalize the issue through everyday coverage, not just special coverage.
- Open the feedback channels to provide ongoing conversations online, in the paper and on TV and in community gatherings.

Explore the process

- Report all we can about who is raped and who rapes.
- Explore whether police have the expertise to investigate these crimes.
- Learn all we can about how courts treat rape and sexual abuse cases.
- How good is our victim support system?
- What is the trial and plea bargain process? How many years do criminals get/serve? What happens when a case goes to trial; how do juries react? What do we know about judges' attitudes, about jury instructions and about how victims are treated?
- What is the prison experience for attackers? Can they be rehabilitated? How are they rehabilitated? When does the rehabilitation counseling occur in the prison term? Is it more effective to treat at the beginning or end of the prison term?
- How are sex abusers released back into society? What works or does not work? Is there ever life after being a rapist? Should there be?

Societal and sexual attitudes

- Have we reached a time when young people no longer think of rape as rape? Have we reached a time when it is OK to steal a little sex, as the cad in the quaint old movies stole a kiss at the door at the end of the evening?

- Have music, popular culture and "the media" corrupted our values in front of our eyes while we, as adults, watched with our hands in our pockets?

- How can we hear the voices of the young people themselves, in loud and unvarnished voices?

The lasting effect

- What laws and tangible changes need to occur?

- How can we educate in the long term?

- How do we measure progress?

Poynter's McBride, in closing remarks to a group of 75 or so journalists gathered at the special Poynter conference, said, "We have to be aware; you can't talk to a group of this size without talking to a rape survivor. We can do better in our coverage. But to do so takes intent. You have to intend to cover it better. It takes the effort to want to go beyond the brief story on Page B-3. We have to take time to listen. I think we can cover this better."

■ ■ ■ REMEMBER

Newsrooms should establish guidelines for covering stories involving suspects who have not been charged. Juveniles deserve special protection from the public's glare. A universal ban on "off-limit" stories such as suicide, bomb threats and rape may rob the public of important information about issues going on in their community.

QUESTIONS BEFORE YOU "GO LIVE"

There is no doubt that a journalist can serve a vital public need by reporting live from the scene of some stories. But when journalists report news live, the stories bypass their usual filtering process to test for accuracy, tone and quality. Journalists who produce or report stories live should use special care, sharp skills and plenty of forethought.

That allure to "go live" has become even easier when social media apps such as Periscope and Facebook Live make it possible for anyone to broadcast from anywhere with a wireless cellphone connection. Journalists who "go live" using their cellphone are far less recognizable than are journalists who are tethered to a live truck or stand in front of a TV camera. Do we live in a day when anytime you are in a public place you may fairly be broadcast to the world online without your permission?

Starting in 2015, newsrooms around the world began using camera-equipped drones, and by early 2016 newsrooms including WSB-TV in Atlanta and WFTV-TV in Orlando began using drones to supply live video to their newscasts. NBC News and CNN launched drones to fly over earthquake ruins in Nepal.[23] Real questions will arise in the years ahead about where a person's private space begins. If a drone hovered 50 feet over your back yard while you sunbathe, would that be an invasion of privacy? How about 500 feet? How about a satellite with a camera capable of zooming in to fill the screen with an image of you in your swimsuit in a lounge chair?

Before you use any live signal, on the air or online, ask these guiding questions:

- **Beyond competitive factors, what are your motivations for going live?** Why do your viewers need to know about this story before journalists have the opportunity to edit, question or filter the information off the air? What truth testing are you willing to give up to speed the information to the viewer?

- **Are you prepared to air the *worst possible* outcome that could result from this unfolding story (such as a person killing himself or someone else live on TV)?** What outcomes are you not willing to air? Why? How do you know the worst possible outcome will *not* occur?

- **What expectation of privacy would people whom you show in this live feed reasonably claim?** How does the public's need to know the information you are showing override the person's privacy claim?

- **How do you know that the information you are presenting live is true?** How many sources have confirmed the information?

How does the source know what he or she says to be true? What is this source's past reliability? How willing is the source to be quoted?

- **What are the consequences, short term and long term, of going on the air with the information?** What are the consequences of waiting for additional confirmation or for a regular newscast?

- **When you are covering a standoff between a suspect and police live, always assume that the hostage taker or attacker has access to the reporting.** Often, TV stations now stream breaking news coverage on their phone apps. Stations sometimes stream coverage on apps or social media that they do not break into their air signal to show live. On all platforms, avoid describing or showing any information that could divulge the tactics or positions of SWAT team members or other emergency workers. Be willing to tell viewers why you are withholding certain information if the reasons involve security. Weigh the benefits of reporting the story live to the public compared with the potential harm reporting might cause.

- **Newsrooms should have a general prohibition against telephoning a gunman or a hostage taker.** It is difficult to imagine the circumstances under which a newsroom might ethically and responsibly decide to violate this guideline. Journalists are rarely trained in professional hostage negotiations, and one wrong question or inappropriate word could jeopardize someone's life. Further, just calling the hostage taker could tie up phone lines or otherwise complicate negotiators' efforts to communicate with the person. When hostage takers or people making other threats call the newsroom, journalists should notify authorities immediately and resist the temptation to put the caller on the air live.

- **Things can go wrong very quickly in a live report, endangering lives or damaging negotiations.** Do not report without verifying information you hear on police scanners. Be aware that during live coverage repeating such information could compromise police negotiations or tactics. Be very cautious in any reporting on the medical condition of hostages until after a crisis is concluded. If a hostage taker hears from your reporting that someone he or she may have harmed has died, it could create a new air of desperation. Be cautious about interviewing hostages or released hostages while a crisis continues. There will be time to broadcast such statements once the situation is resolved.

- **What is the tone of the coverage?** How can the journalist raise viewer awareness while minimizing hype and fear? Who in your newsroom is responsible for monitoring the tone of what is being broadcast?

- **What electronic safety net has your station considered to minimize harm?** This might include a tape and signal delay, which could give you time to dump out of live coverage if the situation turns graphic or violent or if it compromises the safety of others?

- **How clearly does the technical crew at your TV station and website understand the newsroom's standard for graphic content?** How well are guidelines understood by directors, video editors, live-shot technicians, photojournalists, webmaster, social media director, pilots or engineers who might have to make an editorial call when the news director or other people in positions of formal authority are not available?

- **What factor does the time of day play in your decision to cover a breaking event?** If the event occurs when children normally are watching television, how does that fact alter the tone and degree of your coverage?

■ ■ ■ REMEMBER

Live coverage is an important tool for informing the public but carries with it a great responsibility for journalists to show restraint and professionalism.

NOTES

1. *Shulman v. Group W. Productions Inc.*, 955 P.2d 469 (Cal. 1998).
2. *Doe v. Sherman Publishing Co.*, 593 A.2d 457 (R.I. 1991).
3. Wilson Andrews, Mary Kate Cannistra, Ben de la Cruz, David S. Fallis, Lauren Keane, Todd Lindeman and Brenna Maloney, "The Hidden Life of Guns," *The Washington Post*, October 24, 2010, http://www.washington post.com/wp-srv/special/nation/guns/.

4. A version of this essay appeared on Poynter.org, December 27, 2012.

5. MSNBC, http://www.msnbc.msn.com/id/18140540/.

6. *The Guardian,* April 20, 2007, http://www.guardian.co.uk/media/2007/apr/20/1.

7. Poynter Online, The Poynter Institute, April 19, 2007.

8. Interview with the author, April 19, 2007.

9. Interview with the author December 20, 2013.

10. "Straighttalk," Sun News Network, June 5, 2014.

11. "Twins' Suicide Pact and the Columbine Connection," *The New York Times,* November 22, 2010, http://thelede.blogs.nytimes.com/2010/11/22/twins-suicide-pact-and-the-columbine-connection/?_r=1.

12. "Colorado Copycats Seek Attention and Payback, Experts Say," *The Denver Post,* July 27, 2012, http://www.denverpost.com/ci_21168563/colorado-copycats-seek-attention-and-payback-experts-say.

13. "A Murky Question from Colorado: Does Media Coverage Inspire Copycats?" *The Washington Post,* July 23, 2012, https://www.washingtonpost.com/lifestyle/style/putting-a-face-on-evil/2012/07/23/gJQALXSK5W_story.html.

14. *Tennessee v. Garner,* 471 U.S. 1 (1985).

15. Note: The author wrote a version of this essay that was published on Poynter.org, April 7, 2015, http://www.poynter.org/2015/graphic-new-york-times-video-seems-justified/333613/.

16. "Man Cleared in Cold Spring Cop Killing Sues KSTP-TV," *Star Tribune,* April 29, 2014, http://www.startribune.com/man-cleared-in-cold-spring-cop-killing-sues-kstp-tv/257020931/.

17. "Ryan Larson Case Shows Damage of Reporting 'Just the Facts,'" Minnesota Public Radio, April 29, 2014, http://blogs.mprnews.org/newscut/2014/04/ryan-larson-case-of-reporting-just-the-facts/.

18. "Father of Barway Collins, 'I killed my Son,'" *The Pioneer Press,* August 2, 2015, http://www.twincities.com/2015/08/02/father-of-barway-collins-i-killed-my-son/.

19. American Foundation for Suicide Prevention, https://afsp.org/about-suicide/suicide-statistics/.

20. Jason Foundation, http://jasonfoundation.com/prp/facts/youth-suicide-statistics/.

21. Source: http://www.cdc.gov/violenceprevention/suicide/statistics/.

22. Source: http://www.cdc.gov/nchs/fastats/leading-causes-of-death.htm.

23. "Networks Use Drones to Cover Nepal Quakes," Poynter.org, May 1, 2015, http://www.poynter.org/2015/networks-use-drones-to-cover-nepal-quake/340409/.

CHAPTER 18

Let's Get Critical

> *The important thing is never to stop questioning.*
>
> —Albert Einstein,
> Scientist

My teenage daughter (the same one who wrote about her "Luckiest Day Ever" in Chapter 2) and I sat on the couch watching *CSI: Crime Scene Investigation* when a commercial came on for a golden-colored "collectable coin." Here is what the commercial said:

> Look closely at history in the making. The $50 gold Buffalo coin is the purest gold coin ever made by the U.S. government. It's the first U.S. coin ever struck using .9999, that's four nine's 24 carat gold.
>
> Its design is based on the famous Buffalo nickel of 1913 to 1938. Wildly popular with investors and collectors, the U.S. government had to stop production because of a shortage of specially made gold blanks. It's no wonder the price of the last edition is going through the roof! Now, you can reserve your own copy of the $50 Buffalo gold clad tribute proof in 31 mg of pure gold.
>
> National Collector's Mint's private, non-monetary minting recreates James Earle Fraser's American Buffalo against a mirror-like background on one side and his iconic Native American

Indian Head stands out in stunning relief on the other. The final issue price was to be set at $50 per proof. But, during our special release, this 24-carat pure gold clad masterpiece can be yours for only $19.95. With gold skyrocketing past $1,000 an ounce, price can only be guaranteed for 7 days.

The commercial goes on to promise a "certificate of authenticity" and urges buyers to call now to "avoid disappointment and future regret," warning that there is a strict limit of "five proofs per caller." I asked my daughter what she thought she would get if she sent in $19.95. She said, "A gold coin worth a lot more."

I asked if she had heard the words "gold clad" in the commercial. She said "no."

"Right," I said. She was promised a "gold clad" coin.

The commercial said the coin is clad in 31 mg (that's milligrams) of pure gold. As I told my daughter, "That means the five-cent coin they were selling was dipped with a micro-thin layer of gold. It does not mean you are going to get a solid gold coin."

On the day I am writing this sentence, gold is trading at $1,271 per ounce. Thirty-one mg is equal to 0.0010934754 ounces, so the gold on that coin is worth less than $1.39.

I found similar coins selling on eBay for $6.95.

The commercial didn't outright lie. It revealed how much gold you were going to get and that it was a "copy" of the famous gold coin. The ad never said this version of the coin is worth any certain price.

Journalists have to learn to listen to information with Superman ears and watch events with X-ray vision. If you are going to work as a journalist, you have to learn to differentiate fact from crap.

In this chapter you will learn the following:

- How to kill "Zombie Stats," by sorting through information to separate fact and nonsense
- What journalists need to know about polling data
- Use critical thinking to investigate charities
- How to learn from my mistakes

Kill the Zombie Stats

An awful lot of what we read, see, hear or think is true, isn't.

For decades, powerful people including Hillary Clinton, Carly Fiorina and Secretary of the Treasury Jack Lew have repeated the claim, "70 percent of the people living in abject poverty are women." The statistic even appeared in the 2012 annual report that Walmart delivered to shareholders. For more than 20 years this statistic has made the rounds, and it is not true. It is a sort of "zombie stat." In fact, the World Bank says, poverty is more or less equally spread between genders and may even lean more toward men.[1]

The fact-finding website PunditFact.com found that the incorrect statistic may have originated in the 1995 Human Development Report by the United Nations.[2]

UN statisticians have since tried to correct the data but it lives on. There is a lesson in this one example that should haunt us. Ask, "How do we know that?"

Misinformation is so widespread that fact-checking websites such as PolitiFact and FactCheck.org have a steady stream of nonsense to debunk. PolitiFact checked more than 200 statements that Hillary Clinton made on a wide range of topics and ruled about half to be "Half True," "Mostly False," "False" or "Pants on Fire" lies.[3] PolitiFact's check of about 180 statements from Donald Trump found about 90 percent of the statements to be no better than "Half True" and about 60 percent were either "False" or "Pants on Fire" lies.[4]

With so much misinformation around, it would be easy to begin to think everybody's a liar and that you can't trust anybody.

BE SKEPTICAL, NOT CYNICAL

Instead of being cynical, I try to be skeptical. Journalists should be skeptical. Thomas Friedman of *The New York Times* put it this way: "Skepticism is about asking questions, being dubious, being wary, not being gullible. Cynicism is about already having the answers—or thinking you do—about a person or an event. The skeptic says, 'I don't think that's true; I'm going to check it out.' The cynic says, 'I know that's not true. It couldn't be. I'm going to slam him.'"[5]

Skepticism leads us to ask better questions. It is the product of curiosity and critical thinking.

I have never known a great journalist who lacked curiosity. If you are not curious, that's a red flag that you may not be cut out for journalism.

Here are some of the best questions that journalists ask:

- What do we know?
- What do we need to know?
- How do you know that to be true?
- What does this really mean?
- Is that really true?
- Who else knows that?
- Is there any other way of looking at that?
- Has it always been that way?
- Who profits from things being as they are?
- What motivations might a source have to say this is true?
- Does this claim seem reasonable?
- Is the person making the claim willing to be questioned about it?

Each of these questions is the product of curiosity and what I would call "critical thinking." Critical questioning as a journalist is simply the process through which we all evaluate what is or is not a "reasoned argument." I'm not talking about the form of critical thinking that's tied to years of academic study. The point here is to see that asking critical questions will allow you to go beyond understanding information to evaluate it.

QUESTION EVIDENCE THAT SEEMS RELIABLE

The Times-Picayune in New Orleans wondered whether composite police sketches, which have become a staple of crime reporting, are really of any value. The paper discovered that the sketches may actually cause harm to both innocent people and the criminal investigation.[6] The stories said,

In a study completed last year, three university researchers showed nearly 400 college students 12 police sketches of suspects—some computerized, some hand-drawn—alongside a photograph of each suspect's face. They were asked if the two images depicted the same person. Overall, the students said 70 percent of the time that the sketches were not of the same person.

American University professor John C. Watson, one of the researchers, called police sketches "highly suspect."

The biggest x-factor in whether a sketch is going to be helpful or harmful is the reliability of the victim's memory, which is often difficult to gauge. Watson said witnesses are under stress during a crime, and emotion makes it hard to nail down important facial details.

The Times-Picayune had a lot of statistical evidence, generated by years of studies. One study found that the sketches are so unreliable that it might even be unethical for journalists to publish or air them.

Despite repeated studies over 30 years that prove the unreliability of police sketches, journalists print and air them. Ask these questions first:

- Where did the description come from?
- What is the past reliability of this department's sketch artist?
- How close was the witness to the criminal?
- What were the conditions at the time?
- Was it dark?
- Was a weapon involved? Often, criminologists say, victims get a great description of a weapon but a less reliable description of the person holding it because the victim is so focused on the weapon.
- Were the victim and the criminal of different races or ethnicities? Cross-race identification also has proven to be less reliable than when the victim and criminal are of the same race.

SEEK CONTRARY EVIDENCE

Did you put as much effort into disproving the allegations as you did in proving them? Great investigators stay open to the idea their original information is not accurate. They do *not* believe everyone is a crook or a liar. Great investigators are neither cynical nor gullible. How hard did you try to give voice to people who would be critical of your findings?

■ ■ ■ REMEMBER

Journalists should be skeptical but not cynical. Ask questions that will reveal the motives of the person or group supplying the information. Where else can you go to verify or contradict the information?

CRITICAL THINKING AND POLLING

Polling is a part of American culture. In fact the U.S. Constitution and federal statutes require a national poll, the U.S. Census, every 10 years.[7] In addition to the U.S. Census, the government questions another 3 million households every year to get detailed data on income, marital status, ancestry and 27 other categories.[8]

Thirty years after the government began conducting the federal census, newspapers began conducting polls around 1820 as part of their election coverage.[9]

By the 1930s, the polls were accurate enough to predict Franklin Roosevelt's landslide election victory. Polling organizations including Gallup found a regular spot in more than 100 newspapers nationwide. Polling became a component of the American political ritual.

By the late 1970s, news organizations including *The New York Times*, *The Washington Post* and NBC, CBS and ABC News all developed their own polling units to probe political questions and to understand the public attitudes around social issues.

Polling is so common today that you can find daily tracking polls on everything from the public's attitude toward the president's performance to opinions on topics in the news. Rasmussen Reports publishes a daily presidential tracking poll.[10] The slogan on its website says, "If it's in the news, it's in our polls."

SHOULD WE BELIEVE POLLS?

A poll's reliability depends on many factors:

- Who paid for the poll?
- Who did the pollster talk with?
- How many people did the pollster talk with?
- Were the people who were polled the "right" people for the topic?
- What did the pollster ask?
- How was the poll conducted?
- Did anything dramatic change after the poll was conducted?

Most of the questions fall under the critical thinking questions, "What do we need to know?" and "How do we know what we know?"

WHO PAID FOR THE POLL?

Let's say I post a poll on my website reporting that, "A new poll shows *Aim for the Heart* to be the finest journalism textbook of this century."

You would be right to ask questions like, "Says who?" You should also ask, "Who paid for this poll?" If you found out that I paid for it, a smart reader would question the poll results.

So it is with political polling. Ask who paid for the polling and ask who did the polling. Some pollsters work for political parties, some for candidates and some work for special-interest political action committees that have a political agenda. It doesn't mean their data is bad, just that you should read it with a skeptical filter.

In Mexico, polling organizations are required by federal law to supply the federal election commission with details about their polling methods and results. There is no such requirement in the United States, but I would not trust a poll that didn't freely disclose its methods.

"How good do you think Al Tompkins' awesome book is?" is biased. "How would you rank Al Tompkins' book?" is more evenhanded.

Serious pollsters probe topics by approaching them in different ways.

"On average, how honest are our city council members?" may associate the word "honest" with the council members. But ask it in a different way and the question might plant a negative notion in the respondent's mind. "On average, how frustrated are you by dishonesty on the city council?" almost certainly frames the council as being untrustworthy.

In a primary with a lot of candidates, the pollster should randomize the order of the candidates so the same candidate does not come up as the last one mentioned in a long list.

Legitimate pollsters may belong to accrediting groups including the European Society for Opinion and Market Research (ESOMAR), the World Association for Public Opinion Research (WAPOR) or American Association for Public Opinion Research (AAPOR). These groups have developed standards adopted by polling and marketing survey groups since 1948. Members are forbidden from using information they gain during polling to compile marketing lists or sell products while conducting a survey. They are forbidden from "negative campaigning" while conducting a survey. Critically thinking journalists should ask who conducted the poll and whether they are members of professional polling organizations.

MARGINS OF ERROR

Every poll that is based on a sample of respondents has some room for error. The 2010 U.S. Census, the largest poll conducted in America, counted 308,745,538 people and still says it missed 2.1 percent of black Americans and 1.5 percent of Hispanics.[12] The margin of error, a percentage that the poll will overcount or underestimate, depends on several factors. Some are controllable and some are not.

Generally, the more people a pollster can survey, the more accurate the poll and the lower the margin of error is likely to be. Pollsters can estimate how accurate their calculations are likely to be compared with what they would have found if they could have interviewed every person in the survey area.

If a sample is properly drawn, if the people being polled are an adequate representation of the population as a whole, then a pollster can interview 1,000 people and expect a sampling error of plus or minus 3 percent. So in a race where a poll shows one candidate with 47 percent and another with 53 percent, the race can be a dead heat.

The Roper Center for Public Opinion Research explains: "Most surveys report margin of error in a manner such as: 'The results of this survey are accurate at the 95% confidence level plus or minus 3 percentage points.' That is the error that can result from the process of selecting the sample."[13]

WHAT ELSE CAN ADD TO POLLING ERRORS?

Unrepresentative sample sizes are one way polls can return a skewed picture of what the public is thinking. But there are other factors to consider. For example, if the pollster is asking a question that produces a lopsided result, you can have more confidence in that finding than if the result is evenly split. When more people agree or disagree, there is less of a chance of error in the estimate.[14]

Depending on what they want to learn in a survey, pollsters design a target audience to survey. It will include a certain number of men, women, young and old, and the poll will hear from samples of different races and incomes that reflect the total population. But there are lots of reasons pollsters may not reach all of those people. They might not get enough people of one group or another to answer the survey, the topic might be too controversial, or maybe people just don't like getting phone calls from strangers. Pollsters call this the "Design Effect."

Pollsters also have a phrase for questions that may be too controversial for people to answer honestly. "Social Desirability Bias" shows up when respondents say what they think is socially acceptable rather than what they truly think about such issues as same-sex marriage, abortion and religion. Pollsters sometimes call this the "Bradley Effect," after the 1982 California gubernatorial election between Tom Bradley, a black Democrat, and George Deukmejian, a white Republican. Pre-election polls showed Bradley ahead by as many as 22 points, but he lost the election. Pew Research said a pattern of polling errors arose when respondents were reluctant to say they were planning to vote against a black candidate.[15]

Sometimes polls can appear to be wrong because, after the survey is completed, a bombshell revelation about a candidate or a terrible or stellar debate performance can change voter attitudes or motivate voters to turn out or stay home on Election Day. As Gallup explains, "An election that has racial overtones, for example, might activate minorities more than usual. An election that has hotly debated labor-related issues might activate union members."

So it is important to know when the survey was taken and what, if anything, has happened since.

And when pollsters underestimate who will vote, the data becomes unreliable. In the 2016 Michigan Democratic presidential primary, for example, Bernie Sanders won by 1.5 percentage points while numerous polls showed Hillary Clinton to have a 21-point lead. Polls didn't foresee the surge of voters under age 30 who turned out for Sanders. One reason researchers may have missed those young voters is because they relied on landline phones and most Americans under age 45 do not have landline phones.[16]

And pollsters are finding that people seem less willing to answer surveys these days.[17]

Nate Silver's FiveThirtyEight.com website also said independent voters turned out in unexpectedly high numbers for Sanders, many more black voters than expected backed Sanders in Michigan and Sanders scored big in a Sunday night debate before the Tuesday vote. The polls didn't account for the surge that followed.[18]

HOW WAS THE POLL CONDUCTED?

The Gallup organization uses random-digit dial (RDD) as its survey design in countries where at least 80 percent of the population uses landline phones.[19] But in developing countries including much of Latin America, nearly all of Asia, Africa and the Middle East, Gallup relies on face-to-face polling.

Cliff Zukin, professor of public policy and political science at Rutgers University and a past president of the AAPOR, wrote that in the 2016 election cycle, pollsters trying to complete a 1,000-person survey have to call 20,000 numbers and when they speak with people using cell-phones, they often pay the person up to $10 per survey to cover data charges. Pew Research now completes two mobile phone surveys for every landline survey.[20]

Exit polls are small samples of voters taken after they leave the voting place. Pollsters use the data to project how all voters or voter segments cast their ballots. Exit polls also give analysts insight into who came out to vote and why. Exit polls are especially valuable because the pollster is gathering data from people who actually voted, not just those who are likely to vote.

Since 2003, Fox, CNN, NBC, ABC, CBS and the Associated Press have centralized their exit polling through Edison Research.[21] Exit polls question 100 to 150 voters in sample precincts. For example, in the 2016 New Hampshire primary, Edison questioned voters in 45 precincts. As the actual election results are reported on Election Day, pollsters compare their exit polling to the vote data and often can accurately and confidently project who will win a race before all of the votes are counted.

Tracking polls can be useful to identify trends. Tracking polls ask the same question at regular intervals so the public can compare responses over time. Gallup, for example, has conducted tracking polls on American attitudes toward religion for decades. Similarly, tracking polls that measure the popularity of the Affordable Care Act and attitudes toward gun control also reveal significant dips and peaks that shape public policy.[22]

Push polls are more of a marketing technique. They sometimes sound like a legitimate poll but include questions that attempt to influence (push) the respondent into having a positive or negative response toward a candidate or idea. Professional polling associations including the AAPOR have formally condemned push polls.[23]

Straw polls are highly unreliable and may have the highest margins of error of all. A TV station might ask viewers to call in and vote yes or no on a question or vote a contestant off a program. The poll only reflects those people who are watching and are willing and able to phone in. And there is nothing to prevent the same person from voting multiple times. Straw polls are not even accurate enough to call a popularity contest. Sometimes candidates used straw polls to test support for an idea.

Online polls would be useful if pollsters could find a way to make the sample more reflective of the population. When the only people being surveyed are those who visit a website, it is a specialized sample that isn't scientific.[24] Pollsters also consider the "probability sample," which estimates whether every person has an equal chance of being selected in a survey. If the probability of being excluded is high, the survey is unreliable. Online polling generally has a "nonprobability" sample, meaning the probability of being included or excluded is unknown. If you show up, you get counted. The AAPOR says it isn't even possible to know the margin of error for polls conducted that way. Another consideration for online polls is that about 40 percent of those 65 and older do not use the internet, but they make up 22 percent of voters. And online polling commonly undercounts Hispanic and blacks.[25]

Even when a poll is not statistically reliable, websites still have fun with popularity polls. Sometimes they ask questions about who should win this year's Oscar or who is the best *Star Wars* character of all time.[26] Just remember that online polls are missing big chunks of the population.

As a journalist, you have to ask how reliable any polling numbers are and how the survey was conducted. Ask what the probability is of being included or excluded.

WHY ARE POLLS NEWS?

In every election cycle, the conversation eventually turns to "Why do journalists cover the horse race? Why not just cover the issues?" I would say let's cover both. Polling gives insight into what voters or even nonvoters want from candidates. Exit polls in 2016, for example, show that young black voters are not voting in larger numbers even though there are more young blacks of voting age than in 2008 and despite the engagement with the Black Lives Matter movement.[27]

Sometimes polls are newsworthy because they can prove or disprove what the candidates say. When Donald Trump said to CNN, "Frankly, Hillary Clinton doesn't do very well with women voters," PolitiFact responded hours later by showing seven out of seven national polls in which Clinton led Trump among women voters.[28]

Polls guide candidates to downplay or emphasize issues or perceptions. A Pew Research poll found Trump and Clinton to be considered the "least religious" of the leading candidates in the 2016 primary. Trump quickly appeared before evangelical groups to try to prove otherwise.[29] Why? Pew says its research shows "being seen as a religious person is generally an asset for candidates; people who think a candidate is a religious person tend to be more likely to see that candidate as a potentially good president."[30] In short, polling can help journalists understand why candidates focus on some campaign issues over others.

Polls can show the public's reaction to candidates' campaign actions. In the 2016 election, polls showed primary voters didn't seem to mind when Republican Trump made outrageous statements about women or minorities.[31]

And polls are vitally important to campaign finance. Contributors tend to back candidates who are most likely to win. When polls show support is dropping, the money dries up, too. When polls show the race to be tight, candidates can use the numbers to push for more money.[32]

The New York Times media writer Jim Rutenberg rightly criticizes journalists who spend too much time guessing who will win and not enough time making sense of candidate positions on important issues. He wrote, "In the end, you have to point the finger at national political journalism, which has too often lost sight of its primary directives in this election season: to help readers and viewers make sense of the presidential chaos; to reduce the confusion, not add to it; to resist the urge to put ratings, clicks and ad sales above the imperative of getting it right."[33]

In some election years as far back as 1980, as many as half of network primary election stories were focused on horse-race coverage. And it's not just TV coverage that loves a political horse race. *The New York Times* public editor Margaret Sullivan studied two weeks' worth of *Times'* political coverage and found, "Of the 234 political stories in that period (an astonishing number in itself), 180 could reasonably be called 'horse-race' stories. That's more than three of every four articles."[34] Another piece of the puzzle is that the horse-race stories seemed to attract more audience. Half of the newspaper's "most popular" stories in the weeks studied were horse-race stories. None of the issue stories were among the most popular stories of the week.

Using Critical Thinking to Investigate Charities

I admit that I was nervous one morning when I introduced a class of TV newscast producers to a new classroom exercise I developed. I knew what their reaction would be when I plopped a 60-page tax return in front of each of the producers. They groaned, they complained and they told me, "I don't do math." They could not imagine getting excited about spending two hours combing through a tax document. My job that day, and my job in the next few pages, is to change that attitude.

Government filings, such as court documents, inspection records and tax returns are the mother's milk of journalism. They are loaded with facts and nuances that can become the foundation of indisputably true stories. But to make sense of mountains of documents, you have to learn to ask critical questions.

WHAT A TAX DOCUMENT WILL TELL YOU

The document I placed in front of those producers is an I-990 tax form. It is a 12-month snapshot of an organization's activities. Any nonprofit or charity (except churches) that takes in $25,000 a year or more must file an I-990 with the Internal Revenue Service (IRS). The document looks very much like the tax documents that we all file, with one big difference: the I-990 is "open to public inspection." It is a public document. That is the trade-off that nonprofits make so they do not pay income taxes. They must disclose all of their income, expenses, assets and accomplishments. They must file these forms every year. You can get these forms in many places. Websites such as Guidestar.com post every I-990 filed in the United States. Charities often must file these forms with state and local agencies as well. Churches, by the way, do not file I-990s because of the separation between church and state, which allows churches to keep their finances confidential.[35]

With a few clicks of the mouse, you can be on your way to telling a story about how much a university foundation or alumni association or even Donald Trump's family foundation made and spent. Pet shelters, United Way, Make-A-Wish, breast cancer support groups and international relief organizations all are examples of nonprofits that must file I-990 reports. The Poynter Institute, where I work, files I-990 reports. You can find out which individuals were paid the most and what the charity says it has accomplished with the money.

Political committees do not file I-990s either, but they have tons of other financial disclosure documents to file with election commissions.

READING THE FRONT PAGE OF THE I-990

I-990s contain four main sections clearly listed on the left side of the page: "Revenue," "Expenses," "Net Assets" and "Activities and Governance."

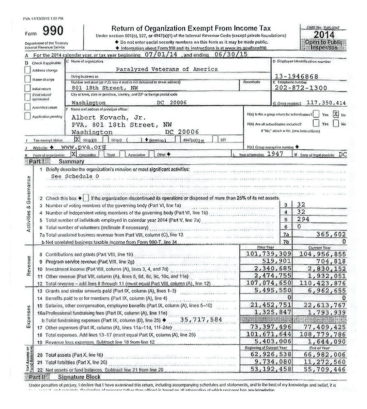

Let's look at the example that I handed to that class of producers. The return we will use is real, filed by a Washington, D.C.–based charity, the Paralyzed Veterans of America (PVA). I chose this charity partly because its name sounds like the sort of cause most people would strongly support, especially in wartime. I also chose it because this charity's tax return raises big questions about how PVA spends the $117 million dollars it raised in a year in the name of injured veterans.

In 2015, the charity spent its money like this:

- Program Expenses: 32.8 percent
- Administrative Expenses: 4.9 percent
- Fundraising Expenses: 62.2 percent

In a snapshot, you would see it spent nearly twice as much on fundraising as it did on programs that it says help veterans. But, as they say on those TV infomercials, "Wait, there's more."

PVA spent nearly $60 million on mail programs for fundraising. But it counted $31,968,627 worth of brochures and other printed materials that it mailed to potential donors as part of its program expenses.

	(A) Total expenses	(B) Program service expenses	(C) Management and general expenses	(D) Fundraising expenses
MAIL PROGRAM FUNDRAISING	59,988,370	31,969,627	1,684,433	26,334,310

That means the program expense category of 32.8 percent is actually less because more than half of the money it says went to "programs" actually is spent on brochures to raise money. PVA tells the IRS that it is part of their "program" to educate the public about spinal cord injuries and the PVA says the brochures do that. And the IRS lets them get by with it even though charity-rating groups don't.[36]

The I-990 shows PVA spent $12.5 million on postage. It spent $6.5 million on mail labels. It paid a marketing team another $5.7 million and brought more than $4 million in "gifts" that it sent to donors.

Let's use some of the techniques we have explored in this chapter and apply some critical questioning:

- If a charity spends more than half of its income on fundraising, does that mean the charity is ineffective?

- Is one year's I-990 enough? Should we examine several years' worth of these filings to determine whether there was anything unusual about this year?

- Does an I-990 really capture the essence of the charity? What interviews would help to clarify your understanding?

- Did the PVA experience unusual growth, losses, change in leadership, new demands on services? How did those events affect this one year's I-990 report?

BIG CLAIMS, LITTLE MEANING

PVA proudly points out in its website (www.pva.org) and in its I-990 that the organization has been around since 1946 and is a "congressionally chartered veterans service." But what does this really mean?

Congressional charters were necessary for corporations operating in the District of Columbia because Washington, D.C., did not have the legal authority to issue corporate charters.[37]

The Congressional Research Service (CRS) issued a report stating, "In effect, the federal charter process is honorific in character. This honorific character may be misleading to the public, however when such organizations feature statements or display logos that they are 'chartered by Congress,' thus implying a direct relationship to the federal

For example the Central Florida Community College address is http://www.cfcc.cc.fl.us. At the same time, Nashville State Community College in Tennessee is not a four-year school but uses an .edu web domain (http://www.nscc.edu). You are likely to find everything from barber colleges to Harvard under the .edu listings. In short, remember that many schools of higher education are not .edu sites, and some .edu websites are not typical colleges and universities.

- .gov is a government designation. The .gov and .fed websites are managed by the General Services Administration (GSA).[39] To qualify for a .gov designation, the GSA says a site must be one of these:

  a. U.S. governmental departments, programs and agencies on the federal level
  b. Federally recognized tribes of Native Americans
  c. State governmental entities/programs
  d. Cities and townships represented by an elected body of officials
  e. Counties and parishes represented by an elected body of officials
  f. U.S. territories

Sites that do not qualify for .gov designation include these:

  g. Local (e.g., city, county, township or parish) government programs or initiatives
  h. Cities, townships, counties, parishes and other local entities that are not represented by an elected body of officials

There are also country extensions. Each means the website originates in that country, such as:

  i. .us is the United States
  j. .ca, Canada
  k. .it, Italy
  l. .uk, United Kingdom

It is fairly easy to find out who owns a website and how to get in touch with the website owner. Go to www.allwhois.org and enter the website name. The name of the registrant will pop up along with a contact phone number.

A QUICK INVESTIGATION CAN
SAVE YOUR REPUTATION

In early May 2016, one of the hottest stories through the news cycle involved a controversial North Carolina law called HB2 that reversed an ordinance extending some rights to people who are gay or transgender. The state law nullified city ordinances in such places as Charlotte that protected people who use public restrooms based on their gender identity.

Some 80 big businesses, including the leaders of Apple and Facebook, protested. Some musicians cancelled concerts to North Carolina. So when a Facebook post appeared saying basketball legend Michael Jordan, who grew up in North Carolina, threatened to move his NBA basketball team from North Carolina, it sounded possible. The post seemed to be legitimate. It included a link that mentioned ABC News and cited a story by the Associated Press.

Michael Jordan To North Carolina: 'HB2 Goes Or The Charlotte Hornets Go'

By abcnews - May 7, 2016 👁 *4765* 💬 *43*

But a careful examination of the URL for the story showed it didn't live on ABCnews.go.com, where the real network parks its stories. Instead this story about Jordan was on abcnews.com.co, which is connected to a satire web company that opposes HB2. To find that connection I just went to allwhois.com and entered the URL. I looked up the owner of the URL and then looked for other websites that owner operated. Many of them are protests about issues that are in the news. Some included fake phone numbers that lead to the Westboro Baptist Church in Kansas, a wildly controversial group that opposes homosexuality.

NOT EVERY CRAZY-SOUNDING STORY IS CRAZY

Sometimes the nuttiest sounding tips turn out not to be so nutty. Fox News, among others, repeatedly passed along the rumors that the federal government was flying drones over the countryside to spy on law-abiding people. At one point, Fox News reported the drones were just like the missile-packing drones used in fighting terrorists in Iraq

Courier-Journal reporter Bill Osinski (who later would be a finalist for a Pulitzer Prize for investigative reporting), Daniel kept changing his story, could not point out where the contest had been and even started suggesting that he had been duped and maybe even drugged by contest organizers. The *Courier-Journal* had been sucked into the hoax as well and was trying to get to the bottom of the whole stinking rotten mess.[43]

Deputy Daniel lost his job. He never did explain why he pulled the stunt. But looking back, any journalist should have been skeptical. What are the chances that Daniel would have been asked, in an international organ-playing championship, to play something titled "The Sheriff Boogie"? What are the chances that this deputy was really the nephew of Mahalia Jackson and toured the globe with her playing for presidents and royalty, as he claimed? Why would he not allow us to film him playing, and why didn't he supply family photos? Why would a contest that he claimed drew thousands of people be held in London, Ontario, a city of fewer than a half million people, rather than Toronto?

Why didn't I find out that there is no American Organists Association? (The professional organization for organists is the American Guild of Organists. The group celebrates early music and baroque music, not boogie-woogie.) Deputy Daniel said he played on a 700-stop organ. I never asked what that means. To put things in perspective, the Mormon Tabernacle organ in Salt Lake City, one of the world's biggest pipe organs, has only 188 stops.[44]

I grew up in the country and I was beginning to realize I was naïve. Until I became a journalist, I didn't have enough influence that made me worth lying to. But now I had a camera, a microphone and a transmitter. I could turn deputies into celebrities.

I was lucky. I had a compassionate boss, Alan Palmer. He hired me from radio, so I think he felt responsible for what he had imposed on the WBKO's television viewers. In the decades I have known him, I have never heard him yell or lose his temper. He never threatened to fire or even suspend me. He knew I needed the job and money to stay in school. When I made a colossal mistake, his face would take on a crimson glow and he would quietly say how I disappointed him. Oh man, that hurt.

I tried to be more curious and less willing to take people's word as truth without evidence. I am not cynical (usually), but I do like proof. A cynic is "contemptuously distrustful of human nature and motives."[45] I do think I have become a lot more skeptical, however. There is a big difference. As journalist David Broder put it, "if the assumption is that nothing is on the level, nothing is what it seems, then citizenship becomes a game for fools and there is no point in trying to stay informed."

■ ■ ■ REMEMBER

Critical questioning and thinking requires the journalist to get beyond the "what" of the story to deeper questions such as Why? How often? Who benefits from the situation being as it is? Who has the power to keep it this way? Who else knows this to be true? Where can I find records to prove this? Who else should I talk with? Where should I go next to develop this story? Be skeptical but not cynical.

NOTES

1. Pedro Olinto, Kathleen Beegle, Carlos Sobrado, and Hiroki Uematsu, "The State of the Poor: Where Are The Poor, Where Is Extreme Poverty Harder to End, and What Is the Current Profile of the World's Poor?" (Washington, DC: World Bank, October 2013).
2. Jon Greenberg, "Meet the 'Zombie Stat' That Just Won't Die," Punditfact .com, July 3, 2014.
3. Source: http://www.politifact.com/personalities/hillary-clinton/.
4. Source: http://www.politifact.com/personalities/donald-trump/.
5. "Listen to Your Heart," commencement address by Thomas L. Friedman at Williams College, Williamstown, Massachusetts, June 5, 2005, http:// www.humanity.org/voices/commencements/speeches/index.php?page=-friedman_at_williams.
6. Brenda McCarthy, "Police Sketches Nabbed Three in Wendy Byrne Murder in French Quarter, but Effectiveness Still Debated," *The Times-Picayune*, Jan. 27, 2009. http://www.nola.com/news/index.ssf/2009/01/effective ness_of_police_sketch.html.
7. Constitution of the United States, Article I, Section 2 and Title 13, U.S. Code. Title 13, U.S. Code).
8. U.S. Census Bureau American Community Survey, https://www.census .gov/programs-surveys/acs/.

9. Irving Crespi, "Polls and the News Media: A Symposium," *The Public Opinion Quarterly* 44, no. 4 (Winter, 1980), 462.

10. Source: http://www.rasmussenreports.com.

11. Source: http://www.gallup.com/poll/111268/How-Gallups-likely-voter-models-work.aspx.

12. Source: http://usnews.nbcnews.com/_news/2012/05/22/11811481-census-bureau-2010-population-count-was-pretty-accurate?lite.

13. Source: http://ropercenter.cornell.edu/support/polling-fundamentals-total-survey-error/.

14. Gary Langer, "Sampling Error: What It Means," ABC News, October 8, 2008, http://abcnews.go.com/PollingUnit/sampling-error-means/story?id=5984818.

15. Pew Research Center, "Can You Trust What the Polls Say about Obama's Electoral Prospects?" February 7, 2007, http://www.pewresearch.org/2007/02/07/can-you-trust-what-polls-say-about-obamas-electoral-prospects/.

16. Source: http://www.cdc.gov/nchs/data/nhis/earlyrelease/wireless201512.pdf.

17. "What's the Matter With Polling?" *The New York Times*, June 20, 2015 http://www.nytimes.com/2015/06/21/opinion/sunday/whats-the-matter-with-polling.html?_r=0.

18. Source: http://fivethirtyeight.com/features/why-the-polls-missed-bernie-sanders-michigan-upset/.

19. Gallup World Poll Research Design: http://media.gallup.com/WorldPoll/PDF/WPResearchDesign091007bleeds.pdf.

20. "What's the Matter With Polling?" *The New York Times*, June 20, 2015 http://www.nytimes.com/2015/06/21/opinion/sunday/whats-the-matter-with-polling.html?_r=0.

21. Philip Bump, "How Exit Polls Work," *The Washington Post*, April 22, 2016.

22. Kaiser Health Tracking Polls: The Public's Views on the ACA: http://kff.org/interactive/kaiser-health-tracking-poll-the-publics-views-on-the-aca/#?response=Favorable--Unfavorable&aRange=twoYear; Gallup religion polling since 1948: http://www.gallup.com/poll/1690/religion.aspx.

23. "Types of Polls." *Boundless Political Science*. Boundless, August 12, 2015. Retrieved May 18, 2016, from https://www.boundless.com/political-science/textbooks/boundless-political-science-textbook/public-opinion-6/measuring-public-opinion-46/types-of-polls-269-1480/.

24. Pew Research, "Evaluating Online Probability Surveys" http://www.pewresearch.org/2016/05/02/evaluating-online-nonprobability-surveys/.

25. Ibid.
26. Source: https://www.washingtonpost.com/ballotbuilder/.
27. "Despite Black Lives Matter, Young Black Americans Not Voting in Higher Numbers," *The Washington Post*, May 14, 2016.
28. "Donald Trump Wrong That Hillary Clinton 'Doesn't Do Very Well With Women,'" Politifact.com, May 2, 2016, http://www.politifact.com/truth -o-meter/statements/2016/may/02/donald-trump/donald-trump-wrong -hillary-clinton-doesnt-do-very-/.
29. "Pew Poll: Donald Trump, Hillary Clinton Seen as Least Religious Candidates," CNN, January 27, 2016, http://www.cnn.com/2016/01/27/ politics/donald-trump-pew-religion-poll-atheists/.
30. Faith and the 2016 Campaign: Pew Research Center, January 27, 2016.
31. "GOP Voters Still Support Trump's Muslim Ban," Rasmussen Reports, April 4, 2016, http://www.rasmussenreports.com/public_content/politics/ current_events/immigration/march_2016/gop_voters_still_support_ trump_s_muslim_ban.
32. "Hillary's Campaign Cites Close Swing State Polls in Fundraising E-Mail," National Review, May 11, 2016, http://www.nationalreview.com/corner/435246/ hillarys-campaign-cites-close-swing-state-polls-fundraising-e-mail.
33. Jim Rutenberg, "The Republican Horse Race Is Over and Journalism Lost," *The New York Times*, May 9, 2016, B1, http://www.nytimes .com/2016/05/06/business/media/the-republican-horse-race-is-over -and-journalism-lost.html?_r=0.
34. Margaret Sullivan, "Waiter, Where's Our Political Spinach?" *The New York Times*, March 5, 2016, http://www.nytimes.com/2016/03/06/public -editor/new-york-times-public-editor-presidential-campaign.html.
35. IRS I-990 bulletin.
36. Source: http://www.give.org/charity-reviews/national/veterans-and -military/paralyzed-veterans-of-america-in-washington-dc-2621.
37. "Title 36 Corporations: What They Are and How Congress Treats Them," Congressional Research Service, April 8, 2004.
38. Source: http://www.tampabay.com/americas-worst-charities/.
39. Source: http://www.dotgov.gov/.
40. Source: http://www.thenewamerican.com/usnews/constitution/item/11607 -epa-defends-use-of-spy-drones-over-iowa-neb-cattle-ranches.
41. Source: http://www.cbsnews.com/news/ap-fbi-using-low-flying-spy-planes -over-us/.
42. "FBI Aviation Purpose and Scope," Statement from the Federal Bureau of Investigation, June 4, 2015, https://www.fbi.gov/news/pressrel/press -releases/fbi-aviation-program-purpose-and-scope.

find context and meaning. Enterprise is at the heart of great journalism. Sadly, I find it missing from many newscasts as I travel coast to coast.

In this chapter you will learn the following:

- Ways to turn the morning editorial meeting into the most important hour of the news day
- How to find new people and places for memorable enterprise stories
- Look for the story behind the story.

ENTERPRISE FROM THE START: MORNING MEETINGS

Exasperated news directors ask me, "Where have all of the great stories gone? Why don't reporters seem to find news? How can our station find stories nobody else finds? Why don't reporters and producers contribute any ideas about what we should cover?" These questions and hundreds like them all point to the same trouble spot in TV newsrooms. Newsrooms need to rethink the morning meeting. If your morning meeting is unproductive, unimaginative and non-inclusive, your newscast will show it.

That crucial hour or so does more to set the tone of a newsroom than any other hour of the day, including the evening news hour(s). That is often the only time in the day when the newsroom meets as a team to discuss values and ideas and, by extension, to develop its culture and style. Often, it offers the most one-on-one conversation that reporters and producers have with newsroom managers. How can we make this important time more useful?

YOU GET WHAT YOU INSPECT MORE THAN WHAT YOU EXPECT

Enterprise reporting takes shape in the daily morning editorial meeting. Morning meetings often begin with an assignment editor reciting the event calendar, but great morning meetings don't end there. Planned events should be the *minimum* of what a newsroom considers for the day's coverage.

How would you describe the tone of your morning meeting? Is it, "Here is what we are going to do. Now, let's go feed the beast"? Or does it begin with, "We are looking for the strongest stories today. We have some events and topics in mind, but if your ideas are stronger, let's go for it." Allow the story motivators that are described in Chapter 4 to shape your story pitches.

Producers and news managers must honor great enterprise ideas by giving them airtime and resources.

A newsroom that honors enterprise sets its own tone—it has decided what it stands for and makes coverage decisions accordingly. A newsroom that emphasizes enterprise reporting is proactive, not solely reactive. A newsroom that emphasizes enterprise reporting leads the audience toward important issues. A newsroom that emphasizes enterprise reporting finds topics that others seldom cover and includes people who are otherwise seldom seen—and includes those topics and people in the newscasts.

Enterprise reporting means thinking more creatively about the standard fare of stories that stations cover. John Lansing, a longtime photojournalist, news director and now chief executive of the Broadcasting Board of Governors, the agency that oversees U.S. government–supported, civilian international news media such as Voice of America, said, "You have to find the words that describe great stories." He added, "Let's say the assignment editor walks into a news meeting and says, 'There is a ground breaking at Fifth and Main for the new arts center. Let's send somebody over to spray it.'" That sort of language, "spray it," conveys a specific idea of what you expect the journalists to cover that day and more importantly how you expect them to cover it. It says you will be satisfied if the person shoots a little video, grabs the press release and leaves. But Lansing said, "If the same assignment editor said, 'The most interesting piece of architecture to be built in America in the last 20 years is having its grand opening. Let's do a piece about the new contemporary arts center. This story should include what this building means to downtown and what it means to the future architecture of our city.' Both story pitches are different ways of looking at the same story." But the second one provides a vision and sets an expectation for excellence.[1]

Great newsrooms cultivate a forward-thinking atmosphere. In these newsrooms part of a reporter's job description is to file daily story notes at

If the meeting is packed with white men in suits, how can you expect to think of stories that minorities and women want to see? If the morning meeting is packed with 30-something-year-olds but nobody more than age 40, how can you expect to know what your most loyal viewers, who are more than age 50, want to see tonight? Does anyone in the room have kids? (Thirty percent of your viewers do.)

INCLUDE THE WEB IN YOUR PLANNING

Make sure your editorial meetings include discussions about how you will file stories for the web and social media as the day unfolds. Talk about how the web version will be different from the TV version.

What documents might the web post as part of the online story? How can online readers interact with the story? What online discussions might pop up as a result of the story? Enterprise is about finding new stories and new ways to tell them. Don't allow your web coverage to be an afterthought. I can always tell if a newsroom is serious about its digital presence by how it talks about or ignores online in the editorial meetings. Stations that value online and social media content plan for it early in the daily news cycle.

EFFICIENT MEETINGS DO NOT EQUAL EFFECTIVE MEETINGS

Nobody has time to waste on an unproductive meeting. Reporters and photojournalists want to get out the door and start shooting their stories. Producers want to start scanning the wires, writing and searching feeds for interesting material.

But efficiency does not always equal effectiveness. Don't hurry through the meeting with such speed that people don't have time to pitch a great idea. And a short morning meeting that ends in confusion about "who is doing what" isn't effective. Newsrooms spend a lot of time redirecting crews and thinking up fallback plans at midday when morning meetings fail to include a full discussion of a story idea. The morning meeting is an investment in the rest of the day.

"The daily meeting is crucial to how I do my work," says Boyd Huppert, award-winning reporter at KARE-TV, Minneapolis. "That is the most important half-hour or hour of the day. If we don't get our plans right then, the rest of the day is a mess."

Be prompt; start your meeting on time. Meetings that always start late tend to train participants to come in late.

BE WILLING TO STOP THE MEETING

More than once I have temporarily adjourned a morning meeting because it was clear we did not have enough good ideas on the table to go forward with a productive news day. By adjourning for a half hour, we were able to make another round of calls to sources and check wires and internet sites to find better leads. Newsrooms should have the courage to stop meetings if they are going nowhere. By making that suggestion, even if you are not the boss, you send a signal that your newsroom has a standard for quality you will not compromise.

■ ■ ■ REMEMBER

Morning meetings set the tone for the newsroom's day. Newsrooms should develop a culture of enterprise reporting, valuing stories that explain the "why, how often and what about that" questions as much as they value stories that only address "what happened."

How to Generate Enterprise Stories

How are you going to find stories that others miss? It starts by breaking out of your routine. Here are a few suggestions.

SEEK THE IDEAS OF OTHERS

More voices add richness, diversity and perspective to your ideas. How can you talk to more people who might have great ideas for stories? My favorite sources included a pharmacist, a pediatrician, a real-estate developer, a mechanic, a junkyard owner, an aviation expert, a veterinarian, a grocery store manager and a county jailer. I had long friendships with a Catholic priest who ran a homeless shelter and a preschool teacher who worked in a tough part of Nashville.

I would ask them what they were seeing that I should know about. I would ask them what was new in their business. When a new prescription drug came out, I would ask my pharmacist friend if it was really new or if it was just hype. I would ask my mechanic friend all sorts of automotive questions including questions about recalls and safety issues. My friend who owned an auto junkyard was a nonstop source of information about criminal investigations because cops were constantly dropping by asking him to be on the lookout for stuff that had been stolen or used in a crime.

My homebuilder/developer friend knew all about the city's planning, zoning, water and sewage ordinances. Another developer was under fire for planning to tear down an old but well-known apartment complex. Neighborhood groups protested the demolition and the retail development plans. My friend helped me understand the sobering economics of renovating such an old apartment building. He had no personal interest in the apartment project, so he became a good source of background advice for our stories.

One of the best places I knew to get a reality check was Marva Southhall's East Nashville preschool classroom. Like most reporters, I usually didn't have much time, so sometimes my visits would just last a half hour. I would just find a chair in the corner of the Caldwell School classroom and listen to the children. They lived in the city's toughest neighborhood. Southhall's class sometimes practiced "Code 1000" drills. The drill involved the children jumping out of their chairs, lying facedown on the floor and covering their heads with their hands in the event there was gunfire outside Southhall's classroom window. One of her classroom windows was pockmarked with bullet holes.

Southhall told me heartbreaking stories of her children, who often did not recognize their real names, just their nicknames. Some children had no idea how to hug or be hugged. Many lacked enough self-esteem to look Southhall in the eye. One young boy had so little self-esteem he could not say a word out loud without covering his mouth with his hand.

Southhall's classroom always reminded me what was important in life. She constantly pushed me to do more stories about children and education and strongly urged me to become a teacher myself. The preschoolers were not the only ones who learned in Southhall's class. I bet there is somebody just like her in your town waiting for you to walk through the classroom door.

BUILD A DIVERSE CONTACT LIST

I can usually tell how good reporters are by how fat their "little black books" are and by how quickly they can find important phone numbers. Enterprising journalists make certain they have a rich mix of sources that they can contact anytime day or night, weekend or holidays. The list includes racial, ethnic, gender, religious and political minorities. Some people collect dolls or coins. Great enterprising journalists collect business cards and phone numbers. I like to store phone numbers in my cellphone contact list and on my computer, but one day, when our newsroom computers failed because of a big storm, I came to appreciate the reporters who keep phone numbers stowed in little address books tucked away in their pockets or purses. About twice a year, I print a paper backup for my entire electronic name and address files. Those files represent a lifetime of work, and I don't trust them to any machine.

LOOK FOR VOICES AND FACES SELDOM SEEN ON TV

Enterprising reporters ask, "Who do we always talk to on this story?" Then they ask, "Who do we *never* talk to?" "Who has a stake in this story other than the usual people we interview?" The seldom heard from, the undercovered, people are almost always more interesting than those who appear on the news every night. Go find them.

Steve Weinberg, an investigative writer and one of the founders of Investigative Reporters and Editors (IRE), told me that he joined a bowling league, in part, to meet more people. He said he was surprised at the diversity in a bowling alley.

You will not connect with your community merely by living there for a long time. We all develop migratory patterns of driving the same route to work, eating at the same restaurants and shopping in the same places year after year. Journalists must understand that they are different from the communities they seek to serve.

And don't forget that your community is constantly changing. It changes with the season, with the ups and downs of the economy. It even changes from what it is in the daylight to what it becomes at night. Discover your community's changing complexion by taking a new route home once in a while. Mark Anderson, the former chief photojournalist at KSTP-TV, Minneapolis, told his photojournalist staff to drive with their windows open so they could hear stories. It is quite a piece of advice from somebody who lives in ice-cold Minnesota, but I have seen stories he found that way, including a story about a remarkable street musician whom Anderson heard as he drove through a small town.

When Melania Trump delivered a speech to the Republican National Convention in July 2016, journalists went nuts over whether she "stole" parts of her speech from Michelle Obama's 2008 address. The news watchdog website NewsBusters said all of the TV networks combined dedicated "130 minutes" or "nearly one third of the available airtime" the next day to the plagiarism scandal. It was exactly the kind of juicy topic that gets journalists talking, but passes right by the average viewer, who worries about health care, crime and employment.[2]

How many people in your newsroom belong to the American Legion or the Kiwanis or go to prayer breakfasts? If your newsroom is anything like the ones I have worked in and now drop in to teach, the answer will be "none or next to none." Journalists must make a stronger effort to connect with people who are not like themselves.

Aly Colón, a former colleague at The Poynter Institute who is now the Knight Professor in Journalism Ethics at Washington and Lee University, encourages journalists to find places where people are likely to stop and talk, mingle and share information about themselves. Barbershops, beauty salons, community centers and ethnic restaurants are what Colón calls "listening posts."

"Some of the most informed people in a community are often funeral directors, day-care center directors, health clinic workers and neighborhood association presidents," he says. But he cautions journalists to use a variety of community listening posts to avoid becoming a pawn of factions or prominent sources in any community.

Social workers at the Nashville Housing Authority helped photojournalist Mark O'Neill and me connect with the small Cambodian, Vietnamese and Ethiopian communities of our town when we wanted to tell stories about Nashville slumlords who took advantage of poor non-English-speaking immigrants.

Journalists should get out in public without their notebooks and cameras. In my workshops I often ask producers and reporters how many of them have ever been to a school PTA meeting that they were not covering. Almost no hands go up. I ask how many have visited a school just to learn what is going on in schools these days. No hands go up. You get the point. TV journalists could narrow the distance between themselves and the public if they would find listening posts in their community.

An anchor with whom I worked, Demetria Kalodimos, hit the road one day, as she often did before she started her regular anchor shift, to deliver a luncheon speech in rural middle Tennessee. On her way home she stopped for gasoline at a country market, a farming community listening post that she knew well. Kalodimos is not only a strong anchor but also a skilled reporter who knows her coverage area thoroughly, so when she saw a number of signs written in Spanish, she knew it was unusual. Like many rural Tennessee counties, this one was nearly all white and certainly not known for being multiethnic. She started asking questions.

Kalodimos learned that middlemen, who were acting as labor recruiters, were encouraging Mexican and Central American migrant workers to work on Tennessee and Kentucky tobacco farms. It was backbreaking labor that usually paid cash. The migrants had begun taking jobs in the important tree and shrubbery nurseries in middle Tennessee as well. Our newsroom was completely unaware of their immigration, but it was becoming common knowledge to our viewers in rural communities who saw the migrants at the country stores, gas stations and coin laundries. Rural hospitals noticed an increase in migrant farm worker injuries. Some injured or sick workers were too frightened of deportation to seek medical treatment.

Kalodimos discovered that the workers were living in unheated shacks. Often a dozen or more migrants shared one filthy room, while their white bosses lived in big, comfortable farmhouses nearby. Kalodimos allowed me to go undercover and play the part of a farmer looking for workers as we set about learning how middlemen recruited the immigrants to work at the farms. Kalodimos' series, *Hard Luck Harvest,* aired right in the middle of the fall tobacco auction season. We showed how there was no reason for farmers to take such advantage of the migrants because there were many legal government-sponsored programs that would help the farmers provide proper housing and health care. Farmers, social workers and community leaders gathered at rural meetings to do something about the horrible living conditions and other concerns. The investigation won a National Headliner Award. All that just because one journalist noticed a few signs written in Spanish and was curious enough to ask questions. That is "enterprise reporting."

BE WILLING TO INTERVIEW
ANYONE WHO HAS A GREAT STORY

Some of my best sources were oddballs, eccentrics and those who had an ax to grind, but it did not make them wrong. I remember Dora Mercer, a colorful woman who lived in a rural Kentucky county. I first heard from her in 1985, when she called and wrote to our newsroom saying that her cows were deformed. She sounded like a nut.

One day we dropped by to see her. Sure enough, her cattle were staggering around. They had sores on their mouths. We noticed that the cows drank from a nearby waterway called Mud River. I learned, through months of interviews and record checks, that Rockwell International's nearby die-cast factory accidentally released PCBs (polychlorinated biphenyls) and other chemicals into the river. We found state records that showed inspectors had been concerned about chemical leaks from the plant as early as the 1950s. We also found records of fish kills near the plant, and we interviewed frustrated state inspectors who had spent years quietly documenting the slow death of the river. There is no scientific proof that Rockwell hurt Mercer's cows. But her questions started our investigation. By 1996, 10 years later, the company spent more than $20 million cleaning the river.[3] We never would have looked into the story if we had not listened to Mercer's seemingly crazy claims.

In my experience whistleblowers are almost always angry, they are packrats, and it never surprises me that they sometimes seem to be anti-social. One guy I found had been fighting the Tennessee-Tombigbee waterway project for 20 years. The $2 billion project was the single-most-expensive public works project in American history, and it was a boondoggle from the very start.

Randall Grace grew frustrated and angry about the government's pie-in-the-sky promises that the Tenn-Tom would deliver prosperity to impoverished Mississippi and Alabama. Grace gave up the fight that took a decade of his young adulthood and built a rustic and secluded log cabin in the wooded hills of Tennessee. He also built a little shed next to the house.

When I finally found him and spent some time with him talking about his struggle against the Corps of Engineers, I noticed the little shed. I asked him what he kept in it. Grace lit up. He had crammed box upon cardboard box of records into the shed. I dug around to find hundreds of pages of clippings, letters and what looked to be thousands of photographic slides of the waterway before, during and after the construction that had cost more than twice what the Corps had promised Congress it would. It was like manna from heaven for me. I could have hugged the guy.

My photojournalist friend Pat Slattery and I once heard about an elderly woman who had spent her whole life fighting the Tennessee Valley Authority (TVA). When we caught up with Corrine Whitehead, we found a firebrand of a woman who had not only saved hundreds of photographs and newspaper clippings that chronicled her lifelong railing against government excesses but also had indexed the clippings and correspondence in files by date and topic. Whitehead's voice reminded me of Katharine Hepburn's. Whitehead wore a shirt collar stylishly flipped up in the back, the way Humphrey Bogart flipped up his trench coat collar in *Casablanca*. A form of polio weakened Whitehead when she was a young woman. Her hands shook as she slowly flipped through her files with us. We tried not to be too gleeful as we sat in the middle of her stash, but we wondered how it could have happened that nobody had ever listened to her story before.

The Kennedy administration ordered Whitehead and her neighbors off their homesteads to build two big hydroelectric dams and two large lakes. Any land that was not flooded would become a public recreation area that the government said would never be developed. For 30 years she was a thorn in the TVA's side. She became one of those gadfly eccentrics who show up at every public meeting and reporters curiously avoid.

In the 1990s, when TVA's budgets got tight, the agency wanted to lease the very land it had ordered Whitehead to vacate. Condo developers and gas station quick markets would be free to set up shop on the land the government promised would remain noncommercial forever.

Whitehead's files allowed us to prove many of the promises the government made to the people of rural western Kentucky. After being hammered on the news day after day, TVA backed off its plans.

Listen to people like Whitehead, Grace and Mercer. They have hearts of gold and closets full of documents that will make your stories golden. Be willing to interview anyone who has a great story.

EXPLORE ALL SIDES TO A STORY

In the *Hard Luck Harvest* series, as in most stories, the more we learned about the issue, the more sides to the story we discovered. We learned that there were many stakeholders in this story, including:

- Farmers
- Workers
- Middlemen
- Hospitals
- Health clinics
- Communities
- Families
- Other migrants
- Social workers
- Lawyers
- Federal, state and local lawmakers
- The INS
- Other workers
- And, of course, the television station

We could have easily gotten bogged down in the pro-and-con story of the Immigration and Naturalization Service versus the farmer. But we would have missed other vital parts of the story, including the story of the lives, hopes and dreams of the workers themselves, many of whom were working to send money back to Mexico to support their families.

Enterprising reporters don't focus just on the extremes of "anti" and "pro." How could you find new voices to cover the battle about abortion, capital punishment and stories about gun control or taxation? The social activists on those issues have websites, PR agencies and news conferences. But the people most closely affected by those issues are seldom in the stories.

By asking better questions, you discover these multiple perspectives that enrich your enterprise reporting. Once you finish an interview, you should ask a few more questions that may take you places you don't expect:

- What else should I know?
- Who else should I talk to?
- If you were me, where would you go next?
- What kind of records or pictures are there of this?

AVOID THE PACK; GO WHERE THE STORY IS GOING NEXT

If you want to find stories, go where the other stations aren't going. Keep asking yourself, "What is most likely to happen next in this story? How can I get ahead of the story?" I think journalists worry too much about what the others are reporting. Inform yourself about what others are covering, but be guided by your own journalistic principles and your newsroom's thoughtful vision. Cover stories that matter to your viewers. Remember, it is good to be different from the pack. You should stand out in the viewer's mind, not blend into the background noise.

COVER FOLLOW-UP STORIES WITH CARE

Return to stories to see what has happened. Viewers love follow-ups. Just about the time you are sick of a story, viewers figure out there *is* a story. Television station researchers tell me that in many markets, especially big-city markets, the most loyal viewers rarely watch more than two and a half newscasts per week. Viewers get frustrated when stations cover an arrest and do not follow up on the court proceedings. They don't track every little event the way journalists do. They don't know every criminal suspect and the crimes the suspect allegedly was involved in as well as a producer who has written 10 versions of the story for 10 newscasts and news cut-ins in two days. We overestimate what viewers know—we underestimate how smart they are.

But journalists must be careful when doing enterprise reporting on follow-up stories. With breaking news, victims can literally be scared speechless. Don't be lulled into thinking that the effects of trauma simply disappear with the passage of time. Be careful when you contact victims for follow-ups.

Michigan State University journalism professor Sue Carter has studied how media coverage affects crime victims and offers some advice about follow-up stories:

- **Anniversary and update stories.** It is a mistake to assume that victims do not suffer pain 10, 20 or even 50 years after the incident. The anniversary itself often stirs up troubling feelings, so be prepared when asking for and conducting an interview.

- **Unsolved crimes.** Try to make it your policy never to run a story about an unsolved crime without notifying the victim or the family first. Particularly in the case of murder, surviving family members feel blindsided when they are not warned that a story will appear about a new suspect or as part of a feature on unsolved crimes.

- **A special word on terminology.** Victims who have had a chance to think about their experience often have strong feelings about "loaded" words such as "victim," "survivor" and "closure." Ask if they mind being called a victim. Many victims bristle at being asked if they have achieved closure; the implication is that they are a failure if they say no, and many would argue that you may someday forgive but will never forget. A better question might be, "How do you feel about the question of closure?"

WRITE THANK-YOU LETTERS

As I mentioned in Chapter 6, ABC's Byron Pitts carries postage stamps and thank-you notes in his briefcase. After he finishes interviewing people, he drops them a short note of thanks for their help. Lots of journalists would not dare go back to some towns where they did stories the locals hated. But Pitts takes great care to treat his interview subjects as humans. Sometimes his subjects send him new stories because they know he will treat them sensitively and with great respect.

Thank-you notes are also a great idea in the newsroom. Send a note to your news director when he or she gives you some extra time or resources to produce a story. Send a note to producers who grant you a little extra airtime to tell your story or to photojournalists who bust their hump to get the extra shot or remarkable sound. Thank-you notes are so much more personal and meaningful than emails or e-cards.

■ ■ ■ REMEMBER

Find community listening posts to inform your reporting. Be open to sources whom others ignore or dismiss. Seek out new sources of information. Follow up stories. Viewers don't watch as often as you think.

LOOK FOR THE STORY BEHIND THE STORY

When your newsroom has an "enterprise journalism culture," it shows up in the way you treat people who call your newsroom. I learned that lesson even before I worked in a newsroom.

Where I grew up in Caldwell County, Kentucky, the school board found the money to build a new bare-bones high school for our rural community. But in its cost cutting the county didn't earmark the several hundred dollars needed to install a flagpole outside the school. Some friends of mine and I, with the urging of our always-patriotic science teacher Dale Faughn, decided we should do something about that.

We called a local construction company and asked the company to donate a load of concrete. We sold Tootsie Rolls and Hershey's bars and raised enough money to buy a flagpole. We leaned on the local VFW to procure a big flag that had flown over the state Capitol.

With all of that done, I mustered up the courage to make a "long-distance call" to the local television station. The station was 50 miles away, but it was only one of three stations that the people in my county could pick up on their antennas. Unless you invested in a big antenna for your home, it was the *only* station you could watch.

I practiced my pitch over and over before making the call. I was sure I could convince the TV station to drive to our school and do a story about our little act of patriotism. On the other end of the phone was the voice of a harried producer or assignment desk manager who, 10 seconds into our conversation, had the idea stuck in his mind that "this is a story about a flagpole." There was a certain "thanks, but no thanks" quality to his voice.

If he had asked, he would have seen the story through a very different lens; the lens through which we were looking. As high school seniors, we had just seen two big events occur. The war in Vietnam had just ended. Only a few months earlier, my classmates and I were eligible for the draft. From the time I was 5 years old, Americans had been fighting in Vietnam. It was cool to hate the government. It was cool to question authority. Now, there was no war and these country boys were no longer in danger of being drafted.

My buddies Mark VanHooser, Jeff Alsobrook, Barry Crowder, Anthony Stallings and I were trying to make a patriotic statement by erecting a flagpole in front of our school. We thought that was news. Although the TV station passed on the story, the local newspaper came by and dutifully snapped a picture of us shoveling in some concrete. The larger story about some grateful kids who wanted to say thanks to their country and the men and women who served it was never told.

I learned something about storytelling and the news business. Seven years later, I produced the 6 p.m. and 10 p.m. newscasts at the same television station that turned us down. I never told my colleagues at WPSD-TV in Paducah, Kentucky, why I aired so darn many stories about kids doing good things at high schools. It was my own private revenge for getting blown off by the assignment desk when I was 17 years old.

That flagpole story taught me a couple of life-shaping lessons. I learned to listen more carefully when viewers called in with story ideas. And I learned that television journalists have become experts at covering "events," but they needed to tell stories that go beyond the "what" of news.

■ ■ ■ REMEMBER

Go beyond the simple question of "what" to ask the more complex question of "why."

Notes

1. Interview with the author, May 10, 2006.
2. Source: http://www.newsbusters.org/blogs/nb/mike-ciandella/2016/07/19/feeding-frenzy-morning-shows-spend-130-minutes-melania-trumps.
3. *Rockwell International Corp. v. Vance Wilhite, et al.*, Nos. 1997-CA-000188-MR, 1997-CA-000210-MR and 1997-CA-000348-MR, Ky. App.

CHAPTER 20

Surviving and Thriving in Today's TV Newsroom

> *If we all do what we can to make the world a better place, the world will be a better place.*
>
> —Martin Fletcher,
> NBC News war correspondent

This final chapter may seem like an odd topic for a book about storytelling and writing.

I include these final thoughts because our business is losing too many veteran journalists to job uncertainty, layoffs, buyouts, early retirement, burnout, low pay, long hours, separation from family, unskilled management and job stress. Researchers at Indiana University said there were 70,000 journalists in the United States in 1971 and that number swelled to 116,000 in 2002.[1] By the end of 2015, the American Society of News Editors estimated the number to be around 32,900. Television stations, on the other hand, continued to add newscasts and saw modest increases in staff according to the annual survey by Bob Papper, professor emeritus at Hofstra University.[2]

No doubt, the number of nontraditional journalists has increased even as newspapers and radios have laid off journalists. Despite rough economic times in the media business, skilled journalists are doing good work in all sorts of newsrooms. I have no doubt we will need skilled journalists to tell stories for decades to come, just as we have needed them in centuries past. The journalists of the future may not be filing stories for the same devices or media they do today, but people have an insatiable need for reliable information delivered quickly.

In this chapter I'll explore what to do on your first day and your last day on the job, followed by these topics:

- How to succeed in a difficult business
- What to do if you get laid off
- How to manage stress at work
- The qualities of a newsroom leader
- How to manage your boss, manage your career and find meaning for your life

How to Succeed

If I were a news director right now, I would hand every new employee a list of "10 Things You Should Know Before You Get Your First Paycheck." It is my checklist for how to be successful in any newsroom. These are not all of the things you have to do to be successful, but if you don't do these things, you won't be successful for long, that's for sure.

1. **Treat the Public with Respect.** Viewers will call you when you are on deadline. Be polite. They will call and complain when you interrupt soaps or football games. Listen to their complaints and thank them for being viewers. Respect viewers enough not to air pointless trashy stories, teases and headlines. Don't insult their intelligence. Remember that every person you feature on the news in any way is a person first, not a sound bite or b-roll. They are people with a boss, family and neighbors who will see them on the news. Without our viewers, we are out of business.

2. **Be Accurate and Truthful.** Do not exaggerate a story or make it appear to be a bigger deal than it is. Viewers want context in stories. Don't just tell them what is going on; find out why, how often and where else. We seek to inform our viewers, not scare them needlessly. This applies to all phases of our newsroom, including weather, traffic, sports and investigative work.

3. **Act as If You Have Some Sense.** Don't drink and drive. Don't post things on a personal internet blog or social network site that will reflect badly on you or the station. What you do to yourself, in many ways, you do to the entire newsroom. For God's sake, if you get arrested for speeding or drinking while driving, don't tell the cops they should give you a break because you are a journalist. The old saying "What you do on your personal time is your business" does not apply to journalists or anybody employed by a journalism organization. You have chosen this craft, which comes with strings attached that prevent you from expressing opinions, participating in political activities and taking stands on public issues that anybody else might be free to do. The fleas come with the dog. Accept it or find another way to earn a living. When you are near a live camera or microphone, remember that whatever you say or do somebody can hear.

4. **Avoid Toxic Communications.** Avoid rumormongers, whisperers and time wasters. Don't send an email to a co-worker when you can communicate in person. Don't deliver bad news by email if at all possible. Watch your tone when all heck is breaking loose in the newsroom. We work in a pressured environment, but so do doctors, hairstylists and teachers. We expect them to keep their cool, too.

5. **Be on Time and Be Ready to Work.** Arrive ready to work. That means you will have read the morning paper, you will have viable story ideas and you will know what is going on in the world. You will not last long in a newsroom if you do not have story ideas. Be ready to talk about them when you hit the door. This applies to everyone in the newsroom. Everyone.

6. **Come to Work Every Day With the Enthusiasm You Had on Your First Day.** Yes, we have tough competitive challenges in our business, but that is not new and it is not unique to us. Hospitals,

insurance companies and Realtors have tough competitors, too. You have the opportunity to change the way the world sees itself every day. You have the opportunity to give voice to the voiceless and hold the powerful accountable. You have the ability to talk to the world via the internet and to talk directly to tens of thousands of people over TV and mobile devices. What will you do with that opportunity today?

7. **Know That You Will Make Mistakes.** We all do. Try to keep making new mistakes, not repeating the old ones. When you make a mistake, own up to it, do your best to fix it and learn from it. If it is a mistake that the news director or station lawyer needs to know about, make sure you are the one who delivers the news—quickly, clearly and completely. If you make a mistake on the air, and if the mistake hurts somebody else, report a correction clearly, quickly and played as prominently as the mistake was. If the mistake occurs online, correct the mistake, make a note at the top of the story that the story has been appended and keep a list of corrections and clarifications on the website.

8. **You Were Hired to Do a Job, but It Does Not Mean You Will Do That Job Forever.** Do the job you were hired to do first, but don't be afraid to dream about taking on new responsibilities. There are 1,500 universities with some sort of journalism training pumping out thousands of graduates a year. But the station chose you. That means it believes in you, or you would not have gotten a key to the building. Be honest about your hopes, and the company should pledge to be honest about whether those hopes seem plausible. Commit yourself to a life of constant learning.

9. **It Is Your Job.** Starbucks adopted a philosophy that says, "We are not in the coffee business serving people. We are in the people business serving coffee."[3] Read just part of Starbucks' business philosophy statement below and apply it to a newsroom.

Our Customers

When we are fully engaged, we connect with, laugh with and uplift the lives of our customers—even if just for a few moments. Sure, it starts with the promise of a perfectly made beverage, but our work goes far beyond that. It's really about human connection.

Our Stores

When our customers feel this sense of belonging, our stores become a haven, a break from the worries outside, a place where you can meet with friends. It's about enjoyment at the speed of life—sometimes slow and savored, sometimes faster. Always full of humanity.

Our Neighborhood

Every store is part of a community, and we take our responsibility to be good neighbors seriously. We want to be invited in wherever we do business. We can be a force for positive action—bringing together our partners, customers and the community to contribute every day. Now we see that our responsibility—and our potential for good—is even larger. The world is looking to Starbucks to set the new standard, yet again. We will lead.[4]

Wow! Such high goals from a chain of coffee shops. Starbucks is not after just "good" service. The corporate strategy includes "legendary service" as a goal. The company demands a consistent standard so that no matter where you go, you will get the same high quality of service and coffee. No wonder so many people make Starbucks a habit, a ritual. Think what a TV station could do!

Starbucks says in its mission statement, "Profitability is essential to our future success." There is absolutely nothing about being profitable that conflicts with what we are trying to do as journalists. Our profits can help us do our journalism and remain independent. Our profits help us to pay employees a fair wage and provide benefits to keep staffers' kids healthy and help staff plan for the future.

If you see an opportunity to improve the station's service to the public, act or speak to somebody who can act. Innovation in the newsroom does not have to come from the boss' office. It should come from every employee. You were hired because they thought you were smart and talented. Show them why they were right.

10. **Build a Legacy.** If you signed on with a station just to get a paycheck, then it might be best to part ways now. You can get a paycheck anywhere, and, frankly, you could make easier money, and probably more money, doing something else. But in this job you can leave a legacy for your community. You can improve education, you can help the homeless, you can inform the public about candidates who will run the government, you can warn your neighbors about threats that might affect their families. A station shouldn't measure your success by how many awards you win. Success should be measured by how you improved your community by seeking truth and telling it clearly, forcefully and fully. You should be here not just to make a living but to make a mark.

CONTINUAL LEARNING

After 43 years as a journalist and journalism teacher, I can say with some authority that I have never known a time when it was more important for journalists to seek constant skills training. In fact at age 59, I finished a master's degree in digital journalism and design just so I could stay on top of the technology that was changing newsrooms. It is nothing my company required me to do, it is not something the company paid for, it is something I wanted to do to remain credible and relevant.

Continual learning is essential and it is not something that newsrooms do well. Often when companies start cutting budgets, the training budget is the first line to be cut. How shortsighted!

Once again, to use the Starbucks model, Starbucks consistently spends more on training than it does on advertising. The result is obvious. The company sends a signal to the employees that they are valued. An article in *Workforce Management* said, "Starbucks employees have an 82 percent job-satisfaction rate." That is 32 percent above the industry average.[5] Another survey of Starbucks employees showed they were far more satisfied with their compensation, benefits and career opportunities than workers at Dunkin' Donuts and Peet's Coffee & Tea, big competitors.[6]

Commit yourself to constant learning, even if your company will not pay for it. It is vital to your survival in this industry. If you are a reporter, be sure you learn the skills of photojournalism. Photojournalists must become versatile enough to report. Producers have to become jacks-of-all-trades, and managers must have a broad awareness of all of the jobs they are asking their staff to perform.

The most successful journalists I know study the work of others and have wide networks of contacts at other stations in other cities. They often discuss story ideas with others and adapt good ideas from other places. They dissect the winners of national contests and figure out what made them so effective. To this day I volunteer to judge in many national journalism contests including the Investigative Reporters and Editors (IRE) national contest, the Scripps Howard Foundation's National Journalism Awards and the prestigious Alfred I. duPont-Columbia University Awards. A key reason I judge is because I want to see the freshest and best new work being produced in the world and discuss it with other journalists. It is a way to constantly learn new techniques.

I know that many teachers use this textbook, so let me send a message to them, too. I find it odd that so many educators have stopped learning. They are still teaching old-school skills for jobs that no longer exist. When students see their teachers learning new skills, think what an inspiration it will be for the students to become constant learners. Teachers, please keep learning. Keep trying new things. Scare yourself a little bit by volunteering to teach something you have never taught before. It will keep you fresh and make you grow.

When my wife was in her mid-50s, she decided to become an ordained Methodist minister. It was amazing to me that this woman, who had been a remarkably successful psychotherapist for more than two decades, would suddenly take on such a challenge. After three years of commuting from Florida to Chicago to study at Northwestern University, and two more years of probation and continual study, she was ordained. Our young children watched their mother pore through thick religion and philosophy books, write weighty papers and fret over pressured exams. One semester she had more than 40 pounds of textbooks to read. I know—I weighed them!

While I studied for my master's degree late into the evenings after a long day at work, my teenage son and I would sometimes commiserate about term papers that were due or semester projects that we thought were pointless. I credit those impressionable days when our kids watched their parents demonstrate constant learning as one reason our children became strong students. They don't wait until the last minute to write book reports. They don't whine about how much homework they have to do. They saw what dedication looks like and made it part of the work ethic of their lives.

Surviving Layoffs, Cutbacks and Reassignment

Journalism is a rough and competitive business. It may be, for some, a sort of calling, a mission or a public service, but it is also a business. And businesses sometimes lay off workers, even good ones, to save money.

Losing a job is traumatic. And it is not all about money. Your job is, in some measure, a reflection of who you are and what you stand for.

We all worry about losing our job in this business. I always worried about losing my job to either a fickle boss or a penny-pinching station owner, or because of a momentary lapse of judgment that got on the air.

The single best piece of advice I can give you about such things is not to allow your job to define who you are as a person. Rather, allow who you are to define how you do your job.

Good people lose their jobs through no fault of their own. Stations and corporations cancel shows, audience's tastes change, bosses change, stations sell, merge or change strategy. Sometimes new bosses want to shake things up or bring their pals from other stations with them. Sometimes companies need to meet Wall Street expectations so they trim jobs to boost the bottom line. Those things happen in other businesses too. But it still sucks to lose your job.

Smart journalists are ready for the storms ahead. They have up-to-date résumés stored on their home, not work, computers. They have up-to-date résumé reels to show a potential employer. They have copies of great job performance appraisals on file away from work. They have ready letters of reference and a wide range of industry contacts on whom they can call if the budget cutters come calling.

Financial independence is vital. You simply must have some money in reserve. I know many journalists don't earn much dough, but a six-month reserve would give you the time you need to land a job if you lose the one you have. It gives you the courage to leave a job that becomes untenable.

WHAT TO DO IF YOU GET FIRED OR LAID OFF

The news business, especially the print journalism part of our industry, has shed tens of thousands of jobs since 2006. The American Society of Newspaper Editors says about 33,000 workers in the print world lost their jobs from 2006 to 2016.

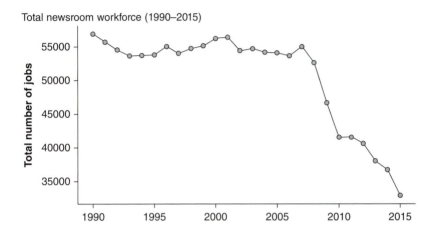

Total newsroom workforce (1990–2015)

Hofstra University's annual survey of TV stations shows broadcast news' employment picture is not nearly as bleak. The peak of employment in TV was 2001, but even while print sheds jobs, broadcast stations were slowly hiring staff.[7]

If you work in the media business, it could happen to you. You might lose your job.

When it happens, it won't be warm and full of hugs. In all likelihood you will be called to the boss' office or a conference table in the human resources office, and you will be handed a packet of materials that explain severance benefits, insurance and such. It may be coldly businesslike. These meetings are often factual and may seem unfeeling. Most likely, the folks delivering the news have knots in their stomachs, but they can't show it. They have a job to do, just as you did when you covered some awful story as a reporter. They have a sort of script they have to stick to, something the company lawyer drew up in case you decide to sue.

The company probably has already cut off your access to your computer. Don't be surprised if you are escorted out of the building after the meeting. It is a rotten thing, but it is standard procedure for companies that cannot risk angry employees damaging company property or upsetting the rest of the staff when they see you crying. It is best if you prepare yourself for such an event. I will be thrilled if you never need the information on the next few pages, but it's here just in case.

KNOW WHY YOU LOST YOUR JOB

The day you lose your job is self-examination-and-honesty time. Get real and don't blame others. I have fired a few, and I mean darn few, folks in my days as a news director. None was surprised. Layoffs are a different issue. Often workers are blindsided by a budget cut. If you were fired for "cause," and by that I mean you were fired because of something you did or didn't do, begin right away figuring out what you need to do differently. You may need counseling for substance abuse, anger or behavioral issues. You may need to learn new skills to work in today's newsroom.

WHAT DO YOU REALLY WANT TO DO NEXT?

Do you have the drive to get back in the journalism game, or is there anything else that you have been hungering to try? Would you be great at it? Do you have the skills you need? Will anybody pay you to do this work? Is it worthwhile work? I have had friends who left TV news and became successful lawyers who serve the poor and disadvantaged. I have journalism friends who have gone to work for nonprofits, become ministers, started work for the government and even one who became a commercial pilot. Many former journalists become teachers and professors. Some take jobs as freelance journalists. But most go back to work for another TV newsroom. Make sure if you choose that route that it is what you really want. Big interruptions in life may open the door for change that can refresh your spirit and make you grow. Play to the strengths you have built in journalism. You have lots of skills. You have worked on deadline, you know how to assimilate lots of information quickly, you are used to working long, unpredictable hours.

HOW MUCH MONEY DO YOU
WANT, AND HOW MUCH DO YOU NEED?

I usually have changed jobs to earn more money. But when I moved from TV to my current job at The Poynter Institute, I took a big pay cut. The reason: I wanted this job and the change that it represented in my life. Money will not make you happy. Now if you don't have enough money, believe me, you can be mighty unhappy. But money alone is not enough of a reason to take a job. Don't let money get in the way of your life's passion. Just take my advice on this one. Don't let a little bit of money get in the way of accepting a job offer. If you want the job, go get it. That said, make the best business deal you can with your new employer and never ever fear talking about money with your boss. Don't talk about it all the time, but don't avoid it either.

FIND A WAY TO WORK THROUGH YOUR ANGER

You have every right to be upset if you have put your heart into your job and lost it anyway. Anger is usually a mask for fear. You naturally fear that no matter what job you land next, the same old thing will happen. Don't go on your Facebook site and pour your heart out. The anger you are feeling is normal, but anger is not going to get you a new job, and revenge is not the answer. Be careful with whom you share your frustrations and do so only in a private way. When you publicly burn a bridge, potential employers will avoid you.

LEAVE ON THE BEST POSSIBLE TERMS

It would feel great to yell at the person who fires you, wouldn't it? Wouldn't it feel swell to set the record straight about how that person drove the company into the ground and it should be that person, not you, losing the job?

Take notes. Listen carefully. Stay calm, even though your stomach is churning. Now is not the time to settle old scores. You probably can't tell, but your boss is most likely an emotional wreck, too.

Trust me. I've been there. Pay attention to the issues that will be covered in the packet they hand you and maybe in the face-to-face meeting.

LEARN ABOUT YOUR SEVERANCE PAY

Are you eligible for a severance plan? How will it be paid and when? Severance is not required by law. It is something companies often offer full-time workers as a way to keep down litigation and help workers get started again. Sometimes companies demand an employee sign a contract saying they won't say anything disparaging about the company in exchange for the severance. Severance is commonly one or two weeks' pay for every year of service. Ask if the severance will be paid in a lump sum or in installments. If a lump sum might help you start your own business or achieve some other goal, then the layoff might be a positive turning point. Make sure you understand the tax implications of a lump sum versus a monthly payout. Would it benefit you to get the payout that stretches across two calendar years?

WHAT ABOUT INSURANCE COVERAGE?

When you lose your job, you are eligible for COBRA (Consolidated Omnibus Budget Reconciliation Act), which allows you to continue your health care coverage after you leave your job. It is not cheap. You pay for your own health insurance under COBRA, and generally you can purchase it for only 18 months. If your employer has been paying part of your health insurance costs, you are about to absorb a big expense you are not used to. Remember to also ask about dental, prescription medicine and optical insurance coverage.

YOU CAN NEGOTIATE

If, for example, your company offers year-end bonuses and you get laid off in November, ask for a prorated bonus payout. If you have a company-issued laptop or other take-home gear, ask if you can keep the gear or buy it at a discounted price. If the company is reducing head count, it probably doesn't need the equipment either. If the company wants you to stay on for another few weeks to train another employee, you have some leverage to ask for some of these extras.

UNEMPLOYMENT INSURANCE

If you lose your job through no fault of your own and if you have worked enough to meet your state's requirements to be covered by unemployment insurance, you will qualify for unemployment benefits. But if you are fired for violating a written company policy, if you quit your job in a huff or you quit out of fear, you may not qualify. A minute or two of blowing off your temper steam can cost you big bucks.

Once you file for unemployment—and don't be shy about filing, you paid for the plan—the unemployment office will require you to actively search for a job. In many states you can sign up for benefits online. If you get wind that layoffs might be on the way, get as smart as you can ahead of time about how to apply for benefits so you can cut down the waiting time to getting paid.

THE EFFECT ON PENSIONS AND RETIREMENT FUNDS

What will happen to your 401(k) and/or pension fund? Ask if there are any "exit fees" to get your money out of the accounts your company has directed you to invest in. If at all possible, resist the temptation to cash out your 401(k) plan. It will cost you big penalties plus taxes on the withdrawal. It can easily cost you a third of your savings. If you have borrowed from your 401(k), you may have to pay it back or pay a 10 percent penalty plus taxes on the loan balance. Depending on how long you have worked for the company, you may have "vested" stock or pension funds. If the company is laying you off because it is having financial troubles, you might want to think about how long you want to hold on to company stock.

JOB COUNSELING

Does the station offer job counseling? A layoff can be a good time to look at the employment horizon and see what else you might want to do. A job counselor can help figure out what you are good at and what you might love to do next. He or she can also help you honestly assess what has been working and what needs work in your career. Finally, job counselors can offer helpful advice on how to manage stress, land a job interview, prepare a résumé, network with employers and negotiate your new deal.

A BUYOUT OR EARLY RETIREMENT

Humane companies look for volunteers to leave the workforce before they start laying off workers. They offer buyouts or early retirement to workers. These can make a lot of sense to workers who are near retirement or who want to change jobs anyway. I have known plenty of people who loved this option, such as women who wanted to start families or folks who wanted to expand their part-time side businesses to full-time.

They may have been ready to leave their jobs anyway, but this payout makes the option more attractive.

If the company offers you a buyout, you have a few things to consider:

- If you don't take the buyout, then what are the chances you will get laid off anyway?

- Does the buyout forbid you from working for a competitor? Noncompete clauses can handcuff you from finding work without moving.

- Is the buyout enough of a lump sum to give you the opportunity to do something else you want to do?

- Do you want to hang around a sinking ship? What will the workplace be like? Will people be doing a lot more work because people like you left?

- Do you have another job lined up? If so, you can double dip—take the buyout and draw your pay from the new job. Make sure you understand the tax implications of taking a lump-sum buyout versus installments. I have had friends who took the installments and then the company filed bankruptcy. Now, not only did my friends not get unemployment benefits, but also they became bankruptcy creditors and years later might get a settlement of pennies for every dollar the company owed them. Take the lump sum and run if the company is not financially sound.

When I was news director at WSMV-TV, we had to lay off more than a dozen really good folks. It was heartbreaking for everyone. A few of them took the severance package, which provided two weeks' pay for every year they had worked. Company buy-outs are not always awful news. One worker in my newsroom took the buyout and started his own production company with the money, having worked at the place for more than 20 years. He said he would never have been able to live that dream if it had not been for the buyout package.

IT IS NOT A BAD IDEA TO CONSULT AN ATTORNEY

It can be money well spent to have a lawyer look over severance agreements and noncompete clauses. You should especially consult an attorney if you have solid reason to believe that age, ethnicity or gender is a factor in your losing your job. But don't be petty. Stay realistic. If you know you are being called in to be laid off, it is usually a bad idea to show up with your lawyer in tow, unless you know this situation is going to end up in a lawsuit anyway. Bringing the lawyer along just sets a tone that invites the company lawyer and talks gets seriously ugly fast. If the company asks you to sign an agreement not to take a job at a competing station or not to appear on another website, don't sign then and there. Ask to take the agreement home and read it over. Then, it would be a smart idea to ask an attorney to take a look at it. Keep the temperature of the conversations as low as you can.

AVOID PITY PARTIES

You have a job to do when you are jobless. You have to reset your life's course and chart a new plan. Get on with it. When I was fired for being a bonehead while working in local radio, I landed a better job at another, much better radio station in less than a week. I never took a job for granted again, and I often hired others who had been laid off or fired from jobs because I found that once you have lost a job, you are much more grateful for the next one.

HIRE A GOOD EMPLOYER

Yes, read that sentence again. Work for good people. Do not take a job with a company you don't believe in. Do not take a job when you know the person you will answer to is a slimeball or a stooge or is unethical. It won't get better with time. Just as your employer should ask you good questions, you should ask questions, too. "What do you stand for?" "What do you think makes a great employee?" "How do people get ahead in this company?" "Who is your mentor, and what did you learn from him or her?" "What is the single worst thing that I could do to disappoint you?" "What could I do to make you most proud?" Ask how you will be evaluated. Let the employer know that you want to be great.

You may just find that losing a job, while rough, even devastating, can make you stronger, smarter and, in the end, happier. You can go over the problems, you can go under them, you can go around them; you have to go right through them. Get going.

A WORD TO WORKERS WHO
DO NOT LOSE THEIR JOBS

The weeks after a layoff can be especially difficult.

The folks who keep their jobs may feel guilty that others, especially those with young children, lost their jobs. They may wonder if it is acceptable to communicate with former workers.

Your friends need your support. Don't shut them out. It may not be appropriate to share company information or secrets with former employees though, and you should make that clear to them.

I think one especially devastating tactic that I have seen too many times is when the laid-off worker is escorted out of the building without being allowed to say good-bye. It is an indignity that just seems unnecessary. With rare exceptions the same workers whom we trusted to be professional in their jobs will act professionally at this dark hour. All the same, be prepared for the possibility that you will not get to say good-bye to office friends.

Also be alert to how your boss is feeling after layoffs. The news director or general manager can't go around telling everybody how sad he or she is, but let me tell you that cutting a person's job is the single most gut-wrenching thing I had to do as a boss. You know that you are creating chaos for an entire family. You know that kids are going to get uprooted from their schools and moved. Spouses will worry, and homes will have to be sold. The boss may well be fearful of his or her job as well. Have some empathy for how others are feeling. Offer a kind word or two.

STRESSED AND OVERWORKED

"This is a 24/7 business and there is no off season," says Patti Dennis, vice president for news and director of recruiting for Tegna Media, one of the largest local TV station owners in America. News veterans such as Dennis have learned to create routines in their lives to help offset job stress and balance erratic schedules.

Dennis says she keeps photos of her daughters and her husband in her office to remind her to stay grounded and centered.

"If you want to be in this business long, you want to be in the middle of where things are happening," she says. "That means if you make plans with your family and a big story breaks, your family gets pushed aside. Sometimes you just stay (at the office) because you want to be a part of the coverage." Dennis has spent plenty of nights at the office. She worked two and a half days straight during the Columbine shooting coverage, catching naps on a beanbag chair in the station's greenroom.

To spend time with her family, Dennis says her family has had to learn to live their evenings backward. "The kids do baths and homework first. I try to leave work no later than 7 p.m. [a typical day is 11 hours], and we eat dinner at 8:30. My family thinks that is normal. My children will have husbands someday who will ask them, "Why do we eat so late?" Dennis calls family dinners "a protected time." "We turn off the TV, we pray and then we talk."

Dennis thinks it is important that news parents realize when they need down time. "You make yourself say it is okay to leave work and have lunch with your kid at school," she says. "I have a cell phone, and I go sit at school and have lunch. I try to do it once a week."

Clearly, a career in broadcast journalism can be hard on families.

The stressful environment of newsrooms has become so deeply engrained in newsroom mythology that Hollywood's movies make fun of it. I laugh out loud at films such as *Broadcast News* or *The Paper* because they are exactly the kinds of zoos I have worked in. An hour before newscasts, people begin to talk so loudly and so quickly that they sound like cartoon characters. These patterns of deadline stress run so deep that we accept stress as an unavoidable part of newsroom culture. Journalists try to relieve stress with a quick drink after work or a workout at the gym. Both are temporary solutions. The workout is a healthier alternative, but even that cannot right a life that is seriously out of balance.

My wife, Sidney, is a marriage and family therapist and a United Methodist minister. She had consulted for dozens of Fortune 500 companies and government agencies that know something about stress, including the Internal Revenue Service. I asked her to draw on her therapist experience and her years being married to a news director to come up with some tips for journalists who are trying to balance their personal relationships and their work. Here is what she recommends:

- **Your partner is not a mind reader.** You know it has been a busy news day; your partner does not. If you are going to be late for dinner, pick up the phone and call. Your partner most likely understands the nature of the news business but does not understand why it is so difficult for you to call when you are running late. When you don't call, your partner can make only one assumption: The story that is keeping you at work is more important than your relationship.

- **Put your own oxygen mask on first.** Airline flight attendants tell passengers that in an emergency the passengers should put their oxygen masks on first before trying to help others. There is a good lesson in this. Journalists must care for themselves and their relationships before they can hope to help their viewers. If your life is out of balance, your stories will reflect that. Worse, others around you will begin to feed off your actions. Newsroom leaders, even informal leaders such as photojournalists, producers and reporters, set the tone for how others act. Attend school plays, Little League games and PTA meetings. The most stressed people I know are those who have few interests outside of work. Volunteer to take on assignments for others so they can attend important family events, too. Build a culture in your newsroom for caring about life beyond the newscast.

- **Pictures help.** You live a stress-filled life. Keep pictures in your work space that remind you of times when you had relaxed fun. Many successful executives I have worked with surround themselves with family pictures that help keep them focused on why they do the important work they do. Usually journalists enter this profession because they want to make the world a better place, not because of the fame or money. Most successful people have an underlying belief that their work is important. It is what keeps them in their jobs when times get tough and stress throws their lives out of whack.

- **Ten minutes and 10 seconds.** I often tell couples who walk into my office that their first homework assignment is to spend 10 minutes a day talking with each other for one week. When they come to see me a week later, I am not surprised to see that most stressed-out couples can't even complete that one simple assignment. Then, I assign them to spend 10 seconds a day kissing.

It is surprising how much couples find to talk about after that exercise.

- **The three most important moments.** The three most important moments in a couple's day are when you wake up, when you say good-bye for the day and when you see each other after the workday is through. How do you say good morning or good-bye? How do you say hello at the end of the workday? Those interactions set the tone for how your partner will think of you all day and how you will interact with each other at the end of the day.

- **Final thoughts.** Your partner and your family share you with the audience. We don't like sitting alone in the bathroom with the kids and the family dog while you cover the tornadoes that are hitting your town. We don't like it when you have to work on Christmas and Thanksgiving. We don't like it when you get called out to cover a big gas leak that keeps you from attending the kid's birthday party or when you miss the funeral of a family friend because it's sweeps month and the office says it can't do without you. They always say that. Be with us as often as you can. Life is short.

So many times in the workshops and seminars I have led, single journalists (especially producers) tell me they are unable to get out and meet other singles because of the long and irregular hours. When you are just getting started, you probably will move around, which can also be toxic to relationships.

When Vernon Stone, a media researcher, asked television journalists about their personal lives, he got an earful. A TV reporter/weekend anchorwoman, age 31, wrote, "I'm probably not married because I move so much, six jobs and cities in nine years since getting out of school. Each time I had to leave alone."

"My partner and I can't set a wedding date because we can't find jobs in the same city," explained a female TV producer, age 26.

"Someday I'd like to get married and have kids," a female TV reporter, age 24, said. "I've even met a wonderful guy here in town. But I'm so ambitious I'd leave town to get a better job." Stone says a lot of young singles in the news business will avoid long-term relationships because they know they will be moving in a couple of years.

Many of the survey respondents felt married to their jobs. A female TV reporter, age 26, said, "I often feel I've put my life on hold. Meanwhile, I have virtually no social life."

"I broke up with a live-in girlfriend because she felt my job meant more to me than she did. And it did," a TV anchorman, age 27, said in Stone's survey.[8]

I am convinced that reporters, photojournalists and producers would be more effective journalists if they could find more balance in their non-news life.

TIME MANAGEMENT

Time is the supreme currency in television. We never seem to have enough time to do all the research we want on stories. There is never enough time to get from one interview to another. There is never enough time to think about the teases that producers write. There is never enough time to hold a truly meaningful morning meeting. We are always in a rush. If only we had more time.

From handheld electronic organizers to leather-bound planners, I have tried every time-management tool known. Some help me keep track of schedules better than others, but none of these organizers gives me more time.

In a newsroom, time management must be a team sport. Reporters, producers and photojournalists know that, in a newsroom, the way that others manage their time directly affects how you will manage your time. Photojournalists know that when a reporter drones on endlessly in an interview or delays writing the story until the last minute, the story editing will be a last-minute rush job no matter how well photojournalists have done their job. Producers who manage their day with maximum efficiency can't overcome reporters who needlessly file stories at the last minute. Reporters who work efficiently have no control over producers who on a whim change the show rundown at the last minute and now want a live shot, which will require the reporter to dash out the door and meet the live truck.

Newsrooms that value time management must value goal setting. They must also respect how individual decisions affect others. As a manager I became interested in how much time I wasted every day just waiting for others to show up to meetings. It was not uncommon for me to have six or seven meetings of various sorts a day. If I waited 5 minutes to start each one—and 5 minutes was the minimum I usually had to wait—that meant that I was wasting 35 minutes a day just waiting for meetings to start. Multiply that times five days a week, and I was idling away almost a half a workday each week! That is equal to two workdays a month or more than two full workweeks a year. I grew to have little patience for people who would show up to meetings late and unprepared. It is usually better to delay a meeting than to go forward with it and be unprepared to conduct a meaningful discussion that will produce results.

When you get to meetings, explain your ideas clearly and efficiently. Don't argue just to make noise, but don't go along with notions with which you disagree just to save time. Respect the fact that other people have time pressures, and do all you can to recognize what affect your decisions have on their lives.

One of the Ten Commandments is "Thou shalt not steal." Keep it by not stealing others' time.

A producer friend of mine told me about how frustrated she was that on Thanksgiving Day the reporter working that holiday shift balked at doing live shots. The crews wanted to finish their stories and go home. I asked my friend how important the live shots were to the viewers, not just to the producers. I asked whether the reporter might use the time that would be spent driving to the live shot in some more productive way, such as setting up a story for the next day or making sure all of the supers (the superimposed names of the people being interviews, the reporters, the locations) were correctly typed. I asked if the good will that might result from allowing the reporter and photojournalist to duck out of the office a half-hour early on a holiday might build goodwill that the producer could cash in some other day.

To be honest, I am not certain that producer ever found a way to see the bigger picture. She was going to have to work until 6:30 p.m., so why shouldn't everyone else?

AVOID OFFICE GOSSIP AND POLITICS

Journalists are professional skeptics, gossips, busybodies, politicians and complainers. We snoop into other people's business for a living. The very qualities that make journalists good at what they do often make us difficult to work with.

The story goes that someone once asked one of the world's most renowned mathematicians to pass along his formula for success in the workplace. He came up with a formula.

$$A = \text{success at work}$$

So the way to achieve "A" is:

$$A = X + Y + Z$$

In this case, he said, "X is represented by doing meaningful work and Y is appropriate compensation for the work done."

"What is Z?" someone asked.

"Z is knowing when to keep your mouth shut around colleagues," he said.

I have found that the least productive people in my newsroom were the worst gossips. I am not sure if they were unproductive because they spent their time gossiping or if they gossiped because they themselves were so unproductive. Self-confident people have no need to harm others with idle rumors. I have to admit that when I was a reporter, I spent too much time mining newsroom sources to learn who was moving up, down or out the door. Those of us who worked in the special projects and investigations unit lived in daily fear that our unit was going to be dissolved. Even when our news director would assure us we were not going to be fired, we wondered why he took time to say that. Certainly that meant that somebody was considering it or he would not mention it for a denial.

When I became a news director, I learned that most office gossip was born when there was not enough real information available to people. The rumors would fly highest when I could not reveal information about an employee's firing or personal troubles. The best rumor control in any newsroom is an open pipeline of information from the managers to the newsroom and from the newsroom to the managers. When somebody comes to you with gossip about another person, let him or her know you are not interested.

Leaders in the Newsroom

Some journalists work a full, productive career in newsrooms and do not alienate their co-workers in the process. What habits have they formed to stay focused on the important work they have to do? I consulted three respected reporters, Nancy Amons (WSMV-TV, Nashville), Chuck Goudie (WLS-TV, Chicago) and Bill Sheil (WJW-TV, Cleveland). Together, we developed a blueprint for journalists who want to become newsroom leaders—the kind of people who do not just survive but thrive, even in tough times.

BECOME THE GO-TO PERSON IN DAILY AND BREAKING-NEWS EVENTS

Reporters, producers and photojournalists become indispensable when they become the go-to person in their newsroom for daily events, not just special sweeps or promotions projects. Even on daily deadline stories, look for the story that others who do not have your enterprising eye will never find. Pitch in without being asked. Go for the "big get" that others might give up on after day one. When the big story hits, be the producer who volunteers to pull together special coverage. Be the reporter who has prepared for this day by keeping emergency contact information ready at his fingertips. Be the video journalist or photojournalist who already has charged her camera batteries, packed her gear and filled the news car with gas. These people have a "Put me in the game" attitude. They have a bias toward action.

BE ON THE TRUTH SQUAD

Allow others to learn from their mistakes, but do not allow the kinds of mistakes on the air that will cause real harm. Think of this the way a flight instructor thinks of it: A student pilot will make mistakes, but the instructor cannot allow the plane to crash and burn. So the instructor waits until the critical point that the student realizes the mistake but the plane can still be controlled. Flight instructors never permit the sort of mistake that can be made only once.

Journalists can follow that guide. I can remember, as a reporter, seeing information in other people's lead-ins or teases that I knew or believed was not true. Yet I wanted to be careful about the delicate position of questioning somebody else's story or the contents of another producer's newscast. My former Poynter colleague Jill Geisler says journalists must learn the difference between "rescuing" and "redecorating." You rescue stories that will be wrong and cause harm if they air as is. You redecorate when you substitute your words for the writer's words, editing mostly for style and not for truth and substance. Writers hate that kind of editing. It steals credit for the work, and it undermines the writer's confidence.

So don't become the newsroom's "Bigfoot," but do not be timid or quiet when your newsroom is about to broadcast information you can help prove is incorrect or out of context. Ask, "How do we know that?" "What assumptions did our source make that we will pass along to the viewers as fact?" To build the kind of culture that would invite such input, be sure you are open for others to ask questions about your work that could make it stronger. Whenever possible, ask challenging questions in private, not in front of the boss or colleagues. Remember the old saying, "Criticism should arrive in private, but delivering praise should be a public event."

BE A TEACHER, MENTOR AND COACH

Be willing to teach others how to use enterprise and investigative tools such as internet sites, public record databases and other resources. Be selfless. Be willing to turn over information to others and resist the temptation to do everything yourself.

- Coaches teach people, while fixers focus just on the story or the copy.
- Coaches work front end before problems develop. Fixers work on deadline at the last minute.
- Coaches deflect credit, but fixers steal credit by "saving the day" at the last minute.
- Coaches focus on what works in a story, but fixers focus on only what is broken.
- Coaches teach by asking questions to help others strengthen their story or idea, but fixers make firm statements about what is wrong with a story.
- Coaches find themselves being needed less and less, but fixers must fix the same problems over and over.

UNDERPROMISE, OVERDELIVER

Even when I thought I had a very good story, I would usually tell my boss I thought the story would be "pretty good." I have worked with plenty of reporters who, every day, would promise the greatest story ever told on television, only to produce garden-variety pieces. I am not suggesting you undersell your story so much that producers do not know where to properly play it. But I would avoid hype and self-promotion. When you say you have the goods, producers and promotions directors want to book it. Don't promise a blockbuster story unless you can overdeliver it. Success has many authors; failure is an orphan.

BE THE CHAMPION OF YOUR OWN PROMOTION

Reporters and producers should advocate stories to the marketing and promotion department. Take ownership of the need for the promotions to be fair and accurate. Remember that you have a duty not only to your station/network but also to the people involved in and affected by the stories. An awful lot of legal problems that TV newsrooms encounter have little to do with the stories they air. The stories sometimes go through not one lawyer but two or more in what celebrated investigative reporter Roberta Baskin once described to me as a "double-lawyerectomy." But the promotions and headlines and teases often do not undergo such scrutiny. It is especially true for daily news stories. Take responsibility for everything that is said on the air about your story.

TAKE OWNERSHIP OF MANAGEMENT DECISIONS AND FIND WAYS TO BE OPENLY SUPPORTIVE

But don't be a management "suck-up." Be a part of a team in which your future and the future of the entire team are invested. Make the group decisions as good as they can be and support them without violating your principles. Even when you disagree with a decision, focus on the decision or policy you want to change, not the individual who made the policy. Take a lesson from politicians on this point. You don't hear politicians say, "My colleague is an idiot and a liar." They say, "My esteemed colleague has more experience than I do in this area, but we don't always agree, and this is one of those areas where we need to find more common ground." Disagreements in newsrooms are fine; in fact, we should encourage the robust contrarian voice in our newsroom. But personal attacks have no place in any news organization.

BE AN ADVISER TO YOUR BOSS

Be strong enough to give your boss the good news as well as the bad. Help your boss know what is really happening out in the trenches. John Lansing, a longtime broadcast executive, says he appreciated people who brought him bad news, "Because it means you are being honest with me."[9]

Don't communicate with your boss only when you have bad news or need something. Help him or her know when some little thing is going well in the newsroom. Deliver some good news to your boss once in a while. Even better, deliver some good news that is not about something you did. Tell your boss about a co-worker who made an extra effort or showed uncommon caring to resolve a viewer's complaint. Dub off, or make a copy of, a story that somebody else did but the news director might have missed.

When I was a news director, I became aware that not much good news comes walking through the office door each day. The most common sound any news director hears is "Knock-knock; got a minute?" I knew full well that not one person who asked for a minute of my time wanted only a minute. The never-ending parade at my door included

> "Knock-knock; got a minute? I think you should know I am getting a divorce."

> "Knock-knock; got a minute? I think I am going to quit."

> "Knock-knock; got a minute? I am having problems with my kid. I need to be off early every Wednesday so we can go to counseling."

> "Knock-knock; got a minute? The TV media critic called me and asked about rumors that our weekend anchors are fighting. Should I have spoken with him?"

> "Knock-knock; got a minute? Don't be surprised if the chief of [fill in the name of a city/town/village or state police department] calls to complain about me. I just want you to know he is a jerk and don't believe anything he says."

"Knock-knock; got a minute? My [grandmother, grandfather, cat, car] died. I won't be in tomorrow."

"Knock-knock; got a minute? Corporate needs you to submit a plan to cut spending by $100,000. They need it in 48 hours."

"Knock-knock; got a minute? One of the photographers wrecked a station car. It's the second time this year. Did you know he has a drinking problem?"

"Knock-knock; got a minute? I don't think I will be able to turn that project for sweeps. Will that be a problem?"

Before I sat in that office myself, it never occurred to me that a news director would hear so many stories of sorrow and woe that had next to nothing to do with the stories we were putting on TV that night. Yet, these issues were far more important because they had to do with the people who were putting the stories on TV.

Know your boss' schedule. If he or she is busy with a big request from corporate, it may not be the best time to drop by and "chew the fat." If your boss is under pressure to cut expenses, it is not the best time to go in to ask for a raise. I also learned to ask the boss' secretary about who had been in the boss' office before I stepped in there. If a "problem child" had just been warming the chair, I might reschedule to a time when I could get a warmer reception.

MANAGE THE BOSS

I often hear reporters and producers claim that their boss does not know them. They say the boss thinks of them only as employees, not as real people. Bosses feel the same way. If you really want to be effective, get to know your boss' style. I worked for two general managers (GMs) in my career as news director. The first of them, Mike Kettenring, believed in an ordered life. He loved for me to generate detailed reports. The more paper, it seemed, the better. Kettenring, a deeply principled man, was schooled by the Jesuits. He rose to station management having been a news director. He wore stiffly starched shirts and was so organized that he wanted his reports delivered with three holes prepunched and ready to be inserted into chronologically arranged binders behind his spotless desk. If I told Kettenring he could expect a project to be completed by June 14, then I would get a note from him on June 7 saying, "Status? Respond by June 10." Feeding his need for paper was, at times, maddening. We were very different kinds of people, but, because of him, I came to learn the value of a more disciplined life. After decades in broadcasting, he became a widower, and chose to become a Catholic priest. He runs a parish church and school in New Orleans. No person, with the exceptions of my mother and my wife, influenced my life more.

My next general manager, Frank DeTillio, was a master salesman. Once a person told DeTillio his or her name, DeTillio never had to ask again. He takes pride in remembering people's names. By the second meeting, he makes it his business to discover something unique about the individual; where the person grew up, went to school, what that person's father did for a living. He is a marvelously warm, fun-loving and caring man who became frustrated with my nonstop snowstorm of written reports to him. I had grown into that habit with Kettenring and assumed all general managers wanted a daily dose of paperwork from me. I couldn't understand his need to see me face-to-face every day. DeTillio taught me the value of learning the needs and desires of the customers and viewers and, so long as it didn't violate our company principles, to adapt to that style.

The main lesson from these two different styles is to learn how your boss wants communication with you. Does he like information in a written report, email, voice mail or face-to-face? Does she want you to go through a formal chain of command, or does she appreciate a less formal and direct style? Does he like people to drop by the office, or does he want you to make an appointment? Is she a detail-oriented person, like my first GM, or does she want executive summaries, as my second GM preferred? Does your boss want to be called at home when a story breaks, or does he want you to handle it and to call only in an extreme emergency? Managing the boss is not the same as "sucking up to the boss." Managing the boss means seeing the whole person, just as you want her to see you.

HAVE YOUR FACTS STRAIGHT

There is nothing more frustrating for a news director than when a producer, for example, marches in and says that the graphics department has gotten an over-the-shoulder graphic wrong for the third straight week. So the news director marches in to the head of the graphics area and begins to vent about the need for accuracy and accountability. The graphics folks tell the news director that the producer has a habit of coming in at the last minute with requests and rarely fills out a written graphics order, complaining that she doesn't have time for their silly written requests. The artists say they are trying to understand what the producer wants while they are working on a half-dozen other requests—and that is how the mistakes happen. As the news director, you now have to remove your foot from your mouth and the egg from your face. You will have a difficult time believing the producer again. You might also wonder if the producer is that careless in leaving out essential facts in newscasts.

I deeply appreciated those who would come to a short meeting with a list of things they needed action on. They would offer options. They would have done their homework.

Reporter Nancy Amons once came to me with a request to buy a fast new computer that she said she needed to do some complex database work in her investigative reporting. She didn't just "drop by" the office. She made an appointment, got there on time and didn't waste time with chitchat; she came right to the point. Amons said she knew money was tight. She said she understood the difference between "want" and "need" and wanted to convince me that this was a "need." She handed me color brochures of the machine. She had a copy for herself so she could answer questions as we went along. Amons had researched the costs, including shipping costs and tax. She knew what the associated software would cost and volunteered to teach herself how to use the spreadsheet programs she would have to know to use the machine. She gave me a couple of less expensive options but explained why they were not great choices for what she planned to do. She said there was no need for a new monitor; the old one would work fine. She just wanted the computer. When I said yes and she got the machine, Amons sent me a note of thanks, and within a short time after the new computer's arrival she produced a story that we could not have produced without the database work.

I remember how she came into the office and told me that because of my good decision to buy the computer, *we* had produced an important story. We both knew the truth; it was her reporting and vision and not mine that produced the work, but it made me more eager to purchase other equipment and software. Amons always managed me more than I managed her.

VALUE THE JUDGMENTS AND CONTRIBUTIONS OF OTHERS

The best journalists I know are highly skilled and experienced, and they listen to and respect the ideas of others, including directors, graphic artists and photojournalists. Colleagues who are not involved in minute-to-minute coverage may see stories quite differently from journalists who get caught up in the daily news grind. Allow others to help you discover that there is not one truth but many truths.

DISCOVER ALL YOU CAN ABOUT YOUR VIEWERS AND SEEK TO SERVE THEM

Draw from personal experience, research and a wide network of diverse contacts. Viewers are usually not at all like journalists in the way they live, think or view the content and execution of newscasts. I sometimes ask my workshop participants to hold up their hand if they have a hunting license, even in rural areas of this country. Almost no hands go up. I ask how many go fishing once a month or more. A few more hands go up. I ask how many drive a pickup truck. A few more hands go up. I ask them how many hands I would see if I asked their viewers those questions. They often laugh and say they see my point. Journalists are not at all like many of their viewers. Our communities are far more diverse than most of our newsrooms.

BE A WRITING AND ETHICS EXAMPLE

Uphold high standards for storytelling and newsgathering. Find ways to recognize the good work of others, even if you are not their boss. By affirming the work of others, you are sharing and multiplying your own values. In every newsroom I have worked in, the most powerful leaders were not the people in formal authority but were the most respected journalists who taught and supported others. Managers should not be the only ones in the newsroom who are willing to make tough ethics calls. Manage up your ethics.

ANTICIPATE MAJOR EVENTS

Be an example of front-end thinking. You know there will be elections, holidays, Olympics, inaugurations, trials, hearings and legislative sessions. If those who are responsible for planning for big events do not think as forwardly as you would like, take responsibility to do so yourself. You can help others to think ahead about the graphics, technical capabilities, personnel and information you will need to cover a big planned story.

KNOW INDUSTRY TRENDS AND
HOW RATINGS AND WEB METRICS WORK

It is naïve to think that a journalist's job is just to report the news. Journalists should understand their own business to argue in favor of strong coverage. I have known so many reporters who got stuck doing silly stories because some manager said research indicated that story was what the viewers wanted to see. Use your critical-thinking skills and ask more questions. Ask to see the research, not as a challenge to the story idea but to understand what the viewers seem to be saying. Even if a manager is unwilling to share the research documents, maybe he or she would be willing to conduct a newsroom meeting to explain the results and how those results affect storytelling and story selection.

The number of reporters and producers and photojournalists who admit to me that they don't understand how the ratings system works surprises me. Here are a few things all broadcast journalists should know about ratings.

Nielsen Media Research has become the de facto national measurement for the television industry in the United States. Nielsen uses a technique called statistical sampling to rate shows, which is essentially the same technique that pollsters use to predict outcomes. For that reason I urge all journalists to remember that ratings are "estimates," not "facts." They are *not* accurate to a 10th of a point, as so many stations pretend them to be when they are claiming a rating victory.

Nielsen Media Research collects information from about 25,000 metered households each day.[10] The meters are little black boxes, which include a computer and a modem that monitor what the household has watched that day. Every night the box sends the data to Nielsen, which downloads the information. Of course, the meter has no way of knowing how many people watched TV or even if anybody was in the room.

Paper diaries, which Nielsen phased out, were prone to socially based responses such as "I watch PBS all the time," while meters are more likely to show that people really watch *America's Funniest Home Videos.* Younger viewers were less diligent than older viewers in filling out diaries. According to Deborah Hamberlin, former vice president for entertainment at NBC and now a vice president at the CW Network, "Younger-skewing programs and stations are underreported in diaries but almost always do better when they are metered." Diaries had a short life span; each week diaries were sent to different households in the market. The meter sample stays in place for up to five years.[11]

Nielsen moved its measurement system to "People Meters" in larger TV-viewing markets. These meters track viewing daily, down to the minute. As People Meter use spreads, there will be less need for ratings sweeps months because there will be a nonstop flow of data on who is watching what program. People Meters require viewers to log in as they watch TV. With the set box recorders there is no way to know if nobody is watching, if one person is watching or if a crowd of 20 is watching the program. Every 70 minutes, if there has been no button-pushing activity or television on/off changes, the People Meter lights flash and ask the viewers to confirm that they are still watching.[12]

How to score a ratings point: For your station to get credit for a quarter hour, a meter must record that a TV set was tuned to your station for five minutes. The five minutes do not have to be consecutive, and it is possible for more than one station to get credit for a single quarter hour.

The lead-in: If you look in all of the metered markets, you will find very few stations that lose the lead-in program and win the news program, especially in early evenings. You must promote the programs that play just before your early and late news and promote the news itself. Nothing else is as important as those three priorities if you want to deliver and retain viewers.

Ratings and shares: In most markets only 400 households are metered and fewer are actually counted on any given day because of cable outages, power interruptions or other issues. This means that three or four households could determine one household ratings point. A rating point is the size of an audience expressed as a percentage of the total target audience universe. Share means the percentage of all televisions in use that are tuned to a specific station or program. Most stations have someone, usually in the sales department, who specializes in analyzing ratings trends. Take that person to lunch and get a lesson in ratings and audience flow.

In addition to understanding how the ratings system works, I offer what to some might be a controversial suggestion: Journalists should learn more about who pays their bills. Plenty of right-minded journalists disagree with me on this point. They say that a journalist's only concern should be telling the news. I may have thought that when I was a reporter. But when I became a news director, I had a new appreciation for reporters who knew when they were about to step on the toes of a major advertiser. I appreciated the awareness, not because we were going to avoid stepping on those toes but so we could forewarn the sales and station management that there was going to be trouble on the phone soon. As a producer or a reporter, you are only one of several stakeholders at the station. Other people, including account executives and other managers, will be affected by your reporting. Be an aggressive and fair journalist *and* respect others.

BE PREPARED FOR RIPPLE EFFECTS FROM HARD-HITTING STORIES AND NEWSCASTS

Sales and management are not the only ones who will be affected by your stories. Other reporters may have a harder time getting information from the police after you rip the police department for a problem you discovered. Lawsuits that get filed over your stories, even if they are groundless, touch many lives beyond your own. Colleagues may be called to testify about a story; the station may have to spend thousands or even millions of dollars defending your reporting. Be bold and aggressive, but be sensitive to the ripple effect of your stories. Be open and even invite conversation from colleagues about the challenges your stories create for others.

DON'T GET CARRIED AWAY WITH GADGETS

I tell college professors that I would much rather see college journalists learn the skills of powerful writing and photojournalism than how to use the latest social media or smartphone tool. Some skills transcend time while the tools of delivering journalism change constantly. I am not giving you permission to become an electronic Luddite, but don't chase every shiny bead. Pulitzer Prize–winning journalist and columnist Thomas Friedman said in a commencement address at Williams College in 2005,

> I started as a reporter in Beirut working on an Adler manual typewriter. I can tell you that the stories I wrote for *The New York Times* on that manual typewriter are still some of my favorites. In this age of laptops and PDAs, the Internet and Google, MP3s and iPods, remember one thing: All these tools might make you smarter, but they sure won't make you smart; they might extend your reach, but they will never tell you what to say to your neighbor over the fence, or how to comfort a friend in need, or how to write a lead that sings, or how to imagine a breakthrough in science or literature. You cannot download passion, imagination, zest and creativity—all that stuff that will make you untouchable. You have to upload it, the old-fashioned way, under the olive tree, with reading, writing and arithmetic, travel, study, reflection, museum visits and human interaction.[13]

LAY DOWN DEEPER ROOTS

I wish that reporters and photojournalists could find a way to stay in their professions longer. I wish more journalists would establish deep roots in one community rather than shallow roots in many communities as they move from market to market with the regularity of college football coaches. When reporters constantly move from market to market, the viewers lose. The viewers often know more about their town's history and values than the journalists do. I think daily journalism is an honorable craft, and it is made even more honorable when you truly care about the people and the community you are serving, regardless of the market size. Some of the most satisfied and accomplished journalists I know, people I have mentioned in this book, are people who have planted themselves in a community for decades.

THE MEANING OF LIFE

"I figured out what life is all about," Ron Tindiglia told one of his friends while on a fishing trip. After nearly 30 years as a broadcast news management icon in New York and Los Angeles, Tindiglia was dying of cancer.

It was such a typical sound bite from this man who touched so many. For three years before his death, I was privileged to learn so much from this master of news management. He often called to ask what I was doing. I would tell him about all of the big plans I had for our newsroom, about good things we had done and he was like an adoring father. He rarely told me about his own achievements; he just asked about mine. I considered him my most trusted rabbi. At his funeral I realized that there must have been 200 people who thought they had the same "best-friend" relationship with him. There, at his funeral, he had one more thing to teach us.

We learned it from friends who delivered his eulogy. They used Tindiglia's voice to tell a story, from which we would all learn the meaning of life.

"See, life has stages," he said. "The first stage is the stage where all you want to do is get 'stuff.' In order to get stuff, you work to get money. In this phase you work to make a living. The work is a means to an end."

The second stage, he said, is about getting "better stuff." Just having stuff is not good enough anymore. Now we need bigger, better more expensive stuff. The clothes, the cars, the house, the good stuff. Instead of buying used cars, you buy a new one. You work so hard that you need a motorcycle or a big stereo to medicate your stress and unhappiness. You deserve the luxury; you work hard for it.

Then, if you are lucky, you become discontented with the second stage and you pass into the third phase of life. The third phase has to do with the search for life's meaning. It is no longer about stuff. In fact it is the "anti-stuff" phase. Work takes on a new urgency, a new depth and a new importance. The third phase is about leaving a legacy. It is about living out what you have spent your life claiming that you stand for.

What a privilege it is to be a journalist. Nurture, value and defend the individual's right to express ideas even if they are unpopular. Do all you can to keep government records as open as possible and to keep the press as free as possible to report the truth, however you find it. Our democracy depends on the free flow of information to the people.

Consider the fact that there has never been a famine in a country that has a free and aggressive press. Journalists like you would find out why the food is not getting to where it is needed most and would hold the system responsible. The Constitution of the United States mentions only one profession for specific protection, journalism.

Respect the viewers. Speak to their hearts and minds. Don't waste their time.

Tell the truth as fully and courageously as possible.

Seek many voices.

Practice ethics.

Enterprise more.

Respectfully question everything.

Reject conventional wisdom.

Strive for excellence.

Use active verbs.

Take better care of yourself.

Aim for the heart.

NOTES

1. Michael Schudson and Tony Dokoupil, "A Long View of Layoffs," *Columbia Journalism Review*, March/April 2007.
2. Source:http://www.rtdna.org/article/update_tv_and_newspaper_staffing# sthash.11hwT6Su.dpuf.
3. Interview with Starbucks former CEO and current chairman Howard Schultz, "The Art of Creating Passionate Consumers," *KNOW* magazine, spring 2005.
4. Starbucks.com company mission statement, http://www.starbucks.com/mission/default.asp.
5. Maryann Hammers, "Pleasing Employees, Pouring Profits: Caffeine Addicts Aren't the Only Fans of This Corporate Legend, Which Serves Up Warm Fuzzies With Its Cold Frappuccinos," *Workforce Management*, Oct. 1, 2003.

6. "Is Starbucks Really a Great Place to Work?" The Society for Human Resource Management, September 25, 2015 http://monitor-360.com/blog/tag/starbucks/.

7. Bob Papper, "Newsroom Staffing," RTDNA Research, July 26, 2016.

8. Vernon Stone, "TV and Radio News Jobs Keep Many Unmarried," University of Missouri Department of Journalism, May 25, 2001.

9. Conversation with the author, Dec. 4, 2001.

10. Nielsen Media Research, http://www.nielsen.com/us/en.html http://www.nielsen.com/us/en/solutions/measurement/television.html.

11. Deborah Hamberlin, "Must Read TV," *NBC Promotions Newsletter* (Winter 1997), 6.

12. "How Does the People Meter Work?" Nielsen Media Research, http://www.nielsen.com/us/en/solutions/measurement/television.html.

13. Thomas L. Friedman, "Listen to Your Heart," commencement address at Williams College, Williamstown, Mass., June 5, 2005.

Index